Religion in
Multidisciplinary Perspective

Religion in Multidisciplinary Perspective

Philosophical, Theological, and Scientific Approaches to Wesley J. Wildman

Edited by

F. LeRon Shults and
Robert Cummings Neville

Cover image by Beth Neville. The left-hand side of the image is the Uluru Red Rock from Uluru-Kata Tjuta National Park in Australia from which Wildman comes. Beth and I could not climb it but we had cocktails and a concert at its base. The right-hand side of the image is the Garden of the Gods in Colorado which, for several years, was the community that hosted the Institute for American Religious and Philosophical Thought where Wildman was. Beth Neville climbed it as a child and Wildman's wife, Suzanne, climbed it during our conference.

Published by State University of New York Press, Albany

© 2022 State University of New York

All rights reserved

Printed in the United States of America

No part of this book may be used or reproduced in any manner whatsoever without written permission. No part of this book may be stored in a retrieval system or transmitted in any form or by any means including electronic, electrostatic, magnetic tape, mechanical, photocopying, recording, or otherwise without the prior permission in writing of the publisher.

For information, contact State University of New York Press, Albany, NY
www.sunypress.edu

Library of Congress Cataloging-in-Publication Data

Names: Shults, F. LeRon, editor. | Neville, Robert Cummings, editor.
Title: Religion in multidisciplinary perspective : philosophical, theological, and scientific approaches to Wesley J. Wildman / edited by F. LeRon Shults and Robert Cummings Neville.
Description: Albany : State University of New York Press, [2022] | Includes bibliographical references and index.
Identifiers: ISBN 9781438487410 (hardcover : alk. paper) | ISBN 9781438487427 (ebook) | ISBN 9781438487403 (pbk. : alk. paper)
Further information is available at the Library of Congress.

10 9 8 7 6 5 4 3 2 1

Contents

1   Introduction to the Work of Wesley J. Wildman   1
     F. LeRon Shults and Robert Cummings Neville

Part 1. Philosophical Approaches

2   The Model(ing) Philosophy of Wesley Wildman   13
     F. LeRon Shults

3   Wildman's Reconstruction of Philosophy of Religion   37
     Timothy D. Knepper

4   Wesley Wildman's Lessons for and from Ethics   53
     Sarah E. Fredericks

5   Pragmatist Inquiry and the Problem of Value   79
     Nathaniel F. Barrett

Part 2: Theological Approaches

6   Pragmatism and the Future of Philosophical Theology   107
     Michael L. Raposa

7   Committing Theology in the Secular University   129
     Kevin Schilbrack

8 Wesley Wildman's Theology 153
    Robert Cummings Neville

9 Wildman's Effing Symbology 181
    Nancy K. Frankenberry

10 Nature and *Homo religiosus* in Wildman's *Science and Religious Anthropology* 209
    Robert S. Corrington

Part 3: Scientific Approaches

11 Relating within Wildman's Integrative Engagement with Psychology, Spirituality, and Humility 223
    Steven J. Sandage

12 Wildman's Contributions to the Neuroscience of Religious and Spiritual Experiences 249
    Patrick McNamara

13 Religious and Spiritual Experiences: An Imagined Dialogue with Wesley Wildman 259
    Anne Taves

14 The Man Who Receives Too Many Emails: Exploring the Construction of Wildman's Institutional Reality 273
    Richard Sosis

15 Response to Religion in Multidisciplinary Perspective 289
    Wesley J. Wildman

Author Bios 327

Index 331

1

Introduction to the Work of Wesley J. Wildman

F. LeRon Shults and Robert Cummings Neville

Wesley J. Wildman is the most original, audacious, creative, encyclopedic, and integrative thinker working within and across the fields of philosophy, ethics, theology, and the scientific study of religion in our time. Scholars in each of these disciplines are likely to be familiar with his contributions to their own field, but few are aware of the multidisciplinary breadth of his work. This multidisciplinarity is a defining feature of Wildman's pragmatic comparative inquiry into religion (as with every other topic). The chapters in this volume critically and constructively engage some of his most significant and provocative transgressions of disciplinary boundaries. The purpose of this book is to invite readers into the web of ongoing conversations that are occurring in the wake of Wildman's scholarly production. This chapter provides a brief introduction to the content and trajectory of his constantly expanding corpus and a preview of the following chapters, each of which explores some aspect of his philosophical, theological, scientific, or institution-building efforts.

Wesley John Wildman was born in 1961 to a warm-hearted, working-class family in Adelaide, Australia. He was raised in the Methodist Church, which became part of the Uniting Church of Australia during his teenage years. Wildman was ordained in the Uniting Church after receiving a bachelor of divinity degree from the University of Sydney in 1985. Earlier he had received a bachelor of arts degree in mathematics, physics, and computer science from Flinders University in 1980 (at the age of nineteen) and achieved first class honors in pure mathematics in 1981. After his BD, he pastored for a year in Sydney and then went to the Graduate Theological Union in Berkeley, California, where he received a PhD in philosophy of religion. During his years at the Graduate Theological Union, he also served as an associate pastor of a local church in Piedmont, California, and acting assistant professor at Stanford University. In 1993, he joined the Boston University School of Theology, where he revived a flagging doctoral program in science, philosophy, and religion. Two early graduates of the program, Nathanial Barrett and Sarah Fredericks, contributed chapters to this volume. Over the decades, Wildman has been involved in several multiyear research projects, such as the Comparative Religious Ideas Project and the Simulating Religion Project; founded the Center for Mind and Culture in Boston; and established the multidisciplinary journal *Religion, Brain & Behavior* (these are described below in the chapters by Neville, Shults, and Sosis).

Wildman's academic position at Boston University is in theology, interpreted broadly to include engagement with philosophy and ethics, and more recently in statistics and computer science. His first book, *Fidelity with Plausibility: Modest Christologies in the Twentieth Century*, was a significant revision of his PhD dissertation and came out in 1998.[1] It had two parts, the first of which consisted of "reflections on Ernst Troeltsch and the origins of the crisis of plausibility in contemporary Christology." Here Wildman established himself as a "mediating theologian," requiring Christianity to relate positively to modern science and the Enlightenment generally in order to be plausible. The second part was an explicit rejection of "absolutist Christologies," which are the most common kind in the tradition, and a recommendation of projects that he refers to as "modest Christologies," such as those proposed by John Hick and John Cobb Jr. His critical engagement of these thinkers' approaches to ultimate reality already anticipated arguments that he has fleshed out in more detail in later books (discussed below). In 2009 Wildman published two books on what Christian theologians call "ecclesiology," with collaboration from Stephen Chapin Garner, a former student and local pastor. *Lost in the Middle?* and *Found in the Middle!* were multidisciplinary (social scientific and theological) analyses of contemporary American Protestant church life with the aim of showing how Christians can be theologically liberal, in the sense of modern plausibility outlined in *Fidelity with Plausibility*, at the same time that they could be evangelical, in the sense of enthusiastic devotion to religious experience and regular congregational participation.[2] He rejected both extreme liberalism in ecclesiology, which he took to be destructive of church life, and extreme conservative evangelicalism with its supernaturalism and right-wing cultural politics.

During the decade that followed, Wildman has produced six volumes that provide a systematic presentation of his "religious philosophy."

- Volume 1: *Religious Philosophy as Multidisciplinary Comparative Inquiry: Envisioning a Future for the Philosophy of Religion* (2010)[3]

- Volume 2: *In Our Own Image: Anthropomorphism, Apophaticism, and Ultimacy* (2017)[4]

- Volume 3: *Science and Ultimate Reality* (not yet published)

- Volume 4: *Science and Religious Anthropology: A Spiritually Evocative Naturalist Interpretation of Human Life* (2009)[5]

- Volume 5: *Religious and Spiritual Experiences* (2011)[6]

- Volume 6: *Effing the Ineffable: Existential Mumblings at the Limits of Language* (2018)[7]

The remaining chapters of this book examine the key arguments he sets out in these volumes, and so our discussion here is brief. Rather than outline them in the order of publication (the logic of which had to do with balancing academic life and dealing with publisher timetables), here we present them in the systematic order in which Wildman conceptualized them from the beginning (the logic of which he spells out in the prefaces of the various volumes).

Volume 1, *Religious Philosophy as Multidisciplinary Comparative Inquiry*, outlines the intellectual project that Wildman will carry out in the remaining volumes. The book begins and ends with a consideration of the academic viability of "religious philosophy" (an overarching phrase he typically prefers to "philosophy of religion" and "philosophical theology," although these subdisciplines often overlap). Here Wildman presents his program to deal with "big issues" in religion, including the great normative questions such as the nature of ultimacy. Rejecting the limitations imposed by some scholars within analytic philosophy and postmodern philosophy, Wildman argues that religious philosophy should include considerations from the social and natural sciences as well as from philosophy, history of religions, and theologies from multiple traditions, all of which he engages in this first volume. His general theory of inquiry is based on the pragmatic traditions, especially the philosophy of Charles S. Peirce. Wildman claims that the same logic of inquiry runs through all disciplines, scientific, philosophical, historical, and theological: a logic of "problem solving." He argues that religious philosophy (in the bold sense he proposes) is historically rooted in six ancient, grand, and sometimes overlapping traditions of thought that he calls the ontotheological, cosmotheological, physicotheological, psychotheological, axiotheological, and mysticotheological. Wildman observes that all of these are now in crisis and suggests that each can be helped by adopting his program of multidisciplinary comparative inquiry.

Volume 2 (conceptually) in this series is *In Our Own Image*, a sustained essay on assessing models of ultimate reality. Wildman distinguishes three basic families of models: ultimate reality as an agential being (e.g., a monotheistic, not-less-than-personal God), ultimate reality as ground of being (e.g., Nirguna Brahman, Perennial Philosophy, Tillich's God beyond God), and subordinate-deity models in which a finite God is a component of ultimate reality (e.g., James's, Whitehead's, or Cobb's God, polytheisms). Each of these families has many variants, and Wildman compares them by analyzing the extent to which they follow three strategies for resisting anthropomorphism (resisting intentionality attribution, rational practicality, or narrative comprehensibility). He points out the strengths and weaknesses of all three classes of models and evaluates their variants in light of the criteria set out in volume 1 above. Wildman's own preference is for a version of the ground of being model of ultimate reality, which he defends as providing (among other things) greater internal coherence, better comportment with the findings of the natural and social sciences, and higher consistency in following all three strategies for resisting anthropomorphism than its competitors. From beginning to end, Wildman also insists that the logical object of the ground-of-being metaphor is beyond modeling or language of any kind, embracing an apophaticism whose virtues he explains throughout the remaining volumes.

In the preface of volume 3, *Science and Ultimate Reality*, Wildman explains that this third volume of his religious philosophy should be conceived as a companion volume to *In Our Own Image*. The latter introduced the method and criteria for adjudicating between the great models of ultimate reality and concluded that ground of being theism meets them better than its rivals (albeit not by as much as Wildman expected at the beginning of his multidisciplinary comparative inquiry). *Science and Ultimate Reality* completes this analysis by focusing on a series of fields not explored in volume 2. For example, he explores the implications of discoveries related to Big Bang cosmology and evolutionary biology for the human understanding of ultimacy. This leads him to an examination of some of the classical debates among theologians and philosophers over the best way to interpret the apparent design in the cosmos and in biological organisms. Wildman also tackles the thorny problem of divine action, arguing that here too ground of being models are less problematic than personal theism and subordinate deity models. In this case, Wildman arrives at this conclusion after a series of chapters dealing with the philosophical problems of causation and relations, and the relevant scientific findings from fundamental physics and mathematics as well as emergent complexity.

Volume 4, *Science and Religious Anthropology*, was actually the first volume of Wildman's systematic religious philosophy to be published. As the preface to that book makes evident, he already had the other volumes clearly in mind. In this context, he defends the thesis that human beings are religious by nature (*homo religiosus*), using a broad definition of religion that refers to the way in which humans bind themselves (*religio*) to that which they take to be of ultimate, existential, spiritual, or social concern. As the subtitle of this book suggests, however, he also insists that (a religiously sensitive) metaphysical naturalism provides the most plausible theoretical framework for making sense of this dimension of human life. In other words, there is no place for supernatural beings or revelations in his ontological inventory. The bulk of this volume is a series of chapters in which he sets out a thoroughly naturalistic religious anthropology, drawing heavily on findings in contemporary science that have provided new perspectives on human evolution, social groups, brains, bodies, sexuality, and the microbial and ecological habitat for human life.

Volume 5, *Religious and Spiritual Experiences*, is the fifth volume in Wildman's religious philosophy. This book began as a series of lectures that were part of a grant-funded project at the Danielsen Center at Boston University. A true heir to William James's philosophical, social-scientific, and neurological approach in *The Varieties of Religious Experience*, Wildman provides a rigorously naturalistic account of religious experience as consisting of certain kinds of intense experiences that can serve as "gateways to ultimacy." Building on his understanding of humanity as *homo religiosus*, and of ultimate realities as the depth dimensions of nature, Wildman engages the neuroscientific literature that has altered the theoretical (and practical) landscape for understanding religious and spiritual experiences and sets out a new set of distinctions to map the territory. He also addresses one of the most controversial issues in this field that has a special bearing on philosophy of religion: are such experiences cognitively reliable? Wildman concludes that they are (or they can be), but only if such assessments of their reliability are grounded within a naturalistic cosmology, an ecological-semiotic account of perception as dynamic engagement, and a symbolic account of religious cognitions (conditions that he outlines in detail).

Volume 6, *Effing the Ineffable: Existential Mumblings at the Limits of Language*, is the final volume in the religious philosophy series. As Wildman pointed out already in the first volume, religious philosophy should be not only multidisciplinary and cross-traditional but also pluralistic in its styles of inquiry—including the phenomenological, the comparative, the historical, the analytical, the theoretical, the literary, and the evaluative. Each of these styles is evident in all of the books discussed so far, but this concluding volume stands out for its intensive literary and phenomenological style. Wildman develops a theory of language for dealing with the ineffable and draws upon literature from a broad range of religions. The book itself is divided into three parts: Ultimacy Talk, Ultimacy Systems, and Ultimacy Manifestations. These parts are loosely correlated with three traditions within philosophical theology, each of which Wildman is deeply immersed in: the American pragmatist tradition, the analytic tradition, and the continental tradition. All of the chapters in this volume point in the direction of a proper spiritual engagement with an ineffable ground of being. The book concludes with a powerful autobiographical essay that describes one of the intensive experiences that drove (and continues to drive) Wildman to keep trying to eff the ineffable.

The six volumes of his systematic religious philosophy are only the tip of iceberg that is Wildman's scholarly corpus. He has published several other books including, most recently, a collection of (robustly naturalistic) sermons, *God Is . . . Meditations on the Mystery of Life, the Purity of Grace, the Bliss of Surrender, and the God Beyond God* (2019); and a book on the future of technologically enhanced spiritual experience, *Spirit Tech: The Brave New World of Consciousness Hacking and Enlightenment Engineering* (coauthored with Kate Stockly).[8] Wildman has also edited or coedited eight books, most of which have explored the relationship between science and religion and/or contributed to the scientific study of religion. He has also published a plethora of scholarly articles—more than 130 at the time this volume went to press. Many of these expand on philosophical, theological, and ethical issues treated in his books, while others explore other scientific disciplines and spiritual paths. Over the decades, he has become increasingly productive in the scientific study of religion, a productivity that has accelerated in recent years as he has led several funded research projects dedicated to multidisciplinary theoretical integration and the use of novel methods such as computational modeling and social simulation.

It is not possible to provide a comprehensive assessment of Wildman's work in a single book, but the chapters that follow represent our joint attempt to contribute to (and promote) such an assessment by engaging most of the core elements of his corpus. The first four chapters focus primarily on Wildman's contributions to *philosophy*, or, at least, they approach some aspects of his multidisciplinary comparative inquiry through a philosophical lens. Shults's chapter compares and contrasts the ways in which Wildman approaches the "modeling" of religious phenomena, especially human experiences of ultimate reality, in his apophatic theology and in his contributions to the computational science of religion. He also critically evaluates Wildman's broad usage of the term "religion" in social science and his ambivalent usage of the term "God" as a way of referring to ultimate reality. Knepper's chapter engages Wildman's proposals for reconstructing the philosophy of religion as an academic discipline. Although he agrees with the overall project, he expresses concerns about the use of the phrase "religious philosophy" and commends a more explicit acknowledgement of the role of Christian theism in the decline of philosophy of religion in recent decades.

Fredericks explores the strengths and weaknesses of Wildman's method of inquiry in relation to debates within the discipline of philosophical ethics. She argues that the latter has much to learn from his emphasis on comparison, fallibility, and multidisciplinarity, but also that Wildman's approach could be enhanced by the incorporation of insights from contemporary ethical discourse about power and diversity. Barrett's chapter, the last in this philosophically oriented cluster, examines the relationship between Wildman's pragmatist method of inquiry and his axiology (theory of value). After clarifying some of the tensions between classical pragmatism and Whitehead's aesthetics of intensity, he draws out the implications for the future of pragmatism in general and for pragmatist contributions to the scientific study of religion in particular.

The next four chapters are more focused on the *theological* dimensions of Wildman's work, although here too it is impossible to separate them from the philosophical and scientific dimensions. Like Barrett, Raposa's chapter takes up the theme of Wildman's pragmatism, but in this case the focus is on the implications of his approach for the future of philosophical theology. Here Raposa offers an appreciative analysis of Wildman's "religious philosophy" (though he shares with Knepper a concern about the phrase itself) but defends the value of (a certain kind of) anthropomorphism in theology. Shilbrack's chapter explores the tension between theology, as traditionally understood, and the academic commitments now prevalent in secular universities. After a careful analysis of the tasks and criteria that are appropriate in such contexts, he argues that Wildman's multidisciplinary, comparative method of inquiry is the best hope for the future of theology in the modern academy.

The chapter by Neville, who has been Wildman's colleague for more than a quarter century, explores some of the key similarities and differences between their theological approaches. Scholars who have followed the interactions among Wildman and Neville over the years will be pleased to find the latter's concise analysis of their differences in relation to theology's public, the role of comparative erudition, hypotheses and understanding, the function of anthropomorphism, language about ultimacy and apophaticism, and the place of religious symbolism in philosophy of religion. Frankenberry's chapter is critical of Wildman's (and Neville's) theory of meaning and approach to symbology. Building on insights from Davidson and other pragmatic philosophers, she challenges the whole project of hermeneutical and mystical theology represented by Wildman and argues that we should acknowledge that religious claims are palpably false without any effing qualifications.

A final cluster of chapters provides a series of critical evaluations of various aspects of Wildman's contributions to the *scientific* study of religion. Corrington's chapter compares and contrasts his own version of "ecstatic naturalism" with Wildman's, discussing the potential of each to engage the modern secular (and scientific) interpretation of humanity. Focusing particularly on religious naturalism and the concept of the sacred, Corrington argues that their approaches are complementary (and necessary) but acknowledges that Wildman's may have a better chance of facilitating radical changes in contemporary religious self-understanding. Sandage's chapter explores Wildman's "relational" disciplinarity, with special attention to the way in which he integrates theology and psychology. In addition to describing Wildman up as a model integrationist (especially in his pluralism and realism), Sandage also offers some psychological reflections on his treatment of the virtues of humility, loneliness, intensity, and bliss.

McNamara's chapter addresses some of Wildman's contributions to the neuroscience of religious and spiritual experiences, including his direct contributions through empirical research on such experiences and his indirect contributions as a mover and shaker in a number of academic and policy-oriented organizations. Like Raposa, McNamara also challenges Wildman's interpretation of the role of anthropomorphism in human evolution and his metaphysical rejection of supernaturalism. Taves also critically engages Wildman's understanding of religious and spiritual experiences. Her chapter appears in the form of an imagined dialogue with Wildman, in which they explore the similarities and differences in their respective views of such experiences. Sosis's chapter focuses primarily on the way in which Wildman has contributed to the scientific study of religion through his work as a founder and leader of institutions (e.g., the Center for Mind and Culture in Boston) and as a founder and editor of leading journals (e.g., *Religion, Brain & Behavior*).

Wildman himself gets the last word. In the final chapter, he provides a response to his friendly critics. Our hope is that the chapters in this volume will both further the conversations within and strengthen the multidisciplinary inquiry across the various fields in which Wildman has worked, including philosophy of religion, religious naturalism, spirituality, theology, ethics, computer science, and the scientific study of religion.

Notes

1. *Fidelity with Plausibility: Modest Christologies in the Twentieth Century*, with a foreword by John B. Cobb, Jr. (Albany, NY: State University of New York Press, 1998).

2. *Lost in the Middle?* with Stephen Chapin Garner (Herndon, VA: The Alban Institute, 2009) and *Found in the Middle!* with Stephen Chapin Garner (Herndon, VA: The Alban Institute, 2009).

3. *Religious Philosophy as Multidisciplinary Comparative Inquiry: Envisioning a Future for the Philosophy of Religion* (Albany, NY: State University of New York Press, 2010).

4. *In Our Own Image: Anthropomorphism, Apophaticism, and Ultimacy* (Oxford, UK: Oxford University Press, 2017).

5. *Science and Religious Anthropology: A Spiritually Evocative Naturalist Interpretation of Human Life*, with a foreword by Philip Clayton (Burlington, VT: Ashgate Publishing Company, 2009).

6. *Religious and Spiritual Experiences* (Cambridge, UK: Cambridge University Press, 2011).

7. *Effing the Ineffable: Existential Mumblings at the Limits of Language* (Albany, NY: State University of New York Press, 2018).

8. *God Is . . . : Meditations on the Mystery of Life, the Purity of Grace, the Bliss of Surrender, and the God beyond God*, with a foreword by Robert Allan Hill (Eugene, OR: Cascade/Wipf and Stock, 2019) and *Spirit Tech: The Brave New World of Consciousness Hacking and Enlightenment Engineering*, with Kate J. Stockly (New York, NY: St. Martin's Press, 2021).

PART 1
PHILOSOPHICAL APPROACHES

2

The Model(ing) Philosophy of Wesley Wildman

F. LeRon Shults

Wesley J. Wildman has been a model for me in many ways over the years. My first encounter with him at the American Academy of Religion a quarter century ago woke me from my dogmatic disciplinary slumbers. As a young scholar I was somewhat proud of my interdisciplinary sensitivities—until that fateful afternoon in Chicago where he presented a vision of the potential role of the natural and social sciences in the study of religion that stretched my mind in ways I had never imagined possible. Throughout our collaborations on a variety of projects over the years since then, he has also provided for me a model of philosophical courage and academic leadership. For reasons that will soon become clear, he gets my vote as America's next top model(er). Most importantly, however, he has been a model friend—consistently meeting me with that rare combination of genuinely empathic concern and intensely ruthless candor. I find it disingenuous to refer to one of my best friends as "Wildman," and so I beg the reader's indulgence as I just call him "Wesley."

As those familiar with our writings and public presentations will know, Wesley and I agree on almost everything, or at least on most of the big things (e.g., the value of naturalistic metaphysics, pragmatist epistemology, and Nietzschean-inspired ethics). Focusing on our agreements, however, would be quite boring—not to mention very un-Wesleyan (in the nominational, not the denominational sense). And so I focus instead on the main (and, as far as I can tell, only) issue in the philosophy of religion on which we do not always agree. I say "not always" because sometimes in our conversations

I experience flashes in which I suddenly think he might be starting to agree with me. These do not occur very often, but often enough that I hold out hope that he is beginning to see the light (of my position). I'm teasing, of course. I seriously doubt we will ever resolve this difference, but it is great fun to argue about it. More importantly, the argument is worth having because of the serious practical implications of our competing claims.

I set the stage for explaining the difference between us by outlining Wesley's *philosophical* (apophatic) modeling of Ultimate Reality and his *scientific* (computational) modeling of real human engagements with what he calls the axiological depth-dimensions of nature. These two sorts of modeling are central aspects of his approach to the philosophy of religion and to the scientific study of religion, respectively. His work in the computer modeling and simulation of religion and other social phenomena is not as well-known as his work in the philosophy of religion, at least among philosophers, ethicists, and theologians (who likely will be the main readers of this book). On the other hand, for most of the computational social scientists who will pick up this book, Wesley's apophatic theology is not likely to have registered on their academic radar. It might seem that these two ways of "modeling" have nothing to do with one another.

However, I suggest that attending to the relationship between them can illuminate some of the (robustly naturalistic) epistemological and metaphysical intuitions that regulate and integrate Wesley's broader efforts in multidisciplinary comparative inquiry. The first section describes, compares, and contrasts the formal operation of these philosophical (or theological) and scientific approaches to "modeling" in his corpus. The second and third sections provide a brief exposition of some of Wesley's own material models of "God" and "religion," two highly contentious terms over which he and I cannot seem to stop contending. The final section makes explicit the key point on which we differ and clarifies (my perception of) the main reasons for this difference. Once again, but here for the first time in writing, I invite Wesley to embrace the iconoclastic urges of his inner Nietzsche more fully and join me in "doing philosophy (of religion) with a hammer."

Computational and Apophatic Models: Always Wrong, Sometimes Useful

"Essentially, all models are wrong, but some are useful."[1] This oft cited adage in the field of computer modeling and simulation might be worrisome for someone obsessed with apodictic knowledge, but it is music to the ears of a philosophical pragmatist and evolutionary scientist like Wesley. What makes the mental models of Homo sapiens interesting is not their capacity to represent some allegedly absolute truth but their role in helping members of this highly social species adapt long enough to survive and reproduce before they die (and perhaps enjoy themselves a bit along the way). It might initially seem surprising that computer scientists and engineers are so comfortable with knowing they are always wrong. But even the best mathematical and computational models are "wrong" in roughly the same sense that a good geographical map is "wrong"—both are simplifications involving abstractions of a far more complex reality.

However, computer models can also be as "useful" as maps, again in roughly the same sense. A map is not the territory; if it were, it would not be very practical to carry around. What makes a map useful is that it adequately captures the structures and features of a territory that are most relevant for the navigation of the latter. Finding one's way to the next town requires knowledge of the roads that go around the mountains but not the insects that go around the molehills. This also applies to computational models used to analyze and simulate the dynamics at play in industrial supply chains, successful marketing campaigns, or obesity epidemics: they are useful insofar as their causal architectures adequately capture the structures and features that make the dynamic system *work*.

What exactly is a computer model? I'll give some concrete examples of Wesley's own use of these techniques in the scientific study or religion in section 3, but let me offer some introductory comments here. Andreas Tolk has recently offered the following definition, "Modeling is the task-driven, purposeful simplification and abstraction of a perception of reality that is shaped by physical, ethical and cognitive constraints . . . Simulation is the execution of a model."[2] There are many types of models (e.g., agent-based, systems-dynamics, discrete event, etc.), but what most have in common is that they attempt to provide an interpretation of some structured reality or process in order to achieve some theoretical or practical goal. What about simulations? If statistical analyses take a "snapshot" of correlations among variables at a particular time and place, simulations provide "movies" of the interactions among variables over time within a multidimensional parameter space. What makes a model useful is that its simplified ("wrong") causal architecture can be executed in a way that adequately simulates the relevant dynamics and features of its real-world target.

Apophatic models are also always wrong. As Wesley consistently emphasizes, all models of ultimate reality (or ultimacy, or God) are inadequate and literally false. The fate of every attempt to model ultimate reality will be "cognitive breakdown." Even theologians who believe in divine revelation and embrace anthropomorphic images of God usually still acknowledge that every model of ultimate reality fails to refer to its logical object literally. This is due both to the inherent incomprehensibility of conceptions of the truly infinite and to the inherent limitations of evolved human cognition. Although he defends the value of theology as an intellectual endeavor, Wesley insists that "it *is* obvious that speaking of ultimate reality must fail, ultimately . . . we know from the outset that any properly ultimate reality . . . necessarily must surpass the cognitive grasp of any being whatsoever, including human being."[3]

But can apophatic modeling also be useful? Wesley thinks it can be, and in at least two senses. First, apophaticism, properly understood, is not a complete turning away from language but a radically permissive approach "promoting precision and play, and inspiring vigorous conceptual wrangling until the very last and best of our concepts fracture into shards at our clay feet."[4] He commends an apophatic wholeheartedness that recognizes the "treachery of words" when dealing with ultimate reality, but "liberates us to play, and play hard, celebrating our species' linguistic genius and taking delight in mocking our linguistic pretensions . . . words both empower and mislead, both refer and distort—and nowhere more than in our outrageous attempts to speak of ultimacy."[5] Apophatic modeling can engender a healthy intellectual competition among Great Models from the world's religious traditions, each of which claims to do a better job of naming the unnamable before collapsing into silence.

Acknowledging the fallibility and final fallaciousness of all apophatic models, Wesley nevertheless playfully leaps into the academic arena and stakes his claim: ". . . the model of ultimate reality I am describing falls, like all ultimacy models fall, but it falls later in the plunge to silence, a mark of being closer to the truth of the matter."[6] We return below to his proposal for a collapsing metric by which to judge apophatic models and provide a brief exposition of his own naturalistic ground-of-being model of ultimacy, but the point here is that Wesley's mystical theological approach not only *relativizes* all models but also *relates* them to each other by rating their relative adequacy and "explaining the sense in which they truly express ultimate reality—both through *describing it more or less accurately* and through enabling people to *engage it more or less authentically.*"[7]

The final highlighted phrase in that last citation brings us to the second sense in which Wesley finds apophatic modeling to be potentially useful. In addition to promoting intellectual wrangling, such models can also facilitate human *engagement* with ultimate reality or "God." Acknowledging that the religious symbols in apophatic modeling are always broken, Wesley argues that the intensity of human life depends on them. "Without religious symbols to help us conceive our world and orient ourselves to it, the moral character of human life would be perpetually superficial and localized. The world would remain a terrifying jumble rather than becoming a kind of cosmic home."[8] Although this kind of theology may not be everyone's cup of tea, apophatically minded religious philosophers can "recognize the virtues of theoretically articulated ultimacy models as intellectual avenues for potentially authentic engagement with ultimate reality."[9]

What exactly is an apophatic model? For Wesley, apophasis begins with the acknowledgement that we simply cannot describe ultimate realities. In one respect, then, apophasis is "*not* a modeling strategy." This is because it "declines modeling for the sake of testimony to a reality that utterly transcends human understanding." However, insofar as they use well-defined negation techniques that provide structure and meaning to their conversations, "there *is* a kind of modeling at work among apophatic mystics and their theological kin."[10] Wesley's scientific and theological kin have something in common: both computational and apophatic models are always wrong—but sometimes useful. Despite this similarity, there is a fundamental difference between these two types of modeling. The computer scientist intends to understand and explain the finite conditions that constrain and enable some complex system within the real world, and there is no predetermined stopping point in her intellectual trajectory toward ever more adequate simulation of the phenomena.

The religious philosopher who intends to speak of the "unconditioned," on the other hand, knows in advance that her fate is apophasis. If "ultimate" reality is alleged to be that which infinitely transcends (and yet somehow immanently conditions) all finite reality, including all human experience and thought, then it cannot be simulated or even conceived by the human mind (or any other computational apparatus). This intellectual trajectory involves "indirect" and "artful" speech, but it must "finally *yield to silence* . . . the deepest theological truth is conjured in the echoes left behind after the *collapse of words*, and not finally expressed in their utterance."[11] An apophatic "model," then, is a human construction that (more or less) artfully and indirectly attempts to refer to that which is beyond finite linguistic reference, to conceive the inconceivable, to describe the conditions for thinking and engaging the indescribable unconditioned—in other words, to "eff" the "ineffable."

In the next two sections, I limit myself to a brief exposition of some of the most salient aspects of Wesley's own proposals for modeling "God" and "religion." This sets the stage for the final section of this chapter, in which I outline the basic disagreement I have with him about strategies for the conceptual and computational modeling of this multidisciplinary terrain.

Modeling "God"

Wesley has an ambivalent relationship to "God." In both of his most recent books, he refers to this term as a "valuable but potentially parochial name for ultimate reality."[12] As we will see below, its putative value lies in its ancient heritage and evocative power, while its parochializing potential lies in its susceptibility to anthropomorphism.[13] The latter is the main reason that "ultimacy" is usually Wesley's "preferred general term for the logical object that is of final concern within religions. 'Ultimate realities' and 'ultimate concerns' are the objective and subjective sides of ultimacy, respectively . . ."[14] This preference seems to go back at least to his collaboration with Bob Neville and others in the Comparative Religious Ideas Project. In that context, he and Bob explained that "ultimate realities" is a vague category of comparison that "means something like this: *that which is most important to religious life because of the nature of reality.*"[15]

In his later monograph on *Religious Philosophy as Multidisciplinary Comparative Inquiry*, Wesley maintained this terminology, defending a form of pragmatic inquiry that engages as many disciplines as necessary when making comparative evaluations of hypotheses about religious matters, including matters of ultimate concern.[16] He also wrote an entire book on *Religious and Spiritual Experiences*, which he argues can engage human beings authentically with "the valuational dynamics and structures of reality itself, and are thus an indispensable opening for understanding ultimate reality and our place within it."[17] More recently, he has explicitly identified his favorite symbols for ultimate reality as "the ground and abyss of being" and "the depths structures and dynamics of nature," which he understands as the "well-spring for all possibilities and their realization, not merely the ones we can appreciate . . . what we actually sense in the moral possibilities around us are definite axiological structures, including a moral logos pointing neither to the Bad nor to the Good but to if-then relationships."[18]

Of course, most symbols for ultimate reality in the religious traditions that flowed from the Axial Age have referred to divine beings that are "morally concerned in a way that is scaled to human interests, as they take shape in relation to both individual existential orientation and regulation of social life."[19] Wesley is acutely aware that his own employment of "God" language within his "naturalistic ground-of-being" model of ultimacy is a "dramatic departure from this pattern." For him, ultimate reality is not an agential-being who cares what human beings do (as in classical theism). And he rejects the idea of reserving the name "God" for a subordinate deity that is distinguished from ultimate reality (as in process theism).

Instead, Wesley wants to use the word "God" (or "God-Beyond-God") as well as "ultimate reality" to refer to the same unconditioned, indeterminate, morally irrelevant "Whence" of human experience. He knows that his approach is not likely to win a popularity contest among the Great Models of ultimate reality, at least not anytime soon. After setting out and defending his position in comparison to agential-being and subordinate-deity models, Wesley imagines his interlocutor's response: "And what is the 'payoff' for all that effort? We get an interpretation of ultimate realty that is so austerely anti-anthropomorphic that the only God on offer is irrelevant to human moral life! Why bother?"[20] Indeed, why does Wesley bother to go to all this trouble? First, he has a pastoral concern for the growing number of individuals with post-supernaturalist worldviews, many of whom may find non-supernatural models of ultimacy helpful in their pursuit of experiences of intensity. Second, he believes that the debate among proponents of the Great Models ought not to be conceived as a popularity contest but as an intellectual endeavor that rigorously contests popular conceptions of ultimate reality, which are generated by evolved cognitive biases that promote uncritical anthropomorphism.

The subtitle of *In Our Own Image: Anthropomorphism, Apophaticism, and Ultimacy* hints at Wesley's main concern with most popular models of ultimate reality or "God." In fact, he frames the debate between three of the Great Models in terms of their strategies for resisting three dimensions of anthropomorphism: Intentionality Attribution, Rational Practicality, and Narrative Comprehensibility. Humans have evolved in such a way that our minds relatively easily interpret confusing or frightening phenomena by relying on these anthropomorphic cognitive defaults. Agential-being models resist Rational Practicality, indulging in theological speculation about ultimate reality rather than focusing only on practical life challenges. Subordinate-deity models resist Intentionality Attribution, at least when it comes to "ultimate reality" (in such approaches, "God" often sounds quite intentional). Religious-naturalist models, the category into which Wesley's own proposal falls, resist Narrative Comprehensibility as well as the other two dimensions of anthropomorphism. This more radical contestation of evolutionary biases is one of the most important reasons for his commendation of naturalistic ground-of-being models of ultimacy.

If all ultimacy models are wrong and must fall into silence, how does Wesley justify ranking these Great Models in order of their anthropomorphic tendencies? Remember that apophatic modeling is not a total refusal to speak in the face of mystery. Rather, apophasis provides a way of ordering speech before its eventual and inevitable collapse. "The apophatic mystic's positive way of naming, the *via positiva*, organizes ultimacy images from the most noble to the least adequate . . . The apophatic mystic's negative way of denial, the *via negativa*, organizes literal ultimacy images from least adequate to most adequate."[21] In other words, the apophatic approach can yield a "collapsing metric," a "conceptual measure that disintegrates as we draw close to ultimate reality but that further away yields meaningful judgments of the relative adequacy of ultimacy models."[22] This metric always collapses because human cognition cannot grasp ultimate reality, but it still provides a strategy for handling the conceptual challenges of apophatic modeling by establishing the order in which the Great Models collapse—identifying the "last" (ultimate) thing that can be said about ultimacy before falling into silence.

Despite the dangers of anthropomorphism associated with the term "God," Wesley still uses it to refer to ultimate reality. This is confusing to both agential-being theists and subordinate-deity theists, all of whom use "God" in much the same way most layfolk do: to refer to a somewhat comprehensible, intentional, morally relevant being. How does Wesley defend himself?

> Against the argument that the word "God" should not be used unless it is personal theism that we have in mind, proponents of naturalistic ground-of-being . . . ultimacy models point to the long contest since the axial age over usage of "God" and cognate words. Judging by this history, confining "God" to personal theism would be changing the rules, not upholding them—and this remains the case even while acknowledging the greater popularity within both folk religion and philosophical theology of understandings of God as personal or not-less-than personal.[23]

Wesley detects a "rule" in the religious philosophical tradition: the debate over whether the term "God" should be used for non-personal models of Ultimacy has been going on for a long time between personal theists and naturalistic ground-of-being theologians, and so the latter should keep using the term for their own models (in spite of the anthropomorphic associations and confusion this causes among religious folk).

Although he regularly breaks other sorts of time-honored rules, Wesley is committed to obeying this one. "This godless world is not without an abysmal ground . . . a Creative Dao, a God Beyond All Gods, or a One Beyond Comprehension. The name of *God* still testifies to this fact, and to the reality it hints at, so long as that name is wrested away from the religious legitimators of cultural meaning making." Wesley approvingly refers to those who affirm "the name of *God* as a pointer to something unconditioned that we seem to encounter in our experience of reality . . ."[24] The same rule seems to apply to other ancient and anthropomorphically tinged terms. For example, he refers to the luminescent creativity and abysmal suffering that "are co-primal in the *divine* nature as they are in our experience . . . All things testify to the divine *glory*. All things without exception."[25] An intense experience of beauty, trauma, or insight can engage us with the axiological depths of reality, within which "we find the *holy*, and it is *sanctified* through being manifested as holy in that experience of intensity."[26]

Sometimes Wesley's obedience to this particular rule about sticking with God-language leads to rather anthropomorphic-sounding expressions. For example, he writes that "We engage God in all our moral decisions, the good and the bad . . . As we transform our environment, we can love passionately, create beautifully, connect deeply, and live justly . . . These are possibilities God *gives* us in creation. On the human scale, God's sustaining of creation constitutes an *invitation* to engage life richly, despite complex choices and inevitable failures, and thereby to engage divine reality itself."[27]

A desire to conform to ancient theological protocols is not the only reason Wesley seems willing to risk confusion (at best) and anthropomorphic interpretations of his position (at worst) by using the word "God" in this unusual way. This willingness is also an expression of his commitment to salvage what he can of "religious" traditions; as their supernatural beliefs and behaviors are dismantled by naturalism and secularism, Wesley wants to find and refurbish those parts of these traditions that post-supernaturalists might be able to use in constructing new modes of intensive axiological engagement with ultimate reality.

Modeling "Religion"

I'm guessing that most of the readers of this volume would sit on the philosophy, theology, and ethics side of the metaphysical chapel in which Wesley marries the disciplines of religious philosophy and computer science. In this section, I provide such readers with a brief introduction to some of the ways in which computational methods have been applied to the study of "religion." Like "God" in the subheading of the previous section, this term also appears in scare quotes for reasons that will soon become obvious. As is the case in almost all scientific approaches to the study of psychological and social phenomena, the use of computer science methodologies requires that the relevant variables be identified and operationalized so that their function within a system or their distribution within a population can be statistically measured and analyzed. As we will see, this applies equally to scientific research on "religion."

My collaboration with Wesley on computer models of religion began as part of our work in an interdisciplinary research project headed by Ian Hodder at the archaeological site of the Neolithic town of Catalhoyuk in what is now southeastern Turkey. Over several intense days in a Turkish hotel, Wesley grilled me on my knowledge of the site and the ways in which theories from disciplines such as cognitive science, moral psychology, and cultural anthropology might shed light on the conditions under which—and the mechanisms by which—Neolithic humans shifted from a social structure sustained primarily by hunting and gathering to one characterized by sedentation and agriculture. That was one of the most challenging and intellectually enjoyable experiences of my academic career—I was hooked! The causal architecture that began to take shape during those days eventually became the basis for a computer model that simulated the role of religion within the dynamics of the complex adaptive social systems leading up to and beyond Catalhoyuk.[28]

Prior to that time, Wesley had already done work on at least three other computational models of phenomena related to religion, including a model of the evolution of groups with (more or less) costly signals of commitment,[29] a model of the transmission of violent tendencies among (some) anabaptist churches during the radical reformation,[30] and a systems-dynamics model of the causes and consequences of secularization.[31] Since that time, Wesley and I have co-authored and co-presented a number of papers on the use of computer modeling and simulation in religion and the humanities more generally,[32] and on the sort of meta-ethical and moral issues that are entangled within such endeavors.[33] We have also developed a model of the role of religious ideas and practices in the shift from pre-axial to axial age civilizational forms in west, south, and east Asia.[34]

Most of our collaborative computer modeling has occurred in the context of the Modeling Religion Project (MRP) and the Modeling Religion in Norway (MODRN) project, which were funded by the John Templeton Foundation and The Research Council of Norway, respectively. As part of the MRP, our research teams developed a variety of computational models. For example, we developed agent-based models that are able to simulate the role of religiosity in managing experiences of mortality salience[35] and the role of identity fusion and other social psychological mechanisms in the generation of mutually escalating religious violence.[36] In each of these latter models, we operationalized "religiosity" as the integration of two distinguishable but interrelated statistically measurable traits: (1) the tendency to look for (and believe in) familiar supernatural agents, and (2) the tendency to long for (and participate in) familiar religious rituals. Both of these dispositions are intensified by mortality salience.

In other words, death awareness can activate two evolved dispositions related to religion: reliance on supernatural causality (to explain confusing or threatening events) and compliance with supernatural conventions (to ease anxiety in ritually cohesive groups). These tendencies can be further amplified by personality and contextual factors that lead individuals to identify strongly with their in-group. This is an example of the "operationalization" of religiously salient variables. By clearly specifying the phenomena we deemed "religious," we were able to construct artificial societies of simulated agents with varying levels of these traits and to develop simulation experiments to test hypotheses about the mechanisms that increment or decrement them in human populations.

The MODRN project also produced several computational models meant to contribute to the scientific study of religion. For example, the variables and interaction rules of the simulated agents in one of our recently published models were formulated in light of factor analyses of international social surveys as well as other empirical research demonstrating the positive correlation between low religiosity and high education and existential security in human populations.[37] But does increased education within homophily networks *cause* religiosity to decline? Our simulation experiments lent plausibility to this hypothesis by forecasting the rates of decline in belief in God and supernatural agents in twenty-two countries up to three times more accurately than linear regression models. This helps to explain why the "godless" prosper in cultural contexts with high levels of education and existential security, such as Scandinavian societies.[38] The MODRN project also published computer models that simulate societies in which one can "grow" populations where there are larger numbers of analytic and altruistic atheists who are affiliated in healthy social networks.[39]

Let's return to the scare quotes around "religion." In all of these computer models, that contentious term is operationalized by referring to beliefs in and rituals around *supernatural agents*—an approach almost universally followed in the bio-cultural study of religion.[40] This approach makes sense not only because it allows scientists to identify statistically measurable traits in a population, but also because *supernatural* beliefs and ritual behaviors are consistent factors found in factor analyses of psychological and sociological data sets. For example, one study found that "supernatural-related belief/practice" is "the only unique diagnostic feature of religiosity . . . and empirically distinct from sociability, virtue, hope, etc."[41] The findings of another set of psychological experiments designed to measure the implicit beliefs of believers and skeptics suggests that "supernatural content" is "the only thing that distinguishes religiosity from non-religiosity."[42] Regression analysis suggests that spirituality—like religiosity—is primarily predicted by "belief in supernatural spirits."[43] Recent factor analyses of survey data also confirm that beliefs and practices related to supernatural forces form a relatively independent cluster of variables.[44]

In his publications within the *scientific* study of religion, Wesley consistently uses stipulated definitions that refer to the alleged supernatural agents and authorities imaginatively engaged by religious in-groups. In other contexts, however, when he is engaging philosophers of religion, philosophical theologians, and scholars in religious studies, Wesley uses the term "religion" in a quite different way. In his book *Religious Philosophy*, for example, he answers the question "What are the universal or partial features of religion?" by describing "the religious" as a vague category that involves the following:

- A way to relate every aspect of life to something ultimate and fundamental, in terms of ideas, values, and practices.

- An answer to concerns about death and immortality, including the ultimate origins, fate, and meaning of human life and all of reality.

- A means of bonding human beings tightly together through obligation, responsibility, and ritual, in order to stabilize social life and realize relational ideals such as peace, pleasure, power, or prosperity.

- A solution to the problem of human evil and a means of healing, liberation, social transformation, and personal self-cultivation.

- A source of orienting narratives by which we discern our place in a cosmological framework and gather the courage to make moral decisions.[45]

Note that none of the descriptions of these features include any reference to *supernatural agents* and that all of them could just as easily apply to individuals and groups committed to atheism and metaphysical naturalism as they do to those committed to the Islamic State or Roman Catholicism.[46]

As a thoroughgoing naturalist, Wesley rejects the existence of any and all supernatural agents, but still calls himself "religious." In fact, when writing as a theologian or philosopher, he tends to call *everyone* religious: the human race is *Homo religious*.[47] He argues that all human knowledge is in some sense religious. "If we understand ultimate reality as the ground of being in naturalistic fashion . . . then *all knowledge*, regardless of subject matter, is the result of engagement with a reality that grounds and transcends us, that we encounter as partially given rather than entirely at our cognitive disposal, that resists our ideas about it to some degree, and that forces us to adapt our interpretations."[48] Indeed, if all human experience is "religious" in this vague sense, then we can "expect to find ultimacy not just in religious practices and beliefs and communities, but lying at the intense root of every aspect of human life."[49] All of this is related to Wesley's use of the apparently oxymoronic phrase "religious naturalist" to describe his own apophatic approach to modeling God or ultimate reality.

When writing for those on the "scientific" side of his academic audience, Wesley uses conceptual or computational models that define religion with reference to particular phenomena related to supernatural agent beliefs and behaviors. When writing for those on the "theological" side, however, he uses the term religion (and God) in a way that refers far more broadly to universal human experiences of natural phenomena. In my view, this not only unnecessarily confuses and complicates the multidisciplinary conversations Wesley aims to foster but also inadequately confronts and contests the religious biases that foster superstition and segregation in our contemporary global context. This brings me, at last, to the main difference between us.

God, Forsaken . . . and No Religion Too

It comes down to this: I want to forsake the use of the word "God" when referring to the truly infinite and the use of the word "religion" when referring to the general capacity of human beings to engage in meaningful and valuable experiences. I want to use these concepts to designate the philosophically incoherent idea of a Supranatural Agent invented by theologians in the west Asian monotheistic traditions and to the supernatural beliefs and practices of laypeople that bind them together in ritually mediated in-groups, respectively. Wesley, on the other hand, wants (sometimes) to use the term "God" to indicate his non-anthropomorphic model of "ultimate reality" and the term "religion" to indicate the axiologically intense aspects of human life.

What is at stake here? Why can't Wesley and I stop arguing about this (apparently) minor difference in our *formal* rhetorical use of a couple of terms? After all, when it comes to our *material* positions on philosophical issues related to metaphysics, epistemology, and ethics (not to mention scientific issues related to the bio-cultural study of shared imaginative engagement with axiologically relevant supernatural agents), we seem to agree on almost everything.

In the introduction to this chapter, I alluded to the fact that our disagreement had something to do with the philosophy of religion. Wesley has worked hard over the years to reform and reinvigorate this academic discipline, which he describes as a form of multidisciplinary comparative inquiry involving "philosophical research into religious beliefs and practices."[50] We both agree that philosophers *of religion* ought to approach their subject matter in a way that is informed by the theoretical insights and empirical findings of the many scientific disciplines that converge within the "bio-cultural" study of religion. We also agree that the *philosophy of* religion should strive to be as unbiased as any other sub-discipline (e.g., the philosophy of language, the philosophy of mind, the philosophy of education). Finally, we both believe that the work of philosophers of religion could have *practical* ramifications in the real world as future generations increasingly let go of reliance on supernatural agents and compliance with supernatural authorities to make sense of nature and act sensibly in society.

However, we disagree on the best strategy for putting the philosophy of religion to good use in helping humanity survive and thrive as we make the transition from cultural configurations whose cohesion relies on hidden gods to new forms of secular organization that rely on healthy governments and institutions. In the previous section, I suggested that Wesley's terminological habits unnecessarily confuse and complicate multidisciplinary conversations and inadequately confront and contest religious biases that engender superstition and segregation. In this section I try to explain why I think this is the case by setting our conversation in the context of the heuristic framework of the theory of theogonic reproduction, which I have developed elsewhere.[51]

The evolution of theogonic (god-bearing) mechanisms helps to explain where supernatural agent conceptions come from and why people keep them around. Why are gods so easily "born" in human minds and so consistently "borne" across human cultures? Most contemporary Homo sapiens are naturally drawn into the bio-cultural force field created by the integration of two reciprocally reinforcing evolved tendencies: anthropomorphic promiscuity and sociographic prudery (see figure 2.1). These cognitive and coalitional

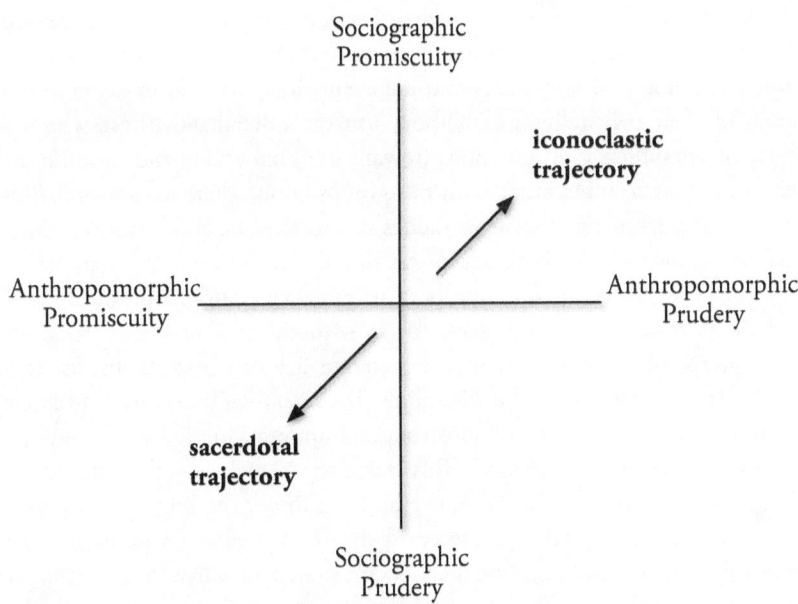

Figure 2.1. Trajectories in the philosophy of religion.

tendencies are part of our phylogenetic inheritance and have been reinforced by millennia of social entrainment practices. In the environment of our early ancestors, the selective advantage went to hominids who were able to quickly detect relevant agents in the natural environment and whose groups were adequately protected from dissolution as a result of cheaters and freeloaders in the social environment.

Think of the horizontal line in figure 2.1 as a continuum on which one can mark an individual's tendency to guess "hidden human-like supernatural force" when confronted with ambiguous phenomena in the natural environment. An anthropomorphically promiscuous person will always be on the lookout for intentional causes, jumping at explanations that appeal to "agency" even (or especially) when such inferences are not easily verifiable or falsifiable. Anthropomorphic prudes, on the other hand, are suspicious about such appeals. They prefer to reflect more carefully before giving in to the allure of facile explanations involving mysterious supernatural agents.

The vertical line represents a continuum on which one can register how tightly a person is bound to those modes of inscribing the social field that are constituted and regulated by the putative supernatural authorities of a religious coalition with which he or she identifies. The sociographically prudish are strongly committed to the divinely sanctioned social norms of their in-group, following and protecting them even at great cost to themselves. They are more likely to be suspicious of out-groups and to accept claims or demands that appeal to the supernatural agents imaginatively engaged in the rituals of their own religious coalition. On the other hand, those who are more sociographically promiscuous (toward the high end of the continuum) are more open to intercourse with out-groups about alternate normativities and to the pursuit of innovative modes of creative social inscription. Such persons are also less likely to accept restrictions or assertions that are based only (or even primarily) on appeals to religious conventions or authorities.

What does any of this have to do with the philosophy of religion? The conceptual framework depicted in figure 2.1 can help us discern two distinct trajectories within this discipline. The *sacerdotal* trajectory (lower left quadrant) has by far been the most popular among philosophers interested in religion and the idea of God. This trajectory is fueled by the integration of the evolved biases discussed above and reinforces the linguistic symbols of transcendence erected and protected by priestly elites, symbols that all too easily activate and amplify their flock's shared imaginative engagement with person-like, coalition-favoring disembodied intentional forces. Unfortunately, these biases are reciprocally reinforcing: thinking about supernatural agents activates segregative inscriptions of the social field, and participating in supernatural rituals activates superstitious interpretations of natural phenomena.[52] These mutually amplifying theistic biases helped hold together some human in-groups (as they competed with and sometimes destroyed out-groups), but they have now become maladaptive in our contemporary pluralistic, ecologically fragile environment.

On the other hand, the *iconoclastic* trajectory (upper right quadrant of figure 2.1) has been the road far less traveled among philosophers of religion. As the central two sections of this chapter amply attest, Wesley strongly prefers this path with its integration of naturalist and secularist sensibilities. He wants to locate the philosophy of religion in the University and resists apologetic approaches within the discipline that defend a particular supernatural coalition. And his apophatic theology clearly involves a more "comprehensive *iconoclastic* protest against anthropomorphism" than most scholars are willing to make.[53] In other words, Wesley is purposely promiscuous in his sociography and a veritable paragon of prudish anthropomorphism. He does the hard intellectual work and makes the necessary emotional effort to challenge the biases that keep most (religious) philosophers under the spell of sacerdotalism.

Wesley and I both do our best to follow this iconoclastic trajectory, but we differ in the extent to which we are willing to challenge the linguistic "icons" of allegedly transcendent supernatural agents around which the priestly and intellectual elites of religious coalitions rally their in-group members, reinforcing laypeople's superstitious beliefs and segregative behaviors while maintaining their own dominant role in mediating ritual access to supernatural agents and policing interpretation of supernatural authorities. My strategy, to paraphrase Nietzsche, is to do philosophy (of religion) with a hammer. This does not *always* mean smashing icons to bits; hammers can also be used to sound out their hollowness or to pry them apart and build something new and useful. But mostly yes: I prefer the smashing. My relatively aggressive iconoclasm is driven primarily by my worry about the potentially deleterious effects of the vestiges of Platonism in philosophy and theology on the psychological and political well-being of contemporary members of Homo sapiens.[54]

The dangers inherent in supernatural beliefs and behaviors are not lost on Wesley. "No matter how invisible they may seem, religious ideas can be socially explosive under triggering circumstances."⁵⁵ Generally speaking, however, his iconoclasm is far gentler than mine. There are at least two reasons for this. First, he believes that the symbols of traditional religious language, even those that are overtly anthropomorphic, are not only potentially valuable for the task of apophatic modeling but actually necessary for any and all attempts at effing the ineffable. "Without religious language, without its technical tricks and its specialized discourse communities, . . . we'd be *mute* in the face of ultimate reality . . . I can say *nothing at all* about it, and it remains unthinkable, without the linguistic exertions of vast religious traditions with their memorial encodings of insight. This fact *morally obliges me to take religion seriously even when its doctrines are fantastic and its fanatics are dangerous.*"⁵⁶

A second reason Wesley hesitates to unleash his inner Nietzsche on the pious but perilous parlance that pervades priestly philosophy is practical. He believes that most human beings are dependent on the structures provided by religious rituals and the nurture of professional pastors to help them cultivate the virtues they need to live well and feel good in the modern world. He worries that hammering too strongly on the psychologically repressive and politically oppressive iconic edifices constructed and defended by followers of the sacerdotal trajectory would leave future generations without the resources they need to guide them into and through intense experiences with the axiological depth structures of reality. I hesitate to criticize Wesley's judgment here not only because I respect his wisdom on all matters, but also because on this particular issue his assessment is based on decades of ethnographic observation at dozens if not hundreds of churches and thousands of conversations with students and colleagues at his day job training pastors at Boston University School of Theology. I find the courage to criticize anyway because of my own experience of (and conversations with others about) the abuses of religion, and of the capacity of individuals in pluralistic, existentially secure, secular contexts characterized by high levels of naturalist and humanist education and freedom of expression, to engage those axiological depths without any help from religious icons.

I say let "God" be forsaken, except as a designation for the anthropomorphic being that the term evokes in the minds of almost all philosophers of religion and all normal people. Richard Dawkins would agree with me. Wesley's response: "why should religious naturalists surrender the word 'God,' which has always been contested, simply turning it over to personalist, supranaturalist theists because Dawkins says they should. Surely it is a word worth fighting for."⁵⁷ Surely not, I reply. And the reason for turning it over is not "simply" because Dawkins (or I) say he should, but because it weakens the force of his apophatic argumentation by confusing his philosophical interlocutors and invites the very anthropomorphic interpretations against which he so vigorously and valiantly battles.

And no "religion" too. Or at least no use of the term to refer to general phenomena that applies to all human experiences and every human group. If religion refers to everything, then it might as well refer to nothing because it fails to pick out any empirically tractable distinction in the real world (such as supernaturalist, as opposed to naturalist, beliefs). The only people who typically use the term in this broad way are conservative apologists when they are trying to defend the value of their own in-groups and liberal scholars when they are trying to obscure the dangers of religion so as not to offend members of out-groups. Wesley is neither. I argue that he should give up this usage even when writing for theologians, and stick with the way in which he employs the term when writing for computer modelers and scientists who study religion. This would have the added benefit of further unveiling the covert operation of the theistic biases that engender beliefs in discarnate anthropomorphic entities.

And this is where this "debate" with Wesley always ends, whether it is carried out in private or over drinks in front of an audience (red wine for me, water for Wesley, hard liquor for everyone else). Despite all that we share in common, we differ in our judgments about the way in which we should use terms like religion and God. Wesley finds my usage insufficiently sensitive to the valuable role that religious ideas and institutions can play in people's lives as our species increasingly shifts from supernaturalism to naturalism. I find Wesley's usage insufficiently sensitive to the damaging role that they play in activating evolved biases that amplify superstition and segregation, thereby diminishing our prospects for making the shift peacefully (or at all). After every iteration of this argument, I think the same thing: even though neither of us will ever budge, it is probably healthy for us to keep having the conversation because the most feasible strategy for managing the shift likely involves a creative tension between our positions. Drinks all around!

Notes

1. George E. P. Box and Norman Richard Draper, *Empirical Model-Building and Response Surfaces* (New York: Wiley, 1987), 424, http://hdl.handle.net/2027/umn.31951d00096163f.

2. Andreas Tolk, "Code of Ethics," in *The Profession of Modeling and Simulation: Discipline, Ethics, Education, Vocation, Societies, And Economics*, ed. Andreas Tolk and Tuncer Oren (Hoboken, NJ: John Wiley & Sons, 2017), 47.

3. Wesley J. Wildman, "Really Ultimate Reality," *Theology and Science* 15, no. 3 (2017): 260. See also Wesley J. Wildman, "Introduction to Negative Theology," in *Models of God and Alternative Ultimate Realities*, ed. J. Diller and A. Kasher (Dordrecht: Springer, 2013), 768.

4. Wesley J. Wildman, *In Our Own Image: Anthropomorphism, Apophaticism, and Ultimacy* (New York, NY: Oxford University Press, 2018), viii.

5. Wesley J. Wildman, *Effing the Ineffable: Existential Mumblings at the Limits of Language* (Albany, NY: State University of New York Press, 2018), 217.

6. Wesley J. Wildman, "Axiological Sensitivity: Its Origins, Dynamic Structures, and Significance for Theological Anthropology," in *Human Origins and the Image of God*, ed. Christopher Lilley and Daniel J. Pedersen (Grand Rapids, MI: Eerdmans, 2017), 152.

7. Wildman, *In Our Own Image*, 41. Emphasis added.

8. Wesley J. Wildman, "Ground-of-Being Theologies," in *The Oxford Handbook of Religion and Science* (Oxford: Oxford University Press, 2006), 624.

9. Wildman, *Effing the Ineffable: Existential Mumblings at the Limits of Language*, 26.

10. Wildman, "Ground-of-Being Theologies," 618–19.

11. Wesley J. Wildman, *Religious Philosophy as Multidisciplinary Comparative Inquiry: Envisioning a Future for the Philosophy of Religion* (Albany, NY: State University of New York Press, 2011), 83.

12. Wildman, *In Our Own Image*, 7. See also Wildman, *Effing the Ineffable: Existential Mumblings at the Limits of Language*, 3.

13. Wesley J. Wildman, "Behind, Between, and beyond Anthropomorphic Models of Ultimate Reality," *Philosophia* 35 (2007): 407–25.

14. Wesley J. Wildman, *Science and Religious Anthropology: A Spiritually Evocative Naturalist Interpretation of Human Life* (Farnham: Ashgate, 2009), 23.

15. Robert C. Neville and Wesley J. Wildman, "Comparative Conclusions about Ultimate Realities," in *Ultimate Realities*, ed. Robert C. Neville (Albany, NY: State University of New York Press, 2001), 151.

16. Wildman, *Religious Philosophy as Multidisciplinary Comparative Inquiry*.

17. Wesley J. Wildman, *Religious and Spiritual Experiences*, reprint ed. (Cambridge: Cambridge University Press, 2014), 256.

18. Wildman, *Effing the Ineffable: Existential Mumblings at the Limits of Language*, 278.

19. Wildman, *In Our Own Image*, 210.

20. Wildman, 210–11.

21. Wildman, *Effing the Ineffable: Existential Mumblings at the Limits of Language*, 34–35.

22. Wildman, *In Our Own Image*, 41.

23. Wildman, 204.

24. Wildman, *Religious Philosophy as Multidisciplinary Comparative Inquiry*, 83. Emphasis added.

25. Wildman, *Effing the Ineffable: Existential Mumblings at the Limits of Language*, 85.

26. Wildman, "Introduction to Negative Theology," 257. Emphases added.

27. Wildman, *In Our Own Image*, 226. Emphasis added.

28. F. LeRon Shults and Wesley J. Wildman, "Simulating Religious Entanglement and Social Investment in the Neolithic," in *Religion, History and Place in the Origin of Settled Life*, ed. Ian Hodder (Colorado Springs, CO: University of Colorado Press, 2018), 33–63.

29. Wesley J. Wildman and Richard Sosis, "Stability of Groups with Costly Beliefs and Practices," *JASSS* 14, no. 3 (2011).

30. L. J. Matthews et al., "Cultural Inheritance or Cultural Diffusion of Religious Violence? A Quantitative Case Study of the Radical Reformation," *Religion, Brain & Behavior* 3, no. 1 (2013): 3–15.

31. Wesley J. Wildman, "Religious Naturalism: Contradiction in Terms of Future Spiritual Juggernaut?," in *A 21st Century Debate on Science and Religion*, ed. Shiva Khalili, Fraser Watts, and Harris Wiseman (Cambridge: Cambridge Scholars Press, 2017), 52–71.

32. Wesley J. Wildman, Paul A. Fishwick, and F. LeRon Shults, "Teaching at the Intersection of Simulation and the Humanities," ed. W. K. V. Chan, *Proceedings of the 2017 Winter Simulation Conference*, 2017, 1–13.

33. F. LeRon Shults and Wesley J. Wildman, "Ethics, Computer Simulation, and the Future of Humanity," in *Human Simulation: Perspectives, Insights and Applications*, ed. Saikou Y. Diallo et al. (Berlin: Springer, 2019), 21–40.

34. F. LeRon Shults et al., "Multiple Axialities: A Computational Model of the Axial Age," *Journal of Cognition and Culture* 18, no. 4 (2018): 537–64.

35. F. LeRon Shults et al., "Modeling Terror Management Theory: Computer Simulations of the Impact of Mortality Salience on Religiosity," *Religion, Brain & Behavior* 8, no. 1 (2018): 77–100.

36. F. LeRon Shults, Ross Gore, Wesley J. Wildman, Christopher J. Lynch, Justin E. Lane, and Monica Duffy Toft, "A Generative Model of the Mutual Escalation of Anxiety Between Religious Groups," *Journal of Artificial Societies and Social Simulation* 21, no. 4 (2018): 1–28.

37. Ross Gore, Carlos Lemos, F. LeRon Shults, and Wesley J. Wildman, "Forecasting Changes in Religiosity and Existential Security with an Agent-Based Model," *Journal of Artificial Societies and Social Simulation* 21 (2018): 1–31.

38. F. LeRon Shults et al., "Why Do the Godless Prosper? Modeling the Cognitive and Coalitional Mechanisms That Promote Atheism," *Psychology of Religion and Spirituality* 10, no. 3 (2018): 218–28.

39. Luke Galen, Ross Gore, and F. LeRon Shults, "Modeling the Effects of Religious Belief and Affiliation on Prosociality," *Secularism & Nonreligion* 10, no. 6 (2021); Ryan Cragun, Kevin McCaffree, Ivan Puga-Gonzalez, Wesley J. Wildman, and F. LeRon Shults, "Religious Exiting and Social Networks: Computer Simulations of Religious/Secular Pluralism," *Secularism and Nonreligion* 10, no. 1 (2021).

40. F. LeRon Shults, *Practicing Safe Sects: Religious Reproduction in Scientific and Philosophical Perspective* (Leiden: Brill Academic, 2018).

41. James Schuurmans-Stekhoven, "Are We, Like Sheep, Going Astray: Is Costly Signaling (or Any Other Mechanism) Necessary to Explain the Belief-as-Benefit Effect?," *Religion, Brain & Behavior* 7, no. 3 (July 7, 2016): 36, https://doi.org/10.1080/2153599X.2016.1156558.

42. Marjaana Lindeman, Annika M. Svedholm-Häkkinen, and Tapani Riekki, "Skepticism: Genuine Unbelief or Implicit Beliefs in the Supernatural?," *Consciousness and Cognition* 42 (2016): 225, https://doi.org/10.1016/j.concog.2016.03.019.

43. Marjaana Lindeman, Sandra Blomqvist, and Mikito Takada, "Distinguishing Spirituality From Other Constructs: Not A Matter of Well-Being but of Belief in Supernatural Spirits," *Journal of Nervous and Mental Disease* 200, no. 2 (2012): 172, https://doi.org/10.1097/NMD.0b013e3182439719.

44. Malcolm B. Schofield et al., "Mental Representations of the Supernatural: A Cluster Analysis of Religiosity, Spirituality and Paranormal Belief," *Personality and Individual Differences* 101 (2016): 419–24, https://doi.org/10.1016/j.paid.2016.06.020; Lemos et al., "Exploratory and Confirmatory Analyses of Religiosity: A Four-Factor Conceptual Model."

45. Wildman, *Religious Philosophy as Multidisciplinary Comparative Inquiry*.

46. For a fuller discussion of potential problems with this usage of the term "religion" and of the importance of balancing iconoclasm with sensitivity to the human need for continuity, see F. LeRon Shults, "Strategies for Promoting Safe Sects: Response to Brandon Daniel-Hughes and Jeffrey B. Speaks," *American Journal of Theology & Philosophy* 39, no. 3 (2018): 80–93.

47. Wildman, *Science and Religious Anthropology*, 218.

48. Wildman, *In Our Own Image*, 197.

49. Wildman, *Religious and Spiritual Experiences*, 256.

50. Wesley J. Wildman, "Reforming Philosophy of Religion for the Modern Academy," in *Reconfigurations of Philosophy of Religion: A Possible Future*, ed. Jim Kanaris (Albany, NY: State University of New York Press, 2018), 253–69.

51. F. LeRon Shults, *Theology after the Birth of God: Atheist Conceptions in Cognition and Culture*, Radical Theologies (New York: Palgrave Macmillan, 2014); Shults, *Practicing Safe Sects: Religious Reproduction in Scientific and Philosophical Perspective*.

52. For a discussion of the empirical evidence for these claims, see Shults, *Practicing Safe Sects: Religious Reproduction in Scientific and Philosophical Perspective*.

53. Wildman, *In Our Own Image*, 71.

54. F. LeRon Shults, *Iconoclastic Theology: Gilles Deleuze and the Secretion of Atheism*, Plateaus—New Directions in Deleuze Studies (Edinburgh: Edinburgh University Press, 2014). F. LeRon Shults, "How to Survive the Anthropocene: Adaptive Atheism and the Evolution of Homo Deiparensis," *Religions* 6, no. 2 (2015): 1–18; F. LeRon Shults, "Toxic Theisms? New Strategies for Prebunking Religious Belief-Behavior Complexes," *Journal of Cognitive Historiography* 5, no. 2 (2020): 1–19.

55. Wildman, *In Our Own Image*, 53.

56. Wildman, *Effing the Ineffable: Existential Mumblings at the Limits of Language*, 289.

57. Wildman, *Religious and Spiritual Experiences*, 25.

3

Wildman's Reconstruction of Philosophy of Religion

Timothy D. Knepper

In this chapter, I address Wesley Wildman's philosophy of religion in general and its influence on my own philosophy of religion in particular. I take Wildman's *Religious Philosophy as Multidisciplinary Comparative Inquiry* as representative, examining it with respect to three issues in which it has had the most influence on my own philosophy of religion: multidisciplinary inquiry and correction, theological inclusion and bias, and religious philosophy and the public. In each case, I do not do so for my own reminiscent indulgence, but because I find these issues crucial for the future success of philosophy of religion, especially as it continues to go through the growing pains of globalization and diversification. In each case, though, I also highlight ways in which my own philosophy of religion has wrestled with, and philosophy of religion more generally should wrestle with, Wildman's solutions to these issues. I state them here as questions: When, if at all, should philosophers of religion abandon fruitless lines of inquiry, and might some lines of inquiry simply be traps of language that should not be investigated at all? Which "theologians" should be allowed a place at the table of philosophy of religion, and if we invite some, must we not we invite all? What are the best rhetorical and practical courses of action to galvanize and empower like-minded philosophers of religion to practice "multidisciplinary and comparative inquiry"?

Wildman's Reconstruction of Philosophy of Religion

I count among my good fortunes the fact that I studied philosophy of religion at Boston University. I was not so sure about this fortune immediately after graduating. There were not many job openings in philosophy of religion, and those that were, were designed for traditional-theistic philosophers of religion.

This was not how philosophy of religion was taught at Boston University, at least not while I was there. We had pragmatist philosophers of religion, comparativist philosophers of religion, Wittgensteinian philosophers of religion, Continental philosophers of religion, fideist philosophers of religion, non-Western philosophers of religion, and historians of modern philosophy of religion. But we did not have traditional-theistic philosophers of religion, not by my reckoning anyway.

Among these many perspectives and approaches, none influenced my own philosophy of religion more than Wesley Wildman's. Twelve years removed from Boston University, this influence only deepens—sometimes in spite of my efforts to resist it.

In this chapter, I address three of these post-BU, Wildman influences: multidisciplinary inquiry and correction, theological perspectives and bias, and religious philosophy and the public. In each case, I do not do so for my own reminiscent indulgence, but because I find these influences crucial for the future success of philosophy of religion. In each case, I also highlight those ways in which I still wrestle with certain aspects of these influences.

Having Hope for Correction

My dissertation under Wesley's direction was tripartite: one part history of mysticism scholarship with respect to the issue of ineffability, one part collection of philo-linguistic tools for the analysis of ineffability discourse, one part actual analysis of ineffability discourse in the Dionysian corpus. The heart of my argument in Part I went something like this: one can never know if a mystical experience is ineffable, since to make it some-thing about which the question of in/effability can be raised is to make it effable in some way; only that which is not any-thing can be ineffable. The issue of ineffability—I therefore claimed—was intractable. One never has extra-semiotic access to some allegedly ineffable thing, for insofar as it becomes a thing it is some-thing that is some-how sayable. My dissertation then went on to argue that scholars should instead study the manageable issue of how ineffability is expressed, especially in the case of so-called "performances of ineffability" that attempt to show that language cannot express something by attempting to make language fail.

I hope I am not delusional in believing that Wesley liked my dissertation. Nonetheless, he disagreed with my intractability argument—who knows whether and how we will be able to study ineffability in the future? We will have to try and see what does and does not work.

If I am not mistaken, then, I am one of the nameless interlocutors in one of the chapter 2 arguments in *Religious Philosophy as Multidisciplinary Comparative Inquiry*. Here, in a section titled "Contexts and the Styles of Religious Philosophy," Wesley sets about illustrating how social and historical contexts are crucial to the seven "styles" of religious philosophy: phenomenological, comparative, historical, analytical, literary, theoretical, and evaluative.[1] His example comes from the study of mystical experience, more particularly the question of whether mystical experiences are the same or different cross-culturally. After briefly summarizing the Forman-ian, perennialist position and the Katz-ian, contextualist position, Wesley underscores the different worldviews, motivations, and environments that underlie this debate. Given this disparity, one might despair of ever resolving this debate. Writes Wesley: "Such interpreters would see this dispute as evidence for their claim that many debates in religious philosophy are intractable, and thus for the futility of inquiry aimed at resolving them."[2] To the contrary, though, Wesley sees this context-based disagreement "as offering precisely the sort of tension needed to refine hypotheses about the cause and significance of mystical experiences."[3] Here, Wesley mentions functional-imaging brain scans and the like: if these "eventually permit correlations to be established with categories used in phenomenological description and comparison, there might emerge a stable set of comparative phenomenological categories that would make the problem tractable in a way that it is not at present."[4] If so, then the features of the context-based disagreement between perennialists and contextualists would serve as an aid rather than an obstacle to inquiry.

This argument is just one example of Wesley's hypothetical-critical method in practice. As a form of inquiry, religious philosophy does as other forms of inquiry do—hypothesizes and corrects. Every hypothesis is in principle correctable. No hypothesis ever rises above the need for correction or sinks below the threshold of correction. And when correction occurs, it does so by means of the feedback potential of reality. Indeed, these three points are just the last three of Wesley's six emphases of his pragmatic theory of inquiry:[5]

> (4) Correction: inquiry is tentative formulation of hypotheses, continually seeking correction.
>
> (5) Fallibilism: beliefs are always subject to correction.
>
> (6) Critical realism: the source of correction is a feedback potential or an experiential resistance to hypotheses; this is the proper empirical basis for speaking of sensible, structured reality external to human experience.[6]

What is key for religious philosophy, then, is how we "marshal corrective resources" within the "sociality of inquiry." Regarding the former (marshalling corrective resources), Wesley indicates that there are five ways in which sources of correction can be developed:

> (1) Developing specialized discourse whose relatively precise and efficient terminology facilitates more and better work with less effort;
>
> (2) Accumulating a great deal of wisdom and encoding it in practices and working assumptions that function as tested guides for subsequent inquiries in religious philosophy;
>
> (3) Allowing multiple experts to cooperate on the same problem, building on each other's results;
>
> (4) Promoting agility in inquiry through group excitement about a recent trend that rapidly catalyzes attention and effort on the emerging problem area;
>
> (5) Introducing a degree of conservatism in inquiry, which resists the hasty abandonment of a promising idea when it comes upon hard times, and promoting problem-solving strategies designed to protect the idea if at all possible.[7]

Regarding the latter (sociality of inquiry), Wesley specifies five dimensions of the dynamism inherent in the sociality of inquiry:

(1) We can discover unanticipated resources that dramatically change the prospects of finding a solution to a problem;

(2) We can arrive at new levels of efficiency in the social organization of inquiries, thereby changing the prospects for making advances in solving complex problems;

(3) We can invent;

(4) We can adjust to new information;

(5) We can bend social will to particular ends.[8]

It is item #5 from the first list and item #1 from the second list that are especially relevant to the ineffability issue. In the case of #5 (from the first list), I believe Wesley would advise scholars of religion not to abandon, whether hastily or not, the ineffability doctrine, which maintains that there is an ineffable core to something religious, be it experiential or metaphysical. Take, for example, Wesley's exposition of the mystico-theological tradition of religious philosophy. With respect to this tradition, Wesley says that "[i]t makes prima facie sense to suppose that everything we know is dependent on something so dense with value and meaning that we only ever engage fragments of it, and also that we can and do engage it in our fragmentary ways."[9] Wesley therefore finds this core hypothesis of the mystico-theological tradition "generally compelling—to atheist, nontheist, and theist alike."[10] Moreover, Wesley notes that, contra the contextualists, the "similarities among mystical-theological conceptual frameworks are more pronounced than the similarities among mystical writing and mystical experiences."[11]

In the case of #1 (from the second list), we now see that Wesley's earlier claim that functional-imaging brain scans might one day resolve the perennialist-contextualist debate constitutes a model example of the kind of "unanticipated resource" that could "dramatically change the prospects of finding a solution to a problem."

Arguably, though, the ineffability issue has not advanced, and the contextualist paradigm is still ascendant in the academic study of religion. Neuroscience—again, arguably—has not been of much use in settling this issue. Even if blood flow is decreased to conceptual-linguistic processing regions of the brain during mystical experiences, that hardly entails that such experiences are ineffable.[12] (Only total decrease would entail total ineffability, but with total decrease we are totally dead.) Moreover, insofar as these are experiences *for experiencers*, it would seem that these experiences must be some-thing of some value that is therefore sayable in some way.

If all this is true—in fact, even if not—we can ask the question, what shall we philosophers of religion do when research fails to advance? When, if ever, is it time to throw in the towel on a hypothesis? Are some religious hypotheses simply dead ends by definition or ambition?

Let us look at some of the things that Wesley has to say about this in *Religious Philosophy*. First, in the context of a discussion of "The Power Source of Inquiry," Wesley details two reasons why "we can correct some hypotheses more easily than others (and some seemingly not at all)," one of which involves "the way the world is," the other, "the way human beings are" (as embodied and social inquirers).[13] In the former case, the correctability of hypotheses turns on the "feedback potential" of the world; in the latter case, how well humans and social organizations can take advantage of this feedback potential.[14] This means that in cases of difficulty, it is never easy to know whether and to what degree these are due to the way the world is or the way that humans are. Later, within the context of a treatment of "Specialized Discourse Communities and Inquiry," Wesley offers an account of three different ways in which specialized languages and communities can advance inquiry, the first of which best fits the ineffability issue: "in domains of inquiry where the feedback potential is weak, there is little agreement on procedures and norms for inquiry"; here, social innovation by specialized discourse communities is required.[15] Finally, in the context of a section on "Approaching Demarcation Problems," Wesley again admits that "[w]hen inquiry does not advance, it is impossible to tell with complete confidence whether this is due to a permanent aporia in the textured fabric of the feedback potential, or to the failure to imagine or sustain a form of social organization adequate to take advantage of available corrective resources."[16]

This, then, is our question: Is the ineffability issue a permanent aporia in the textured fabric of the feedback potential? Or have we scholars simply failed to imagine or sustain a form of social organization adequate to taking advantage of available corrective resources? Is social innovation possible? Or should we just call it quits?

To add another wrinkle, the ineffability issue would seem to be a hall of mirrors: all scholars ever see in it is themselves, usually in a distorted and distended way. Language- and tradition-loving contextualists find all things effable, while experiential- and nature-loving perennialists set aside special things as ineffable. Who is to say who is right? Can anyone be right? Or are some issues of inquiry framed in such a way that they are simply intractable?

Non-issues? Red herrings? Wittgensteinian traps of language where there is nothing at all to find or solve, where all we really need to do is show the trapped fly the way out of the bottle?

There are not answers to these questions in Wesley's religious philosophy. Nor should there be. How can anyone say where and when a line of inquiry should stop? Still, I cannot help feeling that there is not enough recognition in Wesley's religious philosophy of the linguistically bewitching non-issue that tempts the scholar into a fruitless line of inquiry, keeps her there entranced (for fear of abandoning a hypothesis too hastily), and has her chasing feedback potential in some will-o'-the-wisp.

No doubt we owe Wesley a debt of gratitude for showing that nothing is ever really intractable. Yet I continue to wonder whether and when some things are close enough.

Making Room for Theology

In my first evaluation of *Religious Philosophy*,[17] I took issues with Wesley's defense of the role of theology in religious philosophy, all the while abdicating the label *philosophy of religion*. It seemed to me that he had things backward. Was not it *theology* that needed to be tossed overboard for the sake of preserving and protecting *philosophy of religion*? Did not comparative-critical philosophers of religion need to distance themselves from theologically motivated philosophy of religion, whether that undertaken by (Christian) theists for the sake of showing (Christian) theism rational, or by (Christian) postmodernists for the sake of showing (Christian) postmodernity valuable?

Of course, Wesley's position is a bit more nuanced than this. Theology, for him, is "multidisciplinary comparative inquiry into ultimate matters," not "an intellectual activity legitimating the practices and beliefs of a particular religious institution."[18] Such theology, more precisely, is philosophical theology, which Wesley distinguishes from confessional theology. The former refers to "the theologically more aggressive aspirations of religious philosophy," the latter, that which "self-consciously serves the interests of religious institutions."[19] This is not a clear-cut distinction; rather, Wesley uses the categories of social context, purpose, and resource to define two ideal types:

> When theology stresses the social location of religious institutions, the purpose of maintaining or reforming religious identity on behalf of such institutions, and the authoritative resources of

sacred texts and traditions—it tends toward the confessional. When theology's social location is chiefly the social location of the intellectual and literary history of religions, when its purpose is inquiry into ultimacy, and when its resources are description, comparison, analysis, and multidisciplinary theory building—and when it refuses to treat the sacred texts and traditions of any particular religion as decisively authoritative—it tends toward the philosophical (in the sense defended here).[20]

Theologies therefore "tend toward" the philosophical or the confessional; there are no pure types. Another nuance concerns Wesley's diagnosis of and response to the problem of "existential entanglement."[21] The problem here is that philosophers of religion, who ask questions and evaluate claims about the meaning, truth, and value of religious ideas, are themselves existentially entangled in these ideas.[22] The question, then, is "whether these tasks can be pursued without enslavement to covert or explicit ideologies, and whether, in the face of uncertain prospects, it is worthwhile making the attempt."[23] Wesley rejects three solutions to this problem: (1) admitting that impartiality and therefore religious philosophy are impossible, (2) pursuing only the more objective styles of religious philosophy, and (3) insisting that religious philosophers must be religiously unaffiliated.[24] His solution instead lies in "a less defensive attitude to the problem itself" as well as "the social organization of inquiry among religious philosophers."[25] The former includes "a deep understanding of the actual existential potency of ultimate question and a wide appreciation for the diversity of ways such questions are framed and answered."[26] The latter encompasses "demands to learn the key ideas of multiple religious traditions, expectations that students will follow inquiry into whatever disciplines it may lead, and scrupulous monitoring of depth of understanding and breadth of appreciation of religious ideas and practices."[27] But the latter goes beyond such "socialization and training" to "cooperative inquiry and mutual criticism."[28]

A final nuance criticizes extreme forms of objectivity and neutrality (as virtues of inquiry), while simultaneously defending "simplified ideals" of objectivity and neutrality. Wesley begins by maintaining that "[i]f objectivity and neutrality mean lack of involvement—keeping phenomena at an existentially safe distance, or moral impotence—then they certainly do seem unworthy of being called 'virtues.'"[29] In such a case objectivity and neutrality would not only "deny the primal moral responsibility of human beings" but also fail to see things as they really are—"value-laden and interested from beginning to end."³⁰ But Wesley goes on to recognize the place of "simplified ideals of objectivity and neutrality to rule out of bounds intellectual activity that is primarily in service of the interests of a particular religious tradition." (This, he calls the "Loyalty Criterion."³¹) And he argues that "relatively unbiased and ideologically neutral forms of philosophical and theological reflection are possible" in religious philosophy, which "takes the ideals of objectivity and neutrality seriously by establishing procedures of correction that can detect and overcome intellectual defects of bias and ideological distortion."³²

At the time that I wrote my first review of Wesley's book—and even still now—I agree with all of these distinctions. Still, I found it off-putting that so much labor would be invested to defend the role of theology in religious philosophy, given that the label of *philosophy of religion* was dismissed in just one paragraph.³³ Granted, this paragraph does indicate that Wesley would rather have called his project "philosophy of religion" and hopes that one day that name will be available to define a field of multidisciplinary comparative inquires, but it also recognizes that for now "a different name is needed in order to articulate a much-needed contrast with the traditional types of philosophy of religion, which are decidedly *not* multidisciplinary comparative inquiry and which operate largely independently of the academic study of religion" (emphases Wesley's).³⁴

Now, six years later, my position has changed, in part because I am writing an undergraduate textbook on "global-critical philosophy of religion" along with a group of other, like-minded scholars. One of these scholars challenged my initial distinction between "religious philosophies," which I understood to be the historical content for global-critical philosophy of religion, and "global-critical philosophy of religion," which I saw as the present act of philosophizing about religious philosophies. This critique, in a nutshell, was that my distinction reinforced the prejudice that only academically located, confessionally neutral, "global-critical" philosophy of religion is properly global and critical; all other forms of philosophizing about religions are localized, non-critical "religious philosophies."

In writing my textbook chapter on "What is Philosophy?" I ran up against this problem again, this time within the context of a discussion of the appeal to authority. What is a legitimate and illegitimate source of knowledge in philosophy of religion? When is "an appeal" made toward an illegitimate authority rather than a legitimate source of knowledge? The only way out of this dilemma seemed to be that of the Indian *vada* tradition: in global-critical philosophy of religion, one can appeal to whichever sources of knowledge/authority that one wants, but when discussing and debating with others, those sources of knowledge/authority should be calibrated, as far as able (and even when one philosophizes by oneself, so to speak, one should still try to provide "good reasons" for the sources of knowledge/authority that one employs).[35]

So I now find myself in the uncomfortable position of thinking that Wesley's defense of theology does not go far enough. Take, for example, Wesley's "Loyalty Criterion." How can one know when intellectual activity is primarily in service of the interests of a particular religious tradition? And what if some form of intellectual activity is? As far as philosophy of religion or religious philosophy goes, we would not want to "rule out of bounds" such intellectual activity but rather engage it with intellectual activity that is in service of other interests, whether religious or otherwise. Of course, one can also wonder whether "relatively unbiased and ideologically neutral forms of philosophical and theological reflection are possible," as Wesley claims. Given what I have argued in the section above about mysticism, I am not so confident that we philosophers of religion ever get very far from our biases and ideologies. Is not the "solution" then a "big tent" one? Let all the biases and ideologies in; consider all the appeals to knowledge/authority; allow service to the interests of all kinds of traditions, whether religious, secular, or otherwise; but require that dialogical partners calibrate sources and give reasons as much as possible. (Probably this happens anyway, even without our fretting.)

So, again it is the case that we, and especially I, owe a debt of gratitude to Wesley. He has helped me see that theology has a room at the table of philosophy of religion. Now, I suppose I want an even larger table for even more "theologians."

Changing the Field and the Academy

Like many graduate students in the humanities, I gave little graduate-school thought to the public dimensions of my scholarship. My scholarship was for its own sake and for my sake, not for the sake of the world. This continued to be the case even after graduate school, probably due to the research constraints of the tenure process. For three long years, my head remained buried in the critical edition of the Dionysian corpus and Liddell and Scott's Greek-English lexicon.

I suppose, therefore, that I had not really read anything like the Afterword to Wesley's *Religious Philosophy* before so doing. Wesley begins by proclaiming that religious philosophy (as multidisciplinary comparative inquiry) "has a natural and vital place in modern universities, because its secular morality of inquiry comports well with the principles of open and unbiased inquiry that, to varying degrees, guide and inspire the modern university."[36] "Accordingly," Wesley goes on to maintain, "it is time to reassess the place of religious philosophy within the modern university."[37]

From there, Wesley summarizes both a "deconstructive" and a "constructive" case in support of his religious philosophy within the modern university. The deconstructive case, in essence, is that religious philosophy is not confessional theology: although "there are ways of doing theology so geared to special pleading, and so immune to correction from other disciplinary insights that they really do not conform to the morality of inquiry that pervades the academic world," religious philosophy (qua multidisciplinary comparative inquiry) attempts to avoid excess abstraction, disciplinary parochialism, and ideological bias.[38] By contrast, the constructive case argues that religious philosophy belongs within modern universities because of its intrinsic value, morality of inquiry, and native characteristics, which includes inquiry into "questions about the meaning of life and the wellsprings of value," both of which "arise constantly within intellectual work."[39] Neglect of religious philosophy in the modern university only means that these inevitable questions will be dealt with in an "amateurish" fashion. Moreover, religious philosophy is an "efficient" form of inquiry that does not cost the university much.

In the next section ("Religious Philosophy and the Diversity of Higher Education"), Wesley argues that religious philosophy has a natural home in the secular academy; in fact, it "is entitled to support from secular academic institutions."[40] Finally, he concludes his Afterword and book with appeal and admonishment. The leaders of disciplines represented within philosophy, religious studies, and theology departments are told to "lift their eyes beyond the parochial identity politics of their own disciplines and consider the place of religious philosophy amid the wider intellectual currents and social challenges of our troubled world."[41] When they have difficulty doing this, "university academic leadership should demand to know why, and if necessary do it for them."[42] This is because "[r]eligious philosophy lies precisely as close to the beating heart of every secular university's native mission as the existentially potent subject matter of religious philosophy is vital for human life."[43]

To some extent, I have taken all this to heart, mostly within the context of my "global-critical philosophy of religion" project. Again, it was Wesley who helped me see the real-world dimensions—better, the academic-political dimensions—of the project. I was hopeful that the project could have an effect on how philosophy of religion is taught and learned in the academy. I did not realize, though, that it might also just possibly have an effect on lines and hires in the academy—or at least not until Wesley said just this at the end of our first meeting.

What is ironic to me, then, is the hard times that philosophy of religion has fallen on at Wesley's own university. As I mentioned in my introduction, philosophy of religion was lively and diverse during my graduate studies at Boston University. Since then, whether through retirement, relocation, or worse, many of those lines have disappeared and been reallocated for more historically and culturally rooted areas of specialization. Moreover, what has happened at Boston University has happened elsewhere. Indeed, we philosophers of religion should be asking how can we revitalize philosophy of religion in a manner that is engaged with the academic study of religion, steeped in the religious traditions of the world, and relevant to the modern, secular university. Here, we simply ask whether Wesley's "religious philosophy" can deliver these desiderata. Below, I share four concerns that I have about whether it can.

First, I worry that "religious philosophy" is just too expansive, with no focused path and agenda. For Wesley, religious philosophy is a field of diverse and related inquiries at the junction of philosophy and religious studies.[44] It includes a diversity of "styles" of inquiry—those that are traditionally more analytic, such as the analytical, theoretical, and evaluative; those that are traditionally more continental, such as the phenomenological, historical, and literary; and that which is largely neglected by both, the comparative.[45] It seeks "to generate interpretations of every kind of religious phenomena, from the mundane to the sublime and from individual experiences to social practices, with due attention to social and cultural context, and with concern for the questions of meaning, truth, and value, which properly belong to philosophy."[46] It aims to answer the big philosophical questions of metaphysics, epistemology, and ethics insofar as they have "religious significance."[47] And it includes a "strong reading together" of diverse philosophical endeavors, namely the onto-theological, cosmo-theological, physico-theological, psycho-theological, axio-theological, and mystic-theological.[48]

There is nothing here that I disagree with. It is just that I am left without a clear sense about how I can plug into "religious philosophy" in a meaningful and impactful way. Maybe everything I do, everything that every philosopher of religion does, contributes to this expansive vision of religious philosophy. If so, I am left without a clear sense of how "we" philosophers of religion can work together to change the field and the academy, for "we" philosophers of religion (or religious philosophers, if you prefer) seem to be working at cross-purposes. In short, "religious philosophy" leaves me without a strong sense of identity and urgency.

Relatedly, my second concern with "religious philosophy" is that it does not engage the field where it is and therefore is not critical enough. Wesley does include an extended critique of Richard Swinburne's cumulative-case argument, and his treatment of the "six traditions of religious philosophy" contains references to and discussions of contemporary philosophy of religion.[49] But with regard to these six traditions, I have wondered whether Wesley is not too optimistic about them. In some cases, there just does not seem to be the growth that he says there is (e.g., the onto-theological, the mystico-theological); in other cases, there is growth where he says there is not (e.g., theistic attributes, proofs, theodicy); and in still other cases, there appears to be inherent divisiveness between the traditions (onto-theology vs. mystico-theology).

This is a critique that I made earlier with regard to Wesley's treatment of the mystic-theological tradition in general and mystical experience in particular. For me, *Religious Philosophy* expends too little effort in confronting the currently ascendant paradigm in religious studies that holds that ineffability is a prescriptive protective strategy (perhaps even an androcentric one). Wesley's focus on altered states of consciousness and cognitive breakdown arguably disregards the sorts of critical disciplinary perspectives and tools that religious studies has recently brought to the subject of religious experience. And its claim that the mystico-theological tradition is present in all religious traditions (in more or less the same way) is not compatible with the type of careful, comparative enterprise that Wesley espouses. I am therefore unconvinced with Wesley's pronouncement that the mystico-theological tradition is in fact currently "displaying signs of renewal."[50] In fact, it appears moribund, at least from where I look out at the field.

My third concern follows from my second—"religious philosophy" is not radical enough. This is a critique that I have made before with respect to the six traditions of religious philosophy: the onto-theological, cosmo-theological, physico-theological, psycho-theological, axio-theological, and mystico-theological. I have my concerns with using these Kantianesque categories as the categories of global philosophy of religion, as well as with Wesley's "strong reading together" of diverse religious phenomena under these categories.[51] Here, I voice an additional concern: I just cannot see these categories bringing together and galvanizing philosophers of the religions of the world. These categories are just too steeped in Western philosophy and Christian religion.

Finally, I once again wonder about the wisdom of jettisoning the label "philosophy of religion" for that of "religious philosophy." For me, what is most needed is to show how that which often goes by the label "philosophy of religion" is actually "philosophy of (Christian) theism." For me, we (global) philosophers of religion need to mount a campaign to "take back" our field and its title from those (theistic) philosophers of religion who have limited it to what is not multidisciplinary and comparative, to what appears only to want to argue for or against Christian theism, to what is arguably responsible for the decline of philosophy of religion in the modern, secular academy. For me, our strongest case lies in demonstrating that what is commonly called *philosophy of religion* is not philosophy of religion, not in jettisoning "philosophy of religion." This too, though, I have learned from Wesley.

Notes

1. Wildman, *Religious Philosophy*, 48–50. See also Wesley's chapter 1 arguments against Kant's antinomies: (1) they only work as such in a foundationalist epistemology; (2) they are abstracted from the context of the large-scale modeling efforts that produce them and are highly relevant for assessing them; (3) Kant was overconfident about what could and could not be exposed to experience (ibid., 8–11).

2. Ibid., 50.

3. Ibid.

4. Ibid.

5. The first three emphases simply root inquiry in human biology, evolution, and sociality:

(1) Biology: inquiry is an embodied activity made possible by senses and brain.

(2) Evolution: inquiry serves survival through helping human beings solve problems.

(3) Sociality: inquiry is a social process depending on cooperation and consensus. (170)

According to Wesley, the pragmatic theory of inquiry "was the first tradition of world philosophy, and is still the principle philosophical tradition, that takes full and nonreductive account of the emerging evolutionary view of human minds, human sociality, and human experience of the world" (170).

6. Ibid., 170.
7. Ibid., 51–52.
8. Ibid., 120–24. Note that Wesley believes all aspects of handing a problem are inherently social, even when we appear to be working alone (121).
9. Ibid., 303.
10. Ibid. Also note that Wildman finds this to be the chief contribution of postmodernity to religious philosophy: "the recovery of apophatic instincts in a relevant contemporary form" (80), more specifically, an attesting to the "deepest of theological truths," viz. that the "godless world is not without an abysmal ground" and that God is not a determinate entity (83).
11. Ibid., n.49, 335–36.
12. See my forthcoming "Against Absolute Ineffability."
13. Wildman, *Religious Philosophy*, 183.
14. Ibid.
15. Ibid., 189–90. Here are the other two ways in which ways specialized languages and communities advance inquiry:

> (2) In domains where the feedback potential is strong, specialized discourse communities develop specifically to take full advantage of the opportunities to advance inquiry that such situations promise. (191)
>
> (3) Specialized discourse communities sometimes advance inquiry by means of technical and formal languages. (193)

16. Ibid., 216.
17. Knepper, "What's in the Names." This and the next section draw on this review. I thank Springer (*Sophia*) for permission to reuse.
18. Wildman, *Religious Philosophy*, 28, 26–27.
19. Ibid., 29.
20. Ibid., 32. See also Wesley's revisiting of these issues in 236–37.
21. Ibid., 31, 210–14, 233.
22. Ibid., 211.
23. Ibid.
24. Ibid., 211–12.
25. Ibid., 212.
26. Ibid.
27. Ibid., 214.
28. Ibid.
29. Ibid., 24.
30. Ibid.
31. Ibid., 25–25.
32. Ibid., 25, 26.

33. Ibid., xiii–xiv.

34. For Wesley, this terminological move is necessitated by the current state of philosophy of religion, a state that is "haunted" by "two great problems": first, philosophy of religion suffers from "unresolved contradictions about method and scope arising from internal diversity of its activities and fundamental disagreements about human reason;" second, philosophy of religion is "significantly out of step with the academic study of religion" (ix). In the case of the former, Wildman maintains nothing can be done: philosophy of religion neither is nor should attempt to be a discipline of unified method and scope (for this would only mask its ideological narrowness and religious parochialism); rather it is a field of diverse and related inquiries at the junction of philosophy and religious studies. But in the case of the latter, Wildman avers something must be done: philosophy of religion must change not only in substance, so as to take account of the recent dramatic changes in religious studies, but also in name, so as to articulate "a much-needed contrast" (xiv; see also, 309–10). That name is *religious philosophy*.

35. Here, I am particularly influenced by Clayton, *Religions, Reasons and Gods*.
36. Wildman, *Religious Philosophy*, 307.
37. Ibid.
38. Ibid., 311.
39. Ibid., 311–12.
40. Ibid., 316.
41. Ibid., 317.
42. Ibid.
43. Ibid.
44. Ibid., vi.
45. See especially 35–45.
46. Ibid., xv.
47. See especially ch. 1.
48. See especially ch. 8.
49. See especially 102–5 and ch. 8.
50. Ibid., 304.
51. As I mentioned in my earlier review (Knepper, "What's in the Names?"), I wonder whether the way in which Wesley keeps the Western and Eastern strands of religious philosophy largely separate from one another in this section renders problematic his "strong reading together." Non-Western religious phenomena also appear to be shoehorned or appended to modern-Western categories and agendas. (Ultimate reality is too often spoken of as God-like; non-Western phenomena are largely missing from the discussion of the onto-theological, cosmo-theological, and physico-theological traditions; the South Asian and East Asian traditions are mostly relegated to the psycho-theological and axio-theological traditions, respectively, and, even there, not integrated tightly into the recommendations for the future of the tradition.)

4

Wesley Wildman's Lessons for and from Ethics

Sarah E. Fredericks

Because Wesley J. Wildman has not often written explicitly ethical texts, focusing instead on theology, religion and science, philosophy of religion, and most recently the scientific study of religion, devoting an entire chapter to ethics in a volume about his work may seem a bit out of place. Certainly, Wildman has written about ethics. "The Use and Abuse of Biotechnology: A Modified Natural-Law Approach to Bioethics" is the clearest such text.[1] He also writes about axiology, often as a part of a survey of the areas of study in philosophy, religious studies, or religious studies or as he asserts claims about the "axiological features of reality."[2] Wildman frequently names ethical questions when identifying major questions that require multidisciplinary study.[3] However, he rarely does more than mention these applied questions as he focuses on theoretical problems. Thus, at first glance, one may say that Wildman's work is best described as adjacent to ethics than properly about ethics.

A closer look, however, reveals that Wildman's multidisciplinary method for religious philosophy is an ethic for his field insofar as it lays out ideals of human action and how to achieve them. Indeed, in a book chapter reflecting on and expanding the importance of his book *Religious Philosophy as Multidisciplinary Comparative Inquiry* for the academic future of the study of philosophy of religion, he frames his method as having a number of virtues and describes it directly or obliquely as being a "morality of inquiry."[4] This morality is based on that of the modern secular university, which Wildman observes prizes "honest inquiry wherever it may lead" and "efficient economics of inquiry," "refus[es] to honor claims of supernaturally derived information or supernatural authorization of particular religious beliefs," and eschews the "special interests of religious institutions."[5] Wildman outlines how philosophy of religion can fulfill these expectations by following a method that is interdisciplinary, comparative, and open to correction.

As his method of inquiry purports to encompass "every sort of human inquiry," it makes sense that it could also be applied to similar fields such as ethics. Indeed, the method is particularly apt for religious ethics.[6] Both philosophy of religion and religious ethics involve the investigation of religion; arose as academic disciplines out of Western, especially Christian constructive work; and today can occupy uneasy places in the academy that can be suspicious of these disciplines' historical and sometimes contemporary claims to specialized religious knowledge not open to correction. Tensions exist in both fields between those who take descriptive or functionalist approaches and those who make constructive or normative claims. These tensions are only heightened given theoretical and practical concerns about pluralism. Both ethics and philosophy of religion also engage with many different religious traditions for a variety of reasons using multiple methods.

Indeed, using Wildman's method in ethics has several distinct advantages. It encourages ethicists to explicitly connect their work to a theory of inquiry, forcing them to consider the types of knowledge that they take seriously while ensuring that ethics is informed by other disciplines. It articulates a space between relativism and tradition-bound constructive theories that allows for intellectual progress and constructive claims in a time of pluralism.[7] It draws on clear language from the sciences about revision and hypotheses, which can guard against intellectual and practical dangers of moral absolutism that are so easily read into ethics. Finally, it allows for engagement with and pushback by the world, a critical element in any ethical theory and especially so with respect to environmental, biomedical, and political ethics. This aid does not just run one way, however, as the discipline of ethics raises key questions of Wildman's method, including how his study of ideas can be expanded to practices, who has the big questions, who participates in the comparison, and how the effects of the comparison are dealt with.

To substantiate these claims, I first explain Wildman's method for big questions in multidisciplinary comparative inquiry. In the second section, I review the strengths of this method with respect to ethics, focusing on comparative religious ethics and environmental ethics. Finally, I turn to the weaknesses in Wildman's work, indicating how insights from ethics identify and help overcome them.

Wildman's Method: Multidisciplinary, Comparative, Fallible Inquiry into Big Questions

Wildman's methodological approach to the study of religion, whether in religion and science or philosophy of religion, draws upon Ian Barbour's articulation of boundary questions, those questions that are at the boundary between disciplines and therefore require multiple disciplines to answer.[8] Wildman expands Barbour's model significantly, particularly with respect to comparative work and engagement with a larger number of sciences.[9]

Wildman's commitment to big-question problem solving is made explicit in "From Grand Dreaming to Problem Solving."[10] Here he argues that the field of science and religion has spent too much time on "grand synthetic dreaming," specifically in the articulation of ever more typologies or methodologies of how religion and science can relate. He argues that a more productive approach involves "aiming to solve some real problems," a strategy that, he claims, if done well, will simultaneously enrich rich philosophical and theoretical conversations, provide "intellectually compelling solution[s] in the case of theoretical problems, or compelling interpretations and viable strategies in the case of practical problems."[11] By their nature, such solutions will be more attractive to a more diverse group of people than the typical work done in religion and science. Wildman names a few difficult questions: "Why can we still not feed all children and spare them from avoidable disease? How can we manage and transcend differences of personality and ideology, religion and culture? . . . What is the story of complex emergence and life? What systems of political economy work best for given problems?"[12] Elsewhere, Wildman argues that formal education should allow students to focus on particular topics or problems: "'war and peace' or 'global poverty' or 'sustainable energy'" "'worlds of meaning' or 'distributive justice' or 'family conflict,'" topics that should be studied in a multidisciplinary, thematic way because they cannot be addressed by any one discipline.[13] "These questions and thousands of others call for contributions from natural and social scientists, philosophers and theologians, humanists and experts in religion."[14] Big-question problem solving differs from that of an academic discipline in which disciplinary academics lose sight of their discipline's assumptions because they are so taken for granted; consequently, they also lose sight of more complex, urgent, and compelling questions and problems of the rest of the world. According to Wildman, it is better to focus on such topics and questions than on the problems and questions of any one discipline, as these are the issues that matter—both intellectually and to human societies.

Wildman is careful to qualify his focus on such problems. It does not mean "blunting the philosophical edge of science-religion dialogue . . ." or "abandon[ing] the highest standards of rich interpretation and precise argument in exchange for the transient glories of popular relevance."[15] While he is interested in problems with a wide relevance, not just anyone is allowed at his "dialogue table" even if they "feel . . . an interest in a topic." Rather, every participant needs intense, "multidisciplinary training with higher standards"[16] through which "more thinkers [are] able to function as contributing members of multiple disciplines. Most of all, we need people with such talent and preparation that they can tackle the hardest questions of the all-too-familiar problems embedded in ordinary life."[17] Both here and elsewhere Wildman emphasizes the many kinds of academic experts who can participate in addressing such big questions, whether in the realm of religion and science or religious philosophy.[18]

Wildman expands his argument about big questions and the need for multidisciplinary scholarship when he turns from religion and science to religious philosophy, his term for what is often called philosophy of religion. Specifically, he promotes multidisciplinary comparative fallabalistic inquiry for religious philosophy to address a) the disciplinary unease experienced by philosophy of religion as its scholars recognize the significant diversity in subject matter, method, and intention of its practitioners and b) the criticisms from scholars in and outside religious studies who question the coherence and relevance of philosophy of religion to the modern academy.[19] His approach can make sense of such diversity, as it maintains that philosophy of religion is "not a discipline, with the connotations of well-defined method and scope, but rather as a field of diverse but related inquiries."[20] He aims to build legitimacy for this field by building a theory of rationality and demonstrating the connections between religious philosophy and religious studies.[21] In this commitment to multidisciplinary within philosophy of religion, we see Wildman aiming to be true to what exists in the field and capitalize on its strengths to make progress at answering the big questions of the field. These questions include those of "metaphysics, epistemology and ethics insofar as they possess religious significance."[22] For instance, what "explanatory principles" "unite descriptions of what exists into coherent ontological theories of reality."[23] In all of these cases, Wildman argues that inquiry should be multidisciplinary, fallibilistic, and comparative. Let us examine each in turn.

We have already heard quite a bit about Wildman's approach to multidisciplinarity in the context of religion and science research. He makes very similar arguments about religious philosophy: he values multidisciplinarity because it is the way the fields he is involved in, and maybe all fields, actually work and because it enables the use of the various methods and kinds of information needed to address the very complex, compelling, and pressing questions of the world that extend beyond any one field. In *Religious Philosophy as Multidisciplinary Comparative Inquiry*, Wildman makes the particular case that multidisciplinary inquiry in religious philosophy needs to be open to collaboration with the natural sciences, not just to the humanities and social sciences, because the sciences can contribute to study of the big questions. "For example, it no longer makes much sense to study epistemology in isolation from the cognitive sciences, or ethics separately from evolutionary theory."[24] This does not mean that Wildman puts scientific methods or theories on a pedestal, but rather recognizes that they should be recognized as valuable contributors to inquiry. Wildman also supports engagement between scholars of religious philosophy and the sciences because of the sciences' connection to the physical world, something he pursues for its "predictive accuracy and explanatory richness."[25] Finally, it seems that Wildman prizes connections with the sciences because recognizing how the world pushes back on our theories reminds us of the need to keep our theories open to such correction.

Indeed, a "fallibilist, hypothetical" mode of inquiry is the second of three main features of Wildman's methodology. Here he draws on his own experience doing religious philosophy as well as the work of pragmatists, particularly John Dewey and Charles Sanders Peirce, as well as philosopher of science Imre Lakatos's theory of the incremental development of scientific theories and their "conservative implications."[26] For Wildman, all knowledge, theories, and methods of inquiry should be open to testing, evaluation, and correction. Of course this process looks different in the natural sciences or humanities, as one examines physical, ontological, metaphysical, or ethical claims. Aside from different standards in these fields, the world will also push back more clearly on some theories than others. Despite these differences, criteria of success such as clarity, logical consistency, coherence, applicability, adequacy, truth seeking, and problem solving will be pertinent.[27] While these criteria may not lead to one best answer for any question, they can indicate that some answers are better than others.[28]

While Wildman does see his form of inquiry as a search for truth, this is a notion of truth influenced by the pragmatists and Barbour. Specifically, this notion involves a critical realism in which "truth is used typically to indicate correspondence between a proposition and a state of affairs in the world to which the terms of the proposition refer" but where "the means by which we evaluate a truth claim might be many and varied, involving correspondence, coherence, and pragmatic criteria."[29] Given this commitment to fallibilism, any solution to a big question should always ultimately be framed as a hypothesis rather than an absolute answer.[30]

Under this system, continual "dogged work is necessary to make sure that we are not overlooking important new hypotheses or special virtues of existing hypotheses, and the former view inspires us to keep striving for deeper insights and richer appreciation of complexities."[31] This is not a simple one-off process, but rather one that is likely to extend infinitely.[32] Wildman (and I) appreciate this theory of inquiry for a number of reasons, including "that it comprehends every sort of human inquiry."[33] It captures informal everyday inquiry of children and adults about the natural world, social structures, and their own morals. It also applies to the formal inquiry of academics from the ontological and theological (though they have less straightforward pushback from the world) to other humanistic inquiry, and to that of the social and natural sciences. The breadth of this method of inquiry arises because it is developed in light of "the capacities and limitations of human brains, the realities of social life, and the variability in the hypothesis-correcting feedback potential across diverse subject matters."[34]

Admittedly, it can be easy, especially for nonscientists, to be wary of hypothesis-driven methods as so unstable, so open to change at any moment that they seem unworkable in the humanities or for society at large. Critics may worry that hypothetico-corrective methods are not able to capture agents' commitment to particular ideas and practices. Hypotheses may also seem to go against the widespread desire for stability that people seem to have and that communities need to some degree. How, for example, can one have an ethic or a vision of human nature that is changing all the time, critics may ask. Wouldn't this leave society open to constant change and no stability? Thus, such methods may seem at best misguided and at worst a frightening misappropriation of scientific images for humanities research. Wildman is careful to address these concerns. He maintains that the hypothetico-corrective method, while it holds that all is open to correction, also allows people to hold onto some commitments, adjusting other assumptions and theories in order to take account of evidence of many kinds. This, he rightly notes, is what often occurs in practice, even as ideas are also malleable over time. Indeed, this method "fosters tenacious attachment to the core hypotheses being evaluated, seeking every way possible to avoid their falsification."[35]

Wildman sees his fallibilist methodology as an answer to the challenges of religious and cultural diversity. As someone who 1) is keenly aware of very real practical and conceptual differences between religion, theology, and philosophical ideas and practices of various traditions; and 2) holds the notion of truth described above, he needs to have a way to account for and deal with diversity. The hypothetico-corrective method allows just this because it demands that hypotheses are open to assessment and correction not only from one's own experience and tradition but also from others. In other words, Wildman advocates a comparative approach, the third major component of his methodology.

He finds that in religious philosophy comparative judgments are "inevitable" and "pervasive" because of "cultural diversity."[36] Though a difficult process, he argues, comparisons are important to be able to understand something of the various ways ideas and practices manifest in the world.[37] Recognizing the many debates about how to do comparison and, indeed, whether it should be undertaken at all, Wildman finds comparison supportable when a "self-conscious dialectical approach to comparison holds that there should be a dialectical collaboration between data and comparative categories where the task of understanding through comparison can build progressively on previous results. This conception of comparison calls for procedures that gradually refine categories."[38]

This comparative process is one that Wildman, with his colleague Robert Cummings Neville, developed through the Comparative Religious Ideas Project (CRIP), a three-year research project involving experts in many different religious traditions. They helped develop some categories of comparing religious ideas: ultimate realities, the human condition, and religious truth. Drawing on Peircean semiotics, these categories delineate a boundary of what ideas do and do not encompass. They are vague in the sense that they can be specified in multiple, possibly contradictory ways. For instance, the category of the human condition can be specified by "life is a blast" or "life is suffering."[39]

While developing these categories, Neville and Wildman simultaneously articulated their theory of comparison, moving back and forth between comparisons and the theory of comparison, letting each endeavor inform the other. Their theory includes a philosophical articulation of what a comparative category is, how it functions, comes to be, and is refined; as well as criteria for good comparisons. For instance, comparative categories must be tested according to criteria of truth: "tests of consistency, coherence, applicability to the subject matter, and adequacy" as well as "for bias arising from the comparativists' cultural agenda and categories."[40] Each idea to be compared, they argue, should be evaluated along five lines: Does it express the idea "as thought by the people who express it intrinsically"? How does the idea shape the perspective of those who use it religiously or comparatively? How does it interact with other ideas to do so? "The practical representation of ideas . . ." should also be examined.[41] Comparativists must recognize the elements of ideas that "resist representation and translation."[42]

Of course, any claim arising out of such a process of comparison is itself fallible—"further tests might be discovered that would qualify or even disqualify the claim."[43] Wildman and Neville model such comparative endeavors through long-term collaborations among experts who refined and tested their categories over time, ending up with working hypotheses. Such collaboration was and is critical, as no one person had sufficient expertise to undertake such collaboration themselves. Indeed, for Wildman, comparison, a characteristic of religious philosophy, is inherently multidisciplinary, as it should involve whatever disciplines are needed to answer the questions at hand, in the CRIP, about which comparative categories are meaningful. In the CRIP these disciplines include experts in many different religious traditions as well as scholars of historical, philosophical theology, philosophy of religion, and linguistics. Other projects may require collaboration with disciplines further afield, including the social and natural sciences. In sum, then, Wildman's method for religious philosophy is multidisciplinary, comparative, and fallibilist in order to answer big questions.

Advantages to the Multidisciplinary Comparative Fallibilist Inquiry

Having summarized Wildman's comparative multidisciplinary fallibilist method for studying religion, particularly religious philosophy, we can now explore the advantages of this method as it is and as it can be applicable to religious ethics. I particularly examine comparative religious ethics and environmental ethics, as the former has obvious potential for overlap with the comparative aspect of Wildman's work, while the latter illustrates how his engagement with the sciences can be helpful for ethics.

Let me begin by noting some presuppositions that guide my support of Wildman's method to allow it to be obvious to others and so that I allow it to be open to correction. I think that disciplines need to be porous to each other because the world itself resists neat, absolute categorization. For instance, the lines between individual and collective entities are often less rigid than people think, whether one considers the microbes without which our digestion and selves would not exist or how human collectives exist alongside and blur individual boundaries of identity and agency. So too with realms of knowledge, which often bleed into each other. Dividing knowledge about the world into completely discrete, siloed disciplines often obscures what falls between the cracks. A method of inquiry that enables its practitioners to recognize and pursue these interstitial elements even as they recognize the unique contributions of different perspectives is thus key to understanding the world with some fidelity.

Accompanying my commitment to the links between domains of knowledge is the desire for comprehensive knowledge, that is, theories in any domain that explicitly and thoroughly are guided by and ground other domains. For instance, to do comparative religious ethics requires doing ethics in a way that is informed by a theory of what it means to compare and what it means to know as a human. These quests necessarily engage metaphysics, ontology, and epistemology as well as information from the natural and social sciences about human understanding. The ideas of philosophy of religion or ethics in turn inform a political philosophy, economics, practical ethics, and the very disciplines that shape them. In this chapter I am most concerned with the roots of the method: what it means philosophically to compare, the risks of doing so, and how to faithfully represent the subjects and reveal new insights with the comparison, all of which Wildman's work does. Such grounding is appealing to me because I often find comparative work in religious ethics and elsewhere in religious studies unsatisfying because authors jump into comparison without being clear about what they think it means to compare. Having the pragmatic theory of comparison as Wildman articulates (or another theory) allows comparativists to point to such work, and not just any theory but one that goes all the way to epistemology and ontology. In this way, work in comparative ethics is understood as part and parcel of a larger project of human inquiry, has some consistency with other disciplinary endeavors, and has a clarity and rigor at minimum because it leaves itself vulnerable to evaluation along these lines.

Aside from my desire to have comprehensive systems of knowledge, ethics requires an epistemology and theory of inquiry; otherwise there will be no sense of what kinds of evidence and problems ethicists are or should be taking seriously or what it means to know about them or to argue for them. While not every ethicist needs to spend a great deal of time on these matters, being aware of one's position and articulating it (in more detail than often happens) is important both to think through the implications of one's commitments and to make oneself vulnerable to correction by others and oneself. Specifically, being explicit about the sources of knowledge, and modes of inquiry that an ethicist finds meaningful, can help prevent the all too easy tendency to narrow or constrain what we count as evidence to what is familiar, comfortable, or dominant. Many ethicists working in environmental and biomedical ethics, for instance, are now more explicit about sources of knowledge and opening up to more diverse sources, prioritizing religious traditions, law, and the natural and social sciences, as well as traditional ecological knowledge and forms of local, clearly claimed perspectival knowledge. Such moves are important to best understand the situation and to recognize the expertise of various types of experts.

Recognizing the value of different perspectives and the changes that occur through correction over time in the long history of ethics is critical for several reasons. It allows a realist picture of ethics that aligns with multiple examples from human history. It also avoids reifying one point of view with the accompanying political and social disasters for dissenters.

Furthermore, being explicit about one's theory of and sources of knowledge is critical to move people toward recognizing the theoretical limits of their position. For instance, the field of environmental ethics arose as people recognized that their ethical systems did not account for all of what is valuable (e.g., nonhumans) or did not sufficiently protect what had been seen as valuable (e.g., humans). Yet many environmental ethicists aim to find a final, right, perfect solution to ethical questions, ignoring the possibilities that their theories may also be myopic in previously unidentified dimensions, such as the recently emerging nexus of disability studies and environmental ethics. Why not learn from the mistakes of past hubris and adopt a more fallible approach?

Problems can also arise if data are taken as significant when they do not align well with the world and indeed have been superseded in scientific communities. Lisa H. Sideris writes of this problem in *Environmental Ethics, Ecological Theology, and Natural Selection*. There she chronicles how environmental ethicists and theologians, especially in the 1980s and 1990s, often overlooked natural selection, suffering, and death, focusing instead on harmony in nature and "the well-being of each individual creature within the natural community." Sideris argues that this insufficient engagement with science leads to theology and ethics that are out of touch with the world, fail to capture key values, and thus, one presumes, are ineffective at achieving their aims.

Given my predilection for knowledge and experience that are not constrained to particular disciplines, it should not be surprising that I support Wildman's big-questions approach. Too many issues, such as how to respond to climate change or to understand what it means to be human, require such an approach for intellectual and practical reasons. Ethics as a field of inquiry has long recognized the need to look beyond its narrow borders. As H. Richard Niebuhr famously argued in *The Responsible Self*, "In our responsibility we attempt to answer the question 'What shall I do?' by raising as the prior question: 'What is going on?' or 'What is being done to me?' "[44] Niebuhr makes clear that answering these questions requires thinking about what others who affect us think and prioritize, how different societies operate, how "we interpret the natural events that affect us,"[45] and what God is doing in the world.[46] While Niebuhr is particularly interested in how we interpret all of these things cognitively and emotionally, and does not specifically stress the multidisciplinary nature of such inquiry, it is difficult to imagine such inquiry without it. Indeed, many ethicists before and after him have worked to figure out what is going on. See for example James M. Gustafson's "Context vs Principles: A Misplaced Debate in Christian Ethics"[47] as well as much bioethics, environmental ethics, and other fields of ethics that focus on specific types of problems.

The big-question approach, however, is more than "fact finding" in other disciplines and then making ethical judgments. It involves engaging with multiple disciplines to understand what it means to be human in interaction with the world, the constraints we face in articulating and living up to our ideals, and how then practically to try to live up to them. Ethicists would benefit from not only more engagement with religious and philosophical traditions about human nature, capacities, and ideals but also more sustained interactions with insights about these themes from diverse fields including history, anthropology, sociology, psychology, neurobiology, and evolutionary science.

Wildman's multidisciplinary, comprehensive, fallibilistic approach to the big questions is also advantageous as it occupies a space between relativism and tradition-bound constructive and normative claims. While Wildman frames his approach with respect to the challenges of contemporary philosophy of religion, similar challenges abound in ethics, especially religious ethics. Both fields encompass many different methods and aims. Just within comparative religious ethics, itself one part of ethics, we see multiple branches. In light of the challenges of using specialized religious knowledge in the academic study of religion and the intellectual and societal challenges of pluralism, scholars of comparative religious ethics may eschew explicitly constructive or normative work to be descriptive or develop functional accounts of ethics. Others work to articulate normative positions from within a particular religious tradition, a consensus view among several traditions being compared, or a universal normative position. Still others seek a middle path between constructive and descriptive approaches.[48] This diversity arises in part as a response to the questions arising out of the recognition of pluralism—can one be constructive or normative without succumbing to domination and suppression of alternative views? What is the aim of scholarship, as perceived by scholars and the public at large? As noted above, Wildman develops his method for religious philosophy in response to these questions. He argues that the openness of fallibilism can prevent the worst excesses of relativism and tradition-specific inquiry, if it is done in a comparative, multidisciplinary way.

In ethics, I argue, Wildman's hypothetical corrective can function as not just a method but as an ethical ideal, signaling humility and facilitating a willingness to learn with and from others even as one has one's own community and tradition. In *Measuring and Evaluating Sustainability* I developed this idea, calling it the principle of adaptability. I argued that it "encourages us to adapt ourselves and our policies to the world and our knowledge of it, both of which continually change."[49] Doing so demands a precautionary approach and sensitivity to environmental and cultural contexts. In this way, ethics can respond to the intellectual, practical, and ethical challenges of pluralism while still making normative judgments. The ability to weigh in, or at least exclude some possible answers, is critical if one prizes the big-questions approach as so many, if not all of them, involve values. Adaptability functions then not just as a method for humanities research, but also as an ethic, promoting a humble, responsible, responsive approach to knowledge production and implementation.

Ethicists may well ask whether this hypothetical corrective approach is considerably different from, let alone an improvement over, the hermeneutical approach to comparative ethics, which also emphasizes an interaction between people of diverse ethical commitments.[50] At least in William Schweiker's formulation of hermeneutical ethics, there is a great similarity in the criteria used to judge the result of the interpretation and those advocated by Wildman. Schweiker for instance champions "adequacy to relevant material in argumentative exchange"[51] while demonstrating that it is comprehensive, coherent, of broad scope, and revealing deep insight into ethical issues faced by humans compared with alternatives. Similarly, Wildman names "tests of consistency, coherence, applicability to the subject matter, and adequacy"[52] though he (and Neville) also names a number of tests for bias as well as a process of "pragmatic knowledge about the relevant tests for particular comparisons" as discussed above.[53]

The two approaches primarily differ in their emphases and root metaphors for inquiry. Wildman is aware of hermeneutical approaches and draws on them to some degree but deliberately uses language inflected with science and the philosophy of science that is more explicitly about being open to change. The hermeneutical approach emphasizes human texts and cultures far more than the natural world or our biological selves. I worry that the hermeneutical approach will focus so much on human texts and human interpretations that it will underestimate or overlook the many ways the world can push back on theories, focusing instead on a hermeneutical circle within human language, culture, and reason as if that is not connected to the physical, biological, social, and psychological aspects of ourselves and the world. Yet our theories are not constructed in a vacuum. We can receive or seek out feedback about how they align with the world—do they capture what we intend, do they have results that align with our aims and other ethical ideals, and so forth. For example, does a new basic income policy help the poor and middle class as intended? Admittedly, the signals from the world in any of its biological, physical, economic, and social dimensions always need interpretation, but we should not focus so much on interpretation that we forget that there is something to be interpreted.

Wildman rightfully acknowledges that the pushback of the world may be easier in some areas than others. Metaphysics or ontology, for example, are some of the more difficult. Even here he argues that it is possible to have some theories be more resonant with the world than others, narrowing the pool of possibilities. In ethics, the world pushing back can be more obvious than in many of Wildman's examples. People can ask how the implementation of a particular ethical idea works in different communities—what practical results does it have, how does it transform other ideas, does it have counterproductive tendencies? Such evaluations may suggest that the implementation of the ethic needs to change; at other times the ethic itself may need to change.

I also find Wildman's terminology "hypothetico-corrective method" more compelling than Schweiker's terminology of reflexivity.[54] Both Schweiker's choice of the word reflexivity and his examples of the idea emphasizes the interaction with others over the modification of ideas over time.[55] This is in contrast with the explicit and continual openness to correction of Wildman's method even as he recognizes how people will be committed to particular ideas. Commitment to certain ideas in both the general public and among academics is often so strong that people need more reminders of the advantages of being open to correction than vice versa. Thus, Wildman's approach seems particularly apt when working to counter the modern quest for certainty and the many intellectual, social, and political ramifications of promoting one's own ideas over any others.

Finally, the deeper emphasis on multidisciplinarity in Wildman's method, especially with respect to the sciences, makes me favor it over the hermeneutical approach given the importance of attending to the natural world in ethical theory and practice as discussed above in the Sideris case.

Given all of this talk of the world pushing back on our theories, scientific language like "hypotheses," and engagement with scientific disciplines, I am sure that some colleagues will be skeptical. I recognize that some scholars turn to hermeneutics or linguistics-based models rather than scientific-inspired hypothetical-correction of Wildman not just because of disciplinary comfort zones but also for fear that interaction with the sciences too easily overshadows humanistic pursuits and/or leads to a deterministic reductionistic, "value free" view of the world. Yet if one uses Wildman's method, collaborative as it is, one is unlikely to forget or ignore the deep differences and richness of human culture and language or to reduce them all to one model or another.[56]

Ethics Aids the Multidisciplinary, Comparative, Fallible Method

While Wildman's method brings many advantages to ethics, ethics as a field and/or some specific ethical commitments also identifies and can help overcome some limits of Wildman's method. These include the need to invite more people to the comparative table to increase the potential for feedback and to respect the dignity and authority of more people. To extend the multidisciplinary comparative fallibilistic method to ethics, we must also explore whether and how Wildman's method applies not only to ideas but also to practices. A key part of this process will entail considering and dealing with the impact of fallible ideas on peoples' lives. Let us consider each in turn.

Ethical commitments to participatory justice challenge Wildman's method, particularly the way he limits participation in comparative endeavors to those with a) significant academic training and b) willingness to participate in the comparative process as he articulates it. (Though it is also subject to correction, participants seem to need to be willing to change it from within.) This high bar makes sense given the complexity of issues in religion and science and philosophy of religion with which Wildman often engages. An elementary understanding of religion, a particular religion, or the relevant science *may* confine comparative multidisciplinary inquiry, trite observations about the big questions, or reinventing the wheel rather than robust, creative answers to questions. Yet always setting such narrow standards with such a particular vision of expertise is, however, particularly problematic if the big questions are to be relevant for people's practical lives whether because they are directly relevant to policy (how to feed all people) or whether they shape worldviews that influence societal function (what is the human condition).

Participatory justice entails that agents should be able to meaningfully participate in decision-making that affects them. Many advocates of participatory justice support it because they recognize that without representation, the needs and values of individuals or groups are often overlooked in decision-makers either because they are not known or understood by decision-making or because decision-making implicitly or explicitly favors their own priorities. Participatory justice advocates also recognize that prioritizing it is a way to respect the dignity and value of all individuals and collectives by recognizing that they have their own values and significant experience and can be experts in their own right about local ecological knowledge, cultural systems, human interaction, or morality. Proponents of participatory justice such as myself worry that Wildman's expertise model expects scholars to identify and answer the big questions and then maybe allow the answers to trickle down to laypeople. Only then can laypeople provide feedback about any part of the process, that is, if scholars develop processes to hear it.[57] If the goal of multidisciplinary comparative fallibilistic inquiry is to more toward answering big questions, and if Wildman wants the inquiry to be relevant to laypeople, as he indicates when he argues that "aiming to solve real problems is the quickest way to broaden the base of experience informing the conversation, and nothing will engage the large audience of potential stakeholders [in religion and science conversation] more effectively,"[58] isn't it counterproductive to exclude them from most of the process? Do people only want to be handed answers to questions defined by others?

Indeed, opening up the study of big questions to more people and ways of knowing may change the questions asked and the way they are answered to topics more compelling and relevant to the public while still being theoretically rich. As Lea F. Schweitz and I have argued, "These are not abstract questions, which we academics can solve by ourselves. They are particular questions that require the insights of those who live out the questions."[59] For instance, Schweitz describes a module in a religion and science class, sparked by seminarians' questions about identity, memory, and hope in the face of Alzheimer's disease. These questions went well beyond biological, neurological, or psychological questions of aging to explore how science, religion, art (especially oral histories), and personal experience can collectively shape people's understanding of and ability to live with people with Alzheimer's.[60] Schweitz and I maintain that compelling questions come out of such transdisciplinary collaborations involving scholars and others—students, people in the pews, religious leaders, politicians, health care professionals, environmentalists, and children.[61] Indeed, some questions would not arise otherwise.

For example, a host of questions about the existence and implications of environmental guilt and shame became apparent to me because I began studying the environmental confessions of everyday environmentalists, people who are concerned about and try to care for the environment through their daily lives, though they are not environmental professionals or radical activists.[62] Environmental ethicists have largely ignored the moral insights of everyday environmentalists. Instead, they focus on philosophical and theological analyses of what should be or the environmental ethics of environmental radicals, or people whose worldviews and practices are explicitly shaped by a specific religion. As I argue elsewhere, paying attention to everyday environmentalists reveals a generally unstudied exacerbator of anthropogenic environmental degradation.[63] Specifically, studying the informal writings of everyday environmentalists in blogs and environmental memoirs as well as news reports and some social scientific and marketing surveys reveals that everyday environmentalists experience guilt and shame about environmental degradation at both individual and collective levels. Here, both guilt and shame are negative emotions occurring when agents do not live up to a standard that they hold. Guilt focuses on the action itself, whereas shame focuses on how that action reveals something about the agents' identity.[64] While guilt can motivate reparative action, shame often leads to denial of the problem, hiding from it, paralysis in the face of it, or anger.[65] In the environmental context, shame can thus hinder action to limit or reverse environmental degradation. Physical problems for humans and biota continue and perpetuate shame experiences, which in turn perpetuate the devastation of identity and environment.

While environmental ethicists and environmental scholars in general have recognized the multifaceted nature of anthropocentric environmental change—an issue of knowledge/ignorance—economics, politics, cultural and religious values and moral corruption, emotional dimensions, and guilt and shame in particular have received less attention.[66] Recognizing how emotions are affected by and affect climate change will be key to understanding and addressing it. The moral emotions of guilt and shame are not just another component of an answer to existing questions, however. They may also change the question, emphasizing that environmental degradation is not just an economic, physical, and social issue, but also an emotional one. Furthermore, while the emotions of the victims are incredibly important, the emotions of climate perpetrators may also significantly shape their actions and thus the climate. Thus, we must ask how to attend to the emotional and existential challenges of anthropogenic environmental degradation. Elsewhere, I suggest that rituals are the answer, as they allow responses at the emotional, existential, and practical levels simultaneously while being able to operate at individual and collective levels.[67]

These questions with obvious practical significance are not, however, the only kind of question raised by taking guilt and shame experiences of everyday environmentalists seriously. This experience also reveals a collective form of identity and agency that can make more sense of problems like climate change than traditional Western philosophical approaches, which presume that individuals are *the* moral agents and that direct linear causality of individuals is needed for responsibility. Popular narratives and social psychological studies of environmental guilt and shame reveal that these experiences are not just of individual agents or about their individual behavior but are experienced by collectives, which are more than the sum of the individuals in them, and are about the action of the collective. Teasing out the philosophical concepts to make sense of this experience goes beyond the scope of this paper.[68] I bring it up because the notion of diffuse collectives (not bound by an explicit decision-making structure) such as that of developed people in the industrialized world, when paired with notions of individual responsibility, makes sense of the realities of climate change more than individual responsibility alone. Consequently, attending to the ethical insights of everyday environmentalists who are inspired by their emotional experience enables us to have a richer picture of the dangers and impediments of anthropogenic climate change and a more robust theory of identity, agency, and responsibility in general. This constellation of results likely would not be possible if we only engaged with academic experts.

Admittedly, in in the example above, I have broadened the scope of research by 1) paying attention to the questions that people raise in popular literature and when they spontaneously confess to me when they realize that I am an environmental ethicist and 2) looking to their texts as signals of how to answer questions about identity and responsibility in an age of climate change. In short, I have used texts rather than engage in a fully collaborative project as commitments to participatory justice may suggest. Other ethicists who increasingly use anthropological methods push further toward a participatory approach to ethics and comparative religious studies.[69] For instance, comparative religious ethicist Elizabeth Bucar used ethnographic methods and textual analyses in *Creative Conformity* to investigate the ethics of American Roman Catholic and Iranian Shi'i women. She found that their ethics both conformed with their religious authorities and creatively interpreted and asserted their own ethical knowledge.[70] Here Bucar is doing comparative work by developing a category of comparison (creative conformity). She looks to her informants for ethical questions and expertise as she recognizes that they are ethical authorities in their own right who develop ethical content and methods. While Bucar ultimately writes the scholarly work, her interlocutors participate more deeply in her process than in mine in that they could directly push back on her questions and early versions of her interpretation. As such, her work provides us with an example of how to move toward an even more participatory comparative project.

Ethics can also be a useful partner for Wildman's method in that engagement with ethics will naturally push Wildman to elaborate on how his method applies to practices as well as ideas and particularly, the obligations a comparativist has for the practical consequences of one's limited starting points of comparison. In *Religious Philosophy as Multidisciplinary Comparative Inquiry* and other texts on his method, Wildman acknowledges that religion encompasses not just abstract ideas but also practices, texts, artifacts, and so forth. He sees understanding "religion as a whole, in all its intricate variations and manifestations," as the goal of religious studies and regularly refers to ideas and practices as sites of comparison.[71] Yet he focuses on ideas in most of his examples of comparison in the CRIP and elsewhere "because even religious practices are available for comparison as ideas when they are described verbally and framed theoretically."[72] In doing so, he aims to "keep elements of interpretation in the comparative picture."[73]

This focus on ideas makes sense given his comparative goals, yet most of his examples focus on ideas over the interpretation of practices. This tendency could relatively easily be mitigated with different examples, but even then, deeper reflection would be needed to consider the implications of a multidisciplinary, comparative, fallible mode of inquiry for peoples' lives.

Namely, given the focus in Wildman's examples on abstract comparative ideas, questions of responsibility for weak initial comparative categories are relatively easy to set aside. Wildman writes that the

> self-conscious dialectical approach to comparison holds that there should be a dialectical collaboration between data and comparative categories where the task of understanding through comparison can build progressively on previous results. This conception of comparison calls for procedures that gradually refine categories, which helps us fret less over the impurity of the way they are initially produced. This is a particularly important point in comparative religions, where many contemporary comparative categories reflect originally colonial and anticolonial perspectives. Purity of origins is a vain ideal for comparative categories, much as perfectly certain knowledge is a vain ideal in epistemology.[74]

I agree that pure origins for any category and perfectly certain knowledge are vain ideals. We also need to acknowledge the real consequences of limited comparative categories and have a plan of how to deal with them. Early comparative categories of religion that prized text-based monotheistic religions, for example, helped enable Americans to deny First Amendment rights to the free exercise of religion to many Native Americans. Wildman argues that we can "fret less" about where we start the process of comparison because we can always correct it later.[75] Certainly this is true if one only considered the changing of ideas divorced from practices, or if one has an infinitely long temporal and spatial perspective.

However, if one is concerned with the dignity and value of particular human collectives, individual humans, or other biota, then the choice of one not so great initial comparative category over another and their effects in the world are certainly meaningful. Initial conditions can shape the force of the investigation and be difficult to correct later once well established. Of course, such risks cannot be avoided if this is the way inquiry works, as Wildman convincingly asserts. We cannot avoid any inquiry at all because we are afraid of its consequences. To do so is to fail to be human. Yet this does not mean one can dismiss the risks. A multidisciplinary comparative fallibilistic theory of inquiry needs to be accompanied by an account of responsibility for negative social consequences of our comparisons if it is to function as an ethic for scholarship. Here ethical theory and practice about liability and responsibility, especially about unintended consequences, can be helpful. So too can theories of restorative justice—how to make up for or at least deal with harms perpetuated by one's ideas and actions. These harms include the physical, economic, and social harms to other people arising out of the application of the categories of comparison. They also include the harms to the identity and emotions of people harmed by the institution of the categories. Finally, they include the existential harms to the agents who promulgate the comparison—the way that our identity as comparativists is expanded to encompass one who promulgates such comparisons with all of their effects.

Such theories of responsibility and restorative justice are necessary because a complete ethic requires not just statements about ideals and how to live them out such as we see emphasized in Wildman's method, but also ways of thinking through, evaluating, and dealing with the consequences of the ethic. Such consequences may be ideas that follow from the ethic or physical, social, economic, and psychological consequences for the agents employing or affected by those who implement the ethic. Developing all of these resources is beyond the scope of this paper, but is a key step in overcoming the limits of Wildman's method and indeed, any pragmatic fallibilistic method.[76]

Conclusion

Wildman's method for religious philosophy functions as an ethic for scholarship, especially in the humanities, in that it offers ideas for action and a method for achieving them. It offers significant resources for ethicists in a time of pluralism who recognize how the physical, biological, and social world affects our concepts and capacities as humans. Wildman's method delineates a path between the poles of relativism and privileging a religion in comparative religious studies. This is all done to enable people to work toward addressing the big questions that are so intellectually and practically compelling while being humble about what they do and do not know. If Wildman's method is to be extended to ethics, more attention needs to be given to the interlocutors it allows at the comparative table (for their ideas, experience, and to recognize their dignity) and the power dynamics involved in inquiry. Additional attention is also needed regarding how to socially, intellectually, and existentially deal with the often unforeseen negative consequences of a hypothetical approach to inquiry. Fortunately, ethics has and is developing such resources. To work out solutions in more detail will take more time than we have here in large part because if we take Wildman's method seriously, such solutions require a collaborative, multidisciplinary process of inquiry that is open to correction.

Notes

1. Wesley J. Wildman, "The Use and Abuse of Biotechnology: A Modified Natural-Law Approach," *American Journal of Theology & Philosophy* 20, no. 2 (1999).
2. *Religious Philosophy as Multidisciplinary Comparative Inquiry: Envisioning a Future for the Philosophy of Religion* (Albany: State University of New York Press, 2010), 283–93; Wesley J. Wildman, *Science and Religious Anthropology: A Spiritually Evocative Naturalist Interpretation of Human Life* (Burlington, VT: Ashgate Publishing Co., 2009), 174, 216–18.
3. Wesley J. Wildman, "From Grand Dreaming to Problem Solving," *Zygon* (2007): 278; *Religious Philosophy as Multidisciplinary Comparative Inquiry: Envisioning a Future for the Philosophy of Religion*, 3.
4. "Reforming Philosophy of Religion for the Modern Academy," in *Reconfigurations of Philosophy of Religion: A Possible Future*, ed. Jim Kanaris (Albany, NY: State University of New York Press, 2018), 255, 58–59, 69.
5. Ibid., 258.
6. Wildman, *Religious Philosophy as Multidisciplinary Comparative Inquiry: Envisioning a Future for the Philosophy of Religion*, 204.
7. Ibid.; Wildman, "Reforming Philosophy of Religion for the Modern Academy," 256–58.
8. Ian G. Barbour, *Religion in an Age of Science*, vol. 1, The Gifford Lectures 1989–1991 (San Francisco: Harper & Row, 1990), 16–17; *Religion and Science: Historical and Contemporary Issues: A Revised and Expanded Edition of Religion in an Age of Science* (New York: Harper Collins Publishers Inc., 1997), 90–91.
9. Wildman, *Religious Philosophy as Multidisciplinary Comparative Inquiry: Envisioning a Future for the Philosophy of Religion*; "Reforming Philosophy of Religion for the Modern Academy."; W. Mark Richardson and Wesley J. Wildman, eds., *Religion and Science: History, Method, Dialogue* (New York: Routledge, 1996), xii, xiv.
10. Wildman, "From Grand Dreaming to Problem Solving."
11. Ibid., 277–78.
12. Ibid., 278.

13. Ibid., 279.
14. Ibid., 278.
15. Ibid., 277–78.
16. Ibid., 278.
17. Ibid., 277. Wildman points to the science, philosophy, and religion doctoral program at Boston University (from which I graduated) as one place where such training could happen. Ibid., 280. The program has since changed format and institutional structure, illustrating the stakes of multidisciplinary research. Time is needed to know how it pans out.
18. Wildman, *Religious Philosophy as Multidisciplinary Comparative Inquiry: Envisioning a Future for the Philosophy of Religion*, 1–34, 44, 85–124.
19. Ibid., xi–xii, 1–83, 307–19; Wildman, "Reforming Philosophy of Religion for the Modern Academy."
20. *Religious Philosophy as Multidisciplinary Comparative Inquiry: Envisioning a Future for the Philosophy of Religion*, xi.
21. Ibid.
22. Ibid., 1.
23. Ibid., 2.
24. Ibid., 12.
25. Ibid.
26. Ibid., xvii, 156–59, 67–205.
27. Ibid., 5, 42.
28. Ibid., 3.
29. Ibid., 201. Wildman recognizes that this theory of truth is itself a hypothesis and open to correction. See *Religious Truth* for more discussion. Robert C. Neville, ed., *Religious Truth*, The Comparative Religious Ideas Project (Albany, NY: State University of New York Press, 2001), 176.
30. Wildman, *Religious Philosophy as Multidisciplinary Comparative Inquiry: Envisioning a Future for the Philosophy of Religion*, 3.
31. Ibid., 203.
32. Ibid.
33. Ibid., 204.
34. Ibid.
35. Ibid.
36. Ibid., 128.
37. Ibid., 125.
38. Ibid., 147–48.
39. Robert C. Neville and Wesley J. Wildman, "On Comparing Religious Ideas," in *The Human Condition*, ed. Robert C. Neville, The Comparative Religious Ideas Project (Albany, NY: State University of New York Press, 2001), 189.
40. Ibid.
41. Ibid., 204.

42. Ibid., 205.
43. Ibid., 189.
44. H. Richard Niebuhr, *The Responsible Self: An Essay in Christian Moral Philosophy* (New York: Harper & Row, 1963), 65.
45. Ibid., 62–63.
46. Ibid., 67.
47. James M. Gustafson, "Context Versus Principles: A Misplaced Debate in Christian Ethics," *The Harvard Theological Review* 58, no. 2 (1965).
48. Wildman, *Religious Philosophy as Multidisciplinary Comparative Inquiry: Envisioning a Future for the Philosophy of Religion*, xii–xiii, 3–12, 18–33, 136–37; William Schweiker, "On Religious Ethics," in *The Blackwell Companion to Religious Ethics*, ed. William Schweiker (Malden, MA: Blackwell Publishing, 2005), 2–3; Frank Reynolds, "Introduction," in *Discourse and Practice* (1992); Elizabeth M. Bucar, "Mythological Invention as a Constructive Project: Exploring the Production of Ethical Knowledge through the Interaction of Discursive Logics," *Journal of Religious Ethics* 36, no. 3 (2008).
49. Sarah E. Fredericks, *Measuring and Evaluating Sustainability: Ethics in Sustainability Indexes* (New York: Routledge, 2014), 113–14.
50. Schweiker, "On Religious Ethics," 11.
51. Ibid., 13.
52. Neville and Wildman, "On Comparing Religious Ideas," 189.
53. Ibid., 190.
54. Wildman, *Religious Philosophy as Multidisciplinary Comparative Inquiry: Envisioning a Future for the Philosophy of Religion*, 204; Schweiker, "On Religious Ethics," 11.
55. *Power, Value, and Conviction: Theological Ethics in the Postmodern Age* (Cleveland, OH: Pilgrim Press, 1998), 79–80.
56. See, for example, my *Measuring and Evaluating Sustainability* for an extended example of how people of very diverse ethical viewpoints may come to agreement on broad bounds of ethical acceptability with respect to sustainability while retaining their diverging specific commitments.
57. Sarah E. Fredericks and Lea F. Schweitz, "Scholars, Amateurs, and Artists as Partners for the Future of Religion and Science," *Zygon* 50, no. 2 (2015): 419.
58. Wildman, "From Grand Dreaming to Problem Solving," 277.
59. Fredericks and Schweitz, "Scholars, Amateurs, and Artists as Partners for the Future of Religion and Science," 420.
60. Ibid., 429–31.
61. When Wildman advocates for a multidisciplinary approach, he recognizes the various technical terms such as multidisciplinary, cross-disciplinary, interdisciplinary, and transdisciplinary that have been developed to "supposedly express fine distinctions among different methodological approaches to problem-oriented research." He finds that while they are "useful in particular contexts, particularly

for raising consciousness about methodological subtleties, they are of limited value philosophically." Wildman, *Religious Philosophy as Multidisciplinary Comparative Inquiry: Envisioning a Future for the Philosophy of Religion*, 88. While I agree with him that prolonged debate about such terms can distract from problem-oriented inquiry without philosophical benefit, the division between terms can be meaningful even for problem-focused inquiry. For instance, Wildman's choice of multidisciplinary is consistent with his focus on inquiry among academics and, opposed to transdisciplinary, turns our attention away from the benefits of collaboration between academics and non-academics. For a discussion of transdisciplinarity, see Julie Thompson Klein, "The Taxonomy of Interdisciplinarity," in *Oxford Handbook of Interdisciplinarity*, ed. Robert Frodeman, Julie Thompson Klein, and Carl Mitcham (New York: Oxford University Press, 2010).

62. Sarah E. Fredericks, "Online Confessions of Eco-Guilt," *Journal for the Study of Religion, Nature and Culture* 8, no. 1 (2014): 65.

63. In Sarah E. Fredericks, *Environmental Guilt and Shame* (Oxford: Oxford University Press, 2021).

64. June Price Tangney and Ronda L. Dearing, *Shame and Guilt*, ed. Peter Salovey, Emotions and Social Behavior (New York: The Guilford Press, 2002), ix, 24–25.

65. Ibid., 1–2; Ying Wong and Jeanne Tsai, "Cultural Models of Shame and Guilt," in *The Self-Conscious Emotions: Theory and Research*, ed. Jessica L. Tracy, Richard W. Robins, and June Price Tangney (New York: The Guilford Press, 2007), 211.

66. Stephen M. Gardiner, *A Perfect Moral Storm: The Ethical Tragedy of Climate Change* (New York: Oxford University Press, 2011); Dale Jamieson, *Reason in a Dark Time: Why the Struggle against Climate Change Failed—and What It Means for Our Future* (New York: Oxford University Press, 2014); J. Baird Callicott, *Thinking Like a Planet* (New York: Oxford University Press, 2014); Willis Jenkins, *The Future of Ethics: Sustainability, Social Justice, and Religious Creativity* (Washington, DC: Georgetown University Press, 2013); Kevin J. O'Brien, *The Violence of Climate Change* (Washington, DC: Georgetown University Press, 2017); Cynthia D. Moe-Lobeda, *Resisting Structural Evil: Love as Ecological-Economic Vocation* (Minneapolis, MN: Fortress Press, 2013). Love, despair, and grief have all received more attention, maybe because their implications are clearer and because they are not reviled in the way that guilt and shame often are.

67. Sarah E. Fredericks, "Ritual Responses to Climate Engineering," in *Theological and Ethical Perspectives on Climate Engineering: Calming the Storm*, ed. Forrest Clingerman and Kevin J. O'Brien (New York: Lexington Books, 2016). Also see *Environmental Guilt and Shame*.

68. Sarah E. Fredericks, "Climate Apology and Forgiveness," *Journal of the Society of Christian Ethics* 39, no. 1 (2019).

69. See, for example, the panel on the "Emerging Challenges and Possibilities for Ethnographic Fieldwork in Christian Ethics" at the 2019 Society of Christian Ethics annual meeting.

70. Elizabeth M. Bucar, *Creative Conformity: The Feminist Politics of U.S. Catholic and Iranian Shi'i Women*, ed. James F. Keenan, Moral Traditions Series (Washington, DC: Georgetown University Press, 2011).

71. Wildman, *Religious Philosophy as Multidisciplinary Comparative Inquiry: Envisioning a Future for the Philosophy of Religion*, 14, 24, 40, 126, 34, 37, 50, 250, 85.

72. Ibid., 150.

73. Ibid.

74. Ibid., 147–48.

75. Ibid., 148.

76. Actually, all forms of inquiry ultimately come with such responsibility, but it is more acute for fallibilists who admit that they choose a starting point and that it is limited.

5

Pragmatist Inquiry and the Problem of Value

Nathaniel F. Barrett

Wesley J. Wildman's work to date exemplifies the pragmatist imperative to bring all matters of human interest within the reach of forms of inquiry that are critically self-aware, publicly testable, and open to revision. Through ambitious programs of scientific research and a torrent of books and articles, Wildman and his collaborators have made heroic efforts to expand and refine the social and intellectual resources for making progress on Big Questions ranging from the nature of ultimate reality to universal patterns of sociohistorical development. Among these resources is a pragmatist theory of inquiry that shows how progress on such questions is possible.[1]

Developing an adequate pragmatist theory of inquiry is itself a kind of inquiry—a kind of meta-inquiry, perhaps. A pragmatist theory of inquiry includes all forms of mentality within its scope, but its primary focus is human mentality, and its worth is tested by the resources it provides for our inquiries into various problems big and small. In respect of its generality, the theory of inquiry might be considered as a kind of theory of knowledge. For pragmatists, however, an adequate theory of inquiry is not to be obtained by transcendental methods, and its purpose is not to provide a foundation for inquiry, to show how certain knowledge is possible, or to distinguish knowledge from "mere opinion." Pragmatists shun the quest for certainty and absolute truth and focus instead on improving the processes by which our understanding can be improved. Accordingly, a theory of inquiry is derived from reflection on the myriad and continually evolving varieties of human inquiry, including but not limited to varieties of scientific inquiry, and its purpose is to stimulate and refine inquiry by helping it to become more coherent, more responsive to appropriate feedback, and more critically self-aware.

One of the cardinal virtues of a good theory—including a good theory of inquiry—is that it enables important matters to be determined empirically. But pragmatists are not naive empiricists: they are keenly aware that empirical inquiry is always directed by theoretical presuppositions, such that some matters must be decided provisionally to make other matters decidable by a process of inquiry. There is no escape from theoretical bias: the most we can hope for is to be alert to this danger, to develop whatever methods are most effective for making our biases known to us, and to cultivate an ethical disposition that impels us to seek correction. A theory of inquiry is supposed to provide aid for this kind of critical reflection. But insofar as theories of inquiry are still theories, they too can have biases that have important repercussions on our inquiries into other topics.

The task of this chapter is to highlight the topic of value as a critical issue for pragmatist theory of inquiry and to indicate some of its repercussions for investigations of religion. At the same time, what follows is an extended reflection on and response to Wildman's and others' work on these same topics. Nearly everything that is written here comes from conversations with Wildman and with other pragmatist philosophers, living and dead, to whom we are both closely connected. In this sense, this is very much an insiders' conversation, although I have endeavored to make it accessible to readers who are not familiar with its peculiar context. For Wildman, it is likely that I will not manage to say anything new. Be that as it may, the following arguments are intended to challenge his views on several points, or at least to invite clarification.

The key issue around which the following argument turns is the import of Alfred North Whitehead's philosophy for pragmatism. Although technically not a pragmatist, Whitehead is generally welcomed within the circles of American naturalist and pragmatist philosophy in which Wildman makes his home. Among the many reasons for this congenial relation are Whitehead's view of metaphysics as a form of empirical inquiry, his naturalistic understanding of value, and his emphasis on aesthetics as a touchstone for philosophy.[2] When Wildman writes most extensively about value, he acknowledges his indebtedness to Whitehead and to the work of his friend Robert C. Neville, another pragmatist influenced by Whitehead.[3] I share these influences with Wildman, and I would venture to say that they mark us as a distinct breed of pragmatist. Neither Wildman nor I accept every part of Whitehead's system, but within the peculiar intellectual milieu that we share with Neville and a handful of other philosophers, pragmatist and Whiteheadian ideas often mix together so freely that it is difficult to tell them apart.

In this chapter, however, I aim to enliven the conversation by sharpening differences, focusing on a potentially significant divergence between Whiteheadian and pragmatist theories of value. Certainly, within the larger context of modern philosophy, the differences between Whitehead and the classical pragmatists are minor compared to what they have in common. But recently I have become convinced that Whitehead's aesthetics presents an important challenge to pragmatist theory of inquiry that has been overlooked by Whiteheadians and pragmatists alike. In the third section, I articulate the crux of this challenge in terms of a distinction between the Kantian aesthetics of agreement and the Whiteheadian aesthetics of intensity. The rest of the chapter is devoted to tracing out the ramifications of this distinction for pragmatist theory of inquiry and for pragmatist contributions to the scientific study of religion.

Pragmatist Inquiry

In the context of pragmatism, the term *inquiry* is often used to refer to a vast continuum of mental activity running from basic organic processes to the course of human civilization. One of the concerns of pragmatist theory of inquiry is to understand how human inquiry is distinguished from other kinds and, within the sphere of human inquiry, how to articulate and critique the various nested levels of personal and social inquiry.[4] For present purposes, however, we are more interested to point out certain basic features shared by all forms of inquiry.

In the most general sense, inquiry refers to any and all instances in which an organism works toward the improvement of its current situation, however that situation is defined. Because so many typical episodes of inquiry are initiated by some kind of problem, inquiry is often portrayed by pragmatists as problem solving.[5] But at the most basic organic level, the problems of inquiry do not have to be articulated as such. Rather, what is meant by "problem solving" in this more general sense is any attempt to improve a situation that is somehow unsatisfactory. Thus, pragmatists often describe impetus of inquiry as a feeling of dissatisfaction caused by some kind of tension, lack, or conflict. Inquiry is the activity undertaken by the organism in response to this feeling, and it continues until the feeling abates because the tension is resolved, the lack fulfilled, or the conflict overcome—or because attention is diverted to something else.[6]

I wish to underline this point: for many if not most pragmatists, all inquiry is carried forward by the desire to be rid of a disagreeable feeling. At the most basic, organic level, this feeling arises within a particular situation determined by the environment and the basic needs and interests of the organism. Ideally, by struggling to rid itself of the disagreeable feeling, the organism deals appropriately with the situation. A hungry animal's search for food and a frightened animal's search for shelter are thus two common examples of inquiry: hunger and fear are disagreeable feelings that arise within particular situations and, normally, these feelings abate when the animal's behavior results in the appropriate adjustment. Moreover, a disagreeable feeling and its abatement are not just signals that mark the beginning and end of inquiry. Insofar as a feeling is constituted in part by the current situation, it also serves to guide whatever adjustments are called for by that situation.

Of course, the situations of human inquiry are infinitely varied and extend well beyond the simple life-or-death matters that constitute the bulk of inquiry at the basic organic level. But, according to the classic pragmatist view, the most sophisticated varieties of human inquiry are still driven by disagreeable feelings of some kind. Such feelings are famously described by Peirce in his seminal early works as the "irritation of doubt":

> Doubt is an uneasy and dissatisfied state from which we struggle to free ourselves and pass into a state of belief; while the latter is a calm and satisfactory state which we do not wish to avoid. . . . The irritation of doubt causes a struggle to attain a state of belief. I shall term this struggle *inquiry*. . . .[7]

Decades later, Dewey describes the situation of inquiry as pervaded by an "uncertain, unsettled, disturbed" quality, a "unique doubtfulness which makes that situation to be just and only the situation it is."[8]

My insistence on the cardinal place of disagreeable feeling in the pragmatist view of inquiry may seem simplistic and subjectivist. But it is only simplistic if we understand all disagreeable feelings as if they were the same, and not peculiar to the situations that occasion them; and it is only subjectivist if we understand these feelings as if they belonged only to the organism in isolation and not the situation. Dewey is particularly clear on these points, and to avoid any relapse into subjectivism he avoids the language of feeling. But it is clear that when he speaks of the problematic quality of a situation he means something experienced.

With these points in mind, I propose that we characterize the development of inquiry—including the development of pragmatist theory of inquiry—as the acquisition and refinement of methods by which we gain control over the *satisfactions* of inquiry and the processes by which they are procured. Indeed, one could say that all inquiry is some kind of *self-controlled search for satisfaction*; what distinguishes one kind of inquiry from another is the kind of satisfaction that is sought and the kind and degree of self-control that is exercised.

Satisfaction is being used here as a vague term that includes its opposite, *dissatisfaction*, so that it can refer not only to the feelings that bring inquiry to a close but also to the feelings that instigate and guide inquiry. *Self-control* has to do with all means by which we manage to articulate the various parts and processes of inquiry and thereby subject them to criticism and other kinds of correction. Among the most important kinds of criticism—and thus a central topic for pragmatist theory of inquiry—is criticism of the kinds of satisfaction sought by inquiry, more commonly known as the *ends of inquiry*. For the full development of this kind of criticism, it is necessary to have an adequate theory of satisfaction itself, which is a way of talking about aesthetics.

The importance of aesthetics for inquiry has been recognized by pragmatists since Peirce. In the next section, we turn our attention to aesthetics proper: that which is admirable in itself. The reason for introducing this topic in terms of satisfaction is to emphasize its fundamental importance for our understanding of all kinds of inquiry. Even when understood in the most general sense, *aesthetics* suggests a rarefied pleasure, removed from the pursuits of everyday life. We do not normally think of organic processes as *aesthetic* endeavors. By contrast, *satisfaction* seems to fit better with pursuit of the basic necessities of life. In processes of homeostatic regulation, *satisfaction* may refer to the restoration of equilibrium after some disturbance. Given the fundamental role of homeostatic regulation in all living processes, perhaps all forms of inquiry—and the forms of satisfaction that they entail—are elaborations on this basic pattern of disturbance and recovery. A good case can be made that this was Dewey's view of inquiry, and perhaps it applies to Peirce as well.

But it is precisely this assumption that I wish to question: Is all satisfaction a recovery from disturbance? Or is this just one kind of satisfaction?

These questions about satisfaction cut to the core of the basic pragmatist view of inquiry that I have just presented above: Is all inquiry an attempt to rid oneself of a disagreeable feeling? Or is inquiry also sometimes driven by a more positive impulse, the desire to *increase* satisfaction?

If satisfaction is only understood as the recovery from disturbance, there is no way to increase satisfaction except by increasing disturbance, which makes no sense within this picture of inquiry. Moreover, it follows that the overall tendency of inquiry is essentially *conservative*: whenever possible, inquiry maintains the status quo; there is no urge to change for the sake of variety. Inquiry never innovates except in service of maintaining equilibrium within a wider range of disturbances, and this kind of innovation is only undertaken when necessary—that is, when forced by new disturbances. Novelty is permitted only insofar as it is demanded by the problem at hand. There is no allowance for the possibility that novelty can be sought for an increase of satisfaction, that is, the kind of satisfaction that is more than just relief from disturbance.

To my knowledge, these views are nowhere expressly embraced by pragmatists. I present them here as implications of what I perceive as a widespread tendency to understand inquiry in purely negative terms, as a struggle to be rid of an unpleasant feeling. I am suggesting that this is a truncated view of inquiry that stems from a truncated view of satisfaction, which, in turn, may stem from a truncated aesthetics.

In brief, if we understand the aesthetic ideal—that which is desirable in itself—only in terms of agreement, then all satisfaction must also be understood in terms of agreement and the lack thereof, and all inquiry must be understood as a struggle to minimize disagreement. And the problem with mere agreement is that it cannot be *intensified* so as to produce increases of satisfaction that go beyond the mere lack of disagreement. Our everyday experience of satisfaction, however, suggests a much wider range: beyond the mere absence of unpleasantness, there are diverse kinds and degrees of "positively pleasant" feelings, and these must be accounted for by our aesthetics and by our theory of inquiry. Before we turn to aesthetics, however, I want to point out some likely reasons for the tendency among pragmatists to adhere to a truncated view of inquiry.

First, unpleasant feelings can have a forcefulness that makes them seem to have a more prominent role in inquiry than pleasant feelings. Especially in the form of physical pain, unpleasant feelings have an urgency that is generally lacking in pleasure, as well as a distinctive character that serves better to demarcate problematic situations and episodes of inquiry. This asymmetry in our experience of pain and pleasure is reflected at the anatomical level by the ways in which the organs adapted for the experience of pain seem to be more specialized than those adapted for pleasure. For instance, we have specially adapted receptors (called nociceptors) for the detection of various kinds of bodily trauma, and these receptors form the basis for distinctive kinds of bodily pain; but to my knowledge we have no specially adapted receptors for pleasure, not even in the erogenous zones of the body.

Second, in situations of everyday life, there may be a greater need for critical self-control when inquiry is driven by unpleasant feelings. This is because the desire to rid oneself of an unpleasant feeling can be satisfied in many ways, not all of which are adequate solutions (in the long run) to the problem at hand. The proverbial ostrich with its head in the sand is the textbook example of this kind of failure. According to Daniel Kahneman and others, we are prone to a similar kind of error, namely our tendency to substitute a difficult problem with an easier problem that appears the same.[9] Unable or unwilling to find satisfaction within a particular situation, we settle for satisfaction of a different kind that belongs to a different situation, often without noticing.

Indeed, from a pragmatist perspective, it would seem that *all* cognitive errors are versions of this unwitting, self-inflicted bait-and-switch. To end in error, inquiry must be brought to rest, and inquiry can only be brought to rest by some kind of satisfaction. From the standpoint of the original problem, we can say that we should not be satisfied, but it cannot be the case that we have simply gotten the feeling wrong. The anti-subjectivist position of pragmatism entails that every satisfaction properly belongs to *some* situation; therefore, if we really are satisfied—and it is impossible that we can be mistaken about this—we must have succeeded in resolving a situation other than the one with which inquiry began. In short, if all satisfactions of inquiry are situational, then all errors must be consequences of situational displacement. Ensuring ourselves that the satisfaction that concludes inquiry is the *right* satisfaction—the one that we originally sought, or the one we should be seeking—requires critical awareness and self-control.[10]

A third reason may be the special influence of experimental science on pragmatist theory of inquiry. In general, this influence has been positive: the success of modern experimental science is one of the main inspirations of the pragmatic tradition, and, for the most part, pragmatists have learned from scientific models of inquiry while remaining critically aware of the excesses of scientism. However, when advocating for increased "vulnerability to correction" and "responsiveness to feedback," pragmatists sometimes come across as naive falsificationists.[11] The question of when to resist correction and when to yield is a very subtle matter, and pragmatists are only sometimes clear on this point. Moreover, few pragmatists are clear about the varieties of correction and feedback, both negative *and* positive, that are encountered in scientific inquiry. As a result, even where naive forms of falsification are clearly eschewed, there is still a tendency to construe inquiry in purely negative terms, as if progress were made only by discarding hypotheses.

Fourth, the general phenomenal character of satisfaction is surprisingly difficult to describe. This difficulty has something to with the way in which every satisfaction, or lack thereof, is unique to its situation: there is no special quality that attends our experience of a situation to mark its satisfactory or unsatisfactory character. The peculiar phenomenological elusiveness of our experience of value is, I believe, a neglected topic in the theory of value, and its implications for a theory of inquiry are rarely if ever discussed by pragmatists. Unfortunately, a fuller treatment of this issue is beyond the scope of this chapter, but the following point should be kept in mind: no matter how forceful and indubitable our feeling of satisfaction may be, we cannot pin this feeling down by tying it to a clear and distinct element within our experience.

Aesthetics and Inquiry

It is well known that for Charles Peirce, the founder of pragmatism, aesthetics is the most basic and inclusive form of inquiry—the "normative science" that grounds both ethics and logic. At the same time, aesthetics is considered to be one of the most problematic aspects of Peirce's philosophy: it clearly plays a fundamental role within his architectonic vision, yet his remarks on the topic are scattered and vague, and by his own admission it was the least developed part of his system. As a result, anyone who wishes to follow in Peirce's footsteps and develop a pragmatist theory of inquiry must venture a specification of his aesthetic ideal—that which is admirable in itself. And the first step in such an endeavor is to articulate and differentiate among major alternatives.

In this section I articulate a potentially important distinction between two alternative readings of the aesthetic ideal that drives inquiry. This discussion is inspired by a recent work of Richard Kenneth Atkins, *Peirce and the Conduct of Life* (2016), which offers a reading of Peirce's aesthetics that closely follows Kant's view of aesthetic and teleological judgments.[12] My purpose here is neither to critique nor to defend Atkins's reading of Peirce (or his reading of Kant). I simply wish to indicate that his Kantian reading of Peirce's aesthetics entails a particular kind of aesthetic ideal—what I call the *aesthetics of agreement*—that can be helpfully contrasted with another ideal, the *aesthetics of intensity*. The latter ideal is expressly upheld by A. N. Whitehead in his late works, especially *Adventures of Ideas* (1933). Thus, an articulation of these two ideals as divergent alternatives can serve as a heuristic for the investigation of aesthetics and its role in inquiry.

First, to orient the following discussion, let us review the importance of aesthetics for pragmatist inquiry. All varieties of human inquiry are guided by some particular purpose, good, or "end-in-view." In the previous section, this point was made by saying that all forms of inquiry seek some kind of satisfaction. These normative features of inquiry are, in part, products of past inquiry, and although they must frequently be taken as premises, they cannot be simply taken for granted. If inquiry is to be fully self-critical and properly vulnerable to correction, we must also inquire into the kinds of purposes, goods, or ends of inquiry that are worth having, and for this kind of "value inquiry" to function more efficiently, we need a theory of intrinsic worthiness, or that which is admirable in itself. Peirce clearly saw this need;[13] perhaps what he did not see so clearly was how to define the aesthetic ideal, or that which is admirable per se.

Peirce recognized that an endless variety of gratifications and pleasures could qualify as intrinsic goods. From the standpoint of inquiry, however, the problem with these intrinsic goods is that each constitutes an end of inquiry in the wrong sense: considered as a unique aesthetic value, each feeling of gratification constitutes a finality that brings inquiry to a close. Peirce sought a general ideal that would keep inquiry going indefinitely, forever reaching after higher and more inclusive ends-in-view. For this role, Peirce thought that "reasonableness" best fit the bill, because the essence of reason is that it is never fully perfected: there is always room for growth: "reason always looks forward to an endless future and expects endlessly to improve its results."[14]

But what is "reasonableness" exactly? Sometimes it seems as if Peirce's ideal was some kind of supremely general and comprehensive theory of everything. But in other passages his discussion of "concrete reasonableness" suggests that he had something else in mind. Whatever he meant, it seems that Peirce was not sufficiently precise to rule out the Kantian reading offered recently by Atkins. Given Peirce's thorough knowledge of Kant's philosophy, we know that Peirce's aesthetics could have been strongly influenced by Kant. According to Atkins's interpretation, the key to Kantian aesthetics is the notion that pleasure is a state of *agreement*:

When the imagination and the understanding actively reach agreement, there is no tension between them. This results in a judgment of beauty, in the case of aesthetic judgments. The maintenance of this agreement may be called aesthetic pleasure. In the case of teleological judgments, in which there must also be an agreement with the natural object, there is astonishment (in the incompatibility of intuitions and concepts) or admiration (in the continual recurrence of their compatibility). The continual recurrence of the agreement with the natural object may be called intellectual pleasure. With intellectual pleasures, one is in a state in which there is no shock, no astonishment.[15]

Based on this interpretation, Atkins proposes that, for Peirce, the norms of inquiry ultimately come to rest with the aesthetic pleasure of agreement between the mind and the world. To make the case that Peirce also thought of the aesthetic ideal of inquiry as a state of agreement, Atkins points to passages in the "Lectures on Pragmatism"[16] where pain is defined as a "struggle to give a state of mind its *quietus*" and pleasure is defined as "a peculiar mode of consciousness allied to the consciousness of making a generalization, in which not Feeling, but rather Cognition, is the principal constituent."[17] From these passages, Atkins concludes that pleasure is a "state of *quietus* that emerges from a struggle" and that this state, in the context of inquiry, belongs to a state of "agreement between the judgments one makes and the way the world is."[18]

Interestingly, as pointed out by Atkins, Peirce insisted that the pleasure of agreement was distinct from the pleasure of "sensuous beauty," suggesting that his notion of aesthetics was not well served by investigations of commonplace forms of aesthetic enjoyment. Also, to avoid falling into psychologism, Peirce insisted that the aesthetic ideal that guides inquiry must be distinguished from the pleasure we get from whatever happens to agree with our peculiar, parochial mindset. It seems to me, then, that on this reading the pleasure of *quietus* must be relative, always containing within itself some trace of disagreement, some slight disturbance or irritant that keeps inquiry moving forward. As our generalizations about the world become more adequate, the pleasure of agreement increases, and the pain of disagreement decreases: "the struggle of inquiry reaches a minimal intensity, is softened to oblivion."[19]

Thus, as summarized by Atkins, "Peirce's aesthetics is the science of the admirableness of generalizations based on their continually recurrent agreement with the objects or features of reality, and the maintenance of their agreement is a state of pleasure."[20] No doubt some readers will want to dispute this reading of Peirce. Others may want to dispute the notion that continual agreement can be a source of pleasure. But again, my purpose here is to use Atkins's Kantian reading of Peirce to set up a heuristic contrast with an alternative reading. That alternative is the aesthetics of intensity clearly set forth by Whitehead in the following passage from *Adventure of Ideas*:

> Beauty is the mutual adaptation of the several factors in an occasion of experience. . . . There are gradations of Beauty and in types of Beauty.
> "Adaptation" implies an end. Thus Beauty is only defined when the aim of the "adaptation" has been analyzed. This aim is twofold. It is in the first place, the absence of mutual inhibition among the various prehensions. . . . When this aim is secured, there is the minor form of beauty, the absence of painful clash, the absence of vulgarity. In the second place, there is the major form of Beauty. This form presupposes the first form and adds to it the condition that the conjunction in one synthesis of the various prehensions introduces new contrasts of objective content with objective content. These contrasts introduce new conformal intensities of feelings natural to each of them, and by so doing raise the intensities of conformal feeling in the primitive component feelings. Thus the parts contribute to the massive feeling of the whole, and the whole contributes to the intensity of feeling of the parts. Thus the subjective forms of these prehensions are severally and jointly interwoven in patterned contrasts. In other words, the perfection of Beauty is defined as being the perfection of Harmony; and the perfection of Harmony is defined in terms of the perfection of Subjective Form in detail and in final synthesis. Also the perfection of Subjective Form is defined in terms of "Strength." In the sense here meant, Strength has two factors, namely, variety of detail with effective contrast, which is Massiveness, and Intensity Proper which is comparative magnitude without reference to qualitative variety. But the maximum of intensity proper is finally dependent upon massiveness.[21]

I have quoted this passage in full not only because it succinctly expresses Whitehead's aesthetics of intensity, but also because it shows that the aesthetic ideal of intensity, qua "major form of beauty," presupposes something like the aesthetics of agreement as the "minor form of beauty."

Or so it seems. The minor form of beauty—absence of mutual inhibition, absence of painful clash—sounds like the peaceful *quietus* described above as Peirce's aesthetic ideal. In this sense, then, it would seem that the aesthetics of agreement and intensity are not, strictly speaking, mutually exclusive alternatives. However, I believe that on closer examination we find that the pursuit of intensity does in fact diverge from the pursuit of agreement, especially when the latter is taken as the highest ideal. This important point is obscured by Whitehead's idiosyncratic language—for example, his references to "prehensions" and "subjective form"—and by the way in which beauty, qua harmonic intensity, is defined as a complex function of two seemingly opposed features—narrowness and width—or strength and diversity of contrast.

This last point is a critical one: in Whitehead's aesthetics, "intensity" is a function of both strength (narrowness) and diversity (width) of contrast within a single feeling. These are not strictly incompatible features, but their relation is such that it is difficult, if not impossible, to maximize both. Extreme strength of contrast is incompatible with diversity, but the reverse is not exactly true. *Trivial* diversity—for example, the indiscriminate diversity of a large crowd viewed from above as a teeming mass—is deficient in strength of contrast. However, a more *substantial* diversity (what Whitehead calls "massiveness"), as found in any grouping where individuals are clearly distinguished as such, is dependent on some minimal strength of contrast between components of feeling. Thus, while the possibility of increasing intensity by combining strength and diversity of contrast depends on some degree of agreement, agreement cannot be the only criterion or the ultimate measure of aesthetic harmony. Trivial diversity is a kind of agreement that is lacking in "intensity proper," and thus fails to attain the kind of harmonic intensity characteristic of beauty in its "higher form."

Rather than go further into the details of the relation between diversity and strength of contrast, however, let us rely on our intuitive grasp of these matters and take note of the most obvious differences between the aesthetics of intensity and the aesthetics of agreement. At a glance, it should be apparent that we are talking about very different kinds of satisfaction. Peirce (as summarized by Atkins) dismisses sensual beauty; the emphasis of his aesthetics is on *quietus*, peace, and tranquility, which suggests a state of inactivity.[22] By contrast, Whitehead emphasizes beauty, and understands all beauty (including both intellectual and sensual varieties) as a kind of harmonic intensity. Moreover, although in this passage Whitehead analyzes beauty as if it belonged to a single feeling of minimal duration, elsewhere in his works it is clear that intensity is maximized and maintained through rhythm, variation, and the continual entrance of novelty. Dynamism and flux are inherent to Whitehead's aesthetic ideal of intensity in a way that resonates with everyday experience.[23] Whitehead's view suggests that the opposite of aesthetic enjoyment is not conflict, which, after all, provides us with some measure of intensity, but rather triviality and boredom.

Based on these distinctions, further differences between the aesthetics of agreement and the aesthetics of intensity can be unpacked as follows:

	Aesthetics of Agreement	**Aesthetics of Intensity**
Ideals:	peace inclusion togetherness, belonging	beauty participation expression, individuation
Key traits:	compatibility comprehensiveness stability endurance generality	mutual enhancement contrast variety novelty individuality
Opposites:	conflict incompleteness exclusion	dullness indifference triviality

Beginning with the comparison of ideals (beauty vs. peace, etc.), we do not find any obvious incompatibility between the two aesthetics. Indeed, not only would we like to combine these two sets of ideals, but it also seems that they complement or complete one another: what good is peace without beauty, inclusion without participation, belonging without expression? But as we move to key traits, a certain divergence begins to reveal itself: is it possible to maximize both stability and variety, endurance and novelty? Finally, coming to the opposites of each ideal, their divergence is evidenced by the impossibility of simultaneously eliminating opposites of the two ideals: for example, we cannot completely rid ourselves of conflict without falling into dullness and boredom.

Now, ideally, what we want is a comprehensive theory that encompasses both aesthetics and helps us to understand and adjudicate this divergence of ideals. Does this divergence reflect a deep tension inherent to the pursuit of value, or is it simply a product of an inadequate aesthetics? I have argued elsewhere for the former view.[24] Here I am more concerned to point out a critical difference that underlies this divergence of ideals.

The critical difference is that the enjoyment of intensity depends on *limitation*. Because intensity requires selective emphasis and exclusion, it requires decision, in the sense of "cutting off." In the passage quoted above, Whitehead obscures this point when he insists that in the final analysis harmonic intensity depends on "massiveness," which might be taken to mean maximal inclusiveness. But, as I have pointed out above, massiveness, or substantial diversity, is not just "variety of detail," but "variety of detail *with effective contrast*," and although I cannot pause here to argue this point, I think that our everyday experience clearly indicates that the latter cannot be increased without limit.

Because this limit is inherent to the aesthetics of intensity, any process of inquiry that is driven by the aesthetics of intensity must also be inherently limited. By contrast, the aesthetics of agreement imposes no limits on inquiry. Of course, in practice, our agreement with the world may always be very limited and progress may not be guaranteed, but *in principle* there is no limit to agreement. Indeed, it seems that the limitless of agreement is part of its attraction for Peirce as a regulatory ideal of inquiry. Moreover, insofar as it progresses, inquiry that is based solely on the aesthetics of agreement works only to expand the limits of agreement. For this view, progress can be defined as the *reduction* of limitation and can be pictured—in the infinitely long run—as an asymptotic approach to limitless agreement.

What are the consequences, then, of these different views of aesthetics and inquiry? Let us remind ourselves again of the scope of this question. As discussed here, an aesthetic theory is a theory of the basic ideal and impulse that guide and animate all processes of inquiry. We need more than aesthetics to have a complete theory of inquiry, but without aesthetics the most fundamental questions of and about inquiry cannot be asked. Aesthetics not only describes the long arcs of inquiry; it also pertains to its most parochial and momentary "cadences." Truth cannot be reduced to aesthetic satisfaction, but both Whitehead and Peirce believed that the pursuit of aesthetic satisfaction is indispensable to the discovery of deep and lasting truth.

Fortunately, it is possible for inquiry to be productive and self-critical without an adequate view of its aesthetic basis. At the same time, theories of inquiry *do* matter: they make a difference to our particular paths of inquiry, at least by allowing us to achieve at least some extra modicum of self-critical awareness, freedom, and responsibility. As a distinctive form of inquiry, aesthetics emerges whenever the ends or purposes of inquiry are subjected to criticism. It is possible to engage in this kind of criticism without a theory of aesthetics: our explorations of aesthetic experience in the narrow sense, exemplified by the production and enjoyment of the arts, are a prime example of the kind of aesthetic criticism that can proceed without the guidance of an explicit theory. Also, anyone who wonders about how best to live their life engages in a kind of aesthetic criticism; they need not pose to themselves the rather abstract question, "What is the good life?"

On the other hand, precisely because the ends of inquiry can and do evolve even when they are not subjected to criticism, an adequate aesthetic theory is a critical tool for evolutionary and historical analysis and explanation. In short, if aesthetics is essential to understanding how the ends of human inquiry evolve, and if human evolution and history is viewed as a complex, multilayered process of inquiry, then aesthetics is essential to improving our understanding of the evolution of human mentality, society, and culture.

I do not undertake any such in-depth historical or evolutionary analysis here. Instead, I make just a couple of general points in preparation for the next section, which considers how these questions about aesthetics and inquiry might pertain to our understanding of religion.

First, if we take up something like the aesthetics of intensity as part of our theory of inquiry, our view of every level of human inquiry must take both the pursuit of intensity and the inherent tensions and limitations of this pursuit into account.

On the one hand, this means that life at all levels of organization strives not just for survival—for survival is nothing more than agreement between a form of existence and its environment. Rather, life strives for *intensity* (which includes but goes beyond and diverges from agreement).[25] Diverse forms of life seek not to preserve their form, therefore, but to enhance whatever satisfaction is possible through this form. Life is not one side of a simple binary contrast with non-life but rather belongs to a continuum of intensity that includes more or less "lively" or "vivacious" forms of existence.

On the other hand, because of the pursuit of increased satisfaction, life has a tendency to undermine itself. This theory suggests that no path of inquiry that is coherent enough to be identifiable as such—no civilization, society, tradition, human life, or aesthetic pursuit—can advance indefinitely. Those who believe that all evolution is based on norms of survival might seem to agree: the evolutionary record clearly shows that nothing lasts forever. But when history is viewed as a product of the pursuit of intensity, this point is made even sharper. Even more than Darwinian perspectives, the aesthetics of intensity lends itself to a tragic reading of history: all human endeavors at all scales must eventually collapse or decline because no coherent process of inquiry—no search for intensification—can be sustained indefinitely. All good things come to an end; in the most fortunate cases, this end comes because of the limits inherent to the kind of goodness that has been achieved.

Second, adopting the aesthetics of intensity as part of our theory of inquiry suggests that some episodes and pathways of human life are best understood as responses to the inherent limits of human inquiry. All life is affected by limitations and tensions inherent to the pursuit of intensity, but only human life is additionally affected by awareness, however dim and intermittent, of these limitations. Here we begin to see the potential value of the distinction between aesthetic theories that has been sketched in this section: if what I have said about limitation and human inquiry is true, and if the aesthetics of intensity helps to make this limitation apparent while the aesthetics of agreement does not, then it seems that our choice of aesthetic theory can make a crucial difference to our understanding of the problems of human inquiry and the kinds of cultural resources that we have developed in response to these problems.

Reflections on the Scientific Study of Religion from the Standpoint of Aesthetics

In this final section, I draw out further implications of the preceding discussion for the scientific study of religion and raise some questions for Wildman about his work in this field. In particular, the main questions that I wish to raise are the following: Does he take a clear stand on the aesthetic questions raised in the previous sections? If not, how might a more resolutely aesthetic view of inquiry change his approach to the scientific study of religion, if at all?

Wildman is an extraordinarily versatile scholar—I cannot think of anyone so adept at approaching religion from so many different angles—and the complexity of his approach to religion leaves room for interpretation on these questions. Sometimes, when writing in a more theological vein, Wildman adopts a stance that seems very close to the aesthetic perspective that I am advocating. But I find this stance difficult, though certainly not impossible, to reconcile with his generally welcoming stance toward cognitive and evolutionary theories of religion, a field that is thoroughly dominated by "functionalist-adaptationist" thinking and utterly blind to aesthetics.

The former, aesthetic stance is most clearly evident in his recent essay, "Axiological Sensitivity: Its Origins, Dynamic Structures, and Significance for Theological Anthropology," written for a collection of essays that celebrate the work of theologian J. Wentzel van Huyssteen.[26] In that essay, Wildman proposes that "human beings are spectacularly sensitive to axiological possibilities and that pondering our axiological sensitivity and everything that comes with it, from language to art, takes us deeply into the biological and theological distinctiveness of our species."[27] The bulk of the essay is devoted to retelling the story of human evolution from an axiological perspective.

From this perspective, value is not a special construction of human consciousness: "Axiological sensitivity lies at the root of perception and cognition, so the story of the origins and development of axiological sensitivity is as old and tangled as the history of bodies interacting with environments."[28] Indeed, showing his Whiteheadian side, Wildman goes so far as to propose that "reality is physical-valuational hybridity all the way down," such that the axiological sensitivity of life in general can be seen as manifestation of the axiological character of reality in all its forms.[29] Against this deep evolutionary background, Wildman suggests that there is something unique about human axiological sensitivity, which is reflected in the "great leap forward" (approximately 50,000 years before the present) that separated modern humans from other hominid species.[30] Wildman further suggests that a "ravenous hunger" for value and meaning lies behind many if not most innovations of human culture, from music and art to mathematics and religion. This aesthetic view of human evolution is wonderfully summarized in the following passage:

> [W]hen evolutionary pathways open up for us intensifications of ordinary sense experience, we find that entire ranges of axiological possibilities latent in the environment spring to life, with attendant joy and suffering. This is why we are the species that builds art museums, enjoys fine cuisines, proves mathematical theorems, has experiences we call spiritual and religious, is plagued by suicide, and endlessly talks about everything.[31]

The concluding section of Wildman's essay enters into reflections on the existential problems that attend our sensitivity to value and the implications of these problems for our understanding of religion. Wildman observes that we seem to be in desperate need of an "absolute grading of axiological possibilities."[32] That is, faced with inevitable choices of life that "cut off" some value possibilities in favor of others, we seek reassurance that these choices can be justified by some kind of metaphysical foundation that ranks value possibilities within a single, absolute hierarchy. One could say that this need is an expression of axiological anxiety, one of the most bitter fruits of our unique axiological sensitivity. Wildman suggests that much of religious thought—or theism, at least—can be understood as a reaction to axiological anxiety, and he expresses his preference for a non-theistic religious stance that rejects "absolute grading" and attempts, instead, to come to terms with the "full richness of the axiological landscape" of human experience, including its darker truths.[33]

I find it curious that in the course of this brief evolutionary narrative—which, in large part, I wholeheartedly endorse—Wildman hardly draws on his expertise in cognitive science of religion and the distinctive evolutionary perspectives on religion to which it has given rise. Late in the essay, cognitive science is briefly invoked to criticize the anthropomorphic tendencies of folk religion and theology as products of "cognitive error."[34] What is especially interesting to me is that this critique of theism comes right after Wildman's discussion of our need for "absolute grading," which seems to present a different and, I think, more sympathetic (but still naturalistic) view of theism as a response to axiological anxiety. Both might be true: theism and other anthropomorphic religious beliefs might be products of cognitive error *and* axiological anxiety, so we need not be forced to choose between these kinds of explanation—at least not without further consideration of the relevant evidence. But it is worth noting that these explanations come from totally disparate theoretical frameworks that are deeply at odds with respect to the nature and importance of value in human evolution.

Insofar as there is a problem here, I suggest that it may be disguised by a double ambiguity. First, as discussed above, there is lack of clarity within pragmatism about the aesthetic ideal of inquiry: in particular, pragmatists have failed to distinguish between the aesthetics of intensity and the aesthetics of agreement. Second, there is a superficial similarity between the aesthetics of agreement and natural selection. As mechanisms of evolution, the aesthetics of agreement and natural selection are totally different, but insofar as both push toward some kind of optimal state of "agreement" with the environment, they can be easily harmonized or even conflated. Together, these two ambiguities make it possible for pragmatists to overlook potentially deep differences between pragmatist theory of inquiry and standard evolutionary explanations—that is, functionalist-adaptationist explanations—of human behavior. Let me briefly clarify this point.

First, it should be emphasized that any theory that gives some kind of aesthetic preference a role in the process of evolution is completely alien to standard frameworks that adopt a "functionalist-adaptationist" approach to evolutionary explanation. These frameworks are able to explain how aesthetic preferences are shaped and directed, but they cannot explain what these preferences are or how they ever arose in the first place. Even those who defend the independent role of sexual selection are typically blind to this gaping hole in our understanding of animal behavior and its evolutionary past. For example, the ornithologist Richard Prum has made a controversial argument that the evolution of colorful bird plumage (and other features important to mate selection) is driven primarily by female birds' preference for beauty rather than the alleged connection between such "costly" features and fitness of some kind. Prum's "aesthetic view of life" strongly resonates with the pragmatist prioritization of aesthetics, but there is a key difference: for Prum, aesthetic preferences can be presumed as primitive facts without any promise of explanation.[35] He sums up his position as follows: "beauty happens" and "pleasure happens."[36] Like many scientists, he fails to recognize that references to beauty and pleasure—like all references to value—constitute a critical gap in our current frameworks of scientific explanation.[37]

Turning back to pragmatism, it should be clear that the central role of aesthetics in pragmatist theory of inquiry constitutes an attempt to fill this critical gap. Wherever there is mentality, there is some pursuit of an aesthetic ideal. Moreover, according to Whitehead and Peirce, traces of mentality can be found throughout nature, including even non-living processes. The advantage of this approach is that aesthetic preferences and other "value dispositions" need not float in from nowhere at some arbitrary threshold of complexity. On the other hand, it is important to recognize the enormous burden of this approach: to accommodate value within our frameworks of scientific explanation requires a comprehensive reconstruction of our understanding of nature, life, and mind.[38]

With this burden in mind, I find Wildman's combination of aesthetic and standard cognitive explanatory perspectives perplexing. The dissonance is especially jarring when Wildman observes that "the scientific study of religion shows that human beings will behave in exactly the way we do—as meaning-making engagers of axiological possibilities—regardless of whether there is a Kant-style metaphysical foundation for morals."[39] I agree with the basic point that Wildman is making (that our yearning for some kind of "absolute grading" does not prove that one exists), but I am baffled as to its alleged basis in the "scientific study of religion." In my reading of the literature of cognitive science of religion and related fields, I cannot think of anyone who has even ventured the hypothesis that religiosity is based in our nature as "meaning-making engagers of axiological possibilities"—anyone except, of course, Wildman and myself.[40]

If I am right about the absence of axiology in the scientific study of religion, then what does Wildman's statement mean? A bit of wishful thinking? Whatever it means, I am seizing upon it as an opportunity to make a larger point. Perhaps it reveals something about Wildman's peculiar way of understanding the import of scientific research—that is, his way of viewing this research through the distinctive lens of a pragmatist-Whiteheadian axiological perspective. Although I cannot defend this point in detail, I believe that it *is* possible to register contributions from standard cognitive theoretical approaches to religion within such an axiological framework. But the reverse is certainly *not* the case: as it stands, cognitive science has no theory of the unique axiological sensitivity of the human species, let alone a theory that treats this sensitivity as the main driver of human evolution.

So if there is a bone to pick here, the problem that I have is not with what Wildman says, but rather with what he does not say. Or, to be more precise, perhaps the problem is just with what he does not say loudly enough in the right contexts. In my view, Wildman's arguments about the importance of axiological sensitivity pose a deep challenge to the scientific study of religion because they go to the heart of what it means to adopt a naturalistic, evolutionary perspective on human thought and behavior. To be clear: Wildman and I, and other similarly minded pragmatists, are passionate advocates for evolutionary naturalism. We insist, however, that our experience of value must be incorporated into our understanding of nature. As I have just indicated, this is a major undertaking that is largely neglected by scientists and philosophers alike (especially as compared with the problem of consciousness, which is more widely recognized). Wildman is well aware of this challenge, but as far as I know he has not taken advantage of his position as a scientific researcher to make this challenge better known to scientists. In the essay that I have been examining here—which is directed toward an audience of theologians, not scientists—he decries the neglect of axiology as a major blind spot of modern Western intellectual culture.[41] But the incapacity to deal adequately with our experience of value is, if anything, even more pronounced within the human sciences, including sciences of human cognition and evolution.

Insofar as Wildman and I are in basic agreement about the importance of axiology and its problematic place within modern thought, there is no need to belabor these points. The question that I have tried to raise here has to do with the possibility that the pragmatist theory of inquiry has been neither sufficiently clear about value nor sufficiently persistent in its pursuit of greater clarity, allowing pragmatists to slip back and forth across this great intellectual fault line, perhaps without even noticing. In previous sections I have argued that this lack of clarity can be traced back to the work of Peirce, whose writings on aesthetics are scant and vague. Pragmatists are fond of talking about how vagueness can be good for inquiry—but only if it is recognized. My reading of Whitehead has led me to believe that many pragmatists are insufficiently aware of the vagueness of their position with respect to value. Although I have not provided nearly enough evidence on this point, I think the problem is carried over into the later works of Dewey, which are ambiguous with respect to the distinction I have drawn between the aesthetics of agreement and the aesthetics of intensity. In parts of *Art as Experience* (1934), Dewey presents some of the most comprehensive and articulate examinations of aesthetic intensity that can be found anywhere in philosophy (as far as I know). But in other works, such as his "Theory of Valuation" (1939), Dewey seems to come firmly down on the side of the aesthetics of agreement.[42]

One of the possible consequences of this lack of clarity about value is a corresponding lack of lack of clarity about key terms of inquiry such as "correction" and "feedback." When it goes unnoticed, this vagueness makes it all too easy for pragmatists to unite their views with disparate perspectives on diverse areas of human life. For example, the terms "correction" and "feedback" may seem equally appropriate for speaking about natural selection, on the one hand, and the intensification brought to experience by a fine work of art, on the other. Although not necessarily incompatible, these two uses of "feedback" and "correction" are totally disparate, and currently only one of them enjoys scientific credibility in a wide range of disciplines.

Moreover, to return to a critical point of earlier sections, this lack of clarity makes it easy to overlook key differences between *positive* and *negative* kinds of feedback. Natural selection is essentially a culling process; insofar as it involves any feedback at all, it is purely negative.[43] Homeostatic regulation and cybernetic control systems are also essentially negative feedback processes.

My point is that many widespread forms of scientific explanation—but by no means all—are founded on processes of negative feedback. Where these forms of explanation are dominant, a pragmatic theory of inquiry that is insufficiently clear about feedback may appear to be more compatible than it really is, depending on how we understand the aesthetic basis of inquiry. The aesthetics of agreement supports a kind of inquiry based solely on negative feedback—the elimination of disagreement—while the aesthetics of intensity both includes and goes beyond agreement.

So what changes if we consider aesthetics as a fundamental driver of human evolution? More specifically, how might it change our view of religion? Here I can only suggest, in broad outline, how an aesthetic perspective might change our understanding of the relevant facts. For this purpose, the "aesthetic view of life" defended by ornithologist Richard Prum provides a helpful reference point. Although I have criticized his view of beauty and pleasure as primitive facts of animal life, many other features of his view resonate strongly with the pragmatist-axiological view that I am advocating here. For one, we share the view that natural selection, though important, is not the only mechanism of selection. Prum argues that animals have "aesthetic agency": they have aesthetic preferences and are able to influence their own evolutionary trajectory through choices based on these preferences. I would say that the influence of aesthetic choice on human evolution is even more pronounced, especially if we include cultural evolution. Second, Prum is sharply critical of the tendency of biologists to assume that adaptationist explanations are the only kinds of explanation that count. Similarly, I have been critical of a similar "functional-adaptationist" bias within the cognitive science of religion. At the same time, Prum is careful to point out that aesthetic selection is comparible with natural selection and other mechanisms of selection; moreover, he argues that by adopting a more pluralistic view of evolution, we are able to respond to a fuller range of evidence, rather than choosing only the evidence that fits with our preferred mechanism of selection. I think that we should adopt a similarly pluralistic stance toward the scientific explanation of religion.

Now, in light of Wildman's views on axiological sensitivity and its importance for human evolution, it would seem that there is nothing here that he does not already endorse. But, like I said, if there is a problem, it is with the fact that these axiological views, despite their profound divergence from standard frameworks of modern science, have not (yet) led Wildman to mount a serious challenge to the dominant functionalist-adaptationist approach in the scientific study of religion. By a "serious challenge," I don't mean the kind of critique that remains at the theoretical level.[44] Again, Prum's example is pertinent. His advocacy for a more pluralistic approach to evolution involves more than just a critique of the adaptationist bias among his fellow scientists: he also presents a wealth of evidence in support of his alternative view. Similarly, we need more than just a critique of theoretical bias in the scientific study of religion: we also need evidence-based arguments in support of a more versatile approach that includes our aesthetic preferences. Who else but Wesley Wildman is up to the task?

Notes

1. See Wesley J. Wildman, *Religious Philosophy as Multidisciplinary Inquiry: Envisioning a Future for the Philosophy of Religion* (Albany, NY: State University of New York Press).

2. On Whitehead's view of metaphysics as inquiry, see Chapter 1, "Speculative Philosophy," in *Process and Reality, Corrected Edition*, ed. David Ray Griffin and Donald W. Sherburne (New York: Free Press, 1978), 3–17. On the importance of aesthetics in Whitehead's thought and his affinity with pragmatism, see Steve Odin, *Tragic Beauty in Whitehead and Japanese Aesthetics* (Lanham, MD: Lexington Books, 2016).

3. For Wildman's thoughts on axiology, see "Axiological Sensitivity: Its Origins, Dynamic Structures, and Significance for Theological Anthropology," in *Human Origins and the Image of God: Essays in Honor of J. Wentzel van Huyssesteen*, ed. Christopher Lilley and Daniel Pedersen (Grand Rapids, MI: Eerdmans), 132–55. Relevant works of Robert C. Neville include his axiology of thought: *Reconstruction of Thinking* (Albany, NY: State University of New York Press, 1981); *Recovery of the Measure* (Albany, NY: State University of New York Press, 1989); *Normative Cultures* (Albany, NY: State University of New York Press, 1993).

4. Brandon Daniel-Hughes, *Pragmatic Inquiry and Religious Communities: Charles Peirce, Signs, and Inhabited Experiments* (Cham, Switzerland: Palgrave Macmillan, 2018).

5. Wildman, *Religious Philosophy*, 175.

6. Especially in the context of human inquiry, this last possibility is important to keep in mind. Because of the extraordinary flexibility and subtlety with which we are able to define situations of inquiry, it is easy for our attention to be diverted from one problem to another—so easy that we often do so without noticing.

7. From the 1877 essay "The Fixation of Belief," see *The Essential Peirce: Selected Philosophical Writings, Vol. 1 (1867–1893)*, ed. Nathan Houser and Christian Kloesel (Bloomington: Indiana University Press, 1992), 114.

8. *Logic: The Theory of Inquiry*, vol. 12, *John Dewey: The Later Works, 1925–1953*, ed. Jo Ann Boydston (Carbondale, IL: Southern Illinois University Press, 1986), 109.

9. *Thinking Fast and Slow* (New York: Farrar, Straus, & Giroux, 2011).

10. Many kinds of criticism and control are directed toward the situation: specifying and defining the problem at hand, and ensuring that inquiry proceeds so that satisfactions are tied to specified problems. But other kinds of criticism and control are directed toward satisfaction as such: for instance, aesthetic inquiry of an artist seeking a certain quality of expression, or the "inquiry" of a host who is trying to help guests relax and enjoy each other's company.

11. "Naive falsificationism" is the view that experimental science proceeds by a simple process of falsification—that is, an extreme version would be the idea that if data from a single experiment do not support a hypothesis, the hypothesis is refuted and can be discarded. The authoritative discussion and critique of "naive falsificationism" is found in Imre Lakatos, "Falsification and the Methodology of Scientific Research Programmes," in *Criticism and the Growth of Knowledge*, ed. Imre Lakatos and Alan Musgrave (Cambridge: Cambridge University Press, 1970), 91–195.

12. Richard Kenneth Atkins, *Peirce and the Conduct of Life: Sentiment and Instinct in Aesthetics and Religion* (Cambridge, UK: Cambridge University Press, 2016).

13. CP 1.573–82; CP 1.591–1.615. See *The Collected Papers of Charles Sanders Peirce, Vol. 1*, ed. Charles Hartshorne and Paul Weiss (Cambridge, MA: Harvard University Press), 311–38.

14. CP 1.614–15. See *Collected Papers, Vol. 1*, 335–38.

15. Atkins, *Peirce and the Conduct of Life*, 147.

16. From "The Seven Systems of Metaphysics," in *The Essential Peirce: Selected Philosophical Writings, Vol. 2 (1893–1913)*, ed. the Peirce Edition Project (Bloomington, IN: Indiana University Press, 1998), 189–90.

17. Ibid., 190; quoted in Atkins, *Peirce and the Conduct of Life*, 148. Peirce's language here is redolent here of Kant's tripartite distinction between sensation, intellect or understanding, and feeling, in which case the term "feeling" probably refers to something like "affect" or "emotion."

18. Atkins, *Peirce and the Conduct of Life*, 148.

19. Ibid., 153.

20. Ibid., 151.

21. *Adventures of Ideas* (New York: Free Press, 1933), 252–53.

22. Although Atkins insists otherwise; see *Peirce and the Conduct of Life*, 153.

23. See also John Dewey, *Art as Experience*, vol. 10, *John Dewey: The Later Works, 1925–1953*, ed. Jo Ann Boydston (Carbondale: Southern Illinois University Press, 1989), especially Chapter 8, "The Organization of Energies," for an excellent discussion of the inherent dynamism of aesthetic intensity.

24. Nathaniel F. Barrett, "The Problematic of Harmony in Classical Chinese Thought: A Whiteheadian Analysis," in *Through a Prism: Neglected Aspects of Alfred North Whitehead's Metaphysics*, ed. Helmut Massen and Aljoscha Berve (Cambridge, UK: Cambridge Scholars Publishing), 161–85.

25. Whitehead, *Process and Reality*, 105.

26. See n. 3 for full reference.

27. Wildman, "Axiological Sensitivity," 134.

28. Ibid., 140.

29. Ibid., 144.

30. Ibid., 136.

31. Ibid., 140.

32. Ibid., 153–54.

33. Ibid., 154–55.

34. Ibid., 152.

35. Richard O. Prum, *The Evolution of Beauty: How Darwin's Forgotten Theory of Mate Choice Shapes the Animal World and Us* (New York: Doubleday, 2017).

36. These phrases are actually intended by Prum as a shorthand for what he argues is the "null hypothesis" against which adaptive hypotheses should be tested.

37. The gap between value and standard evolutionary explanation was clearly pointed out seventy-five years ago by the gestalt psychologist Wolfgang Köhler. See his "Value and Fact," in *The Selected Papers of Wolfgang Köhler*, ed. Mary Henle (New York: Liveright, 1971), 356–75. See also *The Place of Value in a World of Facts* (New York: Liveright, 1976).

38. For examples of this kind of work, see Whitehead, *Process and Reality* (n. 2 above); Neville, *Recovery of the Measure* (n. 3 above). My own attempts at reconstruction can be found in Nathaniel F. Barrett and Javier Sánchez-Cañizares, "Causation as Freely Chosen and Singular Optimality," *Review of Metaphysics* 71 (2018): 755–87; Nathaniel F. Barrett, "The Nature and Origin of Cognition as a Form of Motivated Activity," *Adaptive Behavior* (forthcoming 2019).

39. "Axiological Sensitivity," 153.

40. To be clear, I am referring only to the restricted context of discourse about "cognitive-evolutionary theories" of religion: within this context, I do not know of anyone else who advocates an axiological approach.

41. Wildman, "Axiological Sensitivity," 143–44.

42. Dewey, *Art as Experience*; "Theory of Valuation," in *John Dewey: The Later Works, 1925–1953, Vol. 13*, ed. Jo Ann Boydston (Carbondale, IL: Southern Illinois University Press, 1988).

43. Here I am drawing on arguments that natural selection does not push for optimal fitness, but only eliminates traits that do not "satisfice," that is, meet certain minimal criteria for persistence in a population. See "Evolutionary Path Making and Natural Drift" (Chapter 9), in Francisco J. Varela, Evan Thompson,

and Eleanor Rosch, *The Embodied Mind: Cognitive Science and Human Experience* (Cambridge, MA: MIT Press), 185–204.

44. The best critique of the standard approach in cognitive science of religion that I know of is Barbara Herrnstein Smith, *Natural Reflections: Human Cognition at the Nexus of Science and Religion* (New Haven: Yale University Press, 2010).

PART 2
THEOLOGICAL APPROACHES

6

Pragmatism and the Future of Philosophical Theology

Michael L. Raposa

I

This chapter is intended as a response to one aspect of Wesley Wildman's elaborate and remarkable proposal for the future of "religious philosophy" conceived as "multidisciplinary comparative inquiry." (For reasons that I sketch in the chapter, I am less nervous about the problematic connotations of "philosophical theology" or "philosophy of religion" as a label for such inquiry than I am about those associated with his preference for "religious philosophy.") My primary focus is on the importance of neither the multidisciplinary nor the comparative features of the sort of inquiry that he prescribes, but rather on its nature as "pragmatic." Wildman's reasons for embracing a pragmatic theory of inquiry are carefully delineated in his books and articles, and his argument for the superiority of such a point of view over alternative perspectives is persuasive.

Here I review some of those arguments while also offering a mild critique of Wildman's proposal, a critique that is similar in certain respects to the one that Charles Peirce articulated when he contrasted his own "pragmaticism" with the philosophical pragmatism of some of his contemporaries. Among my concerns are the following: the identification of inquiry too narrowly as a form of "problem solving"; an admirable emphasis on the importance of "consensus" and "correction" as the goals of interpretation, but at the expense of what I call "semiotic complementarity"; mirroring Peirce's response to Dewey, the conflation of "logic" with a "natural history of thought"; a somewhat truncated account of the role that *attention* plays in the process of inquiry; finally, a bit less than full appreciation of the importance of the logic of vagueness for understanding the task of philosophical theology.

For the purposes both of review and of critique, I need to invest some intellectual energy also in determining why Peirce felt it necessary to defend a certain kind of "anthropomorphism" in logic, science, and metaphysics, while Wildman has so rigorously attempted to remove all traces of it from his religious philosophy, opting instead for an austere "apophaticism." Does this mean that their perspectives on this issue are diametrically opposed? Immediate appearances to the contrary, I suggest that it does *not* and then try to explain why this is so. The observation that there are a variety of different senses in which a philosophical theology may be conceived as "pragmatic" should not blind an observer to the real and important continuities that link one to another. And so I also intend in my chapter to trace some of the features that link Wildman's proposal to the more distinctively Peircean perspective that informs my critique. In general, that critique consists more of a series of questions than it does of rebuttals; and so I hope that it will serve to facilitate lively conversation.

II

The concern with careful and rigorous methodology is a distinguishing feature of much of Wildman's published work. Nevertheless, it is the central preoccupation of an illuminating study published in 2010 as the first of his six-volume "Religious Philosophy Series," a book titled *Religious Philosophy as Multidisciplinary Comparative Inquiry*.[1] (Sections of this book provide for my chapter its primary subject matter.) It was a bit misleading in my introductory remarks for me to contrast an emphasis on Wildman's pragmatism with his insistence on either multidisciplinarity or comparative analysis. As it should soon become clear, on Wildman's account, one cannot possibly hope to be pragmatic without also attending to these other features of inquiry. But before explaining why this is so, consider first the care with which Wildman reviews and evaluates the various labels that are typically used to describe the scholarly study of religion; prominent among these are "religious studies," "the philosophy of religion," and "philosophical theology." What is at stake in choosing one label over the others, and what are the features of an approach labeled as "religious philosophy" that recommend it to Wildman as being especially felicitous?

To those for whom this concern about proper nomenclature might seem a bit too fastidious, I should note that for more than thirty years I have been teaching at Lehigh University in what was established right around the middle of the twentieth century as the first department of "Religion Studies" in any college or university in the United States. The department's founder, A. Roy Eckardt, felt quite strongly, because there was nothing "religious" about the sort of inquiry in which scholars of religion engage, that "Religious Studies" was a misleading designation. Moreover, because nothing that these scholars do *as* scholars should be identified as constituting a religion, to identify it as the "Department of Religion" was even more problematic. Finally, while Eckardt himself was trained in and produced scholarship that might be classified as a somewhat radical form of Christian "theology," Lehigh had severed its official link with the Episcopalian Church in 1900 and after half a century had established its status as a nonsectarian university. Thus eschewing "religious studies," "religion," and "theology" (one or another of these providing the name for departments at other American colleges and universities), under Eckardt's leadership Lehigh's "Department of Religion Studies" was organized and christened.

I relate the Lehigh story because when I first learned about it my initial reaction was that Eckardt and his colleagues had demonstrated a preoccupation with academic terminology unwarranted by the significance of the issue. But after several decades of both attending to Peirce's careful, persistent emphasis on developing an "ethics of terminology" and either witnessing or being engaged in various academic conflicts resulting from a confusion about where and how to sharply draw certain disciplinary boundaries, I am now inclined, much like Wildman, to take such matters more seriously.[2] And I am now also prepared to echo my distinguished predecessor Roy Eckardt by raising a question about what makes the philosophizing that Wildman proposes to engage in a specifically "religious" activity? If the subject matter is religious but the method is philosophical, then he would appear to be doing the philosophy of religion. If the specific purposes of inquiry are at least vaguely religious (e.g., probing the nature of ultimate reality) but, again, the method is philosophical, then it would seem more appropriate to label his project as an extended exercise in philosophical theology. I prefer the latter designation.[3] Wildman himself gives it a partial endorsement; because religious philosophers can have theological interests and objectives, he reports that he will refer to what he is doing as philosophical theology when he feels a "need to contrast it with confessional theology, which self-consciously serves the interests of religious institutions."[4]

Why is the careful intellectual exploration of whatever might appropriately be labeled as "ultimate" in human experience not *best* to be classified as philosophical theology? Like Eckardt, Wildman is concerned not only with the words that we use to describe the form of inquiry in which we are engaged, but also with identifying the ideal social location within which such inquiry might best occur and flourish. Wildman's primary worry is with the way that other labels have been typically employed in colleges, universities, seminaries, and religious communities. It is more about the history of their usage than it is about the meanings of the words combined, so that in a sense his analysis and conclusions are to be regarded more properly as descriptive than purely prescriptive. Wildman even admits to preferring the "philosophy of religion" as a label for his enterprise and hopes for a future when such a designation might be reclaimed. (Note the subtitle of this first volume in the series.) "At present," however, he needs a different name tag to contrast his multidisciplinary, comparative, and pragmatic approach to inquiry with the way in which the philosophy of religion has traditionally been, and continues to be, pursued.[5] Even his policy of endorsing the qualified usefulness of "philosophical theology" as a label is problematic, he admits, because of the typically limited way in which so many philosophical theologians have understood the nature and scope of their task.

Interestingly, one of the features that recommends "religious philosophy" to Wildman as an alternative is the fact that it is "helpfully vague."[6] And because I follow Peirce in taking the logic of vagueness quite seriously, it is a crucial matter to decide in any given case whether the use of fuzzy terms is indeed helpful or not. I am warning in this instance that "religious philosophy" is not vague enough a term to offset the disadvantage of its use possibly being interpreted as an indicator that there is something intrinsically "religious" about the mode of inquiry that Wildman is recommending to his readers. I would argue instead that he should aggressively deny exclusive property rights to those others who are pursuing investigations—in a way that he regards as infelicitous—in both the philosophy of religion and philosophical theology. (I think, in fact, that there is a much greater, messier pluralism of such approaches than his account suggests.) This is perhaps a very minor issue; in the more recent publications in his series, appearing after this first volume where he discussed the matter in detail, Wildman seems to refer to what he is doing as philosophical theology at least as frequently as he refers to religious philosophy.

I belabor the point at the outset here because Wildman takes such great pains to distance his project from any form of reflection that is rooted in premises or presuppositions privately available only to a specific religious community, privileged by a special revelation. He conceives of religious philosophy as a subdiscipline within the broader field of religious studies and identifies the modern secular academy as the ideal location for pursuing this kind of inquiry. On my understanding, philosophical theology (fundamental theology is the label preferred by Roman Catholics) has always been taken to designate just such a mode of inquiry, one occurring prior to or apart from any reference to the doctrines of a particular religious tradition. Like philosophy in general, it is what Peirce would refer to as a *cenoscopic* discipline, a science that appeals only to the deliverances of our everyday human experience, a form of experience commonly accessible to anyone wishing to inquire and not limited to those who have some exclusive access to it—for example, as the result of a private revelation or through work in carefully designed laboratories with the use of special equipment.

This raises an interesting question for me about whether or not Wildman would regard his religious philosophy as being cenoscopic in this Peircean sense, given his very positive evaluation of the contributions of the specialized natural and social sciences to the kind of multidisciplinary inquiry that he is advocating. This is a question to which I plan to return at a later point in my chapter. Now while not a methodological issue, Wildman's substantive position rejecting all forms of anthropomorphism in thinking about ultimate reality could be taken to suggest that he might also be a bit nervous about the *theos* in theology. Yet the word "God" has been used frequently enough to designate a reality that is clearly impersonal in nature, perhaps most famously and self-consciously by John Dewey in *A Common Faith*;[7] and Wildman himself seems quite comfortable with such a practice.[8] Any examination of the topic of anthropomorphism will also have to be briefly delayed. More immediately, it is important to get a clearer sense of what it means for Wildman to describe religious philosophy as "pragmatic," as well as to understand his principal motivations in deciding to adopt such an approach.

III

Although it is commonplace for scholars to frame pragmatism as embodying a distinctive philosophical theory of *truth* or *meaning*, I concur wholeheartedly with Wildman's judgment that its principal value consists in the original perspective that it supplies on the nature and purpose of human *inquiry*. Very early on in *Religious Philosophy as Multidisciplinary Comparative Inquiry*, he makes it clear that to refer to some form of rationality as "pragmatic" is also to regard it as being both "fallibilist" and "hypothetical."[9] Taken all together (and in a fashion entirely consistent with what Peirce, James, and Dewey intended), these concepts signal a clear commitment on Wildman's part to a rigorously scientific method, albeit broadly conceived and nuanced in a way appropriate to his subject matter. This means that there cannot be any a priori path to determining the truth about religion. Moreover, it means that nothing taken as true can ever be placed beyond the reach of reasonable doubt, indeed, that every effort possible should be made to subject the candidates for "truth" to vigorous critique and constant testing. This is hardly an embrace of skepticism. It is rather a very firm and healthy embrace of the experimental method, one that regards even the most well-entrenched components of a particular point of view as hypothetical and so vulnerable to revision or even rejection.

As he developed his economy of research, Peirce advocated the selection in certain instances of what might be regarded as the *most vulnerable* of hypotheses for testing; if quickly and easily falsified, this would result in the competition among hypotheses being made narrower and the path to the truth somewhat shorter. But for Wildman, the making of any hypothesis more vulnerable to correction is an ongoing strategy, even and especially if it seems to be the likeliest candidate for the truth. This is just good science. For religious philosophy, one of the ways to achieve such a goal is to be persistently comparative in one's approach. The beliefs endorsed by a particular religious community or enshrined in their traditions will be rendered more vulnerable by the simple recognition that they are not the only items on the menu, that believing in such a fashion is hardly the only game in town (at least if one regards the "town" in global terms). What Jews, Christians, and Muslims believe about the ultimate reality as a personal deity cannot be evaluated simply by delineating the logic of such a concept, by measuring its internal consistency and explanatory power. It is necessary also, for good pragmatic reasons, that one compare such a belief to what others—for example, in religious traditions developed in South or East Asia—have thought and argued about ultimacy. This kind of comparative analysis can even take the form of a "reverent competition," as Wildman has vividly displayed in a recent book contrasting anthropomorphic conceptions of the ultimate with alternative points of view.[10]

In a different but related sense, the insistence on a multidisciplinary approach to religious philosophy also seems intended to increase the vulnerability of religious claims and ideas as a strategy to test their general fitness. That a belief may seem relatively secure after having been subjected to philosophical scrutiny does not mean that it will remain so when all of the most recent results of inquiry in the physical and social sciences have been brought to bear on the consideration of it. Here there appears to be a certain slippage in Wildman's account, if not, then a failure on my part to interpret him correctly. The concern here again is one about disciplinary boundaries. Wildman is dedicated to building them higher and stronger in some cases, for example, when he wants the distinction between religious philosophy and an apologetic or confessional form of theology to be made clear. But he is interested in keeping the walls quite low when one turns to the range of disciplines clustered under the general label of "religious studies." Wildman is himself remarkable for having developed expertise in a number of these areas. A commitment to multidisciplinarity, on his view, means that the religious philosopher ignores at his intellectual peril the sort of investigations being pursued by social and natural scientists interested in religion.

So here is my concern; let's call it a question. Is the stipulation that one should never ignore the results achieved by specialists working in such disciplines, or is it also the case that one needs to use their methods? I would endorse the former but worry about the latter. The nature of my worry is complex and multifaceted. In part, it overlaps with whatever motivated William James's desire to circumscribe the results and significance of an approach to the study of religion that he called "medical materialism."[11] James was not suggesting that it is either impossible or unimportant to explore precisely what is happening physiologically and neurologically when persons have powerful religious experiences. Yet it remained the case, at least for James, that attending to such questions tells one nothing essential about the meaning or value of such experiences. Insight concerning the latter will come from exploring the "fruits" rather than the "roots" of a certain kind of experience. Such exploration can surely be deemed scientific, and it will be quintessentially pragmatic; after all, William James was one of the founders of pragmatism and he called passionately and persuasively for the creation of a new "science of religions."[12] But this would require having a nuanced and expanded view of what it means to do "science" or to conduct an "experiment."

Wildman certainly understands this latter requirement. As attentive as he is to the theories and arguments of specialists in cognitive science, evolutionary psychology, or quantum physics, he is also sophisticated enough to recognize that productively evaluating and comparing religious beliefs, experiences, and practices will involve the employment of a highly subtle and specialized methodology. His general label for that method of inquiry is "pragmatic," and fallibilism, along with an impulse to seek the continuous correction of hypotheses, is among its "six main emphases."[13] So return to the issue of whether or not such a discipline is cenoscopic. Does successful inquiry in religious philosophy, in contrast with cenoscopy, necessitate appeal to the kind of experience that is not commonly or readily accessible to any honest investigator?[14] How would Wildman draw the line between religious philosophy as a scientific discipline, broadly conceived, and the more highly specialized sciences?

It is important to note that among the other "emphases" characteristic for Wildman of a pragmatic theory of inquiry are "biology," "evolution," and "sociality." To be sure, such a characterization of pragmatism is also entirely consistent with the original insights of thinkers like Peirce, James, and Dewey. Yet such insights are sufficiently vague that they might be unpacked in a variety of different ways (significantly different enough even early on in the history of pragmatism that Peirce was motivated to change the name of his philosophy to "pragmaticism" to distinguish his perspective from others). On Wildman's account, "inquiry is an embodied activity made possible by senses and brains"; it is focused on the goal of "survival" by means of "problem solving;" and it depends "on cooperation and consensus."[15] This account deserves closer scrutiny.

It would seem impossible to be a pragmatist and yet fail to recognize that inquiry is an "embodied activity." Two cautions are in order here, however. That it *is* so embodied does not entail that we can either reduce inquiry to an examination of what is revealed by our senses or describe it exhaustively by giving an account of what is going on in our brains whenever inquiry occurs. The latter mistake was what motivated James's concern about the possibly dangerous hegemony of a medical materialism. The former is tied to an empiricism narrower than any that a pragmatist should be blithe to defend. As Peirce put the matter, an idea receives its logical license only if it *both* enters consciousness through the gate of "perception" and exits through the gate of "purposive action."[16] Some contemporary neo-pragmatists have lingered at the second gate, and ignored the first, at the risk of nudging pragmatism toward a radical constructivism.[17] Wildman's emphasis on "biology" gestures toward the first gate, but there is no reason to assume that he gets stuck there. Consider next what he has to say about "evolution."

That pragmatism in general is a philosophy that originated and developed in the second half of the nineteenth century pretty much directly in response to Darwin and Darwinism is a thesis that has been capably defended.[18] For Wildman, what this means is that inquiry conducted in a pragmatic vein will have "survival" as its primary objective, with such a goal to be achieved to the extent that inquiry takes the form of "problem solving." Now this seems true as far as it goes, and it serves the invaluable purpose of distinguishing Wildman's approach to philosophical theology from any number of other, non-pragmatic perspectives that permit a deep chasm to open up between theoretical inquiry and practical behavior. But here I would want to stake out a distinctively Peircean position on the nature of inquiry, even if that means reading Peirce in a different way from how many other scholars have interpreted him.[19]

The standard interpretation regards Peirce's famous article on "The Fixation of Belief" published in 1878 as canonical, thus also portrays inquiry as an act of scratching the itch of doubt whenever it arises, and so fits perfectly with any account that emphasizes problem-solving. Twenty years later, during the first of his Cambridge Conference Lectures on "Philosophy and the Conduct of Life," in what seems like a complete reversal of opinion, Peirce distanced himself from any argument for a direct continuity between theory and practice, announcing instead that they have nothing at all to do with one another![20] The tendency among some interpreters is to dismiss that lecture as an embodiment of sarcastic hyperbole, formulated at least in part as an irritated reaction to the manner in which William James had insisted on framing the lecture series. I tend not to "dismiss" anything that Peirce wrote, but I agree about the evidence for hyperbole and sarcasm. What else could have motivated the founder of American pragmatism on this occasion to drive such a deep wedge between theory and practice? Yet I also regard the Fixation article as a highly infelicitous formulation of Peirce's theory of inquiry, problematic in a number of respects.

It would move me too far off topic to explain in detail why I think that this is the case. The relevant point here is that Peirce never really believed that inquiry arose only in response to the stimulus of doubt or that it consisted primarily in problem solving. Following Darwin and others, he articulated a theory of evolution, but one in which the explanatory role and range of the principle of natural selection was somewhat circumscribed. Importantly, Peirce's only extended treatment of a religious topic, his 1908 article on "A Neglected Argument for the Reality of God," is also one of his clearest presentations of a general theory of inquiry.[21] As portrayed in that article, inquiry arises in a spirit of playfulness (what he called "musement") and not for the purpose of solving a particular problem. Now while some scholars have certainly argued for the "survival value" of play behavior in humans and other animals, I think one would have to be something of a "spoil sport" to posit that as the primary purpose or meaning of play.

In any event, a pragmaticistic theory need not identify inquiry with problem solving. Of course, Wildman is not committed to Peirce's or to my position on this issue. For other pragmatists, like John Dewey, for example, inquiry might be more accurately described as a response to the stimulus of doubt, or as the need to address some "problematic situation." And so the question is worth raising about how closely Wildman's own pragmatism would follow Dewey in this regard. He worries about the "relativizing" tendencies of William James and some contemporary neo-pragmatists;[22] but Wildman typically endorses both Peirce and Dewey as solid representatives of the pragmatism he espouses. In my view, there are significant differences between them. Moreover, especially for a discipline like philosophical theology, I think it is at least sometimes the goal of inquiry to raise or to generate problems rather than to solve them; as I suggest below for at least one case, the urgency to solve a particular problem can itself be problematic.[23]

Turn, finally, to Wildman's pragmatic emphasis on the social dimension of inquiry, so that its progress requires cooperation and its primary goal is consensus. Not only does Wildman underscore the importance of a vibrant community of inquiry in his theory, he has continuously promoted it in practice. Anyone who knows anything about his work and career will recognize with great admiration that, in addition to being a brilliant and original thinker, he has also been an extraordinary collaborator. Here he actually resembles Peirce, who combined the same sort of genius and creativity with a conviction that one individual's results and progress pale in significance to what a dedicated community of inquiry might achieve in the long run (a conviction maintained despite Peirce's tragic isolation in the Pocono mountains for much of the last three decades of his life). For both Peirce and Wildman, their comfortable familiarity with the methods and investigations of natural scientists helps to explain this emphasis; in the domain of the physical sciences, the necessity of collaboration, the importance of intersubjective correction, and the building of scholarly consensus have all long been recognized as essential.

For the sake of the conversation, I tweak this pragmatic emphasis on sociality just a bit. Whatever the importance of collaboration for inquiry, it needs to be recognized that it can take a variety of different forms. "Teamwork" is indispensable for winning football or basketball games, but it is not *always* the desideratum for inquiry. In the humanities most especially, it seems to me, inquiry often unfolds quite productively as a form of "parallel play," with individuals working separately, albeit surely with some awareness of what certain others have thought and accomplished. Nor does the deemphasizing in a particular case of active, ongoing collaboration belie the need for communication. The results of inquiry are negligible if they are never discussed or shared. Even our parallel play is rooted in sociality.

Likewise, consensus is important but not always the most desirable outcome of inquiry. Sometimes our disagreements are more productive than our agreements, and not always simply because they spur further investigation and so contribute to a final consensus down the road. As he developed his logic of relations, Peirce became convinced that there are forms of generality more important than those designated by class concepts. The latter explore the relation of similarity, focusing only on those features that make all of the members of a class to be of the same kind. In addition to "All X are Y," Peirce became increasingly interested in propositions such as "X gave Y to Z" and in the patterns of behavior that govern such relationships. (He called these logical "systems" as opposed to "classes.") Although the argument is too complex to develop it fully here,[24] I would like to suggest that the rigid adherence to a certain ideal of consensus can be dangerous for communities, for political communities to be sure, but also for communities of inquiry. Two interpreters may construe a symbol in very different ways—not necessarily in ways that directly conflict, but different nonetheless—thus contributing to a richer, deeper, more nuanced understanding of the object of their interpretation. (On the assumption that powerful religious symbols are likely to be multivalent, there should be nothing surprising about this kind of result.) In such a case, it is the diversity rather than the agreement of interpretations that one values. This type of semiotic complementarity is to be distinguished as a goal of inquiry from the convergence of opinion. Both seem crucial for building pragmatically successful communities of inquiry.

IV

I want now to offer a brief interlude before concluding this conversation by turning to the topic of Wildman's staunch resistance to all forms of anthropomorphism. I am impressed by the careful attention that Wildman pays to the concept of *attention* itself in providing his readers with a picture of how inquiry proceeds. "At the heart of the way problems emerge from the flow of experience," he reports, "resides the abstracting power of conscious attention."[25] Without the power that attention supplies, not only would problems never arise to confront us, but there could be no such thing as inquiry. Theories of inquiry or interpretation that properly recognize the significance of such a power are also careful to register "the biological rootedness of human life and consciousness"; here Wildman mentions both Heidegger and Peirce as exemplars (although interestingly it is Peirce who wrote "The Fixation of Belief").[26]

While Wildman observes that "cognitive scientists have isolated more than one kind of attention," it is this capacity for abstraction, "as attention slices through the flow of experience to conjure determinate objects and classes of objects," that he singles out as being of special significance for understanding human inquiry.[27] Our exercise of such a capacity, to be sure, is shaped by our "interests," which can be analyzed to some extent in biological terms. Yet despite all of the constraints imposed by nature, culture, history, language, social location, and so forth, it seems that we do have a certain limited capacity to abstract problems from the chaotic flow of experience, and then, as we go about trying to solve them, the ability to "manage" or "refine" the way in which we frame such problems. This, Wildman concludes, is what the "art of inquiry" consists in.[28]

Peirce described a way of paying attention that involves focusing on selected features of experience and ignoring others, a mode of abstraction that he called "precission."[29] This seems very close to the kind of abstractive attention that Wildman perceives as essential to inquiry; indeed, for Peirce precision is crucial for success in inductive reasoning. At the same time, to return to Peirce's Neglected Argument, he prescribed there a type of reasoning that is rooted in a different way of paying attention. Rather than a "slicing," a forceful narrowing of attention to this rather than that, what Peirce called musement is a playful state of being fully "awake," a readiness for whatever might appear either "within" or "about."[30] It precedes the singling out of some determinate object or problem for special attention, but is itself a form of attention nevertheless, this one crucial for success in abduction or hypothetical reasoning.

Now I am intrigued by how at one point in his discussion Wildman observes that "our embodied cognitive faculties play around within the flow of consciousness in highly distinctive ways—and with apparent spontaneity that suggests the playing around may have produced quite different outcomes."[31] Such cognitive play seems more akin to Peirce's musement than to the forceful slicing of attention through the flow of experience in order to focus on some object or problem. One of my questions for Wildman is to what extent he thinks the production of "different outcomes" is self-controlled. Is the "contingency of abstraction" something that we can account for at least in part by talking about a human freedom that displays itself in skillful cognitive play? (Peirce believed that success in musement could best be achieved only with continuous practice.)

I think that this discussion is related to other questions that I have about Wildman's additional assertion, here following John Dewey, that a "pragmatic theory of inquiry must be committed to the thesis that biology and inquiry precede logic experientially and not the other way around"; that is to say, "logic has biological roots."[32] Now there is a complicated story to be told about how Peirce understood the relationship between logic and psychology. Yet he was quite critical of Dewey's attempt to represent logic as the "natural history of thought" rather than as a normative science.[33] This does not mean for Peirce that when we do logic we cease to be embodied selves. But every person is also a living symbol for Peirce, a self continuously interpreting itself to future versions of itself, that is, those continuously coming into being in the flow of time. This space between present and future is the space within which freedom as self-control can be effectively exercised, primarily by shaping habit formation. It is also a metacognitive space (perhaps better thought of as metasemiotic) delineated and shaped to a significant degree by the way that we pay attention. Peirce sometimes described logic as the science of second intentions applied to first intentions.[34] Because we have some control over this sort of application, an ability to direct attention either poorly or well, logic is properly speaking a normative science and so it cannot simply be conflated with a natural history of thought. Even if it has biological roots, nevertheless, it must ultimately be judged by its fruits. (And the ability to solve problems effectively should be counted as just one among these potential fruits.)

The role that attention plays in shaping various kinds of logical inferences is an important topic, neglected by neither Peirce nor Wildman, and a good deal more could be said here by way of pursuing a comparison of their respective approaches to that topic. On my reading, there are additional differences, subtle but important, between the two. I do not think, for example, that it would be accurate to conflate Peirce's logic of abduction with Wildman's characterization of hypothetical reasoning as a strategy enabling "inference to the best explanation"; nor would Peirce likely be comfortable with characterizing abduction in any of its forms as "intuitive."[35]

At this point, however, my energy might be more productively invested in another type of comparison, one that juxtaposes Peirce's vigorous defense of anthropomorphism in both philosophy and science with Wildman's equally vigorous and sustained critique of it, most especially as it shapes certain perspectives in philosophical theology.

V

A full-blown treatment of Wildman's commitment to apophaticism in philosophical theology, along with his rejection of anthropomorphism in all of its forms, would take us far beyond the territory marked in advance for this discussion of his pragmatic theory of inquiry. Some treatment of these topics is justified by the fact that they are hardly irrelevant to such methodological considerations. Here I confine myself to the illustration of such relevance, refraining from a more general commentary on Wildman's critique of anthropomorphism.

At this point, it will not surprise my reader if I begin by turning once again to Charles Peirce for guidance.[36] On Peirce's view, the claim "that a conception is one natural to man" can readily be translated into the judgment "that it is anthropomorphic."[37] Indeed, "anthropomorphic is what pretty much all conceptions are at bottom." Moreover, to label an idea as anthropomorphic is "as high a recommendation as one could give to it in the eyes of an Exact Logician." As Peirce indicated in his correspondence with William James, while others might be inclined to categorize pragmatism as a form of "humanism" (and here he had the British pragmatist F. C. S. Schiller clearly in mind), he preferred the word "anthropomorphism," the latter being far more "expressive of the *scientific opinion*."[38] It is a philosophy thus conceived as anthropomorphic, in Peirce's estimation, that most fully qualifies as a "good sound solid strong pragmatism."

What is it, more precisely, about the "scientific opinion" that recommends such a label for pragmatism? Anyone who rejects this recommendation should be advised "to remember that every single truth of science is due to the affinity of the human soul to the soul of the universe, imperfect as that affinity no doubt is."[39] That such an "imperfect" affinity exists is a conjectured presupposition that Peirce embraced as the best way to account for the otherwise inexplicable success with which scientists have so rapidly and efficiently discovered truths about nature; while they err with regularity, their success is vastly disproportionate to the infinite number of candidate hypotheses available for the explanation of any given phenomenon. It is not a mysterious presupposition but rather one buttressed by an evolutionary theory explaining how our capacity for reasoning must have developed in continuous adaptation to the natural world in which human beings live and move and have their being. Human reasoning, especially in its initial phase as abductive or hypothetical inference, is rooted in instinct and shaped by practical concerns. Peirce's defense of anthropomorphism thus embodies a claim about the role that instinct plays in abduction, a claim presupposed by his philosophy of science and explicated in terms of his understanding of human evolution.[40]

So anthropomorphism is not opposed to philosophical naturalism on Peirce's view; it just *is* the form that his naturalism takes. What would cause us to think that a human mind would *not* be adapted to the purpose of understanding the natural world, that human reasoning is *not* productively guided by instinct? In the very same letter to William James in which he defended anthropomorphism as "strong pragmatism," Peirce also quickly observed how it implies theism, not belief in James's finite God, but the affirmation of a supreme "Ideal" conceived quite vaguely as "a living power." Echoing the declaration made two years earlier about our human "affinity" to the universe, Peirce now gives it an interesting theological twist: "Moreover, the human mind and the human heart have a filiation to God." Not only then is it natural and instinctive to believe in the reality of a personal God, but pressing the point even further, in a review published in 1903, Peirce warns that "if we cannot in some measure understand God's mind, all science . . . must be a delusion and a snare."[41]

Now for an alternative story about why human beings might have a natural tendency to believe in a personal deity, consider the version that Wildman prefers. Evolutionary psychologists have suggested that a hyperactive tendency to detect "unseen presences" in natural environments would have had great adaptive utility for some of our early hominid ancestors. The "skittish" behavior developed in conjunction with such a tendency may have been irrelevant in the vast majority of cases where such presences were imagined rather than real. But in the few cases where what was unseen posed a real threat, both the tendency and behavior could have resulted in survival for those ancestors. Here, then, is a simple evolutionary account that might explain the anthropomorphic propensity displayed by humans to believe in the existence of invisible agents who can affect their lives and destiny.

Note that this account is quite different from Peirce's hypothesis about human instinct, about the human mind being naturally attuned to the ideality of nature, mind to Mind. Indeed, the contrast between these explanations is quite pronounced. The tendency among members of our species to generate anthropomorphic hypotheses is reckoned on one explanation of it (Peirce's) as the sign of a highly fallible but nevertheless invaluable instinct for reasoning correctly. It is as valuable for human purposes as the instinct to build nests is for birds or to make honey for bees. From another perspective (Wildman's), this predisposition is a natural source of false inferences, its survival value for our ancient ancestors more than overshadowed now by its negative effect on human beliefs and practices. Yet I have frequently noted how in the Neglected Argument Peirce at least supplied the rubrics for an experimental test of his hypothesis about instinct—one involving the regular practice of musement—however difficult it might be in practice to conduct such a test or to evaluate its results. One might ask then what sort of experiment or evidence would be relevant to an assessment of the certainly plausible but nevertheless highly speculative proposal of the evolutionary psychologists whose views Wildman believes are so important for understanding religion. What might recommend or count against it? Why should one regard it as more "scientific" and so prefer it to Peirce's hypothesis? Understand that evidence marshalled in support of the presence of certain "cognitive defaults" in human beings is not what is needed here. Peirce observes the same kind of cognitive (and emotional) predisposition to anthropomorphize. So did Sigmund Freud for that matter, rooting such a tendency in infantile feelings of helplessness and the universal psychological machinery of wish-fulfillment.[42] This indicates that the presence of such a predisposition might be explained in very different ways, employing starkly contrasting intellectual resources and strategies.

Freud and the evolutionary psychologists focus on the "roots" of belief in a personal deity. Pragmatists like Peirce and James tend to emphasize the observable "fruits" of such belief, not as isolated facts, but as forming a pattern and so signifying something meaningful about the possible source and object of belief. Wildman is sympathetic to both approaches. On the one hand, he is quite interested in examining the potential biological and psychological roots of particular religious beliefs. On the other hand, he is a pragmatist who is interested in the practical fruitfulness of such beliefs, the problems that they may have arisen in response to, and the manner in which they enable their believers to adapt and flourish. And he fully admits that psychological arguments about evolutionary conditioning and cognitive biases (of the contemporary variety, not Peirce's!), although they cannot be ignored as serious challenges, do not automatically "defeat" theism.[43]

Despite the sharp contrasts, there are important continuities between how Peirce and Wildman approach this issue. Like Wildman (and perhaps unlike James, although Wildman's judgment of him may be a bit harsh), Peirce is a realist, committed to exposing all beliefs to the corrective shock of "secondness" (Wildman's "feedback"), a correction that only ongoing experience can provide. The results of an isolated act of musement, conducted by a single individual, would be meaningless for Peirce. That is why musement has to be a regular exercise, an experiment to be repeated frequently and by as many different individuals who will accept Peirce's invitation to do so.[44]

Despite their very different evaluations of anthropomorphism, interestingly enough, both Peirce and Wildman are emphatically apophatic in their philosophical theologies. Radiantly optimistic about what humans can come to know about the world through the disciplined application of a pragmatic theory and method of inquiry, nevertheless, at the end of the day both of them are theologians of mystery. When it comes to any sort of talk about the nature of God and divine attributes or purposes, Peirce is quick to insist that we only "catch a glimpse of" or "wildly gabble about" such matters. Wildman's apophaticism cuts against the grain of any anthropomorphism, the latter representing for him an attempt to domesticate the divine reality, to reduce an indeterminate ultimate reality to the level of a determinate being displaying agency, possessing consciousness, having goals and purposes, and so on. Peirce's apophaticism is fueled by the extraordinary seriousness with which he takes the logic of vagueness. Belief in God is true, indeed, indubitable for Peirce, only at the highest level of vagueness. God is only very vaguely personal, moreover not in any anthropocentric sense, because for Peirce human beings are not assumed to represent the paradigmatic case of what it means to be a "person." On the other hand, if one delineates with philosophical precision the various divine attributes, as Wildman does in characterizing different forms of theism, the problematic nature of such belief is readily exposed. While Peirce is very vague then, Wildman is quite explicit about what it means for people to believe in a personal God. Rejecting such a deity, Wildman is nevertheless committed to a (presumably fallible) belief in ultimate reality as the "Whence of nature."[45]

If so little can be known about God, then what is the pragmatic value of an exceedingly vague conception of such a reality? For Peirce, the meaning of a vague symbol will often be best embodied in the feeling responses to that symbol, as well as in the conduct that it inspires. Wildman admits that this is a strength of anthropomorphic theism, that it is well-equipped to elicit powerful feelings and to decisively shape human behavior. And so he actually has a position quite close to Peirce's here. Limits on the adequacy of our conceptions imposed by an apophatic philosophical theology are not simultaneously limits on what we can feel or do. And what we feel and do in response to whatever we conceive the ultimate reality to be, pragmatically speaking, is an interpretation of what that conception means. From a Peircean perspective at least, a cultivated habit of love, manifested both in patterns of feeling and of conduct, will constitute the most adequate interpretant of any sign representing the ultimate nature of reality as a vaguely personal and creative Love.[46] Wildman has written a good deal but is still developing his own account of how attending to a conception of ultimacy as the impersonal, indeterminate ground of all reality can be linked to certain spiritual experiences and practices.[47]

This points to another important contrast between Wildman's religious philosophy and a Peircean approach to religious questions. For Peirce, it is the "humble" nature of his argument for God's reality, its accessibility to anyone who agrees to engage in musement with the appropriate level of commitment and spirit of disinterestedness, that recommends it as plausible. Moreover, once entertained, the hypothetical idea of God's reality, vaguely conceived, will prove to be increasingly irresistible, not only because of its beauty, but because of its pragmatic utility, so that the muser will be disposed "to shape the whole conduct of life and all the springs of action into conformity with that hypothesis."[48] In a striking way that manifests more as elitist than as "humble," Wildman warns, for most people because of the "unattainably high levels of training and knowledge in ideas that are virtually impossible to understand" as a prerequisite for interpreting and then embracing the view of ultimacy that he endorses.[49] Indeed, such an idea must be rated "low" in terms of its ability to "captivate the hearts and minds of large numbers of ordinary people without specialized training."[50] Wildman seems to agree with Peirce that what we feel and do in response to some conception constitutes its pragmatic meaning. Nevertheless, that meaning is available only to a very few, and so it would appear that whatever form of religion might be linked to Wildman's religious philosophy, it is not one intended for "ordinary people."

There is an additional, perhaps too cryptic comment that I will make about the relevance of a logic of vagueness for any philosophical theology conceived as a pragmatic form of inquiry. Because he is quite philosophically precise about what it must mean to believe in God as personal, Wildman is convinced that the traditional form of such belief must ultimately be shipwrecked on the rocky shores of the problem of evil. His pragmatism is organized around the task of problem solving, and either a process theism (a less than ultimate God that does the best that God can) or the kind of ground of being theology that he embraces (an ultimate reality that has no agency, intentions, or purposes, the consideration of which would cause such a problem) can resolve the problem of evil in ways that classical theism must fail to do. Indeed, Wildman's very moving and personal "Afterword" to the second volume of his Religious Philosophy Series can be easily read as evidence that his rejection of anthropomorphism is deeply motivated by issues of theodicy.[51]

I want to conclude with a modest and here undeveloped proposal for developing a "theology without theodicy." There can be meaningful responses to the problem of evil that do not include "solving" it. On the one hand, Wildman does want to preserve the experience of evil as something profoundly dark, disturbing, and mysterious. On the other hand, he needs a religious worldview for which that experience will not represent a philosophical problem. Peirce's pragmaticism, combined with his logic of vagueness, supplies resources for a type of inquiry that neither turns away from such dark mysteries nor tries to explain them. While the philosophical tools here are Peircean, the darkness being explored is more akin to Ignatius's "desolation" or to John of the Cross's "dark night" than to anything that can be described in our metaphysics. Finally, it is not the problem of evil but the paradox of love (love for a God who is experienced both as real and as no-thing) that summons us to inquiry.

Notes

1. Wesley J. Wildman, *Religious Philosophy as Multidisciplinary Comparative Inquiry: Envisioning a Future for the Philosophy of Religion* (Albany: State University of New York Press, 2010).

2. Such was his preoccupation with the ethics of terminology that Peirce frequently engaged in the practice of inventing new words when he felt that all of the old ones that were available had multiple or confused meanings. "Pragmaticism" as distinguished from "pragmatism" is perhaps the most notable case in point.

3. Although I should also admit, and for some of the same reasons as Peirce's with regard to "pragmaticism," that I coined the word "theosemiotic" in 1989 to indicate my own distinctive understanding of the nature and purpose of a philosophical theology pursued using Peircean resources. This allows me to circumvent the problem of wrestling with all of the other ways that philosophical theologians have understood their task.

4. Wildman, *Religious Philosophy*, 29.

5. Ibid., xiv.

6. Ibid.

7. See John Dewey's *A Common Faith* (New Haven: Yale University Press, 1934).

8. Wesley J. Wildman, *In Our Own Image: Anthropomorphism, Apophaticism, and Ultimacy* (Oxford: Oxford University Press), 204.

9. Wildman, *Religious Philosophy*, xvi.

10. The reference here is to *In Our Own Image*.

11. Consult the first of James's Gifford Lectures, on "Religion and Neurology," in William James, *The Varieties of Religious Experience* (New York: Macmillan Publishing Co., 1973), 21–38.

Consider also the pragmatic critique of the cognitive science of religion that Scott Davis supplies in his book *Believing and Acting: The Pragmatic Turn in Comparative Religion and Ethics* (Oxford: Oxford University Press, 2012).

12. James's proposal for a "science of religions" appears in Lecture 18 ("Philosophy") and Lecture 20 ("Conclusions") of the *Varieties*. I offer an analysis of this proposal, in comparison with Peirce's thought, in my article on "From a 'Religion of Science' to the 'Science of Religions': Peirce and James Reconsidered," *American Journal of Theology and Philosophy* 27 (May/September 2006): 191–203.

13. Wildman, *Religious Philosophy*, 170.

14. From Peirce's perspective, "if philosophy glances now and then at the results of the special sciences, it is only as a sort of condiment to excite its own proper observation." CP 1.241. (All references to Peirce in this abbreviated fashion are to *The Collected Papers of Charles Sanders Peirce*, ed. Charles Hartshorne, Paul Weiss, and Arthur Burks (Cambridge, MA: Harvard University Press, 1935, 1958). CP 1.241 should be read as "volume 1, paragraph 241.")

15. Wildman, *Religious Philosophy*, 170.

16. Peirce, CP 5.212.

17. See my criticisms of Robert Brandom and Richard Rorty in "Instinct and Inquiry: A Reconsideration of Peirce's Mature Religious Naturalism," in *Pragmatism and Naturalism: Scientific and Social Inquiry after Representationalism*, ed. Matthew Bagger (New York: Columbia University Press, 2018), 27–43.

18. An early defense of this thesis is presented in Philip Wiener, *Evolution and the Founders of Pragmatism* (Cambridge: Harvard University Press, 1949). Consult also my discussion of the importance of Darwin and evolutionary theory for Peirce in the first chapter ("Scientific Theism") of *Peirce's Philosophy of Religion* (Bloomington: Indiana University Press, 1989).

19. For a fuller account of my reading, consider "Pragmaticism among the Pragmatists: A Brief History and Future Prospects," *Cognitio: Review of Philosophy* 16, no. 2 (2015): 321–34.

20. Peirce, CP 5.358–87 and CP 1.616–77.

21. Peirce, CP 6.452–93.
22. Wildman, *Religious Philosophy*, 170.
23. Peirce urged overlooking "temporary urgencies" in order to facilitate genuine inquiry. I am not as confident as he was about reaching the truth "in the long run."
24. I do develop the argument at some length in a book titled *Theosemiotic: Religion, Reading, and the Gift of Meaning* (under contract with Fordham University Press).
25. Wildman, *Religious Philosophy*, 89.
26. Ibid., 91.
27. Ibid., 89, 91.
28. Ibid., 92.
29. For Peirce on precission, see CP 1.549.
30. For Peirce's description of musement, consider CP 6.452–65.
31. Wildman, *Religious Philosophy*, 90.
32. Ibid., 178.
33. Peirce, CP 8.188–90.
34. See Peirce, CP 2.548, CP 3.490, and CP 4.38.
35. See Wildman, *Religious Philosophy*, 173.
36. The remarks that follow here are adapted from a much longer discussion appearing in the third chapter of my book in progress on *Theosemiotic: Religion, Reading, and the Gift of Meaning*.
37. Peirce, CP 5.47.
38. Peirce, CP 8.262.
39. Peirce, CP 8.262.
40. For a more detailed account, consult my essay on "Instinct and Inquiry."
41. Peirce, CP 8.168.
42. Freud's classic account of this tendency to anthropomorphize nature and natural forces appears in *The Future of an Illusion* (London: Hogarth Press, 1927).
43. Wildman, *Religious Philosophy*, 105.
44. I first proposed that musement should be regarded as a kind of experiment in *Peirce's Philosophy of Religion*, 134, 148, 169.
45. Wildman, *In Our Own Image*, 200. I can only assume that discerning the "Whence" of nature would have to involve something very much like what Peirce described as the practice musement, but I am not convinced that Wildman would agree.
46. This is the argument presented in *Theosemiotic*.
47. At least this is what I take to be the subject matter of a work in progress titled *The Future of Spirituality*.
48. Peirce, CP 6.467.
49. Wildman, *In Our Own Image*, 65.
50. Ibid., 217.
51. Ibid., 220–27.

7

Committing Theology in the Secular University

KEVIN SCHILBRACK

Introduction

The most significant aspect of Wesley Wildman's work, in my judgment, is that he argues that philosophers who study religion should move beyond their traditional but relatively narrow focus on theism to construct comparative evaluations of religious philosophies around the world. He describes this ambitious project this way: "When religious philosophy seeks to evaluate answers to the big questions of religion (for example, the meaning of life), it must assemble competing constructive theories pertinent to the big question and try to detect the superior candidate(s) through arguments about both the premises of competitor theories and criteria used to claim theoretical superiority."[1] This vision of a philosophical project that excludes no religious worldviews would include the questions about God that traditionally constituted philosophy of religion, but it also leads beyond them into largely uncharted comparative waters. As the world shrinks and evaluative cross-cultural conversations are increasingly needed, I would argue that this comparative project can and should find a natural academic home in philosophy of religion, which has long been developing the evaluative tools that the project needs. In fact, I would argue that Wildman's vision should be the future of the discipline.

The primary obstacle for Wildman's vision, however, is a serious one: it flies in the teeth of the way that many scholars today think that religion should be studied in secular universities. Some of these scholars (especially many working in phenomenology, anthropology, or history of religions) hold that religious studies has a primarily interpretive remit, and they understand this to entail that religious studies scholars should be empathetic or relativistic or nonreductive and therefore should not be in the business of judging and ranking worldviews. Other scholars (especially many working in sociology, psychology, and cognitive science of religion) hold that religious studies has a primarily explanatory remit, and they understand this to entail that religious studies scholars should be neutral or scientific or reductive and therefore should not be in the business of judging and ranking worldviews. Both camps agree—against Wildman—that the academic study of religion should not be a place where religious worldviews are judged and ranked. As opposed to making interpretative or explanatory claims, making evaluative claims about religions, they say, is a "theological" project that does not belong in the academy.

If one uses the term "theology" to refer to any kind of religious philosophy, theistic or not, that is, to any reason-giving about how people should think and live that refers to a superempirical reality, then it is not wrong to call Wildman's project a philosophical kind of theology.[2] But how can one make the case for including a theological project in the academic study of religions? A widespread view holds that including theology crosses the line between (as the *Schempp* decision influentially put it) teaching about religion and teaching religion.[3] Making normative religious claims may belong in religious schools, but under what conditions could this kind of work belong in a secular university?

Some have argued that theology should be excluded from religious studies because the academy should be resolutely scientific, but I judge that that kind of scientism is no longer persuasive.[4] Normative claims cannot simply be excluded from academia, because taking an evaluative stance is something that scholars cannot avoid, no matter how empathetic and focused solely on interpretation they are, or no matter how neutral and focused solely on explanation they are.[5] In terms of commitments to particular values, every scholar stands somewhere. But this argument that normativity is inevitable in scholarship does not settle the issue, because the next question is crucial: *which* values are appropriate for the particular situation of the academy? Put more sharply, even if the scholarship of everyone who studies religion is informed by *some* norm, what distinction can scholars make between academically appropriate and academically inappropriate norms? Can one distinguish between teaching religion and teaching about religion? These are foundational but still unsettled questions for the academic study of religion. Moreover, as scholars come to terms with the imperialist and colonialist genealogy of the study of religions, to examine the norms by which one makes cross-cultural evaluations like those that Wildman is seeking is particularly urgent. Wildman recognizes this: "The case needs to be made within the university for the inclusion of religious philosophy so understood."[6] The aim of this chapter is to make that case.

The case I make addresses two foundational issues. The first concerns the specific tasks that belong in the secular university, that is, the questions that scholars of religion should be asking. The second concerns criteria that scholars should meet when they answer them.

Three Models of Theology in the Secular Academy

One problem with many of the debates regarding whether theology belongs in the academic study of religion is that people use the term "theology" to name very different kinds of thinking and writing. It is crucial for those in this debate to be more specific about the intellectual tasks that are or are not appropriate for a secular as opposed to a religious institution. Toward that end, I distinguish between three models of what it is that a theologian might do in the secular academy: just the first task, just the first and second, or all three.

On the first model, letting theology into the academy means only that one include the task of *describing* theological claims. Here, scholars focus on the normative religious claims of some community—what Ninian Smart called the doctrinal or philosophical dimension of a religion[7]—and those who seek to describe religious philosophies accurately share with all the other scholars in the academic study of religion the hermeneutic goal of interpreting, grasping, or understanding the object of study. A solely descriptive project then traces out the normative religious claims of some community systemically, sees how they hang together, and perhaps sorts them into types. If a scholar does this work across cultures, one could call it a form of comparative theology.[8] But academic theologians who limit themselves to this descriptive model would not also make judgements about those claims as true or false, rank them as superior to other theologies, or recommend them as good for people to follow. Those who bring theology into the secular academy in this sense simply describe the normative religious claims of others but do not make normative religious claims themselves.

They treat religious philosophy as an object of study but do not engage in it as subjects. This solely descriptive approach is implied in the quote from Spinoza, which some use as a slogan for the study of religion: "I have taken great care not to deride, bewail, or execrate human actions, but to understand them."[9] Achieving this nonjudgmental stance requires one, for the sake of academic inquiry, to set aside or restrain one's own judgements of what is real, true, just, and good, and this process of "bracketing" one's normative views has been taken as the methodological sine qua non for many scholars in the study of religions.

For most scholars, simply describing a religious philosophy does not necessarily count as "doing theology." Theology here is an object of study, and one can certainly give accurate and empathetic descriptions of theological claims with which one disagrees. In fact, including theology in this descriptive sense is necessary if a scholar then wants to go on to give a reductive explanation of why different communities deploy the religious philosophies they do. But (as I argue in the next section) one cannot describe or explain a religious philosophy with understanding unless one uses some evaluative norms, and, when those norms are religious, one's descriptions and explanations will be at least implicitly theological.

On a second and more robust model for theology in the secular academy, a scholar would not only describe religious claims but also *evaluate* them. A scholar who evaluates the claims of some religious community is required, as before, to understand, grasp, or interpret them accurately, but the task now includes what we might call a second stage that takes what has been understood and critiques or assesses it.[10] Previously, care was taken to represent the religions without judgment, but the inquiry here is now explicitly normative: Are the religious practices in question virtuous? Are the religious social structures oppressive? Are the religious experiences veridical? Are the religious claims plausible, coherent, warranted, or true? Comparative scholarship in this evaluative mode could assess whether the teachings of some religious community are more or less in conflict with the natural sciences than those of another, or whether the institutions of one religious community are more or less patriarchal than those of another.[11]

Those scholars who evaluate theologies necessarily share with those who merely describe them the goal of grasping religious claims according to the self-understanding of those they study, but they differ in that their task can be called "critical"—it also weighs those claims in ways that can contradict the reasoning given by the religious community in question.[12] The academic study of theology that is critical in this sense assesses the reasons given in some particular religious community in the light of one's own account of, for example, justice, the nature of ultimate reality, or what constitutes human flourishing. If making evaluative claims about religious philosophies is theological, then these scholars are to that extent theologians. Nevertheless, like those who stop with the task of description, evaluative scholars study the theologies of actual religious communities and do not develop their own. That is, this kind of scholar produces normative religious claims about theologies, but they do not then go on to propose their own teachings as rival to the theologies found in the religions of the world. On this model, the study of theology is evaluative but not constructive.[13]

On a third and even more robust model, one not only describes and evaluates the theological claims of others but also *constructs* one's own. Here, the academic study of religious philosophies would include not only describing or evaluating them in, so to speak, the third person, but also speaking and writing them constructively in the first person. It would include the development of a religious philosophical position, the best account one can articulate of superempirical realities and what they mean for how people live.

I use this concept of "superempirical realities" to refer to alleged realities that are not empirical and whose existence is not the product of anything empirical. It is meant to include both realities that are said to be like a person (e.g., Allah in Islam, Devi in Hinduism, Òrìṣà in the Yoruba tradition) and those that that are not (e.g., the Stoic Logos, the Neo-Confucian Supreme Principle, the Dao), but to exclude realities that are the product of human activity (e.g., one's nation or wealth).[14] This concept provides a way to distinguish between constructive philosophies that ground their recommendations on such realities and are therefore on this definition religious, and constructive philosophies that do not and are therefore on this definition nonreligious. Whether it is theistic or not, a constructive religious philosophy written by a scholar in the secular academy would be shaped, as all thinking is, by one's own particular location. Moreover, given the diversity of religious philosophies already being practiced, any constructive religious philosophy developed in the secular academy will disagree with others. In fact, it is likely that religious philosophers' constructive proposals will grow from the critiques of theologies that they made when they were wearing their evaluative hat. Nevertheless, advocates for this model can argue that when constructive religious philosophers work according to the criteria used by constructive philosophers in general, their discipline is just as appropriate for the academy. Paula Cooey, for example, makes this argument, pointing out the double standard: "No one is suggesting that philosophical construction, for example, John Rawls's work on justice or Martha Nussbaum's work on pleasure, be discounted as scholarship, or excluded as course material from the classroom."[15] The argument is that there is no way to exclude constructive religious philosophical thinking from the academy without simultaneously excluding a great deal of constructive thinking about ethics, metaphysics, political theory, feminist critique, and postcolonial thought.[16]

Which Theological Tasks Belong in the Secular University?

I have distinguished three different tasks with which a scholars might engage theology. I now want to argue that the secular university should include all three.

The answer to the question of whether theology *in the descriptive sense* belongs in simple: if a religious community has developed a theology, then to do justice to the object of study, the academic study of religion has to include it. A complete account of a religion will include not only its narrative, ritual, social, and legal dimensions but also any theologies it has developed. Including theology in this descriptive sense ensures that one sees the religious communities that develop doctrines and philosophies not simply as credulous storytellers or as practitioners swept up in collective effervescence, but also as reflective people interested in the coherence and credibility of their commitments.

A theology or a religious philosophy is a form of second-order reflection in that it takes an existing set of religious beliefs, practices, experiences, and institutions as its object and seeks to present them so that they hang together in a way that is coherent and plausible. The members of a religious community who engage in these reflective practices are typically motivated to do so not simply because they enjoy self-examination but rather because their form of life faces some internal or external challenge. They take up theological reflection and reason-giving when they find themselves struggling with conflicting interpretations or rival forms of life. In some situations, the religious community creates a division of labor and designates certain individuals to do this intellectual work, but one can also find reflection and reason-giving in everyday religious practices, including prayers, protest marches, architecture, how parents raise their children, how people treat their money, and when they go to war. The theology practiced by the members of a community designated by authorities to do so and practiced by all the members insofar as they are reflective people are not different in kind.¹⁷ Even if reflective intellectual work is easier to recognize when it is in a text, therefore, theological responses can also be found in the discourses and practices of those who are not intellectuals, and a complete descriptive account of such a religion will not fail to include them.

Underlining this fact is important because there continues to be a bias among many scholars of religion that religion is an aspect of human culture that *by definition* does not give reasons. One influential set of scholars treats a religion as essentially an experience of something mysterious, ultimate, or sacred. On this account, religious texts seek to express this experience and religious practices seek to lead people to have it, but it is difficult if not impossible to put the object of that experience into words, let alone give discursive reasons why one should act in accord with it. If this experientialist account of religion is right, then the only way to evaluate a religious community's claims is by seeing the world as its members do. On this account, those who seek reflective arguments for a religious worldview are misguided. Another influential set of scholars treats a religion as simply an ideology imposed on people for which questions are not permitted. On this account, religious texts assert the eternal validity of the group's teachings, and religious practices inculcate proper behavior, but religious communities do not make claims that are open to debate. If this ideological account of religion is right, then the study of religion should focus on how social groups use religion to create authorities and to control people. Again, those who seek reflective arguments for the religious worldview are misguided.

To be sure, some theological texts (including some classics of religious philosophy) do hold that the evidence for the religious worldview is found in an experience that cannot be put into words or that human reason is not to be trusted and so one should defer to the proper authority. In other theological texts, however, one finds attempts to show the coherence of the teachings and practices of the community, to rule out implications that are problematic, to develop them in new ways that avoid error, to offer self-correction, to show the faulty logic or evidence for rival views, and so on. The details of how and when and why religious communities reflect on their form of life are various and fascinating.¹⁸ When one speaks of the category of "religious practices," therefore, it is important to keep in mind that it includes not only rituals, but sometimes also the reflective theological practices of debate, commentary writing, system construction, and apologetics. Of course, one should not make the mistake of saying that what a religion teaches is found most authentically in the texts of the group's intellectuals, as opposed to the worship services, feast days, dances, or ascetic disciplines of those members of the community who are not intellectuals. This is a hard habit to break for academics who are themselves most comfortable learning from books. But even as scholars of religion develop an account of religion that is more than just belief, they should not make the opposite error and fail to include reflective intellectual texts and practices.

In sum, then, the academic study of religions has to include theology in at least the descriptive sense. The tasks of evaluating someone else's theology or constructing one's own are much more controversial.

I have been distinguishing between the tasks of describing, evaluating, and constructing theologies, and it is useful and legitimate to do so, because one might describe a theological claim without deciding whether one thinks that the claim is right or wrong, and one might evaluate a theological claim as right or wrong without deciding what would be better. But even though it can be useful to *distinguish* between descriptive, evaluative, and constructive approaches in this way, it does not follow that these approaches can be *separated* in the sense that one could produce descriptions that that are free of evaluative norms, not produce evaluations of what is wrong with some claim without any sense of what would be better. In the academic study of religions, this distinguishability but inseparability deserves more attention.

One cannot produce descriptions that are free of evaluative norms. A person can repeat words mechanically without understanding them, for instance, if one mimics words in a language one does not know. One might therefore wonder whether a scholar could work with a translation manual, replace the words from a theological text with equivalent words from the manual, and come up with a description of what the text says. In this way, like the person in John Searle's Chinese Room thought experiment,[19] a scholar could describe a theology without understanding it and therefore without any sense of how it might be evaluated. Analogously, one might assume that a scholar who describes a religious practice could observe the practice and then transcribe what he saw in theory-free "observation sentences" that were not encumbered by any grasp of the self-understanding of the participants. With such examples, empiricists and positivists not content with merely distinguishing the task of describing facts from that of assessing values have sought to separate them completely. But for half a century now, post-positivist philosophers of science have argued that even simple acts of observation are conditioned by the perceiver's theory-laden, interest-laden, value-laden judgments. Historians, anthropologists, and other scholars interpreting religious texts and practices do not simply observe and repeat facts mechanically. What they describe depends on what they understand, and understanding texts and practices includes understanding norms with which one could evaluate them or construct alternatives.

Here is a nonreligious example of what it means to say that a description includes evaluative norms. Imagine that someone understands that *Malik was angry that he was not invited to the party*. To grasp this description of a person, one must understand not only what it means to throw a party and send out invitations, but also that anger is an emotion that requires a responsible agent as its object.[20] It follows that even if one does not make a judgement whether Malik should be angry in this instance, even if one has never consciously reflected on the norms with which one might answer this question, and even if one could not put those norms into words if one tried, nevertheless one has to understand that Malik would not be justifiably angry, for example, if it turns out that the invitation was sent but lost. If one understands the descriptive claim about Malik's anger, then one must already have norms with which one could make a judgment about it. In this way, there are evaluative norms integral to meaningful human discourse and behavior, and it is not possible to describe that discourse and behavior in a way that lacks them.

The same situation obtains with regard to describing theology. Simply understanding a theological claim already carries with it norms by which the claim could be evaluated. As with the claim about the party invitations, someone who describes some theological claim about justice, the nature of ultimate reality, or what constitutes human flourishing might not have formulated a position on whether the claim is true. She might be personally or professionally uninterested in taking an explicit position on this. Thus, my argument is not that a scholar who simply describes a theology "implicitly" takes a normative position or that all scholarship on religion is "really" theological. I hold that describing and evaluating cannot be separated, but I continue to distinguish and do not collapse them. Nevertheless, to the extent that one comes to understand a claim about some allegedly superempirical reality, one also comes to understand what it would mean to hold it incorrectly. There will be norms integral to making sense of the theological claim, norms that would let one engage in theological evaluation and construction if one so chose. Consider examples like the Advaita Vedānta claim that *Brahman and Atman are not-two*, the Mu'tazilite claim that *God's attributes are not distinct from God's essence*, and the Madhyamika claim that *dependent origination is interminable*. My argument is that understanding such claims entails knowing both how and how not to use them. Unlike everyday empirical claims like *the apples are on the table*, whose uses are widely shared, the use of superempirical claims like these is relatively limited, socially speaking, and almost certainly requires training in the discursive norms of that community, and therefore even describing these claims with understanding is not easy. However, if a person does not simply mechanically repeat the words that *Brahman and Atman are not-two* but describes this religious philosophy with understanding, then not only must they understand that "Brahman" refers to the ultimate reality and that "Atman" refers to the individual's true self, but they must also be able to recognize rival ways of talking about these two alleged realities that would be dualistic and that would be contradicted by the claim. A scholar's understanding is enabled by her grasp of how one would draw out the implications of the claim, apply it in different situations, and consider it plausible. To the extent that one is not able to disentangle legitimate uses of the claim from those that imply dualism, one has not yet understood what one is saying. In short, if a description of a piece of human discourse or behavior aims at *making sense* of it, then the description cannot be independent of the scholar's assumptions of what is rational, real, good, or true.[21] The same holds when one explains a religious philosophy: evaluative norms are always already operating. Furthermore, insofar as considers a claim irrational, harmful, oppressive, or false because it says X rather than Y, then by imagining this Y, one's evaluation is not independent of one's constructive views. For personal or professional reasons, scholars who describe religious philosophies might not care to make explicit the evaluative-constructive norms that undergird their work. But it does not follow that those norms are not present.

If this argument that describing and explaining religious philosophies always operate according to normative assumptions is persuasive, then the debate about theology in the academic study of religion should undergo a shift. The debate should not be whether evaluative and constructive norms should be permitted in the secular university, because descriptive and explanatory scholarship already includes them. It also cannot be whether evaluative and constructive thinking should only be the *object* of descriptive or explanatory projects, because those norms are already in the subject position. Instead, the debate about whether theology belongs in the secular university has to take into account the fact that normative assumptions are already operating in academia implicitly and uncritically, and reflect on them critically. It should ask: what assumptions about what is rational, real, good, or true are made in a given account of religion? On what grounds should one accept or reject these norms? What norms are best for the study of religion? To argue that these are legitimate questions for the academic study of religion does not imply that this field should not take methodological naturalism as a ground rule. But it does imply that evaluative and constructive thinking cannot be excluded from the secular university.

The Criteria for Theology in the Secular Academy

The argument of the previous section is that (1) because every task in the study of religion involves making sense of the phenomena, scholarship on religions always includes the scholar's own evaluative-constructive norms about what is real, true, just, and good; and (2) scholars in the secular university should seek the best evaluative-constructive norms. The academic study of religion is a multidisciplinary field, and not every scholar in this field will take as their task critical reflection on questions about reality, truth, justice, and value—but some should. For most of human history and in most cultures, these norms have been grounded in an allegedly superempirical reality, that is, in a being or structure whose existence is said not to depend on human efforts, and this claim too should be an object of critical reflection in the secular university. In short, then, the academic study of religion should permit all three tasks described above: the description, evaluation, or construction of religious philosophies.

More controversial than the questions that scholars ask, however, is the way that we answer them. I therefore want to shift from the discussion of the tasks pursued in the academic study of religious philosophies to the criteria we accept. Here, the central issue is not whether religious studies scholars engage in describing, evaluating, or constructing norm-laden views; I think that those three kinds of intellectual engagements take place throughout religious studies and throughout the secular university. The central issue, rather, is whether a scholar's descriptive, evaluative, or constructive claims are open to confirmation or disconfirmation from those who do not already accept the epistemic authorities of the religious community in question. What criteria must scholars of religion meet?

One straightforward way to approach this question sorts the answers into three camps. On my definition, a theology or a religious philosophy makes claims predicated on superempirical realities. The first camp is composed of those "secularists" who would exclude theology from the academic study of religion because, they say, claims about such realities by definition cannot be confirmed or disconfirmed by any sharable reasoning or evidence. Theology therefore fails to meet the criteria of inquiry accepted by every other discipline in the secular university and does not belong. There would be a confusion of goals involved in the very idea of an "academic theology." In the second camp are those "inclusivists" who claim that theological claims often do not meet shared criteria, but that in some cases they *could*. When theological claims can only be justified in terms of epistemic authorities of the religious community in question, those theologies are confessional and do not belong in the academy. But when they are open to support or challenge from other perspectives, then they do belong. On this view, an "academic theology" is possible. The third camp is composed of those "sectarians" who hold that, given the distinctive task of theology and the secular commitments of the secular university, theology is enfeebled by the attempt to operate according to secular criteria and should instead only be practiced in specifically Christian academic environments. Theologians should respect the particularity of its vocation and should not seek to meet criteria that are not their own.[22]

These three camps disagree with each other on whether theological claims can meet the criteria of inquiry in the secular university and on whether they should. All three agree with each other, however, that the secular university requires scholars to make their claims vulnerable to some sharable reasoning or evidence. But is this requirement sensible? Some Christian theologians have recently argued that even when theological claims operate according to their own criteria, criteria not shared by any who are not traditional Christians, such a theology is nevertheless an appropriate discipline for the secular university. Paul Macdonald champions this position, which he calls, blending the second and third camps above, "inclusive sectarianism."[23]

The key argument of inclusive sectarianism is that hopes for and pretentions to universally accepted criteria for what counts as reasoning or evidence are no longer plausible. There are only particular or tradition-specific criteria, and so, properly speaking, every discipline operating in the secular university is sectarian. It follows that scholars who operate according to the particular sources and norms of their own religious community cannot be justifiably excluded. Macdonald offers a Christian version of this argument. His starting point is sectarian: "Christian theology is based in and centered upon what Christians profess but cannot prove is God's self-revelation. . . . The Christian theologian's principles are accepted on divine authority."[24] However, there is no "objective cognitive vantage point from which it is possible to survey the true and real 'as they are,' independent of how they may appear from within any given perspective." The concepts of "reasonableness" and "evidence" do not translate without remainder or distinction across all the disciplines that the university houses. For this reason, those who practice disciplined inquiry in the academy "should not be asked to make arguments the conclusions of which everyone accepts or whose premises are derived from authorities that everyone accepts." Macdonald therefore contrasts the "academic theology" that the inclusivists seek with what he calls "traditional theology." Traditional theology concerns truths "that lie outside the realm of human knowing" but it should not have to "de-dogmatize its reasoning or discourse about the divine."

According to this inclusivist sectarianism, the secular university should adopt an epistemological pluralism that recognizes multiple epistemic authorities. Scholars in the academic study of religions would be allowed to evaluate the theological claims of others and to construct religious positions of their own, according to the lights of the authorities they recognize, and such work should not be excluded from the academy if they refuse to argue for their position according to some putatively disinterested criterion. As Macdonald puts it, "I think that the secular university is *already* or at least *should be* sectarian, in the following sense: *all* intellectual inquiry in the secular university proceeds from somewhere, rather than nowhere in particular—that is, some external vantage point furnished by the 'secular perspective.'"[25] As Kathryn Tanner puts it, "The primary justification for inclusion [of a form of inquiry in the university] is the ability to produce an interestingly different angle on life . . . an interestingly different contribution to the mix."[26] On her model, the university is the site of a cultural contest that does not require participants to operate according to a single norm but only to have something distinctive to say about the world and one's place in it. For both Macdonald and Tanner, the secular university can and should recognize the importance of letting confessionalist theologians stay true to their own distinctive values and interests.

I think that the question of whether there are universal criteria of rationality that would apply to every discursive community is, even in our present postmodern context, still a live issue. As we see in the discussion of theology, this epistemological question also represents an important challenge for the secular university. But we do not have to settle this question to make progress on the issue of what is required of a discipline included in the secular university.

Some in this debate have assumed that there are universal criteria of rationality that should govern all thinking. They hold that logical principles are inevitable or that the natural sciences represent the paradigm of rational inquiry or that there are transcendental features of any communicative act. Let's call this the "universal criteria" position. The notion that there is a single set of criteria that should govern all intellectual traditions is the view that the inclusivist sectarians reject. They argue that, as one moves from one intellectual tradition to another, what counts as reason and evidence varies. Let's call their view the "plural criteria" position. A problem with this argument, however, is that one can reject the plural criteria position without arguing for (let alone proving) the universal criteria position. That is, though many in this debate may have assumed the universal criteria position, the exclusion of confessionalist theology does not require it. A third possible position in this debate is the pragmatist one that because the secular university is a place of collective inquiry and debate, no discipline in the university should insulate itself so that it answers only to its own criteria. Call this the "no silos" position. Those who hold the "no silos" position may or may not hold that there are universal criteria of rationality, but they do not assume any tradition-neutral vantage point. The "no silos" requirement is not that a discipline belongs in the secular university only when *everyone* must accept its premises or its conclusions, but rather that it belongs only when its premises or conclusions can be debated with at least *some* others. The "no silos" position provides a vision of the secular university where sociological claims about groups might be undermined by individualist psychology and where chemical claims about molecular properties might be supported by theories in physics. But this vision would not include disciplines that made claims about, say, moral actions that could not be confirmed by ethics or claims about the origin of species that could not be disconfirmed by biology. The "no silos" position asks forms of inquiry that seek to be a part of the secular university to make themselves vulnerable to debate with others.

To accept the "no silos" position, scholars in the secular university would have to separate two questions. The first question asks whether the claims one makes are faithful to or authorized by the tradition one seeks to represent. The second asks whether those claims are true. There is a tendency for intellectual traditions, both religious and not, to collapse these two and to treat their epistemic authorities as synonymous with truth. They then hold that when one's claims are faithful to those authorities, those claims are true (or, at least, that members of the tradition must take them as true). To collapse these two questions is to claim that the epistemic authorities in one's tradition have a perfect or unsurpassable access to truth, an access that cannot be challenged from any other perspective. To separate them is to recognize that one's epistemic authorities, no matter how illustrious, are fallible. The most sustained argument I know that Christian theology must not confuse these two questions is that of Schubert Ogden.[27] In Ogden's terms, theologians have to separate the criteria that they use to judge the "appropriateness" of their religious philosophy from the criteria that they use to judge its "credibility." That is, the judgment one makes whether one's claims are Christian does not answer the question of whether they are true. For Ogden, the criterion that determines whether what one says is Christian is whether it is appropriate to or fits with the earliest apostolic witness found in the New Testament. The question of whether what one says is credible has to meet a completely different criterion, namely, whether what one says can be validated in the light of common human experience.[28]

Wesley Wildman also holds that theologians must separate these two questions, which he calls the questions of "fidelity" and "plausibility." Fidelity concerns whether one's project belongs in the tradition to which one claims membership. Plausibility is "judged by what passes for consensus in as wide an interdisciplinary, crosscultural domain of intellectual debate as possible."[29] Separating these questions enables Wildman to distinguish between an "absolutist" and a "modest" theology. An absolutist theology collapses these two criteria, and so it does not accept what Wildman calls "a secular morality of inquiry" and would not belong in the secular university, whereas a "modest" theology holds that "nothing is finally so sacred that it may not, ought not, be questioned."[30] For a secular morality of inquiry, "inquiry is unbridled by religious or other ideological institutional interests, it does not indulge special pleading or favoritism, it is fully responsive to the insights of whatever disciplines have a claim in the subject matter, and it honestly and assiduously seeks out sources of correction wherever they may be found."[31] An academic theology that operates by this morality would have these six virtues: "(1a) it does not conform to the authority structures of religious communities; (1b) it does not operate within the ambit of assumptions about putatively supernaturally authorized revelatory information that pervade confessional forms of theology; (1c) it does not serve the institutional or intellectual interests of any particular religious groups; yet (2a) it functions in full awareness of these and other features of religious traditions; (2b) it incorporates every kind of naturally-derived human knowledge as it bears on religious subject matters; and (2c) it strives for consistency with the less theoretically aggressive styles of philosophy of religion (especially the phenomenological, comparative, historical, and analytic styles)."[32]

One way to see the implications of the approach defended here is to contrast the proposal that the academic study of religion must be *secular* with a proposal that it must be *nonreligious*. Sam Gill, for example, distinguishes between the academic study of religion and the religious study of religion. He defines a religious study of religion as a study of religion "primarily for the purpose or purposes stipulated by the religion studied . . . for example, to find God, to transcend desire, or any other reason that religious practitioners have for their religious practices . . . rather than the purpose or purposes stipulated by the academy."[33] On Gill's account, the purposes of the scholar and those of the religious person do not overlap, and, to be academic, the study of religion has to have nonreligious purposes. Of course, some scholars study religions to know themselves better, to cultivate tolerance of difference, to understand the nature of things, or to find peace. If these are religious purposes, then they presumably would be inappropriate goals in the academy. On Wildman's account, by contrast, as long as scholars separate the question of fidelity to a religious tradition from the question of plausibility to the wider public—that is, as long as they operate according to a secular morality of inquiry—these purposes would not be academically inappropriate.[34]

I have argued that the academic study of religion should include not only the description but also the evaluation and construction of religious philosophies. The "no silos" position requires scholars to separate the question of whether their evaluation of a given religious philosophy or their construction of their own is faithful to the epistemic authority of some particular religious community from the question of whether their views are plausible to as wide an interdisciplinary, crosscultural domain of intellectual debate as possible. When scholars do separate these two questions, thereby making their views vulnerable to support or critique from other perspectives, then an evaluative and constructive religious philosophy would belong in the secular university just as evaluative and constructive nonreligious philosophy does. Nevertheless, the evaluation of another's religious philosophy is a difficult and politically charged issue. Some scholars will want to avoid using criteria of plausibility that are not accepted by those they evaluate, and they can do so by developing an "immanent criticism" that the religious community in question fails to satisfy its own standards.[35] Other scholars want to use criteria that are shared with those they evaluate because the criteria are commonsense, logical, or transcendental. Others, however, justify their judgments using criteria not shared with those they evaluate by arguing that, for example, given a commitment to racial equality, racist religious teachings are unjust or that, given natural selection as an explanation for the origin of species, religious teachings that contradict this explanation are false. Such evaluations could be done in a mode that is, so to speak, hypothetical: evaluative scholars might argue that if one takes a preferential option for the poor, or if one accepts Mengzi's account of the cultivation of virtue, or if one agrees with Tillich's account of broken symbols, then religious teachings that conflict with these commitments are to that extent wrong. Insofar as the judgments are offered in this hypothetical way, the critical evaluations open the door for debate about the criteria themselves.[36]

An Example of Comparative Religious Philosophy

This chapter's argument that evaluative and constructive theological scholarship belongs in the secular university when it operates according to a secular morality of inquiry may seem abstract or "meta." It may therefore be valuable in closing to illustrate what Wildman's comparative philosophical theology or religious philosophy looks like in practice.

Philosophers of religion have traditionally focused on theism, often developing models of God's nature and arguments about God's existence and then evaluating whether certain models or arguments are more persuasive than others. For example, Anselm argues that God is such that God cannot be conceived not to exist, and Gaunilo responds that this ontological argument leads to absurdities. Or Paley argues that functional complexity in the natural world points to a supernatural hand, and Hume seeks to undermine that case. But what would it look like to make evaluations across religious traditions and to weigh the relative plausibility of entire systems of thought?

One way to approach a global philosophy of religion might be to set up a contest between a Christian philosophy, a Buddhist philosophy, a Hindu philosophy, and so on. Wildman, however, sets up the contest so that it is not between but rather across traditions. The key step is that Wildman defines "ultimate reality" as that on which every being depends ontologically and which depends ontologically only on itself, but he leaves open the question of whether the ultimate ontological conditions of everything that exists is a person-like God.[37] Given this distinction, one can recognize three kinds of religious models of ultimate reality, each of which is found in multiple religious traditions: (1) "agential-being models" that identify ultimate reality with God, (2) "subordinate-deity models" that include both ultimate reality and God but do not identify them, and (3) "ground-of-being models" that offer some account of ultimate reality but not one of God.

One finds agential-being models of ultimate reality in the Christian Augustine and Aquinas, the Muslim Ibn Sīnā, the Jewish Maimonides, the Hindu Udayana, and in a variety of forms in monotheisms around the world. As I noted above, agential-being models have received the preponderant attention from philosophers of religion to date. One finds subordinate-deity models that propose a person-like God who is not metaphysically ultimate in ancient Manichaeism and Zoroastrianism, in Chinese concepts of Tiān and Shàngdì, in the demiurge of Plato's *Timaeus*, in Philo, and in process theology. Ground-of-being models that propose ultimate conditions of reality without a person-like God are found in Chinese accounts of the Dao, Buddhist accounts of *pratītya samutpāda*, Upanishad-based accounts of *nirguṇa Brahman*, accounts of *natura naturans* in Spinoza and contemporary religious naturalists, accounts of Being Itself in Aristotle, the neo-Platonist Plotinus, and Paul Tillich, and in the God beyond God proposed by perennial philosophy. As Wildman puts it, each of these three models "boasts a long heritage, impressive explanatory power, significant cross-cultural visibility, and considerable internal diversity."[38] Each is not simply a logically possible model of ultimate reality, but also a time-tested and widely appealing "Great Model." These then are the three positions that Wildman puts into a comparative competition.

As noted above, Wildman holds that a secular morality of inquiry is one that is open to support or critique from whatever disciplines have a claim in the subject matter. Wildman's comparative project exemplifies those desiderata when he puts the evaluation of these three models in the context of recent work in the scientific study of religions and, in particular, in the context of cognitive scientific theories regarding anthropomorphism. He argues that in every culture in human history, we can find practices based on the belief in invisible, intentional beings, though typically the practitioners have not also needed or cared to develop something as abstract as a model of ultimate reality. There is therefore in fact a fourth religious position, namely, the position that involves interaction with supernatural agents but does not offer any answer to the question of that on which every being depends ontologically. This anthropomorphic position is so natural to human beings that Wildman calls it our "evolutionary default." Wildman attends to three dimensions of these anthropomorphic concepts: they explain events in terms of the benevolent or malevolent purposes of invisible agents ("Intentionality Attribution"), they aid in solving immediate problems ("Rational Practicality"), and they inspire memorable and appealing narratives with tangible personal implications ("Narrative Comprehensibility"). Despite these uses, however, anthropomorphism is fragile, because as one comes to see that people invent and make religious use of supernatural agents, the plausibility of the evolutionary default position is undermined. Exactly this, Wildman writes, is the central result of the last century of scientific study of religion: "evolutionary models show this, cognitive neuroscience shows this, experimental psychology shows this, and developmental psychology shows this; the evidence grows increasingly strong with each passing year."[39] Wildman argues that it is precisely as a response to the weaknesses of the default position that the three Great Models were developed: some asked the question of ultimate reality and moved away from Rational Practicality; some abandoned supernaturalism and moved away from Intentionality Attribution; and in all cases the attempts at increased plausibility moved away from the simple story promised by Narrative Comprehensibility. In these ways, the three Great Models are actually the results of a flight from anthropomorphism and, in their different ways, toward apophaticism.

Wildman uses multiple criteria to sort the strengths and weaknesses of each model. His aim is not to produce a knock-down proof that only one model is credible but rather a comparison of their plausibility relative to each other. Each Great Model has advantages over the others, though each also suffers from disadvantages. As Wildman scores the competition, ground-of-being models—that is, the least anthropomorphic and the most apophatic of the three—score the highest, though, remarkably, the scores of each model are not far apart. (Somewhat tongue in cheek, Wildman says that ground-of-being models score a 53, agential-being models a 44, and subordinate-deity models a 40). So that others can see the competition and perhaps weight the criteria differently, Wildman shows all his work.

Though this comparative project is deeply informed by the scientific study of religion, especially cognitive science, it is in the end an evaluative and constructive piece of religious philosophy. Because it deliberately and explicitly conforms to a secular morality of inquiry, it is hard not to think that religious philosophy, integrated in this way into the academic study of religions, represents the future of theology in the secular university.

Notes

1. Wesley Wildman, *Religious Philosophy as Multidisciplinary Comparative Inquiry: Envisioning a Future for Philosophy of Religion* (Albany: State University of New York Press, 2010), 39.

2. Wildman usually avoids the label "theology" for his work precisely because it suggests that it is tradition-limited, sectarian, or confessionalist. His preferred term is religious philosophy, but he grants that "philosophical theology" also fits. See his *Religious Philosophy as Multidisciplinary Comparative Inquiry*, 26–34; and his *In Our Own Image: Anthropomorphism, Apophaticism, and Ultimacy* (Oxford: Oxford University Press, 2017), x.

3. For a critique of *Schempp* as a myth of origins for the academic study of religion, see Winnifred Fallers Sullivan, "Teaching Religion: Refusing the *Schempp* Myth of Origins," *The Immanent Frame*, https://tif.ssrc.org/2016/08/15/teaching-religion-refusing-the-schempp-myth-of-origins/.

4. Here I have in mind the arguments of Donald Wiebe. See Wiebe, *The Politics of Religious Studies: The Continuing Conflict with Theology in the Academy* (New York: St. Martin's Press, 1999) and *The Science of Religion: A Defense* (Leiden: Brill, 2018). I agree with Wiebe that the academy should operate according to the strictures of methodological naturalism, but I distinguish between a strict naturalism like his and a nonreductive, nondogmatic "liberal" naturalism. For this argument, see Schilbrack, "A Better Methodological Naturalism," in *The Question of Methodological Naturalism*, ed. Jason N. Blum (Leiden: Brill, 2018).

5. I develop an argument like this in Schilbrack, *Philosophy and the Study of Religions: A Manifesto* (Oxford: Blackwell, 2014) ch. 7, as does Thomas Lewis in his *Why Philosophy Matters for the Study of Religion—and Vice Versa* (Oxford: Oxford University Press, 2015), ch. 2.

6. Wildman, *In Our Own Image*, x.

7. Ninian Smart, *Dimensions of the Sacred: An Anatomy of the World's Beliefs* (London: Harper Collins, 1996).

8. An example of a comparative theologian who deliberately refrains from evaluating the religious worldviews described is Francis X. Clooney, *Comparative Theology: Deep Learning across Religious Borders* (Oxford. Wiley-Blackwell, 2010), e.g., 10–11. The goal of the "new comparative theology," on this descriptive model, is to reorient the theological task away from the judgment or even latent competition between traditions and toward comparisons predicated on aesthetic appreciation and moral identification with the religious other. On this, see John N. Sheveland, "Solidarity through Polyphony," in *The New Comparative Theology: Interreligious Insights from the Next Generation*, ed. Francis X. Clooney, S. J. (London: T&T Clark, 2010), 171.

9. Benedict de Spinoza, *Complete Works*, tran. Samuel Shirley (Indianapolis: Hackett, 2002), 861. Spinoza's slogan also seems to inform the Berkeley Public Theology Program, which asserts that public theology involves "comparison and description of the commitments and modes of inquiry of all [religious] traditions." For a critique of the limitations of Berkeley's model of public theology, see Martin Kavka, "The Risk of Teaching Theology in a Public University: A Response," *Religion Dispatches* (May 26, 2016), http://religiondispatches.org/the-risk-of-teaching-theology-in-a-public-university-a-response/.

10. By speaking of "stages," I mean to distinguish between descriptive claims (like "Aquinas speaks of God as *actus purus*") and explicit evaluative claims (like "In so doing, Aquinas made a brilliant contribution" or "In so doing, Aquinas made a terrible error"). The latter depend on the former but not vice versa. As I argue in the third section of this chapter, I do not mean to suggest that one's descriptions or interpretations in the first stage are free of normative commitments.

11. Comparative theologians who operate with this understanding of academic theology include Michelle Voss Roberts and John Thatamanil.

12. I think that it is important not to cede the label of "critical study of religion" only to those historians, social scientists, and other theorists who seek to explain religious phenomena in terms of *causes* not recognized by practitioners. The philosophers, ethicists, and theologians who evaluate religious phenomena in terms of *reasons* not recognized by practitioners are engaging in a study of religion that is equally critical. On the parallels between these two forms, see Schilbrack, *Philosophy and the Study of Religions*, ch. 7.

13. Kathryn Tanner accuses Schubert Ogden of holding this second model and of restricting theology in precisely this way: "in Ogden's case, theology [in the secular university] seems solely critical, rather than constructive, in that its concerns are limited to the assessment of theological proposals already on the ground. Theology's job as a discipline of the humanities, in other words, is not to produce a religious stance but to evaluate it. As something like a humanistic discipline, theology is thereby eviscerated of part of its normative focus: those who do theology in the sense of actively proposing what it is that Christianity should stand for in contemporary times, become the object of study rather than participants in academic theology. One can study what theologians say or put one's own theological sensibilities into the subjunctive mode as perspectives that students might temporarily imagine themselves occupying, but the assertion of a judgment concerning what is proper for Christians to say and do in response to the challenges of contemporary life is all off-limits in the university." See Tanner, "Theology and Cultural Contest in the University," in *Religious Studies, Theology, and the University: Conflicting Maps, Changing Terrain*, ed. Linell E. Cady and Delwin Brown (Albany: State University of New York Press, 2002), 201. The claim that Ogden—famous for his arguments that in contemporary times Christians should develop a combination of Bultmann's demythologization and Hartshorne's process theism—does not think that academic theology includes constructive thinking is a strange misreading of Ogden, and Tanner does not provide any evidence that Ogden excludes constructive theology.

14. See Schilbrack, *Philosophy and the Study of Religions*, ch. 5.

15. See Cooey, "The Place of Academic Theology in the Study of Religion from the Perspective of Liberal Education," in Cady and Brown, *Religious Studies, Theology, and the University*, 180.

16. The case for including constructive thought in the secular academy is especially important, I judge, given how congenial it is for a neoliberal university

that sees education solely as a training for the workplace to exclude the educational task of constructing accounts of the real, true, moral, and just.

17. I owe this good point to Kathryn Tanner, "Cultural Theory," in *The Oxford Handbook of Systematic Theology*, ed. John Webster, Kathryn Tanner, and Iain Torrance (Oxford: Oxford University Press, 2007), 528. And it is worth remembering that many religious philosophers did not recognize boundaries between theology and religious practice: what scholars today consider Anselm's theology, for example, he wrote as a prayer.

18. The best account I know of the uses of religious reason-giving is that of John Clayton, *Religions, Reasons, and Gods: Essays in Cross-Cultural Philosophy of Religion* (Cambridge: Cambridge University Press, 2006). Clayton points out that many philosophers of religion today assume that members of a religious community develop reasons for their form of life (such as arguments for the existence of God) to respond to an extrareligious challenge from secular critics. More often, however, they do so to respond to an interreligious challenge from another religious tradition or to an intrareligious challenge within the community. What counts as a good reason then shifts according to these discursive contexts.

19. See Searle, *Minds, Brains, and Science* (Cambridge: Harvard University Press, 1984), ch. 2.

20. For an analysis of the logic of anger, see Robert Solomon, *The Passions: The Myth and Nature of Human Emotion* (Notre Dame: University of Notre Dame Press, 1983), 283–86.

21. Delwin Brown suggests this link between understanding and evaluating when he asks: "What is the difference between thinking about the logic of a particular complex of beliefs as it relates to other beliefs and to its material context, and doing what the adherent does when he or she thinks analytically about the main beliefs? One can think about ritual without doing ritual, but can one think about a set of beliefs, as analytically as one might think about the components and functions of a ritual process, without doing something very close to what reflective practitioners might do when they think about the same set of beliefs?" (Brown, "Academic Theology in the University or Why an Ex-Queen's Heir Should be Made a Subject," in Cady and Brown, *Religious Studies, Theology, and the University*, 129).

22. The labels of secularists, inclusivists, and sectarians come from an excellent map of this debate by Paul A. Macdonald Jr., *Christian Theology and the Secular University* (London: Routledge, 2017), ch. 2. Macdonald discusses Richard Rorty, Donald Wiebe, and Russell McCutcheon as examples of the secularist camp; Delwin Brown, Sheila Greeve Davaney, John Caputo, Jeffrey Robbins, and William Hart as examples of the inclusivist camp; and Gavin D'Costa, Paul Griffiths, David Hart, and John Milbank as examples of the sectarian camp. For a slightly different map of the debate, see Linell E. Cady and Delwin Brown, "Introduction," in Cady and Brown, *Religious Studies, Theology, and the University*, 4–10.

23. Macdonald lists Kathryn Tanner, Denys Turner, and David Ford as other Christian theologians who argue for some version of this alternative.

24. Macdonald Jr., *Christian Theology and the Secular University*, 20, 21. The other sentences in this paragraph were drawn from the following pages: 5, 65, 86, 5, 3, 68, 67.

25. Macdonald Jr., *Christian Theology and the Secular University*, 81.

26. Tanner, "Theology and Cultural Contest in the University," 206.

27. The distinction pervades all of his work, but see especially Ogden, *On Theology* (San Francisco: Harper & Row, 1982), ch. 7; and on the requirement that not only secular universities but any university that describes itself as a place of higher education must grant its faculty the academic freedom to invalidate church teachings, see Ogden, *Doing Theology Today* (Valley Forge: Trinity Press), ch. 6. One might think that separating these two criteria is a modern development, or that it emerges in what might be called liberal theology. But their separation is really a response to the challenge of living in a pluralistic context, and that challenge does not appear for the first time only in modernity. Delwin Brown has argued that for Christian theologians, the separation of criteria of plausibility and authority first emerged with medieval thinkers. See Brown, "Academic Theology in the University or Why an Ex–Queen's Heir Should Be Made a Subject," 130.

28. Of course, the criteria for how one adjudicates these two questions are themselves contentious: one might object that Ogden takes the discipline of history too seriously when he says that Christian claims must fit with the earliest apostolic witness, or one might object that he takes the discipline of metaphysics too seriously when he says that claims about God must fit with common human experience. Perhaps there are better criteria for these questions (and Wildman's approach differs from Ogden's). But there is no non–question-begging way to argue against the separation of the two questions. That is, one cannot make a credible argument that one's epistemic authorities are perfect unless one separates appropriateness and credibility.

29. Wildman, *Fidelity with Plausibility* (Albany: State University of New York Press, 1998), xviii.

30. Wildman, *Fidelity with Plausibility*, xvi.

31. Wildman, "Reforming Philosophy of Religion for the Modern Academy," in *Reconfigurations of Philosophy of Religion: A Possible Future*, ed. Jim Kanaris (Albany: State University of New York Press, 2018), 261.

32. Wildman, "Reforming Philosophy of Religion for the Modern Academy," 255.

33. Sam D. Gill, "The Academic Study of Religion," *Journal of the American Academy of Religion* 62, no. 4 (December 1994): 966.

34. The question of *why* one should practice the study of religion is remarkably undertheorized by religious studies scholars. The best discussion I know of the purpose of this field is Richard B. Miller, *The End and Future of Religious Studies* (forthcoming).

35. Jeffrey Stout, *Democracy and Tradition* (Princeton: Princeton University Press, 2005).

36. This public reason-giving is the condition that Tal Lewis puts on including evaluating theological claims in the secular academy: "What is important is . . . to be willing to offer justification for the norms that we invoke. Participants in the academic study of religion must be willing to bring the norms themselves into debate and subject them to critical inquiry" (Lewis, *Why Philosophy Matters*, 45–46).

37. Wildman, *In Our Own Image*, 8. An earlier draft of this closing section of the paper appeared in the journal *Reading Religion* (http://readingreligion.org), and I am grateful for the permission to use that material here.

38. Wildman, *In Our Own Image*, 5.

39. Wildman, *In Our Own Image*, 84.

8

Wesley Wildman's Theology

ROBERT CUMMINGS NEVILLE

Wesley J. Wildman's theology can be understood from reading his writings, from being his student, and from being his friend. Although I've read his writings and have learned many new things from him as a student (especially how to manage my computer), my understanding of his theology comes most profoundly from being his friend for more than twenty-five years. We have been colleagues in curricular matters at Boston University, collaborators on projects such as the Comparative Religious Ideas Project and the Science and Religion Program, and I even had a role in setting up his Center for Mind and Culture. But most importantly we have been friends, sharing families, the adventures of children, traveling together, crying and laughing together, and being mutual shrivers. Although I cannot express it well, I know a lot about how his theology feels for him and how he feels the world through it. For all our theological similarities and differences, we have come to relate to one another with mutual love. Of that I am more confident than I am of my own theology.

In this chapter, I aim to articulate some of the main lines of Wildman's theology, although others in this volume do that too. I aim also to give a critical reading of his philosophy, indicating where I disagree with him. Because our conversation has gone on for many years, this involves elaborating a bit of my own theology as he has criticized it, exposing our back-and-forth for a wider audience. For those interested in the public record of this conversation, the place to begin is Wildman's "Neville's Systematic Theology of Symbolic Engagement."[1] As he and I have often said, despite the differences between us, those very differences stem from our separate enterprises of artistic intellectual creativity.² We offer our systems as different works of theological art, both to be enjoyed as enriching the theological world. To ask which of us "wins" the theological debate is a category mistake. In Wildman's language, we put forward two systematic ways of effing the ineffable.

Theology's Public

Although Wildman is an ordained minister in the Uniting Church of Australia, from the Methodist branch of that union (I am an ordained United Methodist minister), his theology is not aimed at Methodists, or Christians of any sort, in a confessional way (nor is mine). Rather, as he argues in his 2010 *Religious Philosophy as Multidisciplinary Comparative Inquiry: Envisioning a Future for the Philosophy of Religion*, he writes theology for the secular academy.³ "Religious philosophy" is the word he used in that book for "theology," "philosophy of religion," "systematic theology," and "philosophical theology," all of which are more or less synonymous for him, although some might be more natural in certain contexts.⁴ More recently, in his 2017 *In Our Own Image: Anthropomorphism, Apophaticism, and Ultimacy* and his 2018 *Effing the Ineffable: Existential Mumblings at the Limits of Language*, Wildman uses "philosophical theology" and sometimes "systematic theology" for what he does.⁵ Basically he and I are both philosophers who focus often on first- and second-order theological topics as they arise in religion, religions, secular culture, and personal life. We are both systematic, having been influenced in this by Paul Tillich. Like Wildman, I have not known exactly what to call myself until recently when I settled on "philosophical theologian," a title supposedly invented for Tillich.⁶

When Wildman claims that theology in the sense of philosophical theology should be addressed to the secular academy, he means two things. One is that its arguments and methods of inquiry should be those that would be respected by the academy. This entails that confessional appeals to special revelation or religious identity are not to be part of academic theology because not all members of the academy could hold to them. This point sets Wildman (and me) apart from a great many Christian theologians who believe they are thinking for the sake of the church with the assumptions of the church taken for granted.⁷ Other religions also have confessional theologians from whom Wildman is distinct. Theology as "faith seeking understanding" is *not* what Wildman does (nor I), although it is what Tillich did. Of course, we have both had some form of religious faith since childhood, and for many years that faith has not been exclusively Christian. Perhaps for us the relation between faith and theology is best expressed as "theological inquiry seeking the best faith." Theological inquiry should be respectable to anyone in the academy, regardless of their faith (or non-faith) position.

The second thing Wildman means by the claim that theology should be addressed to the academy is that the academy itself should be interested in academic theological inquiry into first- and second-order religious and theological topics, which it often is not. Many in the academy today think of theology as exclusively confessional, even overtly or covertly Christian, and work to purge it from the academy. Wildman's own university, Boston University, recently has purged him and his theology (as well as me and mine—I then retired) from any of its units except the School of Theology.[8] Where then will the academy treat serious inquiry into what Wildman calls the Big Questions of theology, for instance, the nature of God or ultimacy, why there is something rather than nothing, the grounds of value and obligation, the nature of the self and its ideals, how to engage others beyond self-interest, and the meaning of life? These might be addressed in philosophy departments, in which case they would be philosophical theology, but most philosophy departments reject such questions these days in favor of small questions and with the suspicion that *any* theology is confessional theology. Wildman's limitation of theology in the academy to what would be respected according to academic norms of inquiry carries with it an important normative implication of what the academy *should* be interested in, namely the big theological questions. Denominational schools of theology are not likely to be trusted to represent the best of academic thinking because they are subject to accusations of confessionalism.

I would add two additional points about academic theology that he does not stress but with which he might agree.

First, academic philosophical theology should write for an audience that potentially includes anyone with an interest in the outcome of the inquiry. This would include all sorts of confessional theologians who would be interested even if they could not bring their "confessions" to bear on the inquiry in a trumping way. In this sense, philosophical theology should be at home in denominational seminaries, and they should look to learn from it. So should secular or nonreligious thinkers who wonder about the big theological questions. This means that philosophical theology should develop discourses that connect with this interest that is broader than the academy alone.

Second, I would be almost as suspicious of the norms of inquiry in the academy as many in the academy are to the trumping norms of confessional theology. Centuries-old traditions of humanistic thinking have existed in the academy of which philosophical theology is a natural part. But these increasingly are being squeezed out or shrunken in these days when the academy principally trains students for jobs and is coming to think that science, technology, engineering, and mathematics (STEM) are the only truly legitimate forms of knowledge with legitimate methods of inquiry. More than any other theologian I know, Wildman has worked to bring the natural and social sciences into the heart of theology, but he knows that their methods of inquiry are not the only ones needed for theology. Although he is clear about the limits of scientific reductionism and appeals to humanistic inquiries of many sorts, he is not as suspicious as I of the negative effects of STEM for the policing of the academy.

Comparative Erudition

An obvious implication for philosophical theology for the academy is that it should be erudite in a wide range of religious traditions so as to be able to address their ideas and concerns. Wildman was involved during the late 1990s in the Cross Cultural Comparative Religious Ideas Project at Boston University, which over a four-year period compared some of the big ideas of Buddhism, Chinese religions, Christianity, Hinduism, Judaism, and Islam on the topics of the human condition, ultimate realities, and religious truth. There were six historians of religion and their graduate assistants plus four generalists including Wildman and me.[9] All of us received crash courses from the specialists on their traditions, and we all participated in discussions of methods of comparison. Wildman and I collaborated on nine essays spread throughout the three volumes publishing our findings, mainly on methodological issues and comparative conclusions.[10]

The comparative method on which Wildman and I agreed and that guided the project compares religious ideas as various specifications of explicit comparative categories. The comparative categories themselves are vulnerable to correction as inquiry proceeds, aiming at fairness and lack of bias. This responded to the common criticism of comparison that it employs the categories of Christianity to compare all the other traditions. When the ideas compared can be expressed as different specifications of the constantly improved comparative categories, the ways the ideas compare can be stated. Wildman himself has gone far beyond the explorations of that project in the development of comparative categories. For instance, in *Religious Philosophy* he concludes that there are six theological traditions or categories of historical development that cut across all the major world religions: the ontotheological, the cosmotheological, the physicotheological, the psychotheological, and axiotheological, and the mysticotheological. I return shortly to his categories for comparing concepts of God or ultimacy.[11]

Wildman is one of the few philosophical theologians who insist on broad erudition in the world's religions as the experiential and cultural base from which to do theology. He also insists that theologians need to be able to address the ideas and concerns of thinkers from all religious traditions and from various secular arenas. He himself is astonishingly expert in both of these conditions for philosophical theology.

An important implication of this approach to global religious erudition is that the primary focus in the study and comparison of religions is the logic of the ideas, not close readings of particular texts. Of course, no one would encourage sloppy readings of texts. Nevertheless, many postmodern thinkers believe that only close readings of particular texts are legitimate, rejecting large theories that express and sometimes compare the logic of ideas and rejecting also philosophical readings of history that are needed to bring distant religious cultures into relation. Wildman and I reject those postmodern limitations to large theory and philosophical history and are suspicious that "close readings" can be blind and naive about their own prejudices without them. Wildman has a fascinating discussion of postmodernism in *Religious Philosophy*, chapter 3.

Hypothesis and Understanding

Wildman approaches theology with a Peircean method of inquiry that he sometimes describes as problem-solving.[12] Nevertheless, the bulk of his theological writing is in setting up the problems to be solved. This is to be expected, because he has to tie his theological conceptions to the historical traditions of theology and also to the other disciplines that bear upon them. The remarkable thing about *In Our Own Image* is that he does bring the discussion to a well-formulated problem, presents alternative hypotheses, and probates them according to criteria he spells out. I sketch his argument in *In Our Own Image* to illustrate and comment on his method.

The topic of *In Our Own Image* is the nature of what is ultimate, if anything is. It aims to set up alternative hypotheses that can be so clarified and distinguished in relation to one another that they can be referred to with acronyms. He finds, after much careful historical and conceptual discussion, three ultimacy (U) models: U1, U2, and U3. U1 is the class of models of the ultimate as an agential-being, God as a being who acts in some sense or other, and some kinds of personal theism. U2 is the class of models of the ultimate as the ground-of-being, Tillich's phrase but a class in which Wildman would put perennial philosophies. U3 is the class of models that have no coherent conception of ultimacy but that would include theologies of finite Gods, such as Whitehead's in which God plus the world is ultimate, with ultimacy rejected as a theological category, and anti-theologies of eliminative materialisms that also reject the category of ultimacy. U1, U2, and U3 are to be considered as candidate hypotheses about ultimacy.

Wildman supplements these hypotheses about ultimacy with philosophical cosmologies that are hypotheses about how human beings might relate in the world to the possible ultimates. Again, he finds three cosmological (C) models. C1 is supernaturalism, in which supernatural beings might be found within the world and in which the Ultimate as agential-being is taken to be supernatural ("supranatural," Tillich would say), for instance as creator of the world of nature.[13] C2 is cosmological naturalism that denies the existence of any supernatural beings and any supernatural God transcending the world but that finds ultimacy within nature itself, under some construction or other of "nature." C3 is any philosophical cosmology that denies the theological importance of any conception of ultimacy. Obvious link-ups exist between the ultimacy and cosmological models. U1 agent-being models easily go with C1 supernaturalism to produce certain kinds of personal theism. U2 ground-of-being models easily go with C2 naturalisms to produce religious naturalisms; they also can go with C1 supernaturalisms that believe in supernatural beings within the world. U3 no-coherent-model ultimacy views go with C2 naturalistic models such as Whitehead's that have a subordinate-deity theism with a naturalistic theory of the world; they go as well with C3 models that reject any notion of ultimacy within the world. Wildman's discussions of the various internal complexities of these several hypotheses and the possible combinations of them are subtle and display his comparative and historical erudition. He has an astonishing sensitivity to conceptual affinities and allergies.

Wildman is eminently worth teasing about his love for denotative acronyms and numbered hypotheses. Therefore, I refer to *In Our Own Image: Anthropomorphism, Apophaticism, and Ultimacy* as IOOI-AAU, pronounced *yuu-ee-ow*, or IOOI (*yuu*-ee) for short. IOOI has three magnificent long chapters on U1, U2, and U3 respectively, with the last devoted to the examination of theologies of subordinate deities such as those in process theology, William James, and others.

How does a philosophical theologian evaluate these hypotheses of ultimacy? Wildman is insistent on the process of evaluation, not content to leave the hypotheses distinguished and logically interrelated. Strangely, Wildman claims that the criteria for evaluation are rather personal, reflecting the interests and commitments of the theologian. The following are the criteria at which he arrives after long discussions the content of which you can guess:

1. Be not less than personal in the conception of ultimate reality.

2. Include a conception of God.

3. Define God as unambiguously, definitively, good.

4. Provide a robust metaphysical basis for the hope for life after death.

5. Demonstrate a high degree of internal coherence in relation to ultimate reality.

6. Eliminate the problem of divine neglect.

7. Eliminate the problem of suffering.

8. Eliminate the problem of divine incompetence.

9. Treat ultimate reality as the object of religious reverence and worship.

10. Comport well with the Central Result of the scientific study of religion (supernaturalism as an evolved cognitive default).

11. Comport well with the natural and social sciences.

12. Support a fair and nonparochial interpretation of religious diversity.

13. Be amenable to both theistic and nontheistic interpretations.

14. Resist the Rational Practicality dimension of anthropomorphism.

15. Resist the Intentionality Attribution dimension of anthropomorphism.

16. Resist the Narrative Comprehensibility dimensions of anthropomorphism.

17. Support robust apophaticism in relation to God

18. Support a powerful solution to the problem of the One and the Many.

19. Captivate the hearts and minds of large numbers of ordinary people without specialized training.

20. Support robust religious institutions.

21. Specify a metaphysics that helps to resolve outstanding problems in philosophy.[14]

Note that these criteria for hypotheses about ultimacy are not easily made consistent with one another. But they do reflect the interests of large numbers of theologians in each case and will determine, among other factors, what each theologian seeks to articulate and defend. Preference is not entirely subjective, however. Wildman assigns high, medium, or low scores to each of the ultimacy hypotheses coupled with cosmological hypotheses, U1-C1, U2-C2, and U3-C2 (subordinate deity) for each of the twenty-one criteria. Weighting high as 3, medium as 2, and low as 1, agential-being models (U1-C1) get forty-four points, naturalistic ground-of-being models (U2-C2) get fifty-three points, and subordinate-deity models (U3-C2) get forty. Weighting each of the twenty-one criteria equally, "objectively" the naturalistic ground-of-being models (U2-C2) are most plausible, and they are most plausible to Wildman for reasons I shall develop. Nevertheless, different theologians weight the criteria differently, so the plausibility scores do not stand as merely objective.

Here I want to draw a major distinction between Wildman's philosophical theology and mine, regarding how we treat hypotheses. I call Wildman's approach an "external" one in the sense that he as theologian mostly stands outside the array of hypotheses about ultimacy as if he could delineate their contours as logical on their own and comprehensible to anyone as at least neutrally different. When he comes to his own theological affirmations, he brings his own preferences for criteria in from the outside. IOOI has many very moving passages about his own theological and spiritual development regarding how to evaluate theological issues. He also has accused me for some decades now of merely having personal preferences for the criteria that count heavily in my theology, for instance, number 18, solving the problem of the One and the Many. He thinks it is perfectly legitimate for a theologian to dismiss that criterion and hold to a hypothesis that simply cannot solve the One and Many problem. (To which I answer that, someday, someone will raise the question of the One and the Many and the very raising of the question will create havoc for theologies that cannot solve it.)

My own philosophical theology I would call "internal" in contrast to Wildman's "external" one. My treatment of hypotheses is "internal" to a philosophical theological system that I have been developing since childhood. Because we have talked about them in depth for a quarter century, Wildman and I treat pretty much the same ultimacy and cosmological hypotheses, as well as criteria for evaluating them, even when we frame them a bit differently. Nevertheless, I arrived early at a hypothesis about determinateness in the world and how it demands what I call an "ontological creative act." I have elaborated this hypothesis from many directions over the years, relating it to alternative hypotheses about ultimacy, the cosmos, ethics, the nature of the self, relations with others, the meaning of life, and so forth. Wildman was a naturalistic ground-of-being theologian from very early years as well, but he has always defended it as the best hypothesis among many, given his criteria-preferences. I have defended my comprehensive systematic hypothesis and its many component hypotheses relative to their alternatives, but with the alternatives considered as within the development of my system. Moreover, I have defended the criteria by which I evaluate the hypotheses within the system in many ways for a long time. My criteria have been vulnerable to correction within the system and are not applied only at the end. Like Wildman, I recognize my particular historical location, but try to control for its influence on the elaboration and defense within the theological system.

Wildman sometimes says that this difference between us is a matter of temperament. I rather say that my way provides a better means for making the whole array of one's arguments vulnerable to correction. Furthermore, I think my way provides a more solid commitment to seeking truth rather than what serves one's interest. One major strength of Wildman's externalist approach is that it allows others to get into it just by following the logic of his analysis. A major weakness of mine is that one slowly has to buy into the system to see how it unfolds, even if one rejects it in the end. Another strength of Wildman's approach is that he can frame his hypotheses in clear, univocal language friendly to denotation, as in the "operational definitions" of the natural sciences. An opposite strength of my approach is that it uses language dialectically, changing meanings by contexts, playing upon odd resonances and connotations rather than strict denotations, thus possibly avoiding the reductionisms that so easily attend scientific operational definitions. Wildman thinks of his philosophical theology, in its approach, as an extension of Peirce's scientific inquiry into theological matters. I think of mine more as the creation of a work of art, the inhabitation of which makes you see differently and understand more of what the world is. My theology comes out to be a non-supernaturalistic ground-of-being naturalism, but a different one from Wildman's. I also share his apophaticism, a point to which I return shortly.

The Backstory of Anthropomorphism

Anthropomorphism in conceiving ultimacy is a basic notion signaled in the subtitle of Wildman's IOOI-AAU. Many religious traditions, especially in the West, conceive of ultimate reality as a God who has something like human agency, intentionality, rationality, perhaps emotions, and perhaps a moral character. No sophisticated theologians would employ crude anthropomorphisms such as that God is a Big Guy in the Sky, as Michelangelo painted him symbolically on the ceiling of the Sistine Chapel. But a great many would develop more transcendent conceptions of divine personhood, claiming that God is "at least personal" if also "more than personal," according to some meaning or other of that "more." Such transcendent conceptions of personhood usually are correlated with human personhood so as to allow personal relations between God and human individuals (e.g., in petitionary prayer) and groups (e.g., in covenants). "Personal theisms" might take the form of belief in subordinate deities or belief in super-transcendent agent-beings.

Wildman and many other scholars in the scientific study of religion, including my coeditor LeRon Shults, believe that anthropomorphism has a kind of primacy in the founding of religion because it is an evolutionary default response to many things. For evolutionary reasons, people came to attribute anthropomorphic traits to all sorts of things, even things that have no real anthropomorphic structures. People attributed supernatural personhood to trees, storms, and pools, and believed in all sorts of supernatural beings, ghosts, living dead ancestors, demons, angels, gods, and demigods. "Hyperactive-agency detection" is a kind of cognitive error, but it had its evolutionary advantage. To hear movement in the bushes, attribute it to a tiger, and run like mad is far more adaptive in the long run than stopping to investigate whether it is a tiger or only the wind.[15]

Among many scholars of religion in the West, it is fashionable to *define* religion as belief in supernatural beings and to *explain* the origin of religion as a result of hyperactive agency detection, an evolutionary default behavior.[16] To the contrary, however, what the evolutionary story explains is primitive science. It explains why people who are not aware of such cognitive errors would believe that the world is populated with all sorts of supernatural beings. Modern philosophical, scientific, and scholarly thinkers about science recognize the cognitive errors for what they are and can develop techniques not to be caught by them (hyperactive-agency detection is only one of several such tempting cognitive errors). Modern science has banished supernatural beings from its categories of things that exist and interact. Those sophisticated people who identify religion with belief in supernatural things banish religion from its list of true beliefs. I myself think these people mostly are criticizing primitive science when they think they are criticizing religion; vast numbers of people today do indeed hold to primitive or "popular" science.

Nevertheless, whether anthropomorphic belief in supernatural beings is relevant to religion depends on whether those beliefs function to orient people to ultimacy, Wildman and I agree, making exceptions for sophisticated beliefs in subordinate deities of the process theology sort. Surely it is the case that Western religions have developed anthropomorphic conceptions of gods and a monotheistic God. But Plato's Form of the Good is not at all personal; Aristotle's Thought Thinking Itself has more to do with his theory of actualization relative to potentials than with personal agency (it is pure, nonagential contemplation). But Judaism, Christianity, and Islam have developed increasingly transcendent conceptions of personhood in trajectories that reach to conceptions that are beyond personhood, such as Thomas Aquinas's conception of God as the Pure Act of To Be. That trajectory allows for thinking of God as an agent, at least as an intentional creator of the world if not an actor within it, although the end of the trajectory—God as Pure Act of To Be—cannot act or intend. Anthropomorphism is surely an issue within Western religions such as Christianity.

In the South Asian traditions around Hinduism and Buddhism there has been no lack of belief in supernatural beings. Just try counting the supernatural sentient beings enlightened in the *Lotus Sutra*! Nevertheless, all such sentient beings were considered subject to karma, and hence not ultimate. Metaphors for ultimacy in those traditions focused rather on consciousness, cultivating pure forms of it, distinguishing consciousness itself from its contents, and extinguishing intentionality, agency, desire, rational commitment, and so forth as having any ultimate reality. Indeed, the very intentional agency the West personified in the most transcendent ways often was taken in South Asia to be the root of the human predicament from which religion seeks liberation and enlightenment.

The Chinese in East Asia also believed in thousands of supernatural beings but very early rejected notions of a High God (Shangdi) for nonpersonal metaphors for ultimacy such as Dao, Heaven, and the Great Ultimate; the Chinese metaphors center around spontaneous emergence. Sophisticated contemporary Buddhists and Hindus, Daoists and Confucians, by and large have abandoned the primitive science of their forebears and practice their religions with no significant anthropomorphic figures except for teachers and cultural legends that are recognized as merely metaphorical.

God and Ultimacy

Wildman's theological approach begins with the assumption that religion historically and for most people now is based on anthropomorphic conceptions of God as an intentional agent. The default anthropomorphism stems from evolved hyperactive agency detections, which in most instances is a cognitive error built in to our biocultural makeup. Ways exist to control for this cognitive error, as well as others, and careful modern science helps. Because we now know how so many of the capacities for intentional action depend on the biological structures of the body, especially the brain and nervous system, disembodied supernatural beings are increasingly implausible. Nevertheless, he gives the anthropomorphic U1-C1 approach 44 points as scored according to his list of criteria, compared with 40 points for the U3-C2 for the subordinate-deity model, which might very well be anthropomorphic too, and compared with 53 points for his own preferred naturalistic ground-of-being U2-C2 model. In the long run, his greatest complaint about the agential-being models of ultimate reality is that they cannot handle the problems of theodicy if they say that God is good as well as ultimate. For Wildman, the trajectory of theology is from anthropomorphism to non-anthropomorphic naturalism (sliding off into apophaticism, about which more shortly).

For me, by some possible contrast, the trajectory of theology begins with a glimpse of ultimacy in the orders of things, including the wonder why anything exists at all, and moves through different symbol systems for ultimacy, including personification, pure consciousness, and spontaneous emergence, finding perceptual satisfaction in seeing the world as embraced in an ontological context of mutual relevance that is best named an ontological creative act.[17] Hyperactive agency detection is important for understanding the development of science but not so much for the development of religion except in the personified theistic West. I am annoyed by thinkers who define religion itself as belief in supernatural beings both because it privileges the West over East and South Asia and because it pays too much attention to the cognitive side of engaging ultimacy at the expense of existential determination of selfhood and religious practices and institutions.

Wildman's flight from anthropomorphism to naturalism is by no means an attraction to scientific materialism. Quite the contrary, he is extremely clear that science picks up on only certain aspects of nature, which is permeated by values of many kinds. He describes nature as structured by "axiological folds," a term he develops, I think, from Robert Corrington's "sacred folds."[18] Axiological folds are structures that yield values of various sorts, values that can be appreciated in human experience and even more greatly appreciated with increasing scientific sophistication about natural structures. I agree with him thoroughly in this and give my own account of axiological folds as relations among densities of being.[19] We agree that the ultimate reality is a ground-of-being that gives rise to a world filled with value.

In his "Neville's Systematic Theology of Symbolic Engagement," Wildman points out as if it were a problem that my view of the ontological creative act is that it has no nature of its own apart from what comes in the creating. This is indeed my view. What is created includes the determinate world that in turn includes whatever characters the ontological act has by virtue of creating. I reject *creatio* or *emanatio ex deo*, which Wildman defends in relation to Plotinus in chapter 3 of *Effing the Ineffable,* and hold strictly to *creatio ex nihilo*, as he says. This might sound odd if you begin by assuming that creation language supposes a creator with a nature; I am urging a purification of that assumption: the nature of a creator is the result of creating. Another way of putting my view is that the world exists only insofar as it is in an ontological context of mutual relevance; that ontological context of mutual relevance consists in the ontological creative act with the determinate things of the world as its terminus. So it makes sense for me to say that the ultimate is just the world so long as by "the world" you include the ontological creative act creating the world in the ontological context of mutual relevance. In *Ultimates* I became clearer than I was before that it is fair to call my theology a "theism" only when dealing with the personification metaphors of West Asian religions. It is not a theism when dealing with the basic consciousness and spontaneous emergence metaphors of South and West Asia respectively.

Wildman, by contrast, in chapter 3 of *Effing the Ineffable,* defends the thesis that there is a theogony by which God develops a character by infinitesimal steps of creating determinateness, which he likens to Plotinus's One giving rise to determinateness. To this, I would ask whether there is any difference whatsoever, no matter how small, between the infinite One and the first step toward determinateness. If there is not, then no step has been taken and the One is alone. If there is, it is a determinate difference, bringing the One into finite relation with the end of the step, and thereby demanding a yet deeper ontological context of mutual relevance to contain the One plus the step, which is my position. If there is a series of infinitesimal steps from the indeterminate or infinite One to full-blown determinateness, either a finite series or an infinite series, each step is a cheat, feigning determinacy and yet denying it. Because any step from an infinite One toward determinacy comes by inserting negations or limitations in the infinity of the One, each cheating step is an addition of negation, or nothingness relative to Infinite Oneness. Therefore, the series of infinitesimal steps, finite or infinite, is just the accumulation of negations. Since any move away from the infinite One is through the creation of negations, why not just call it *creatio ex nihilo*? All that is added to the One to achieve determinateness is negations: the One creates things by creating negations of infinity.

Is it not much simpler instead and in conformity to common sense to say that the ontological creative act creates positive determinate things with all their reality including determinate negations and relations with one another? I admit, with Wildman, that we have two hypotheses here: his, with *creatio ex deo*, moving from the infinite one to determinations by infinitesimal steps, and mine, with *creatio ex nihilo*, a total surd, moving from nothingness to the determinate world in the ontological creative act that is the existence-dimension of all the related things in the world.

Whereas he often speaks graciously of balancing these two hypotheses, claiming they are two ways of construing the abysmal ground of being, I recommend taking the better one (mine ☺). He concludes chapter 3 of

Effing the Ineffable, in reference to the claim that the two hypotheses are balanced alternatives for construing the abysmal ground, by saying:

> It is a slender case. And I may not be a wholly impartial evaluator. But the Abysmal ground view of ultimacy looks significantly better to me than the alternatives. Long live symmetry! And long live the playground where we philosophical theologians perpetually attempt to eff the ineffable.[20]

His argument that the two hypotheses themselves emerge from the ineffable abysmal ground is by analogy with the story of the Big Bang in which there was a period when the electromagnetic and weak forces could not be distinguished, followed by a cooler period in which they become distinct. But he already knows that a temporal story is precisely *not* analogous to the eternal theogony of which time is a result. Is he not pleading for a "rational floor" in which the utterly arbitrary, absurd givenness of the ontological creative act creating the world as its terminus is made to seem more understandable in temporal terms? Long live the asymmetry of the ontological creative act that gives us a world with its pockets of order!

In some places, including chapter 3 of *Effing the Ineffable*, Wildman accuses me of being an occasionalist, thinking that for me the eternal ontological creative act creates each temporal thing in its own time, relations along with the things related. He says this "profoundly obscures the rational conditions for scientific inquiry and human freedom, among many other things."[21] To this I answer that my analysis of determinateness as such applies to any world whatsoever and is vague with respect to whether the world is temporal. But our world is indeed temporal, and so the ontological creative act creates the temporal things in all their connections, with causation as known by science, freedom as known by the pursuit of responsibility, and a whole host of other conditions. We simply have to look to see what the characters of the temporal world are. Great temporal distinctions, changes, and connections suppose that all their elements are eternally created together in an ontological context of mutual relevance containing all temporal transitions.

Apophaticism

Let me now attempt to articulate another subtle contrast between Wildman's philosophical theology and my own, close as they are, beginning with mine this time. I practice theological inquiry in order to develop concepts that guide our engagements with ultimate realities so that we become aware of what is important or valuable in the ultimates and respond appropriately. For all its dialectical twists, turns, and interpretations of the histories of religions, the point of my philosophical theology is to be an index that connects us with ultimate realities and enables appropriate responses. I believe that truth is the carryover of what is important or valuable in the object interpreted into the interpreter such that the interpreter can comport to the object appropriately.[22] I claim my philosophical theology is true, however fallibly, in this sense. Having a philosophical theology means living within the system so as to engage ultimate realities with guidance as to what is valuable and important for the living. Selections among theological hypotheses are just steps for composing the living system and inhabiting it as vulnerable to correction.[23]

For Wildman, the truth of his theology lies in inference to the best explanation among the hypotheses considered. Of course, vast work goes into the framing and contextualizing of the hypotheses and the identification of relevant criteria for choice. But for him, I think, truth consists in the claims made for the best hypothesis. Given the roles for preferred criteria, his appeal to truth is as existential and "subjective" as mine. Nevertheless, for him, the truth of his final hypothesis (subject to revision) is external to his living in it, whereas for me the truth is internal to the living in the hypothesis. The existential quality of his theology lies in living with the balances of the hypothesis. This is very close to the position I take on "religionless religion" in *Religion*, part 4.

Accordingly, for Wildman apophaticism is the denial of the final stability of any hypothesis about the ultimate. Part of this is the general Peircean commitment to fallibility. Wildman holds that the world gives us feedback regularly, if very slowly, to correct our ultimacy hypotheses. Another part of Wildman's apophaticism is that the criteria by which we judge hypotheses about ultimacy are inevitably subject to personal preference.

Apophaticism for me, beyond the general point about the fallibility of all hypotheses, consists in the hypothesis that the ontological creative act is immediate, with no intervening steps of creation that might be plotted in a hypothesis. The ontological creative act is not a thing with a structure beyond what it creates; rather it is the ontological context of mutual relevance containing all existing things by containing them. The act contains no reason why it creates this or that, or why it creates at all. Though fallible, my hypothesis explains *why* the ontological creative act cannot be known except by what it creates.

Behind our differing approaches to apophaticism is a deep puzzle between us. I would like to quote extensively from the third chapter of his *Effing the Ineffable* for the bulk of his argument against my position. In that chapter he has established the character of a fallibilist pragmatist like the two of us as a laid-back surfer-dude who counts on nothing solid but is hyperattentive to the waves and swells around him.

> Consider self-identified fallibilist pragmatist Robert Neville. The philosopher responsible for the only significant advance in the theory of *creatio ex nihilo* since medieval philosopher Duns Scotus, Neville reduced the problem of the One and the many to its purest form—the ontological conditions for determinateness. In *God the Creator* . . . , he demonstrated that there is a best account of the One behind the many using this pure form of the problem as the leading criterion. He gets a solution to the rational floor of inquiry for free, having solved the problem of the One and the many.
>
> But there is a trick in the argument. In Neville we have a fallibilist pragmatist who believes a rational floor of inquiry is indispensable for any type of intellectual activity. But he actually invokes as a premise of the argument that there is a rational floor for inquiry. He doesn't make a big deal about it; the premise is not made explicit. But it is a functional premise nonetheless. If the idea of an ontological ground and the concept of a rational floor are as tightly correlated as they seem, Neville's argument begs the question. It presupposes its own answer. His One is fated to be the triumphant solution because the criteria active within the inquiry are freighted in its favor. He might appear to get a rational floor as a result of identifying an ontological ground but in fact it is the other way around. His uncompromising demand for a rational floor guides his inquiry and yields his *creatio ex nihilo* answer to the problem of the One and the many, eliminating competitor views along the way. Neville's argument is very strong, and possibly logically valid (it is a complicated comparative argument and so validity is difficult to assess). But the rational-floor premise is deeply questionable.
>
> I think this rational-floor premise is worth fighting about. I reckon Neville functions here only partially as the surfer-dude fallibilist pragmatist. It might be the characteristic suit and tie that

gives away his incomplete commitment to the surfer lifestyle—though I do admire the way he dresses down when working in the garden or on sabbatical. It seems as though he is ruling on the issue of whether we need an ultimately rational floor for inquiry without considering the relevant evidence. Surfers are always patient and rarely surprised. It is part of the spirituality of waiting for waves and noticing their endlessly varying shapes and potentialities. Neville might have given more patient thought to whether we truly need his One-style rational floor.

I think we can get by without an ultimate rational floor for inquiry. In fact, about half the time I think we *are getting by without it*. The other half of the time I lean toward thinking that Neville is correct, that the rational floor, and the grounding One that goes with it, really are there. And this raises a question I find stunningly interesting: what if the question of whether there is a rational floor can't be decided?

Very Big Questions can be answered only by examining the qualities of inquiry to see whether rationality or irrationality dominates—an infuriatingly circular process that provisionally presumes rationality and depends on irrationality appearing as failures of putative rationality in the interstices and at the margins of inquiries. When we do this, what do we find? Well, here comes that generalization than which no more outrageous can be conceived: we see a mixed bag of successful and frustrated inquiries. And we must acknowledge the difficulty of deciding whether inquiries are frustrated because we didn't organize them optimally, because the feedback on which we rely to correct hypotheses is absent or weak, or because there is irrational absurdity at the root of reality. If the latter, we must further acknowledge the distracted genius of irrationality: reality supports the very possibility of constructing inquiries that we are prepared to call rational, but now manifested as teasingly rational surds within an irrational ambit having no boundaries, no intelligible features, and no possibilities of final comprehension. Even judgments of rationality necessarily must be merely functional declarations.[24]

Even after all these years of arguing about this, I still do not understand why Wildman believes that I presuppose a "rational floor" for my argument about the one and the many. Certainly it is not a term that I myself used, and "floor" language sounds terribly foundational in a way that pragmatists reject. In fact, my position is that intelligibility is radically contingent on the existence of determinate things. That there is any rationality at all is a radical surd. No reason exists for why there are determinate things. The ontological creative act is absurd, in the sense Wildman means. Sometimes he explains his position on the ground-of-being as its being symmetrical, giving physics the need to account for the breaking of symmetry. This comes from his mathematical sense that basic rationality is symmetry—things balance across the "equals = sign."[25] By contrast, I call my ground-of-being view asymmetrical in the sense that whatever symmetry exists needs to be created: it is an order that needs explanation, and the only explanation is the absurd, arbitrary, gratuitous, ontological creative act whose terminus is whatever is determinate. The ontological creative act is asymmetrical in the sense of moving from nothing to whatever rational somethings there are, an immediate move of sheer creating; "nothing" is intelligible only after the fact of something. I celebrate the title (and arguments) of Tyler Tritten's book *The Contingency of Necessity*, where rationality is included in what he means by necessity.[26]

Given determinate things, however, and I believe there is a given world, the question remains what rationality consists in. Charles Peirce said that it is pointless and immoral as part of inquiry to entertain a hypothesis that says its topic cannot be explained. Wildman agrees, I think, but points out that many inquiries do not work out. They might fail because the inquiries are ill-formed or the circumstances of inquiry are not right. But they also might fail because there is no rationality in what they are trying to understand. In this case, if we could ever tell that this is the case, the inquiries would be right in saying that their topic is irrational.

My own view is that an analysis of determinateness as such might yield a hypothesis about determinateness that would apply to any possible world. I have such a hypothesis and argue that it is a good hypothesis.[27] It is not deductive, but it is dialectical and it depends on step-by-step internal persuasion that this is the best way to think about determinateness. We also can inquire into just what determinate world we have here, and this is an empirical as well as dialectical inquiry. My own hypothesis is that the world is temporal and spatial and that determinate things in it are harmonies, which themselves can be analyzed. This hypothesis needs to be argued from the inside. My general guess about the rationality of the world, given the small sample we know, is that there are pockets of tight order with lots of internal rational connections within seas of very little order, vast seas of space-time with very few complex metaphysicians such as Wildman and me and with little order besides some laws of motion. I don't see how this view of mine supports Wildman's view that I presuppose a floor of rationality. Rather, I aim to work argument by argument, on the inside of philosophical inquiry about how systematic the world is, with mini-inquiries taking their form as we understand the contexts and powers, which in turn calls for the development of larger contextual hypotheses.

To summarize my view of rationality, that there is any determinate world with any rationality to it is an absurd fact, simply given. This is explained in the hypothesis about the ontological creative act creating determinate things within an ontological context of mutual relevance. There are characteristics we can hypothesize to apply to any set of determinate things. There are the particular determinate things we can know, fallibly and hypothetically, by various means. And there is a great deal that we find ourselves not grasping by any modes of inquiry so far. We might conclude down the road that there simply is no kind of order of the sort we are looking for in this or that area of inquiry. This is what Wildman notes when he says that irrationality shows up around the edges of our inquiries, especially their failures.

Here is what I suspect about the root of our disagreement, a point I made earlier. Wildman takes an external approach to the hypotheses he formulates, looking to adjudicate them by criteria from elsewhere. Therefore, he balances the hypothesis that the world has a rational floor with the hypothesis that the world is permeated by chaos or irrationality; he claims that it is a significant achievement to think of this dilemma. He has no prioritizing criteria beyond splitting his time while believing. Half the time he sides with me in the cogency of my dialectical argument for the ontological creative act as the one for the many determinate things; but I suspect bias here because I know how much he prizes our friendship. The other half of the time he sides with the irrationality hypothesis because so much does seem chaotic or irrational; but I suspect bias here too because I know that he knows that one of the offices of friendship between philosophers is the obligation to push my vulnerability as hard as possible.

I take an internalist approach to hypotheses, developing a system around which to assess and coordinate them. I say that sometimes the failures of inquiry come from faults in the inquiry, but other times the inquiry is correct to conclude that there is no rationality of the sort sought in the topic under investigation. Peirce rejected the claim that science presupposes determinism by arguing that just how much rational order exists in the world and of what kinds are empirical questions, not questions about what is to be assumed for inquiry to take place. The traditional, multicultural, grand inquiry, for instance, to correlate the positions of the stars with the fortunes of human affairs has by and large concluded that no close correlation can be found—that the impulse for the inquiry was determined by one of the cognitive errors Wildman points out. Wildman says that even "judgments of rationality must be merely functional declarations." Yes, but when the functional declarations are interwoven in an intricate system whose parts are vulnerable to criticism from many angles, they are not so "merely."

Where do we come out in all this? First, Wildman and I agree that all hypotheses about ultimacy, even the big ones worked into systems such as he and I have, are fallible. We probably would agree even more strongly that anything we think now about ultimacy is probably at least a little wrong and will be corrected in the future. Second, Wildman and I agree that the ontological ultimate (I claim four additional ultimates) is a ground of being, not itself determinate and the ground of everything that is determinate. Third, we have not yet found agreement on what "ontological grounding" means. As I read (and hear) him, he is attracted to something like a Plotinian view in which the primordial symmetry of the One breaks out into determinateness and determinate things, breaking symmetry.[28] I say, somewhat differently, that the one is the singularity of an ontological act of sheer creation, sheer making, that has no nature of its own, One, Many, or Otherwise, except what arises in creating determinate things. The singularity comes from the fact that the act creates all things that are at all determinate with respect to each other by creating them together as an ontological context of mutual relevance; it does not unify them. So in the problem of the One and the Many, I dismiss the emphasis on oneness and substitute for it the singularity of all relations and relata. The ontological act is asymmetrical, not symmetrical as Wildman would have it. Fourth, we agree that inquiry often breaks down, perhaps from its own fault and perhaps because it seeks a kind of order that its topic does not have. Fifth, we disagree about how the world simply might lack order. Wildman would infer that it lacks order if inquiries, in the long run, show more instances of irrationality than rationality. This is his hypothesis contrasting with what he calls the floor of rationality. I would say that how much rational order exists in the world is an empirical matter to be decided by further inquiry; the rationality of inquiry in the long run hopefully can show what aspects of the world are rational and ordered, or chaotic and disordered. For Wildman the big question is whether the world is rational or irrational; for me it is how rational it is, in what sense, and where. He would answer his question by assessing inquiries; I would answer mine by looking at cases. Sixth, we differ about how absurd the existence of the world is. Wildman explains the radical contingency of existence itself by minutely absurd infinitesimal steps toward determinacy from a symmetrical infinite One. I say that the existence of the world is totally absurd, without reason, motive, or even a possible alternative apart from what is given in the world. This is why Wildman says I'm likely to be the only philosophical theologian to be to his "left."

Religious Symbolism and Philosophy of Religion

Permit me to root out one last tension between Wildman and me. He, like me, has been deeply influenced by Paul Tillich, including by Tillich's claim that, because of apophasis, all religious symbols need to be broken. Tillich thought that such symbols still participated in what they point to, and Wildman has approved of my systematic elaboration of that claim, calling upon pragmatist insights of which Tillich was unaware. Nevertheless, Wildman sometimes thinks that broken symbols are mischievous and often used for downright evil; this is the moral outcome of his analysis of anthropomorphism. I, by contrast, try to hedge the broken symbols and use them metaphorically, even musically, to enhance participation in the ultimate reality of the ontological creative act. This leads him to criticize my preaching for allowing my hearers to think I believe the symbols in some literal sense when I do not. I, in turn, praise his preaching for using symbols so musically when he should not be able to do that on his theory of symbolism. Indeed, I delight in his *Effing the Ineffable* for using nine avenues of religious symbols and pushing them in trajectories toward ultimacy, breaking them only at the end.

Wildman rightly notes (along with Tillich and me) that religious symbols are employed to engage ultimacy in many ways besides intellectual ones. Most of the chapters of *Effing the Ineffable*, except chapter 3, are about existential and ecclesiological engagements, not high metaphysics as in *In Our Own Image*. To be sure, unbroken symbols can be mischievous and evil in existential matters and church life. Nevertheless, the "liberal" project of breaking anthropomorphic symbols can be destructive of religious communities and the faith of large numbers of people, Wildman says in chapter 6 of *Effing the Ineffable*. He believes those communities need anthropomorphism for their own solidarity. The anti-anthropomorphic mystical apophatic theology he espouses can only live on the underside of organized religion. He does say that organized religion depends on the experiential intensity of his kind of mysticism to stay vital, and so he sees a struggle between community solidarity and vitality.

I would like to complicate this picture of symbolism in religious life by pointing out that at least three related continua exist in religious communities.[29] First is the continuum stretching from popular religion to the most sophisticated kind of religious thinking in a tradition. Second is the continuum stretching from the need to make symbols intimate to human life to the need to make them properly transcendent, which for anthropomorphic symbols means breaking them. Third is the continuum from thinking about most of the world in completely secular, nonreligious, and nonultimate terms and thinking of the world as suffused with religious meaning relative to ultimacy. We in the Christian and Jewish traditions are accustomed to thinking of religious communities as congregations in which everyone in a geographical area is mixed together—from the uneducated to the sophisticated, from the existentially needy to the anti-idolaters, from those who take the secular world on its own terms to those who see the sacred everywhere. This has not always been the case, even in Christianity and Judaism. Thomas Aquinas would have spoken differently to his seminarians, to monks in a monastery, to nuns in nunneries, to aristocrats, tradesmen, peasants, and villains, shifting his symbols and their interpretation to what each group needs. Buddhists also have distinguished theologians from monks and them from laymen, and men from women. Advaita Vedantins and Confucians often have said that their paths to enlightenment and sagacity are only for some individuals in a community, even only for some individuals within a family, with the others handed over to different traditions of discourse. It seems to me that in nearly all large-scale religious traditions there exist significant groups who would be up for Wildman's anti-anthropomorphic mystical apophaticism (and my ontological philosophical theology) without having to speak that way to other segments of the community. Wildman's worries about the conflict of communal solidarity with intellectual theological honesty are problems mainly for communal organizations in which all kinds of people are mixed together in congregations.

My response to Wildman's dilemma about religious communities is complex. First, I would never fall for the journalistic or sociological tack of identifying religion with religious communities of a social sort.[30] Those communities are religious in a serious sense only when they are venues for engaging ultimacy, and here I would hope they would be compatible with some mystics in the balcony. Homogeneous monasteries, hermits living virtually by themselves, and theologians collaborating with theologians from other traditions in developing their spiritual lives have different social settings for being religious, not all called "communities." Schleiermacher and Tillich thought there was more authentic religion in coffee houses than in churches in their times, although they also spoke for churches.

Second, I would say that it is possible to educate people who think they need anthropomorphism and a "personal God" when they really can learn to be more sophisticated and follow the breaking of symbols, avoiding the mischief and evil of anthropomorphism. Third, I point out again that not every religious tradition starts out with an anthropomorphism it has to get over. Many traditions need to become more sophisticated about other elementary religious symbols. Fourth, the social situation of religious communities is rapidly changing, and not too much worry should be given to the ones we have now, for instance congregations, because religious life is already morphing into new, noncongregational forms.

Finally, I believe in the importance of socially organized religious communities in our time, but more for their political usefulness than their necessity for religion. To counteract the excessive individualism of much global culture, there is great political reason to strengthen the social infrastructure. We need educational communities, recreation communities, economic and special interest communities as well as religious ones. Even if religious communities are totally vapid with respect to fostering engagements with ultimacy, they can be extremely useful for building a rich body politic within which people learn and practice the institutional structures of freedom and equality. This means, I think, that we do not need to worry as much as Wildman does about the religious fragility of religious communities under threat from wild mystics like us. We will find each other irrespective of religious communities.

One of the reasons Wesley Wildman is one of the greatest theologians of our time is that he can preach without the symbols of anthropomorphic deity. I wish he would feel free to preach *with* those symbols, because sometimes they are the best music and do not have to be mischievous or evil. But what he has in *Effing the Ineffable* is a rhetorical blockbuster of an argument for the God beyond gods. I have to say that he remains on my right because he thinks the problem is to get over gods. For those with that affliction, he is the soma of liberation. What an astonishing surd of the universe that I have him as friend!

Notes

1. Wesley J. Wildman, "Neville's Systematic Theology of Symbolic Engagement," in *Theology in Global Context: Essays in Honor of Robert Cummings Neville*, ed. Amos Yong and Peter G. Heltzel (New York & London: T & T Clark, 2004), 3–27. We have both reformulated our positions somewhat since then. See, for instance, Wildman's "How to Resist Robert Neville's *Creatio Ex Nihilo* Argument," *American Journal of Theology and Philosophy* 36, no. 1 (January 2015): 56–64, and my response, 65–68. See also his paper on my interpretation of Paul Tillich in the *Bulletin of the North American Paul Tillich Society*, 2018, and my response.

2. This is not to say that we agree about artistic intellectual creativity.

3. Wesley J. Wildman, *Religious Philosophy as Multidisciplinary Comparative Inquiry: Envisioning a Future for the Philosophy of Religion* (Albany, NY: State University of New York Press, 2010). See especially the "Afterword: Religious Philosophy in the Modern University."

4. See *Religious Philosophy*, chapter 1, for a discussion of the relations among philosophy, religious studies, and theology in "religious philosophy."

5. Wesley J. Wildman, *In Our Own Image: Anthropomorphism, Apophaticism, and Ultimacy* (Oxford: Oxford University Press, 2017). In this volume Wildman summarizes his methodological stipulations from *Religious Philosophy*, often speaking of "trans-religious" rather than "comparative" matters, although the emphasis on comparison across religions is the same. See also his *Effing the Ineffable: Existential Mumblings at the Limits of Language* (Albany, NY: State University of New York Press, 2018). In this chapter, my citations of his work come mainly from *Religious Philosophy as Multidisciplinary Comparative Inquiry*, *In Our Own Image*, and *Effing the Ineffable*.

6. My recent "coming out" as a philosophical theologian is in my trilogy, *Ultimates: Philosophical Theology Volume One*, *Existence: Philosophical Theology Volume Two*, and *Religion: Philosophical Theology Volume Three* (Albany, NY: State University of New York Press, 2013, 2014, and 2015, respectively). *Ultimates* is dedicated to Wildman, and his *Religious Philosophy* is dedicated to me. I cannot find anyone claiming the title of "philosophical theology" before Tillich, for whom Union Seminary in New York named his position beginning in 1940. Many recently have used the title, however, generally to designate the use of philosophy to think about theological topics, in which case it goes back in the Western tradition to Plato and Aristotle. Wildman and I frequently have discussed what to call what we do, and it is no surprise that we both settled on "philosophical theology."

7. One thinks of Karl Barth, of course, as a confessional theologian thinking for the church. But Paul Tillich begins his *Systematic Theology* with the same profession. See my "Theologies of Identity and Truth: Legacies of Barth and Tillich," in my *Realism in Religion: a Pragmatist's Perspective* (Albany, NY: State University of New York Press, 2009), 9–21, for an analysis of their texts on this point.

8. Wildman's *Effing the Ineffable* is dedicated to "my colleagues in Boston University's Graduate Division of Religious Studies: A Fond Farewell," and the dedication is explained in the "Acknowledgements."

9. The specialists and their assistants were M. David Eckel with John J. Thatamanil (Buddhism), Livia Kohn with James Miller (Chinese religions), Paula Fredriksen with Tina Shepardson (Christianity), Francis X. Clooney, S. J., with Hugh Nicholson (Hinduism), Anthony Saldarini with Joseph Kanofsky (Judaism), and Nomanul Haq (Islam). The generalists were Peter Berger, a sociologist; John Berthrong, a Sinologist; Wildman; and me. With the exception only of Haq, the historical specialists were experts in a religious tradition other than their own so as to avoid even the appearance of interreligious dialogue.

10. The volumes were *The Human Condition*, with a foreword by Peter L. Berger; *Ultimate Realities*, with a foreword by Tu Weiming; and *Religious Truth*, with a foreword by Jonathan Z. Smith, all edited by Robert Cummings Neville (Albany, NY: State University of New York Press, 2001).

11. See *Religious Philosophy*, chapter 8.

12. See his explicit discussions of pragmatism and inquiry in *Religious Philosophy*, chapters 6 and 7 and in *In Our Own Image*, chapter 1 and passim.

13. For Tillich's distinction between supernaturalism and supranaturalism, see his *Systematic Theology: Volume II: Existence and the Christ* (Chicago, IL: University of Chicago Press, 1957), 5–10. Wildman's discussion of this is in *Science and Religious Anthropology: A Spiritually Evocative Naturalism Interpretation of Human Life* (Burlington, VT: Ashgate, 2009), 19–23.

14. IOOI, 217.

15. See Wildman, *In Our Own Image*, 82–90, for a more elaborate discussion of this "Central Result" of the scientific study of religion.

16. See Robert Cummings Neville, *Defining Religion: Essays in Philosophy of Religion* (Albany, NY: State University of New York Press, 2018), chapters 1–4, for a better definition of religion.

17. My theory is spelled out in detail in *Ultimates*, with the last part of *Religion* as the extreme statement of my apophaticism.

18. See Robert S. Corrington's essay in this volume and his *Nature's Religion*, with a foreword by Robert C. Neville (Lanham, MD: Roman and Littlefield, 1997).

19. See my *Metaphysics of Goodness: Harmony and Form, Beauty and Art, Personhood and Obligation, Flourishing and Civilization* (Albany, NY: State University of New York Press, 2019).

20. ETI, 79.

21. ETI, 70.

22. See my *Recovery of the Measure* (Albany, NY: State University of New York Press, 1989), divisions 1 and 4, for an explanation and defense of this approach to truth.

23. See my *On the Scope and Truth of Theology: Theology as Symbolic Engagement* (New York & London: T & T Clark, 2004). Compare this with Wildman's *Religious Philosophy*.

24. ETI, 65–67.

25. See *ETI*, chapter 3.

26. See Tyler Tritten, *The Contingency of Necessity: Reason and God as Matters of Fact* (Edinburgh, UK: Edinburgh University Press, 2017). Tritten argues his case from late antique and German Idealist authors, especially Schelling, whereas I argue mine from medieval and pragmatic authors.

27. It is spelled out in my *Ultimates*, part 3, and many other places.

28. See his discussion of symmetry and asymmetry in chapter 3 of *ETI*.

29. These are explained at length in *Ultimates*, chapter 4.

30. See the argument in chapter 1 of my *Defining Religion*.

9

Wildman's Effing Symbology

NANCY K. FRANKENBERRY

Introduction

Like the supersleuth Robert Langdon, the hero of Dan Brown's bestselling novels who relies on "symbology" to solve crimes, Wesley Wildman uses religious symbols to try to "eff the ineffable." Langdon's symbology is a fictional creation, invented by Brown to reveal not ineffable insights into ultimate reality, but insufferable scandals in the Catholic Church. Wildman's multidisciplinary, comparative methodology is on the lookout for inference to the best explanation, while Langdon's single-minded effort sets out to crack the intricacies of the Da Vinci Code. Inspection of their respective webpages reveals that both scholars are masters of symbolic manipulation. On his home webpage, the Boston University professor playfully takes in everything "from unambiguous nothing to ambiguous something and relentlessly, gracefully back again," and describes his most recent book as "a meditation on how religious language tries to limn the liminal, conceive the inconceivable, speak the unspeakable, and say the unsayable."[1] Across the Charles River, the Harvard Symbologist's official website depicts an encoded ancient parchment that may, or may not, be Da Vinci's lost prophecy about the future. We are told only that "the code has yet to reveal its mystery, but Robert Langdon is very close to finding the key to deciphering the message. Leonardo's encoded message consists of twenty-four symbols. Robert Langdon is certain there exists a key, and he is working very hard to find it."[2] In a further parallel, both Boston professors bear a striking resemblance to the irresistible Tom Hanks. Add to that the fact that the two have never been spotted in the same room together, and the suspicion grows that we dealing with One and the Same. Only the perennial problem of the One and the Many is more difficult than the question of how to differentiate Wildman and Langdon.

My aim in this chapter is to demystify metaphorical and symbolic language, which has often been described in almost magical terms, especially in religious studies. Along the way, I hope to differentiate Langdon and Wildman. According to the alternative theory that I develop here, there is no such thing as symbolic meaning. By the term symbolic meaning I refer to something regarded as latent, hidden, or coded as a message in religious texts and rituals whose semantic content is ruled symbolic or metaphorical or figurative, requiring sophisticated hermeneutical translation; even then, it is said, we only see through a glass darkly. In advancing this thesis, I have found Donald Davidson's philosophy very helpful. Consider how he announces the subject of his essay on "What Metaphors Mean":

> [This paper's] thesis is that metaphors mean what the words, in their most literal interpretation, mean, and nothing more. . . . The central mistake against which I shall be inveighing is the idea that a metaphor has, in addition to its literal sense or meaning, another sense or meaning. . . . Some stress the special insight metaphor can inspire and make much of the fact that ordinary language, in its usual functioning, yields no such insight.[3]

Metaphor and symbolism are uses of literal language, according to Davidson, just as much as "assertion, hinting, lying, promising, or criticizing" are uses of literal language.[4] In that case, both Wildman and Langdon face different difficulties, depending on which theory they adopt of religious symbols, metaphors, and meaning. While all signs may be treated as "symbols," as Langdon appears to do, then we are dealing with semiology. But we only produce illusion when we cross the wires and treat all religious symbols as signs, as Wildman appears to do with regard to religious symbols; then we are dealing with Tillichian theology.

In that case, the principal difference between Wildman and Langdon can be expressed in terms of the difference between abstract and concrete levels of discourse. Langdon is in pursuit of a Holy Grail, all of whose symbols are quite concretely visual, or anatomical, or based in human feeling—extensions, we might say, of the human hand. Wildman's symbols are highly abstract conceptual models—extensions, we might say, of the human mind. Thus, Langdon obsesses over the interpretation of ancient symbols such as the pentacle, the chalice, and the rose. And Wildman is preoccupied with conceptual models for ultimate reality. It is clear how to interpret the pentacle, the chalice, and the rose, for each is a sign standing in for something. In *The Da Vinci Code*, the pentacle stands for the "sacred feminine" or the "divine goddess," the chalice for Holy Communion and the blood shed by Jesus on the cross, and the rose stands for the Holy Grail, Mary Magdalene, secrecy, womanhood, and, most obviously, female sexuality. But what is ultimate reality?

What is Ultimacy?

Of the two, Wesley Wildman's position is more vulnerable to critique than Langdon's. It pains me to say this as we agree on so much—the inadequacy and the inevitability of anthropomorphic models, the collapse of the purported Jerusalem-Athens synthesis, and the impossibility today of refusing the challenges of the natural sciences to the truth of basic theistic propositions. There is much wisdom in Wildman's multidisciplinary comparative inquiry, which offers a thorough reshaping of philosophy of religion along the most important interdisciplinary lines found today. More than anyone else of his generation, Wesley Wildman has emerged as a distinguished cartographer of religious philosophies, a self-styled "comparing inquirer," at just the moment that comparative projects are most in demand.[5]

However, comparative projects alone will not suffice to more thoroughly historicize our discipline, a goal distinct from comparison even when it is multidisciplinary. We need to insist, in addition to more comparative work, on the study of collective mentalities, of economic, social, or cultural determinations of individual behavior, and give much more attention to the influences of unconscious motives and forms of self-deception on religious thought and action. In particular, we need to demystify certain myths regnant within the academic study of religion, especially in the philosophy of religion, where the myth of symbolic meaning has galvanized the imaginations of many post-Tillichian scholars.

It remains an open and urgent question to me how to interpret Wildman's symbolic discourse about Ultimate Reality or, as he prefers to say, "Ultimacy."[6] Wildman's impressive achievements in an ever-widening oeuvre are most fully on display in his two most recent books, *Effing the Ineffable:*

Existential Mumblings at the Limits of Language (2018), and *In Our Own Image: Anthropomorphism, Apophaticism, and Ultimacy* (2017). I am chiefly interested in these volumes (the second and sixth, respectively, in Wildman's six-volume magnum opus) because they present Wildman's theories in their most applied form, and they intersect with my own current interest in language, semantics, and holism. In these works, he succeeds brilliantly in (1) calibrating the distinctive strengths and weaknesses of what he distinguishes as the chief forms of philosophical cosmology with religious significance: supernaturalism; ground-of-being cosmologies; and process cosmologies; (2) arguing with admirable precision that ground-of-being cosmologies are scientifically less costly, philosophically more coherent, and religiously more satisfying than the other two alternatives; and (3) demonstrating a compelling case for comparative approaches in philosophy of religion.

Wildman is less convincing about Ultimacy-claims and why "effing the ineffable is our inescapable fate."[7] On the one hand, he insists that philosophy of religion ought to develop conceptual models of Ultimacy, and his own investigation of three such models seems eminently fair and reasoned. On the other hand, it is hard to see the usefulness of the model he chooses in the end, with its attendant symbolic apparatus. By the time Wildman has added up the pros and cons of the anthropomorphic models of a personal God, and what he deems "the subordinate deity" models found in process philosophy and theology, the reader is primed to award pride of place to ground-of-being models, as Wildman himself does. In his words, ground-of-being conceptions of Ultimacy are to be found in "the creative Dao, a God Beyond all Gods, or a One Beyond Comprehension."[8] All these, he says, are "pointers" to "something unconditioned that we seem to encounter in our experience of reality."[9]

We know at least this much about Ultimacy from *In Our Own Image* and *Effing the Ineffable*: it is unconditioned, it is indeterminate, and it is morally ambiguous. It is, in the final analysis, ineffable, but it can be effed symbolically as a means of engaging our naturalistic ground of being. Wildman maintains, like Robert Neville, that religious symbols are always "broken," that they must be "properly interpreted," and that without them "our connection to the divine depths of our experience may remain undeveloped."[10] He adds the important observation that "naturalist ground-of-being models of ultimate reality must explain how engagement works and supply careful interpretations of symbols whose literalized metaphysical sense is held to be mistaken even while the use of such symbols is deemed efficacious for engaging ultimate reality."[11] Indeed, that is exactly the formidable challenge that Wildman's religious philosophy must meet if he is to convince us of the superiority of ground-of-being metaphors of Ultimacy. Yet his apophaticism stands in the way, shrouding Ultimacy not only in mystery but also wrapping it in patent falsity.

By "broken symbols" Wildman seems to mean the same thing that Donald Davidson has in mind when he describes the "patent falsity" of metaphors and metaphorical sentences.[12] Why not, then, simply acknowledge that religious symbols are patently false when their literal meaning is understood, and that there is no code to crack, no symbolic meaning to decipher, no feat of demythologization to execute? Wildman is well enough able to make this evaluative judgment about the anthropomorphic agential-being models and metaphors of ultimacy, but when it comes to ground-of-being models and metaphors, he wants to "break" the symbols used and still retain some symbolic meaning. This is the exact opposite of the Davidsonian strategy, which holds that there is no such thing as symbolic meaning, only literal meaning—defined as the coincidence of speaker's (utterance) meaning and sentence meaning. Employing Saussurian terms, literality is the coincidence of parole and langue. Metaphorical and symbolic language is a matter of use, not of semantics. As such, it is parasitic on an understanding of literal meaning in the first place. That is, the order of dependence is asymmetrical; we cannot derive literal meaning from use any more than we can derive linguistic competence from performance, or a theory of language from a study of speech. Only because we already understand the literal meaning of whatever sentence is in question can we generally tell when an utterance is a lie, a joke, or an irony. Symbols, metaphors, poetry, and even lies are all parasitic, in this sense, on literal or "first" meaning. They do not carry, encode, express, or point to any deeper meaning. We can look to use when we read or hear puzzling sentences, but we will not grasp any meaning other than literal meaning.

It is important not to characterize this objection as a residue of logical positivism or a legacy of analytic philosophy. It is not, as theologians typically complain, simply a matter of saying "if you can't speak clearly, say nothing, and don't tolerate fuzzy speech that masks conceptual unclarity!" The Davidsonian point relies on no such dogma. Neither does it rely on a referential theory of meaning, something that Wildman appears to assume, even while asserting that he does not take a stand in *Effing the Ineffable* on the question of the reference of religious symbols.[13] Rather than embark on a lengthy discussion of why meaning does not entail reference, I simply make one point: we humans lack the vantage point from which we can transcend the language—whether symbolic or metaphorical or literal—in which we are embedded in order to judge that the relation between symbols of Ultimacy and Ultimacy-Itself (as we might call it) is indeed an authentic "engagement." I take this to be a built-in condition of being human, not a matter of temperamental differences between "comparative inquirers" like Wildman and "analytical ascetics" like me.

Three Philonian Inconveniences

According to Wildman, "One of the great mysteries surrounding the function of religious symbols is how, precisely, they facilitate a person's 'participation' or 'taking part' or 'engagement' in that to which they purport to refer."[14] Among the questions he raises about "the work of effing the ineffable" is this one: "How . . . do symbol systems encode and express strategic mechanisms?"[15] Here again the question that cries out for an explanation is how in fact symbolic meaning is produced in religious terms. I find that Wildman leads us to a familiar stalemate. To the extent that he acknowledges the contemporary quandaries with anthropomorphic variations on the three Great Models, he is pushed toward theological agnosticism. And to the extent to which he resists complete and utter apophaticism, he is forced to readmit some anthropomorphic concessions as the only possible defense against sheer agnosticism. No one has depicted this stalemate more skillfully than David Hume in *Dialogues Concerning Human Understanding* (1779). Early on, Philo advises Cleanthes to "mark the inconveniences" of his anthropomorphic view of the Deity. Then, as Dialogue Four opens, Philo issues a sharp skeptical challenge to Cleanthes for rendering Deity too much an open book, as though one could read the very nature of the Divine plainly from the face of nature. While Philo and Cleanthes hurl epithets at each other ("you anthropomorphite!" "you mystic!"), Demea retreats into a kind of theological agnosticism that leaves him with nothing to say except to utter a few biblical bromides about "God's ways are not our ways." The reader is treated to a classic quandary: how to escape from Demea-style agnosticism, which results from emptying all words about Ultimate Reality of their meaning, without falling fatally into anthropomorphism, and how to evade anthropomorphism without sacrificing the possibility of intelligibility that is the only defense against sheer agnosticism? Every way out reduces to atheism or plays into Philo's skepticism.

Wildman is of course sensitive to this problem, but his way of handling the quandary only plunges us into further problems having to do with "ground of being" models. Philo's question to Demea is still a good one: how does a god about whom nothing can be said differ from no god at all?

The second inconvenience that attends Wildman's notion of Ultimate Reality stems from his preference for Paul Tillich's ground-of-being theology.[16] As every historian of the postwar period knows, Tillich exerted the greatest influence over those who could no longer rest content with the old gods or resist the new challenges of modernity. He taught several successive generations a brand-new language, heavy on Germanic obsessions with der Grenze, illustrating how to salvage something suitably deep and ultimate from the scrap pile of post-Kantian idealist theology. More than any other religious philosopher of his generation, Tillich's redescriptions succeeded in adroitly finessing most of the challenges of the modern critique of religion. Wesley Wildman's version of Tillich succeeds in finessing most of the same challenges in our time. But at what cost? That is the major question. One cannot help but note that Wildman's "Ultimacy," like Tillich's "god beyond the god of theism," is compatible with just about every state of affairs.

I am reminded of Malcolm Diamond's use of E. M. Forster's *A Passage to India* to describe his doubts about Tillich's redescription of the central topics of Christian belief. Diamond recalls the dialogue between two missionaries, Mr. Graysford, who is older and conservative, and Mr. Sorley, who is younger and open-minded. In the spirit of liberalism, they concur on the subject of heaven, agreeing that the exclusivism prevalent on earth should never be mirrored in heaven. Forster gives their dialogue an ironical turn in this passage:

> In our Father's house are many mansions, they taught, and there alone will the incompatible multitudes of mankind be welcomed and soothed. Not one shall be turned away by the servants on that verandah, be he black or white, not one shall be kept standing who approaches with a loving heart. And why should the divine hospitality cease there? Consider, with all reverence, the monkeys. May there not be a mansion for the monkeys also? Old Mr. Graysford said No, but young Mr. Sorley, who was advanced, said Yes; he saw no reason why monkeys should not have their collateral share of bliss, and he had sympathetic discussions among them with his Hindu friends. And the jackals?

Jackals were indeed less to Mr. Sorley's mind, but he admitted that the mercy of God, being infinite, might well embrace all mammals. And the wasps? He became uneasy during the descent to wasps, and was apt to change the conversation. And oranges, cactuses, crystals, and mud? And the bacteria inside Mr. Sorley? No, this was going too far. We must exclude something from our gathering, or we shall be left with nothing.[17]

Diamond's point is that Tillich's world seems indistinguishable from the secular world, just as Mr. Sorley's heaven is indistinguishable from earth. In that case, why talk Tillichese? Or why talk Wildmania?

A third inconvenience is provided by Richard Dawkins. Although he is routinely assailed by the pious and the impious alike for lacking "sophistication" and for holding to a "crude" and anthropomorphic picture of God, Dawkins, nevertheless, takes seriously the truth-claims implicit in the beliefs of priests, mullahs, rabbis, and millions of ordinary believers. Unlike those who think that science and religion are converging, Dawkins has understood that the God of the philosophers and the God of the liberal theologians is light-years away from the interventionist, miracle-performing, sin-punishing, prayer-answering God of Abraham, Isaac, Jacob, Jesus, Mohammed, and most religious believers the world over today. From Texas to the Taliban, religious people do indeed hold as true such beliefs as "Jesus rose from the dead" and "eternal punishment awaits sinners." Dawkins assigns these statements a false truth-value without turning to the Theology of Symbolic Forms, as I have called it, or to "broken symbols," as Wesley Wildman and Robert Neville, more charitably, have called it. Dawkins calls a spade a spade and a false statement a false statement. There is no "symbolic meaning" that he overlooks due to a deficient theological education.

In light of Christianity's inextricable ties to factual and historical claims, one wonders what specific propositional content can be given by sophisticated theologians to the claim, for example, that "Jesus is risen." What occurred, exactly? The resuscitation of a dead corpse? Not likely. Too literal for liberal theologians. Then what? And according to which theologian? "Symbolic truths" and "symbolic meanings" are a dime a dozen, and the theologians who convert the literal meaning of religious language into "symbolic meaning" only leave us with another puzzling question: why would people speak in this coded fashion, all the while appearing to be ignorant of the "real" meaning of their own statements?

What is Symbolic Meaning?

I have been criticizing the idea of symbolic meaning for promoting the myth of an additional, special, ad hoc meaning, over and above, or in the depths of, "first" or literal meaning.[18] But when I say that the very idea of symbolic meaning in religion is a myth, or illusory, I do not mean that symbols, taken simply as synonymous with signs or as a subcategory of signs, are in any way illusory, or even unimportant in understanding religious life and thought. In this sense, symbols are a matter for Peircean semeiotics. Robert Langdon understands this as he pursues every symbol for and of the Holy Grail. Reversing the equation, however, and regarding all signs as symbols, some of which are privileged, only produces illusion. It leads theologians to treat religious symbolizations as a special instance of the semiotic, and to promulgate opaque claims, such as "the symbol participates in that to which it points" (Tillich), or "in hermeneutics symbols have their own semantics; they stimulate an intellectual activity of deciphering, of finding a hidden meaning" (Ricoeur).

Armed with insights from American pragmatism as found in the writings of Donald Davidson, Richard Rorty, Robert Brandom, Jeffrey Stout, and others, we are now in a position to correct the entire tradition of hermeneutical theology by seeing symbolic or metaphorical statements as having to do with use or force and not with semantic content. This is not so grandiose a claim as it might seem. One has only to ask the Humpty Dumpty question: which shall be master of which? It then becomes easy to see the way in which symbolic or metaphorical statements are parasitic upon literal semantic meaning. There are no meanings of a metaphorical or symbolic kind over and above the literal meanings of sentences. The distinction between metaphorical and literal meaning as two different kinds of meaning marks another untenable dualism, not unlike "analytic and synthetic statements." We can and should do to "metaphorical" what Quine did to "analytic," relativizing the distinction within a holistic account. In that case, metaphorical and symbolic expressions "belong exclusively to the domain of use," as Davidson says, and they mean "what the words, in their most literal interpretation, mean, and nothing more."[19] Symbolic and metaphoric uses of language thus depend on literal meaning, but as uses they are not rule-governed. No rules determine which metaphors will be apt and which not, or how and when a speaker's sentences may be used to draw attention to one or another aspect. Because they are not covered by any general rules, there is nothing general or philosophical we can say about them that is not ad hoc. And because there is virtually no limit to the aspectual features that metaphoric or symbolic usages cause us to notice, these aspects do not form part of the meaning of the speaker's utterance. In other words, I am denying both the possibility of a theory of religious symbolic meaning (a finitistic account of its content) and the very idea that symbolic language should be accorded any kind of meaning (including speaker's meaning) beyond the literal meaning of words and sentences.

Taken as signs, symbols obviously proliferate in religions and help to propel Robert Langdon on his Mary way. However, they do not "point to" or "participate in" any language-transcendent meanings that are hidden or coded. This claim may sound counterintuitive to many scholars of religion like Wesley Wildman who have been deeply influenced by Paul Tillich.[20] To them, appealing to the semantics of literal meaning seems to summon up some clichéd stereotype of fundamentalist fervor that conflates "literal" with biblical literalism. In the popular understanding, to be "literal" is to be, at the very least, pedestrian, prim, humorless. These misconceptions aside, my argument is that, while metaphoric or symbolic usages of words may be more difficult to understand than their nonmetaphorical, nonsymbolic counterparts, there is nothing "extra" required in order to make sense of them. It is easy to fall into thinking that when we do succeed in making sense of symbolic or metaphorical statements, we are making use of a second species of meaning. But we can correct this upside-down picture in the study of religion by understanding that symbols and metaphors have to do with pragmatics, with usage in a context, and do not have anything especially semantic about them beyond literal meaning. If this theory is correct, it helps to explain the inability of a metaphorical or symbolic usage to be paraphrased, for if a metaphor had a second meaning in addition to its "first meaning," it should be perfectly glossable.[21]

The next step is to allow for the sense in which sentences dripping with symbols and metaphors are, as Davidson reminds us, "patently false."[22] Patently false expressions may nonetheless prompt readers or hearers to notice novel relationships or analogies, even as their literal truth-values are judged false. Juliet is not the sun, Jesus is not the Son of a Heavenly Father, and the Buddha is not literally born from his mother's side before stepping out with blessings in all four cardinal directions. Obviously false sentences can be interpreted in the same way as any nonstandard or anomalous way of speaking or writing is interpreted—by mixing and matching up what is familiar to us with something unfamiliar until we hit upon a new understanding. Sometimes we may have to revise old theories to fit the new way of seeing because "metaphors often make us notice aspects of things we did not notice before" and may bring surprising analogies and similarities to our attention.[23] But this is not tantamount to maintaining the difficult view that metaphors or symbols of Ultimacy have special semantic content. Once we give up the idea that metaphorical or symbolic use of language carries a message, like a ship hauling cargo, and understand that we have no key for deciphering an encoded content even if there were one, we can see that religious critics, theological innovators, and philosophers of religion who devise new and startling sentences about "God," "nirvana," the Tao," or "Ultimacy" are not providing their communities with semantically meaningful content but, instead, with causal stimuli that may, or may not, induce programmatic changes in the way such sentences will come to be used. Once they become widely circulated—as is the current mantra "God is love," for example—they die, and dead metaphors no longer count as metaphorical but as literal. As living, however, metaphors are within the space of causes, not the space of reasons, to recall Sellars, although this distinction, like any dealing with the slender membrane separating life and death, can be blurry. As a metaphor, such as "ground of being," is on the way out, plodding toward the platitudinous, just when does it begin to convey information rather than simply trigger belief revision? It can be hard to say. Yet as it crosses from the space of causes to the space of reasons for revising belief, it does not acquire an elevated character or fulfill an intrinsic feature. It simply assumes double occupancy, useful both as cause and as reason, according to an ever-shifting relation of other causes to other linguistic forms. This is a process that we understand only retrospectively once a metaphor has died into literalness. Then we can both bury it as well as praise it. But, as Davidson observes, "it is no help in explaining how words work in metaphor to posit metaphorical or figurative meanings, or special kinds of poetic or metaphorical truth. Once we understand a metaphor we can call what we grasp the 'metaphorical truth' and (up to a point) say what the 'metaphorical meaning' is. But simply to lodge this meaning in the metaphor is like explaining why a pill puts you to sleep by saying it has a dormitive power."[24]

Why, then, do many theorists of religion treat statements couched in religious symbols as though they accomplish so much epistemologically, if in fact they possess no semantic content beyond their literal meaning, and their literal meaning is patently false? I suspect that it is because the dormitive power of their implicit theory of religious language confuses the effects of using words metaphorically in sentences with the meaning of the sentences, and they proceed to read those effects back into the semantic content of the metaphors or symbols themselves.[25] Without a clear distinction between semantics (what a propositional attitude means) and pragmatics (what its use causes one to notice), we forfeit the ability to explain the very idea of a mistaken or incorrect interpretation of other speakers or texts.[26] And yet this loss seldom poses any deterrent to dormitive power theorists, who appear to believe that words and sentences acquire additional meaning by virtue of being taken as "pointers" or as "carrying over" values, and that a proposition can become more credible by being presented as an approximation.

Between Semantics and Pragmatics

We may find in Davidsonian semantics a convincing theory of meaning, but it does not, alas, serve to rescue the notion of "symbolic meaning" for any heavy lifting in the study of religion. Here are the main elements of that theory, as I would adapt it from Davidson's work. First, I would invoke a distinction between what words mean and what they are used to do. Symbols, metaphors, and all figurative language belong exclusively to use. Use, however, is not meaning.

Second, symbols and metaphors mean what the words, in their most literal interpretation, mean and nothing more. All of the confusions that attend the study of religious symbolism can be traced to the idea that a symbol or a metaphor has, in addition to its literal sense or meaning, another sense or meaning.

Third, it is helpful to bear in mind that the language of religious texts and the speech of religious folk abound with nonassertorial examples of performatives, illocutionary acts, and other uses of language. Use, however, is not meaning. (Even Wittgenstein qualified this famous injunction by saying "in a great many cases, but not all," we can find the meaning by looking for the use.) Not every utterance we are interested in makes assertions or expresses beliefs. People joke, play games, tell riddles, deceive themselves and others, commit malapropisms, speak metaphorically, grimace and smile. But if the interpreter could never figure out what the speaker believes to be the literal truth, there would be no understanding of the joke, the game, the riddle, the metaphor, or whether the grimace was a grudging welcome or the smile a deceptive ruse. Nor would it be possible to understand what it would be for religious folk to be telling a lie or to be self-deceived. This argument is the necessary consequence of theoretical holism.

Fourth, only certain schools of scholarship have been induced to posit the Myth of Symbolic Meaning over and over again in the modern period. All of them, I find, are infected with variations on the same ontological or metaphysical or theological theme: religion has to do with the Sacred, the Numinous, the Wholly Other, the Incomprehensible One, the Really Real, the Ineffable, or Being-Itself. Some scholars have succeeded very well in showing us why their statements are symbolic and not literal statements, but they have flatly failed to explain, for each of these statements, what its symbolic meaning is. The really fundamental, and I have come to think, insoluble, problems in such accounts of linguistic religious symbols arise when we ask what is the meaning of religious language in these theories. Those who go symbolic at this point are usually unable to supply the semantics.

The account of meaning and of metaphor that I am trying to develop here offers a serious challenge to our habitual ways of thinking about these problems in one further respect. "Generally," as Davidson writes, "it is only when a sentence is taken to be false that we accept it as a metaphor and start to hunt out the hidden implication. It is probably for this reason that most metaphorical statements are patently false, [. . .] Absurdity or contradiction in a metaphorical sentence guarantees we won't believe it and invites us, under proper circumstances, to take the sentence metaphorically."[27] Could it be that modern scholarship has turned to the Myth of Symbolic Meaning only because it has recognized in the traditional language of religion its patent falsity or absurdity and, finding that outcome unacceptable, has sought another "deeper" or "higher," at least "different," meaning? How deep? How high? Different in what respect? Even if we could answer such awkward questions, it would still not change the basic fact that talk about the gods is patently false.

Finally, the problem is not only that our interpretation of metaphors such as "ground of being" rejects the literal and conventional sense of the words and leaves us frankly clueless as to any conceptual content at all, but also that, as Davidson points out, "there is no limit to the content that metaphors can suggest."[28] Where do we get off the USE-train? How do we go on? Every case is different, each person her own Pope. What aspectual features of the world are you caused to notice by religious symbolism or metaphorical language? These may be quite different from what I happen to be caused to notice. Linguistic indeterminacy and instability create the conditions that are conducive to relativism. Your guess is as good as mine.

We have now arrived at the point where not only is the objective pole of our ultimate concern indeterminate, but so also is the symbolic language used to eff it! This is in sharp contrast to most of our nonmetaphorical declarative sentences that are indeterminate only in a limited sense. Facing an unusual or unclear use of words in a sentence, we can usually make sense of it if we assign the sentence to a larger or wider pattern that fixes its meaning. Without an assignment that fixes the meaning of an indeterminate sentence and makes it true relative to that natural language, linguistic communication becomes impossible. But metaphors resist being fixed in this way. They cannot by their very nature be assigned a single interpretation of their propositional content. For this reason, they cannot communicate any content directly. This makes metaphors and symbols in religious studies more than just slippery—they are downright muddled. Although they may hint at many different truths, they state none, lack propositional content, and cannot be said to have "meaning."

For theologians, the limitless semantic potential of metaphors offers both good news and bad news. For ground-of-being theologians, the good news is that they may stay in business for a very long, long time, as their interpretations of their favored metaphors may become endlessly creative. The bad news is that ground-of-being theologians will make no headway, discern no meaning, state no truths. Indeed, conflicting or contrary truths may even come to be ascribed to the metaphorically rich "ground-of-being."

Effing the Ineffable

Further problems with the notion of symbolic meaning emerge in connection with ineffability claims. As I seek to show the conceptual connection between the two, I raise questions that invite Wesley Wildman's response in light of the searching and poignant position he develops in *Effing the Ineffable*.[29]

As an aid to understanding ineffabilism, the experience of encountering a great work of art is sometimes invoked, where one will feel unable to tell people just how it was. One then attempts to diagnose this frustrating situation by saying something like "words cannot describe" or "words are only general but Van Gogh's bedrooms and haystacks are completely singular and unique. . . ." This presumes that the problem is the limitations of our language, especially of our psychological vocabulary. Indeed, "joy" and "sorrow" are both too crude and too simple to capture the exactitude and particularity of feeling and sentience afforded by Beethoven's sublime Fifth Symphony. However, in speaking of joy and sorrow, and perhaps their fusion in a third, distinctive feeling, we are capable of conveying something, if not the whole enchilada, then at least some rice and beans.

Even in the realm of the sublime, we are not mute, inglorious Miltons and should not confuse "ineffable" with "incomplete." As a matter of course, we can concede that no description does full justice to the concrete reality of any aesthetic object, because there is always more that can be said about it—or said about anything, for that matter. It is not because of the artwork's language-defying uniqueness or the personal limitations of one's vocabulary. We can grant, also, that a description of a painting or a symphony is unlikely to communicate what the painting or symphony itself does, if "communicating a feeling" means producing that feeling in another person. But why should "communication" mean "duplication" or "reproduction" of the same feeling? You can understand perfectly well what I mean when I say "I'm elated at the good news!" even if you do not feel elated yourself and even if you don't have a clue what the news is. In that case, when someone says "words cannot describe" or "the feeling is ineffable," we can hear it as an attenuated sense of "describe" and a hyperbolic use of "ineffable." Seeing a painting or hearing a symphony or reading a poem is no more ineffable than a thunder clap. The thunder clap also causes a feeling that the description does not. Nor should we confuse "ineffable" with "intangible." Something as vague as national identity may be intangible, but it is not for that matter ineffable.

I am raising the question, then, of exactly what semantic content is expressed in mystical or religious language that either employs or borders on ineffability claims. A recent study by Stephen Bush examines the constructivist position according to which experiences do not precede their expression but rather are discursively constructed, and finds an unresolved issue in Wayne Proudfoot's constructivist interpretation of religious experience.[30] On that account, for a subject to have a religious experience, it is a necessary precondition that he or she have certain concepts. As concepts are required to identify a religious experience, the concepts are a part of the experience. For our own worry about ineffability claims, this would mean that effing religious experiences goes hand in hand with conceptualizing them, so that nothing is, in the end, ineffable, and claims about ineffable experiences or objects of experience are hyperbolic. Bush's argument, however, is not about ineffability. His warning is not to confuse preconditions for constituents.

The use of concepts is a necessary precondition for baking a cake, to give Bush's example, but that does not mean that concepts are constituents, like the milk, eggs, sugar, and so forth, of the cake. Two things that are concurrent may not necessarily be constituent of each other. Wet sidewalks and rain go together, Bush says, but this does not mean that wet sidewalks are constituents of rain. It is logically possible, then, that concepts may not be constituents of religious experiences, even if they are preconditions for them or accompaniments to them. In that case, on the supposition that experience is only in part constituted of concepts, beliefs, and other propositional attitudes, something nonconceptual—and therefore ineffable, we may suppose—could also be considered part of religious experience.

Even so, experiences taken as religious and reported as ineffable are bound up with beliefs and concepts that precede or precondition the very experiences. Because language does not simply function to express experiences but also to color or condition the very having of experiences, it is hard to see the meaning of such locutions as "nonlinguistic experiences." Either we can identify (however incompletely) something that is nonlinguistic, or we cannot. If we can identify it, we are employing language and concepts in the very process and thus exhibiting it as intralinguistic, after all. On the other hand, if it is not possible to identify the putatively ineffable something, how is it distinguishable from nothing at all?

The chief difficulty of saying that ultimate reality is completely beyond concepts consists in still assuming that there is something with a mind-independent intrinsic nature, namely that of ineffability. This is a position that assumes, furthermore, that there is a way things are from their own side, which is not in any way affected by our concepts. To the contrary, both Wildman and I should be able to agree that it is not that there are some objects within the grasp of our cognitive capacities as well as some beyond them, but rather that the very concept of an object is something established by these capacities. Of course, ultimate reality is not an object according to Wildman. Yet, insofar as one tries to eff the ineffable, one takes it as an object of thought. Our ability to grasp the world by concepts is acquired by our knowledge of language. Some would even argue that it is the very same thing as that knowledge. As a public phenomenon, language is an ability we display in interaction with other speakers. We would therefore want to claim that we can be taken to have understood the meaning of a sentence or to have mastered some concept only if we can give a public display of its use or application. A concept for which we could not give the application conditions even in principle, where we could not even tell in the abstract what kinds of objects would fall under it, is not a concept at all. But this seems to be exactly the situation with the concept of ultimate reality when seen as ineffable. If what falls under this concept is said to transcend all our conceptual resources, we would be necessarily unable to apply this concept to anything. Once this concept is ruled out, the only remaining conclusion is that there is no such thing, not even an ineffable one that, unfortunately, hard as we try, simply cannot be effed.

I take it that, for Wildman, meaning effectively determines truth and supervenes on use. I assume the opposite, on naturalistic grounds that Wildman also claims. I assume that truth, not meaning, is a better starting point for a theory of language, and that meaning supervenes on intersubjective understanding. That is, the attitude of holding-true is (among other things) what allows us to translate and interpret one another's utterances or writings with some degree of success on a regular basis. In saying this, however, I do not want to argue for a strong version of truth-conditional semantics according to which meaning is explained by truth-conditions. I hold merely to the project of stating meaning in those terms, thus preserving the important connection between truth and meaning.[31] Reversing the order of Wildman's apparent priority, I make holding-true the basis of all understanding of meaning in order to avoid unnecessary paradoxes and dead-end skeptical arguments. To make convention such a necessary element in language is to get it backward, I say. It is not that convention is a condition of language, but rather, as Davidson has put it, that "language is a condition for having conventions."[32]

Let me be clear about what I am not saying. First, I am not dismissing truth-conditional semantics altogether when I say that I do not support a strong version. I think we can state meaning in terms of truth-conditions, without holding that meaning is explained that way. Second, I am not proposing anything remotely resembling the logical positivists' position that the only meaningful statements are those that involve either empirical facts (of observation) or strictly analytic truths (a priori). This would make a theory of language not only useless in connection with religious language, but useless also with respect to any other application in the field of natural language. Nevertheless, we can endorse Davidson's general argument that knowledge of the circumstances under which someone holds sentences true is key to interpretation, or, as he puts it: "Although most thoughts are not beliefs, it is the pattern of belief that allows us to identify any thought; analogously, in the case of language, although most utterances are not concerned with truth, it is the pattern of sentences held true that gives sentences their meaning."[33]

Recognizing the impingement of conventions on "the pattern of sentences held true," we can also nudge holism in a more historicist direction that considers the importance of time, place, and context when we deal with the vagaries of religious uses of language. This requirement would make truth a relation that holds between a sentence, a speaker, and a time, but it would avoid falling into radical relativism or losing sight of the basic principle that language makes sense only against a background of knowing what counts as a truthful sentence. Language can be understood as relative to circumstances in a limited sense, one that covers a focus on "convention," without ceding the essentials of a Davidsonian theory of meaning. To see why, all we have to do is to turn the argument around and separate semantics and ontology from reference. We can then forego the notion of reference in any strong realist sense without giving up ontology or semantics. All this is possible because language presupposes a generalized grasp of what it is for a word to refer or for a sentence to articulate some truthful proposition.

In summary, while Wildman and I share a common commitment to naturalism, pragmatism, anti-anthropomorphism, fallibilism, and a host of other "isms," we diverge in our theories of meaning. To make convention the final ground of appeal, as Wildman appears to do, winds up relativizing language without leaving anything to which it could intelligibly be said to relate. As a theory of language, conventionalism, if thoroughgoing, explains nothing, and in fact removes the very grounds of rational explanation. Communication does not at all require rule-governed repetition—it simply makes frequent use of it. Therefore, convention does not help explain what is basic to communication—it just describes a frequent feature of it.[34] This feature is contingent.

How then should we take Wildman's interest in "effing the ineffable"? Can there be a "language" whose sentences are untranslatable into any of ours? This way of posing the problem assumes that translatability into a familiar tongue is, for good Davidsonian reasons, a criterion of languagehood. Elsewhere I have defended that thesis, and I do not reiterate the argument here, except to note several of its key steps.[35] The first step treats ineffabilism in religious studies as the methodological twin of incommensurability claims in the social sciences. By a common reductio argument, one can position proponents of ineffabilism with proponents of conceptual schemes so that they must deny the possibility of translation between one scheme and another, in which case they could not know something ineffable existed or that an alternative conceptual scheme existed without describing it or translating it, thus demonstrating its effability and translatability, after all.

The next step is to ask what it means to grasp the meaning of a sentence. One basic part of the answer, though not the whole, involves a revised picture of the mind and its place in nature. This consists in direct interaction between language users and public objects, where the terminal elements in the conditioning process determine the grasp of meanings, no matter the neural networks. As numerous authors have put it, this is a kind of "natural history of what is in the head." Sentences that we learn by being conditioned to hold them true by the presence of objects and circumstances in an environment form a web, providing language all the anchoring it needs to the world, where "world" signifies an ever-changing congeries of conditions. In the presence of words and sentences that are not learned in this basic way, as many religious cases typically are not, we face several choices. Suffice it to say here that all of these involve interpretive strategies that connect comparatively abstract levels of discourse with more concrete ways of talking in one order of derivation or another. My own choice is to interpret abstract God-talk or Ultimacy-talk, for instance, as parasitic upon the more concrete and starkly anthropomorphic character of popular piety. I think Wesley Wildman would agree with this assessment, but I wonder how far he would take its ramifications. Is the presence of popular piety a necessary condition for religious philosophy's comparative labors? If there came a time in the secular future in which popular piety died out completely, what work would religious philosophers have? My guess is that they would fall on exceedingly hard times, eventually becoming extinct, too.

The choice, then, is between three ways of taking talk about the gods. Patently false because unverifiable? That is the discredited way of logical positivism. Patently false but still harboring a germ of "symbolic meaning"? That is the disingenuous way of Theology. Patently false, period? That is the straightforward choice that many of us make these days, unable to understand "symbolic meaning." Those who resort to claims about "ineffability" seem to be admitting that they are not able to understand it either.

The final step in my argument is to say that if we can indeed interpret an alien conceptual scheme (so alien as to be called ineffable), then the ineffable is not Wholly Ineffable and so not, strictly speaking, radically incommensurable. This is on the assumption, to repeat, that intertranslatable languages express a common stock of concepts. On the other hand, if we cannot interpret that which is ineffable, then we have no grounds to attribute any meaning to the concept of the ineffable nor any evidence to support our saying that something is described truly as ineffable.

We ought, therefore, to reject the idea of something ineffable. Should we also reject the idea of "Ultimacy"? If it is tied to the idea of ineffability, yes. Yet, in the face of the reasoning outlined above, many religious believers will still object that human reason is too weak a reed to rely on, and "for all we know, something may be out there"[36]—ineffable, mystical, transcendent, Wholly Other, Ultimate Reality. Our inability to discriminate or identify radically different conceptual frameworks, so the objection goes, is not necessarily a strike against their existence. The "for all we know" objection derives initial plausibility from a sense that we ought not confuse what we can know with what there is, thus wrongly inferring ontology from epistemology. It sounds, at first, fair and suitably modest, just the sort of thing a fallibilist should say. After all, what do we ignorant humans know about the everyday mysteries of the internet, let alone the origin or destiny of the universe that our religious mythologies re-present to us? At the same time, we do know that there are sounds outside of human hearing range; we do not know what it would be like to hear them, yet we still characterize them as sounds. Are not religious cases that involve ineffability claims or Ultimacy similar?

The reply to this objection must begin by pointing out how utterly empty it is. In addition to simply saying "for all we know . . . ," we need some positive reason to accept that something is ineffable or ultimate. Unless a persuasive example can be cited, the discussion will degenerate into a fruitless effort to shift the burden of proof to the other side. Indeed, it is so hard to imagine what anything that different would be like that the example is unlikely to be met.

I think there is an even more decisive objection. The "for all we know" line of thought drives too much of a wedge between what we think we know and what there is. As such, it can never succeed, even in principle, for it threatens to dismantle what we mean by language and to derange our system of concepts. By our concepts and language we mean mental states and the meanings of our words and the contents of our reasons. These are publicly available. What we mean by our words is determined by what we intend them to mean, and what our audience takes them to mean. Meaning is, I repeat, a cooperative social affair, constituted by a triangular relationality between speaker, audience, and shared environment, and governed by the principle of charity. Therefore, no sense attaches to the possibility of concepts to which you could have access but that are in principle inaccessible to me. Alternatively, if they are accessible to you, then you are not, after all, faced with ineffability, and neither am I. Both of us may have to struggle to understand what we mean when an unfamiliar or obscure or vague concept pops up in sentences between us, but we will get the general gist.

A further point to consider in understanding why there cannot be a serious gap between what we know and what there is has to do with locating meaning at the distal stimulus, as Davidson does, not at the proximal stimulus, as Quine and others do in emphasizing the firing of sensory neurons.[37] What we engage with in patterns of interpretable, situated behavior is the object that our words and sentences mean or refer to. It just is our meaning the same thing by our words, regardless of any stimulation inside our heads. Unremarkably, we form our shared verbal behavior in relation to objects and events in the external world. If we said, instead, that meaning is located at the proximal stimuli of nerve endings, we would disastrously divorce truth and meaning, inviting truth relativized to individuals, and from there it would be an easy slide into skepticism. Once something is interposed between the world, as though on one side, and our beliefs and sentences, on the other, the doubt arises that there might in fact be a gap between what we know and what there is. The very intermediary (sensory stimuli) first called in to overcome a possible rift between objectivity and subjectivity turns out, on this theory, to underwrite yet more skepticism.

Far better, in my judgment, to adopt a different picture, according to which meaning and truth are not severed, and concepts are not considered ungraspable nor languages uninterpretable. What does it take to show the indissoluble link between meaning and truth? I think this is the same complicated question whose formal demonstration is simply contained in pairing some sentences (such as "snow is white") on the left of a T-sentence with an interpreting condition expressed in one's own language on the right. Is there still something, some meaning, not yet captured? The "for all we know" objection wants to answer yes. But to suspect a residue where none can be found is to support a host of other problems, such as relativism, skepticism, and the question of other minds. Only if what I mean and think has a necessary connection with the external world that I share with other speakers can I overcome the traditional dualism between inner meaning and external world. Only if the meanings of my words and contents of my thoughts are, in the first instance, dependent on contexts in which they are first learned, and in which I continue to use and think them, can we remove meaning from the relativist's suspicion that it is anchored primarily in subjectivity rather than intersubjectivity. Once we see how meaning is, in truth, anchored in an intersubjective world, the possibility of untranslatable languages and ungraspable concepts—in short, the possibility of ineffability—vanishes. What remains is only hyperbole, an exaggerated claim to the effect that something—an ineffable ultimate reality, a sacred object, or a form of human experience—exceeds all human understanding.

Taken together, the thesis that there is no such thing as symbolic meaning and the thesis that nothing is ineffable are vitally important in the academic study of religion. Because my perspective goes against the grain of recent work by Wesley Wildman about the presumed limits of language and the cogency of symbolic meaning, I have devoted much of this chapter to arguments against these views, as adapted from Davidson's two classic but controversial essays, "What Metaphors Mean" and "On the Very Idea of a Conceptual Scheme." In the first, proponents of symbolic meaning are positioned so that they must deny the possibility of paraphrase, and yet their only way of knowing any symbolic meaning is actually at work would be to paraphrase it, in which case, by making it literal, they will have denied it the status of symbolic meaning. In the second, proponents of ineffability are positioned so that they must deny the possibility of translation between our human form of life—taken as a conceptual scheme—and some other "ineffable" form of being taken as a conceptual scheme. If these parallel moves have been successful, they spell the death knell for the representationalist way of thinking about religious language, as well as the birth of a new, more naturalized understanding of the place of mind and language in nature.

Two questions seem to me most pressing as we tackle the multidisciplinary comparative inquiry that Wesley Wildman has so convincingly laid out. First, how are we to reject supernaturalism or personal theism tout court in a reasoned and non-dogmatic fashion? Second, how are we to espouse both anti-supernaturalism and methodological naturalism without scientism, the reductive doctrine that there is no knowledge other than scientific knowledge, of which physics forms the foundation?

To answer the first question, we can paraphrase Richard Rorty and say that the undiscussability of the supernatural is not the result of the exalted status of the divine but a consequence of trying to bestow that status on something pictured as outside of human schematizing.[38] As Wittgenstein said, "a picture has held us captive." Returning to the topic of ineffability, we can also say, in parallel fashion, that ineffability claims are the result not of trying and failing to say something significant about something profoundly surpassing human understanding, but rather of trying to bestow profound status on "airy nothingness," in Shakespeare's fine phrase, hoping to give it "local habitation and a name." And summing up my argument about symbolic meaning, we can say that the very idea of "symbolic meaning" or "symbolic truth" depends not on finding a meaning or truth that exceeds the literal, but on trying to bestow extralinguistic status on something lacking in any address as fixed by any canonical designator. It is like playing tennis without the net. There is no way in which to keep score if one can never know whether the serve goes over or not.

A second controversial question remains. Does the repeated and intelligent use of the scientific method yield extensive objective knowledge in a way that no other method for fixing belief can? Should we say that science, no longer conceived as narrowly empiricist, settles all questions of ontology so that, as Freud declares in ringing tones in the last sentence of *The Future of an Illusion*, "our science is no illusion, but an illusion it would be to suppose that what science cannot give us we can get elsewhere"?[39] If this amounts to the claim that the world consists exclusively of matter governed by laws of nature that are in principle described by science, and that qualities such as beauty or value are not independent of the mind but are humanly constructed responses to the world, then I advise that we reject the claim. It is nothing but scientism, a reductionism that has no place in the study of religion. The idea that science, especially physics, is the royal road to knowledge and truth is best understood as a variation on the idea that ecclesiastical authorities are in better touch with God than the laity. Stated positively, pragmatic naturalism has no trouble affirming two things. First, human life has an objective value and importance. Our values and moral convictions are not just humanly contrived responses that can be exhaustively explained as the outcome of the evolutionary process. Second, the universe is not merely an aggregate of material particles governed by a set of laws that we happen to experience as beautiful or sublime. The universe is genuinely awesome, and to feel that awe is not an aberrant feature of our mind but a proper response to what we have not made but which has made us.

Ecological studies have shown that human life is intertwined with the movements of the sun and moon, migrations of animals, and the advance and retreat of polar icecaps. Evolutionary theory has found that humankind's roots go back to early primates, backboned fishes, primeval sea worms, and the element-building stars. And biological studies have revealed that life extends to an attenuated pre-life hidden in the heart of inanimate matter. Religious naturalism holds that humans have no privileged position above or outside this web of nature and life. Indeed, we appear to be rather adventitious emergent forms in natural history and in cosmic evolution. As Stephen Jay Gould liked to point out, wind back life's tape to the dawn of time and let it play again—and you will never get humans a second time. Yet here we are, on this sun-drenched planet, looking out at a universe billions of years old, with about four hundred billion galaxies, each with about one hundred billion stars. Staggering in its beauty and unimaginable in its dimensions, the natural universe itself is as promising a candidate as any for Ultimacy, or its variants—God, the Sacred, Tao, Nothingness, Great Spirit, and so forth. Requiring no explanation beyond itself, nature—with all its constituents, principles, laws, and relationships—is far from ineffable, but it may well be ultimate.

In Defense of the Analytic Ascetic

While lauding his skill at creative coordination of discordant notes and integration of far-flung ideas, I invite Wildman's reply to the questions I have raised in this chapter. I have written, obviously, from the perspective of an unabashed "ascetic-analytic," the type that Wildman finds too inclined to "try not to construct anything."[40] Of the four types he identifies, he clearly identifies with the "comparing inquirer" and probably thinks my tendency toward analytical asceticism is a lot less fun. On the contrary, the analytical ascetic drinks freely from a cup that is always running over. She knows how to give herself over to things she does not fully understand. Her book is an open life. If she is, as Wildman says, "averse to direct speech about ultimate reality under any description,"[41] it is because she thinks that symbolic statements without literal meaning are blind, and religious concepts without semantic content are empty.

Let us not disparage the way the analytical ascetic values clarity of vision, coherent intellectual understanding, and spiritual vitality. She honors stillness at some moments and rides the waves of passion and exuberance at others. This world, with what Mary Oliver called its "untrimmable light," is her home, and these are the measures Wallace Stevens knew were destined for her soul. She has tasted her share of lotus, has marveled at moonbeams and mother of pearl, and has scaled the heights and discovered the depths. She is no stranger to the beautifully rendered and deeply moving experiences that Wildman writes about in Part 3 of *Effing the Ineffable*: Loneliness. Intensity. Bliss. It is simply that she sees no necessary connection between these experiences and Ultimate Reality. They are, to her, ordinary enough, which is to say quite extraordinary, while the extreme hypotheticity of Ultimate Reality strikes her as strained. It is not that "words cannot express," for words are ready at hand to do what words only and always do: render the menu, not the meal itself. She suspects that Robert Langdon is really an atheist and that Wesley Wildman is a mystic. They could be One and the Same, after all, and that would be another good Philonian point.

Notes

1. For Wildman's webpage, see http://www.wesleywildman.com/.

2. For Langdon's webpage, see http://www.randomhouse.com/doubleday/davinci/robertlangdon/.

3. Donald Davidson, "What Metaphors Mean," in *Inquiries into Truth and Interpretation* (Oxford: Clarendon Press, 1984), 245–46.

4. Davidson, "What Metaphors Mean," 259.

5. Recent critiques from within Western-centric philosophy of religion call for concerted engagement with global and indigenous religious traditions and deplore the parochial quality of the field. See Kevin Schilbrack, *Philosophy and the Study of Religions: A Manifesto* (Malden, MA: Wiley-Blackfield, 2014) and Thomas A. Lewis, *Why Philosophy Matters for the Study of Religion—and Vice Versa* (Oxford: Oxford University Press, 2015). I find their theses important and unobjectionable, though insufficiently aware of the work of Robert C. Neville for more than forty years, and of Wesley Wildman's further contributions to a comparative, nonparochial, nondogmatic philosophy of religions.

6. During the investigations of the Comparative Religious Ideas Project, culminating in a three-volume study in 2001, the term "ultimacy" was favored as encompassing both "ultimate realities" and "ultimate paths." Wildman's interest in metaphysical theories of ultimacy carried the term "ultimacy" forward.

7. Wesley J. Wildman, *Effing the Ineffable: Existential Mumblings at the Limits of Language* (Albany: State University of New York Press, 2018), 217.

8. Wesley J. Wildman, *Religious Philosophy as Multidisciplinary Comparative Inquiry: Envisioning a Future for Philosophy of Religion* (Albany: State University of New York Press, 2010), 83.

9. Ibid.

10. Wesley J. Wildman, *In Our Own Image: Anthropomorphism, Apophaticism, and Ultimacy* (Oxford: Oxford University Press, 2017), 195.

11. Wildman, *In Our Own Image*, 195–96.

12. Davidson, *What Metaphors Mean*, 258.

13. Wildman, *Effing the Ineffable*, 98.

14. Wildman, *Effing the Ineffable*, 97 (emphasis added).

15. Wildman, *Effing the Ineffable*, 98 (emphasis added).

16. It should come as no surprise that Wildman shares much in common with Paul Tillich, that Teutonic titan of mystical depths and ultimate concern, whereas I am closer to what I find displayed in the writings of Donald Davidson, but also of J. L. Austin, Ludwig Wittgenstein, and Stanley Cavell. What Cavell called "the uncanniness of the ordinary" perhaps best measures the distance between my work and Wildman's. I can appreciate the dictates of ordinary language without experiencing an irritable itch to get "beyond" it, as though there's some *there* there.

17. E. M. Forster, *A Passage to India*, quoted in Malcolm Diamond, *Contemporary Philosophy and Religious Thought* (New York: McGraw-Hill Book Co., 1974), 388.

18. In what follows I draw upon Donald Davidson's position in "What Metaphors Mean," 45–264.

19. Davidson, "What Metaphors Mean," 245.

20. Writers as diverse as Clifford Geertz, Peter Berger, and Robert Bellah conceive of religion as a special kind of symbol system that evokes a sense of ultimate, transcendent, encompassing meaning, where "meaning" has to do with "significance" rather than semantics. Robert Neville and Wesley Wildman fall ambiguously within this lineage. Neville is closer to C. S. Peirce than is Wildman, and Wildman is closer to Tillich.

21. I do not want to be overly insistent on this point, but simply to emphasize that the metaphor-without-meaning view rests on the primacy of semantics over pragmatics. See Donald Davidson, "Locating Literary Language," in *Literary Theory After Davidson*, ed. R. W. Dasenbrock (University Park, PA: Penn State University Press, 1992), 295–308, where Davidson explains, "In my essay 'What Metaphors Mean' . . . I was stubborn about the word 'meaning' when all I cared about was the primacy of 'first meaning'" (307, n. 4). Davidson did not change his mind about metaphors, but he did change his mind about the word "literal," preferring the term "first meaning."

22. Davidson, "What Metaphors Mean," 257.

23. Davidson, "What Metaphors Mean," 261.

24. Davidson, "What Metaphors Mean," 247.

25. This explains, I further suspect, the problem with the semiotic theory of religious symbolism inspired by Charles Sanders Peirce and systematically developed in an original way by Robert C. Neville as the current leading alternative to the theory I am advancing. For Neville, religious symbols are "iconically false and yet indexically true," as he writes in *Symbols of Jesus: A Christology of Symbolic Engagement*. Like Wildman's, Neville's "broken symbols" should be treated as on a par with Davidson's "patently false" metaphors, even though he would recognize only one category of signs—"iconic"—as false. For an important critique of this approach, see David Rohr, "How Can Human Symbols Represent God? A Critique

and Constructive Alternative to Robert C. Neville's Account of 'Indexical' Theological Truth," *American Journal of Theology and Philosophy* 40, no. 2 (2019): 73–97.

26. No such loss occurs in the very different goal of Robert Brandom's work to derive an "inferentialist semantics" from a detailed analysis of pragmatics or social practices, a non-eliminative project that reverses the priority of semantics over pragmatics. See especially his *Between Saying and Doing: Towards an Analytic Pragmatism* (Oxford: Oxford University Press, 2010).

27. Davidson, "What Metaphors Mean," 258.

28. Davidson, "What Metaphors Mean," 263.

29. In linking problems of ineffability with problems concerning symbolic meaning, I am drawing upon material I developed in "Naturalisms, Ineffability Claims, and Symbolic Meanings," in *Methodological Naturalism in Question*, ed. Jason N. Blum (Leiden: Brill, 2018), 104–28.

30. Stephen Bush, "Concepts and Religious Experiences: Wayne Proudfoot and the Cultural Construction of Experiences," *Religious Studies* 48, no. 1 (March 2012): 101–17.

31. I owe this insight to Terry Godlove, who has convinced me, over the years, that the project of *explaining* meaning in terms of truth conditions faces too many obstacles, some of which are spelled out in Michael Williams, "Meaning and Deflationary Truth," *Journal of Philosophy* 96, no. 11 (1999): 545–64. For his own way of handling the question of truth, see Terry F. Godlove, "Truth, Meaning, and the Study of Religion," *Method and Theory in the Study of Religion* (2017): 1–21.

32. Donald Davidson, "Communication and Convention," *Inquiries into Truth and Interpretation* (Oxford: Clarendon Press, 1984), 280.

33. Davidson, "Thought and Talk," *Inquiries*, 162.

34. Davidson, "Communication and Convention," 279–80.

35. In "Religion as a Mobile Army of Metaphors," in *Radical Interpretation in Religion*, ed. Nancy Frankenberry (Oxford: Cambridge University Press, 2002), 185–87. My skepticism about a meaning that cannot be expressed linguistically, or a form of activity that cannot be interpreted as language in our language, is shared by Donald Davidson, who said in a famous essay that it is tempting "to take a very short line indeed" with this question. See Davidson, "On the Very Idea of a Conceptual Scheme," *Inquiries*, 185. However, for most non-philosophers, the long route is required.

36. I have heard these exact words from my undergraduate students for four decades, suggesting that "out there" has become the new post-Hubble version of Plato's Cave.

37. Quine's proximal theory makes our neural nets intermediaries between the world, on the one hand, and our beliefs and utterances, on the other hand. This is Cartesian in spirit and consequence, according to Davidson in "Epistemology Naturalized," *Dialectica* 45, no. 2–3 (1991): 191–202.

38. Compare Richard Rorty, "Cultural Politics and the Question of the Existence of God," in *Radical Interpretation in Religion*, 53–77.

39. Sigmund Freud, *The Future of an Illusion* (New York: W. W. Norton Co., 1927).

40. Wildman, *In Our Own Image*, 4.

41. Wildman, *In Our Own Image*, 4.

10

Nature and *Homo religiosus* in Wildman's *Science and Religious Anthropology*

ROBERT S. CORRINGTON

Wesley Wildman and I share some striking philosophical and theological commitments, not least of which is our mutual affirmation of some form of "ecstatic naturalism." At the same time, we privilege the insights of evolutionary biology, cultural anthropology, liberal Protestant theology (especially Schleiermacher and Tillich), and a pragmatist theory of epistemology. Further, we each have struggled to be as capacious as possible in our understanding of the religious dimension of human experience as it unfolds in and as nature. We are linked in our strong rejection of reductionistic scientism that would purge our understanding of the self and its provenance of any deeply religious elements.

This is not to say that we agree on all, or even some essential, points, but that the family resemblances outnumber these contrasts. However, I bring up a few variations at the appropriate time. I wish to divide this chapter into two interlocking sections. For me, the most important conceptual territory lies in the discussion of religious naturalism and the issues of supranaturalism, supernaturalism, pantheism (which Wildman rejects as absurd), transcendence, and the nature of nature. Second, the depth dimensions of the human process, of *homo religiosus*, must be understood as they relate to nature and the sacred.

Religious Naturalism and the Nature of Nature

Wildman's understanding of religious naturalism is both generous and precise. It is generous in that it finds a place for a large number of what he calls "stakeholders" who have probed into religious phenomena in distinctive ways. His approach here is interdisciplinary in that he rejects the hegemony of any one methodology or conceptual set, say that of clinical psychology. Each legitimate stakeholder has something to contribute to the astonishing contour of horizons that encircles our understanding of *homo religiosus*. It is only by letting the best insights of each stakeholder enter the dialectic that an adequate picture can emerge of what it is to be religious in the context of nature. His perspective is precise insofar as he hews closely to a clearly defined understanding of just what limits scientific inquiry imposes on religious anthropology. He is critical of those theologians who soften the implications of hard science to smuggle in wooden and tribal beliefs. His commitment to universalism is directly tied to his positive evaluation of the deliverances of the sciences to a global understanding of the human process. He is both a universalist and a contextualist, but in different respects.

In affirming an ecstatic naturalism, Wildman, like me, follows in the lineage of Tillich, but with certain qualifications. He is almost strident in rejecting "sup*ra*naturalism," as was Tillich. It seems to me that "sup*er*naturalism" is just a more radical and even less legitimate form of supranaturalism and Wildman, Tillich, and I reject both. Supranaturalism affirms that the divine agent is both beyond the world yet alongside all beings (complexes). From my perspective, process panentheism is a softened form of supranaturalism, while avoiding some of its ontological commitments. For a supranaturalist, god is a determinate being with specific traits that/who created nature by an act or thought outside of the time process. Such a perspective affirms divine teleology, divine law, a self-conscious deity, a *Heilsgeschichte*, an anthropology of sin and grace, and perhaps a dose of apocalypticism. Supernaturalism goes even further and dis-severs the link between nature and its radical Other. In this case, a miracle is defined as a direct violation of the efficient causal laws of nature.

Wildman notes that for Tillich supranaturalism reduces god to a finite being and is thus a form of idolatry. One might be surprised to find Wildman's subsequent deep appreciation of Barth for making this same move in a very different theological context. This is an example of the generous spirit manifest in Wildman's book. On the flip side of the coin, or so the narrative usually goes, Schleiermacher comes in for the same praise, especially around his notion of "absolute dependence" on an infinite that is *unendlich* and thus a type of *Unendlichkeit* (infinity). For Schleiermacher and me, as well as for Wildman in his apophatic theology, the divine has no knowable traits *an si*ch. The genius of Schleiermacher is that he translates the traditional list of divine traits into phenomenological categories as they unfold in our higher consciousness. For example, instead of talking of a supernatural creation out of nothing, Schleiermacher describes the experience of a felt "whence" (a term that Wildman uses) that permeates our religious self-consciousness. Barth is right that this prepares the ground for Feuerbach and what Wildman and I might call the liberation of religious anthropology from dogmatics.

But this is not the end of the story. Tillich also affirms that *nature* is self-transcending in moments of ecstatic eruption from out of its ground and abyss. Here one makes a key distinction that may put Wildman and me on different sides of the fence. Wildman is happy to affirm that *homo religiosus* is self-transcending whenever there is a movement of inner human ecstasy within the confines of a nature that is not itself ecstatic, whereas I would affirm that nature is ecstatic whenever it breaks beyond its own plane of immanence into a stronger self-transcendence. However, nature's self-transcendence does not entail any form of supranaturalism as all such transcendence is always in and of the one nature that there is. Here our two forms of ecstatic naturalism seem to diverge. I call Wildman's form "ecstatic naturalism A" and my form "ecstatic naturalism B," or, as he would put it, ENA and ENB. While I don't like abbreviations, I honor his stylistic convention here.

But what is meant by the concept of the "self-transcendence" of *nature*? Using terminology with which Wildman is comfortable, this momentum is the unfolding of the transition from nature naturing to nature natured. This medieval (and current) distinction is a key to both ENA and ENB, but in different ways. The distinction has less play in ENA than in ENB because the latter is plunging into ontological waters that ENA would put off-limits. ENB defines "nature naturing" as "Nature perennially creating itself out of itself alone as manifest in innumerable potencies and emanations," whereas "nature natured" is defined as "The innumerable orders of the world without any contour or order-of-orders." The latter definition rejects any traditional process notion that nature is a grand organism or super order. There are only orders in a blinding variety of modes.

I suspect that one key difference between Wildman and me is in how we might envision Schelling-like potencies and Emerson-like emanations.

For ENB, potencies, as ejections, explode out of the unconscious of nature and are ontologically prior to the modal realm of actualities and possibilities. On the "gentler" side, there is no singular emanation from the Plotinian One, but an endless series of "smaller" emanations when nature naturing objectifies itself as nature natured. Emerson refers to the resultant product (nature natured) as "an endless chain of countless rings." No doubt, from the perspective of ENA, any talk of exploding ejections from out of the unconscious of nature sounds like upside-down supranaturalism. But as Tillich and his beloved Schelling might half-humorously ask: "But what is an abyss for?" ENB would answer: "To explain the ever-erupting link between the human unconscious and the unconscious of nature." But more of this later.

Can a religious naturalist define nature? Many have tried, but the answer is "no." The reasons are quite simple. First, to define something is to locate it in a genus with a specific difference. If you say that "nature is all that there is," then what possible genus could it occupy or be? And there could thus be no specific difference from something that is not a genus. Heidegger probed endlessly into the "ontological difference" between Being and things-in-being and found himself exasperated on the edges of language when it came to "talk" of Being. One of his more noted strategies was to cross out the word Being in his text; hence he wrote ~~Sein~~ or ~~Seyn~~ to give iconic power to the abyss separating any discourse about things-in-being, even as a totality, and Being. Here we can substitute the word "nature" for Being and write ~~nature~~. Thus, the word ~~nature~~ has no referent. Second, almost all philosophers have tried to find the one trait that is found in "all" orders of the world (nature natured). Many candidates have made their brief appearance on the stage: monads, substance(s), actual occasions, simples, words, spirit(s), matter, energy, secondary qualities, primary qualities, and so forth. Yet if nature is innumerable orders with no one trait in common, and no doctrine of internal relations to link them, then it follows that one can only talk of traits in the plural. ~~Nature~~ has no what.

As noted, Wildman has no truck with pantheism, which he claims has "no exemplars" in either mythology or philosophical theology. In a sense, he is right, and a religious naturalist must reject "strict" pantheism. Schopenhauer made the same point when he argued that if you simply equate god and nature, then one-half of the dyad is superfluous. Pick the half you want and be done with it. I agree. However, the traditional notion of pantheism is not the only form. What I have called a "deep pantheism" does not equate nature with some kind of divine being, but probes into the unconscious depths of the one nature that there is from which all gods and goddesses come, a point we deal with in the second section. Deep pantheism provides a plausible alternative to pantheism, process panentheism, and supernaturalism. This discussion would carry us too far afield.

Homo Religiosus and the Sacred

In this section I discuss the concept of the sacred in ENB and have some comments about the evolutionary context of *homo religiosus*. Wildman is friendly to the general worldview of Mircea Eliade, which starts and ends with the holy and numinous, in the tradition of Rudolf Otto, rather than beginning with a preestablished divine being. One distinct advantage of this starting and ending point is that it is both universalistic and pluralistic at the same time. It is universalistic insofar as it describes human religious experience in all times and all places using the same basic categories. Yet it is pluralistic insofar as it never allows any one manifestation of the sacred to usurp all others in a violent and tribal way. Now, I am reading Wildman into Eliade a bit here to reinforce a point that is dear to both ENA and ENB; namely, that there is no such thing as a self-validating revelation that rests on supranaturalistic warrant. Both forms of ecstatic naturalism utterly reject the concept of revelation if it is defined in traditional terms. Religious anthropology, with its constructivism, has made it clear that there is no way in which *homo religiosus* can pry itself free from culture-specific beliefs and unconscious projections. Yet it is a psychoanalytic fact that the recipient of a "revelation" eschews any pragmatic epistemology that would test the alleged revelation against a community of interpreters and refined introspection. The believer is locked into a nonreflexive content that can often issue in violence and a struggle of the powers as one revelation pits itself against others.

Very often the concept of revelation is directly tied to a belief that one and only one sacred text is the written version of the revelation. This leads to a literalism that ironically serves to deaden the text by flattening out its metaphors and symbols. Wildman is quite critical of textual idolatry. His extensive work in comparative religion makes him immune to such imperial claims. Put simply, the sacred cannot be confined to any given revelation or text. More strongly put, even if we could somehow "sum" all revelations and texts, we would not exhaust the possibilities of the presence/absence of the sacred dimensions of nature. As Karl Jaspers would put it, a text or a revelation is but a "cipher" of that toward which it points, never the thing itself. Tillich, of course, stresses the erotic and participatory dimension of any encounter with the sacred. For both ENA and ENB, neither revelation nor text can overcome the quarantine of apophatic theology.

Yet Wildman is sagacious enough to combine hard-edged apophatic theology with metaphysical boldness, especially when delineating fundamental (ontological) traits of the human process. Here I make a distinction between my use of the word "metaphysics" and my use of the word "ontology." I would argue that to be human is to use signs, a premier form of which is deposited in language. Insofar as one speaks and thinks in signs one has something of an inkling of the way of things, both within and without the self. This inkling will blossom into a deeper hunch about how things are put together and what things nature contains (I am using language loosely here). Simply put, most persons have a sense about the makeup of "whatever is, in whatever way it is." This sense can get deposited in a metaphysics that is always generic in scope, at least in intent. Thus, metaphysics is the broadest semiotic activity known to *homo religiosus*. Ontology, from my perspective, is a subaltern discipline within *metaphysica generalis*. One speaks here of ontologies in the plural—each is regional in scope, yet struggles to serve the larger metaphysical categorial array. Hence, we have an ontology of the self, of the pre-human organic, the inorganic, consciousness, the brain, ethical foundations, aesthetic traits, and so on. To do philosophy is to do a painstaking phenomenological description of regional ontologies as they emerge in a dialectic with the larger metaphysics that both shapes and is shaped by the regional ontologies.

Wildman's ontology of the human process is one that cleaves closely to neuroscience and posits a mind/brain continuity thesis. He is clear that, for him, consciousness cannot prevail outside of brain activity, and hence he rejects theories of the immortality of a soul substance, however defined. For ENB, immortality and reincarnation suggest themselves as the most warranted views on what happens to the core of the self after brain death. But these contraries cannot be settled here, or perhaps at all on this side of "death." What is important in this context is what happens to the self in this life. A key dimension of ENB is its strong commitment to an ontological reconstruction of psychoanalysis and its prospects for linking it to a metaphysics of nature. It is my belief that in this way one comes close to understanding *homo religiosus*.

The entry point to an ontology of the human process is a discussion of what I have called "sacred folds" as they activate the depth unconscious of the human process. What is a "fold" and what makes some of them "sacred?" The concepts of unfolding and enfolding have become commonplace in the literature, but they are used in far too generic a sense. Some ague as if everything is a fold of some kind, whereas ENB argues that only certain loci in nature function as folds in the fullest sense. A fold is best defined semiotically. When a network of interpretants—emotional, dynamic, or logical—heats up and gives off more meaning, the network starts to oscillate and rock back and forth, thereby becoming unstable. At a certain tipping point, the network begins to fold in on itself as its inertial energies find a core around which to rotate. C. G. Jung would understand this phenomenon as the creation of a "feeling-toned complex."

The now in-folded network of interpretants radiates semiotic energy to human sign users who have the innate capacity to respond to it. As more selves become attracted to this ongoing in-folding, the network becomes more powerful as a magnet for unconscious projections. The fold now becomes fuller of signs, qua interpretants, and brings a nascent human community into its orbit. Thus, the fold is sustained and strengthened, at least in the short run, by finite human projections that attach themselves to the fold. It must be remembered that all projections are unconscious and, for the most part, and for many, are beyond conscious scrutiny—hence their uncanny power over the self. At the heart of an individual's projections is the ultimate projection; namely, the transference. It is in the connection between the transference and the fold that the fold become sacred.

Within Freudian psychoanalysis, the transference is understood to be between the analyst and the analysand. For the analysand, the analyst becomes the screen for the unconscious projection of a parental imago that inflates the ontology and status of the analyst. This is potentially dangerous territory, as such a transference can stand in the way of individuation and can also invoke a countertransference in the analyst. ENB radicalizes this understanding of the transference to include non-human complexes, or complexes that get clothed with human traits. There is one more ontological layer to be considered. "Beneath" the transference and its connection to the sacred fold is the transferential field that is the conduit for all human projections, whether they be full transferences or only preliminary to one. The transferential field is not a projection, nor is it teleological in any way. Rather, it is the ultimate enabling condition that stands in the between, in this case, between the unconscious of the self and the unconscious of nature, thereby bringing them into contact with each other.

Homo religiosus becomes religious when it enters a transference relationship to the sacred fold via the enabling condition of the transferential field. It is seized by that which seems larger and more powerful than itself. And, in a sense, this is true. The sacred fold is an autonomous gathering of interpretants that have an inertial trajectory within the self and its regnant community. However, ENB agrees with ENA that the sacred and religious content of the sacred fold is, at least on the surface, a product of personal and cultural inscription as well as projection. There is no identity of contour between and among sacred folds. Each fold rests on its own bottom. Where Wildman and I might slightly part company is related to the question of what is left of the sacred fold after all inscription and projection are prescinded. Is there a core that is a part of nature in an extra-human sense?

I want to radicalize Peirce and claim that interpretant cables or networks can prevail outside of human interpreters and thus have their own energy and power. However, I want to be very clear that ENB rejects panpsychism with its imperil claim that all orders are to some degree mental or, in a weaker form of the position, nascently mental. Mentality is a regional ontological trait that cannot be stretched to the breaking point and shoved down the throat of nature. Note that I am not claiming that ENA is panpsychist. From this radicalization, I want to make the inference that the heart of the sacred fold exists prior, both temporally and ontologically, to the sequent projections and inscriptions that it draws to itself. The principle of individuation applies to sacred folds as well as to human beings.

On the other side, sacred folds are subject to entropy in the long run. Many years ago, I went to Olympia in Greece to see if there was anything left of Zeus at that sacred fold. It was starkly clear that his reign was over, both ontologically and existentially. Sacred folds come into being and go out of being, and no "one" religion is immune from this entropic logic. In the history of a so-called "singular" religion, many sacred folds can prevail in incompatible ways, both synchronically and diachronically. A given sacred fold can set fire to a tribal community and cause a massive uncritical transference to explode into internal and external warfare. Some, I among them, have argued that religious violence is the most lethal kind because it has both the power of the unassimilated unconscious and because it has its complete warrant within itself. Tribal violence and the demonization of the Other have deep evolutionary roots, especially around the problem of cheater detection in a time of scarcity. ENA and ENB envision the same scenario. If (genetic) kinship altruism is to evolve into non-kinship and social altruism, then all potential cheaters must be detected and ejected from the tribe. The best way to overcome cheating is for potential new members to take an oath of loyalty to the tribe that is backed up by a posited deity that is, of course, a projection of the imago and power of the tribal leader. Oath taking solidifies the connection between and among tribal members but can only function if there is a logically necessary demonization of non-tribal communities.

This evolutionary context is important. Wildman, using the latest scientific discoveries in genetics, makes it clear that inheritance is a more complex process than had been previously thought. We now know that the environment can shape gene expression in a causal way and that evolution is not a mere mechanical dialectic between random variation and natural selection. In fact, humans have and can evolve more adaptive strategies through the effects of environmental shaping. Wildman argues that while evolution seems to have no in-built teleology, there is a momentum toward complexification that in turn affects the trajectory of future evolution. Using Peirce's language, he adopts what could be called a "developmental teleology" that is now in the grasp of the human process. One implication of this is that religious self-shaping has a direct hand in our evolutionary development.

Above, the issue of gods and goddesses was broached. There need not be a conflict here between ENA and ENB. Wildman has a secular approach to the phenomena of religion, but never in a reductive sense. He defines his position as "the modern secular interpretation of humanity (MSIH)." Yet he also claims, perhaps rightly, that he also has a theological agenda that works in consort with MSIH. But this agenda is a radical apophatic one that clears away much of the history of theology, both "Western" and Asian. What is left seems to be a variant on Schleiermacher's wonderful phenomenology of higher consciousness with its sense of the potency of the infinite to enter into and alter the structures of consciousness—perhaps even the brain itself. But if we have a taste for and sense of the trait-less infinite, what happens to the finite gods and goddesses who populate religious history, and presumably always will?

ENB, like ENA, is indebted to the grand history of religions approach with its appreciation of the shifting signs and symbols of religion. The question becomes: where do these symbols come from, and how deeply do they go into the abyss of nature's unconscious? Gods and goddesses are concrescences of primal archetypes that emerge out of the fissuring between nature naturing and nature natured. In this sense, they are energy-charged sacred folds that have a nascent potential to become clothed with human Feuerbach-like projections. Both Wildman and I would argue that Krishna never was and never will be an autonomous self-conscious being who prevails outside of human projections. Yet Lord Krishna has had and will continue to have evolutionary effects on the changing shapes of Hindu religious self-conscious. In a sense, Krishna is in the DNA of his devotees and can work his effects there via developmental teleology. Projection generates an ontologically strange kind of counterprojection with real effects. Krishna can change those who are bound up with him.

While Wildman would distance himself from the "wilder" aspects of my archetype theory as it relates to the self-fissuring within the one nature that there is, he would be quite open to the power of at least the cultural inscription that activates, if not power-filled archetypes, then at least universal cultural forms. His distaste for postmodern hyperrelativism and irresponsible linguistic *jouissance* is to be commended in an era in which sections of the academy have narcissistically removed themselves from real social discourse in the tradition of John Dewey. His rootedness in the body and the personal and social brain keep his ontological feet on the ground of actual religious experience as it is lived by human beings.

Conclusion

Wildman is not unaware of some of the difficulties of instantiating MSIH, noting, for example, that Asian religions might have a harder time doing so than the Western monotheisms. Yet our two forms of ecstatic naturalism are in deep harmony concerning the value of MSIH in clearing the decks of dangerous and divisive theological constructs and affiliations. While secularity runs the risk of becoming a religion itself, it can, if used carefully, provide the nonprejudicial clearing within which the world religions can interact with each other in far less tribal and violent ways.

I do worry about one thing. I worry that ENB might run the risk of invoking deep unconscious powers that can unleash the shadow side of the human process and turn *homo religiosus* into a monstrosity. Yet these shadow powers, as so brilliantly described by Jung and Wilhelm Reich (the emotional plague), are always and everywhere afoot. Human history is, among other things, the history of mass genocides, and this process will continue, especially and largely because of climate change. For example, India has built a double-layer fence around all of Bangladesh, and its military kills anyone who gets too close to it. What this means is that with the rise in sea level that has already taken away parts of Bangladesh, its citizens will be unable to migrate to higher land when the situation becomes urgent. The Bangladesh population will suffer mass death in the decades to come. This is religious and national tribalism at its worst.

Yet ENB, by invoking these powers, does provide a mirror onto the human process and calls it to a confrontation with the social shadow that now threatens to accelerate the death rate even beyond its current level. If life is truly governed by the eruptions from the unconscious, both the collective human form and the natural form, then it is only by acknowledging this that any long-lasting amelioration is possible. Thus, while I do worry that my form of ecstatic naturalism might be too "wild," I also believe that its confrontation with the social unconscious is a necessary but not sufficient condition for the full well-being of *homo religiosus*.

Wildman's "tamer" form of ecstatic naturalism has one distinct advantage, namely, that it lowers the ontological stakes between and among religions to such an extent that violence can be outflanked by the implementation of MSIH. I share this dream and understand the power of Wildman's approach. His sharp clarity and profound understanding of the most current work in the universalizing sciences represent a strong curative for supranaturalism and its relation to violence.

It is not necessary to choose between ENA and ENB in some rigid dyadic sense. It is clear to me that we are in the gravest human crisis in species history and that a multitude of approaches are called for to help alleviate unjust and horrific conditions. We are already in the era of mass death and mass migration because of climate change, and religious anthropology is a key player in reshaping our self-understanding of the evolutionary and cosmological frameworks of our travail. Where I tip the hat to Wildman is in my recognition that his use and understanding of science and the intersection of various stakeholders may be more genuinely pragmatic than mine. While we both self-identify with pragmatism and pragmatic epistemology, his form is more grounded in current causal interactions, while my form is more poetically eschatological. In the end, given this hat tip, do I think that ENA is better for our future than ENB? I believe that both are necessary but that Wildman's approach may have the greater chance of making the kinds of radical changes in our religious self-understanding that are called for.

PART 3
SCIENTIFIC APPROACHES

11

Relating within Wildman's Integrative Engagement with Psychology, Spirituality, and Humility

Steven J. Sandage

I start this chapter with a few personal reflections about Wesley J. Wildman. I first met him in 2012 when I applied for a faculty opening at Boston University in pastoral psychology and Wesley was chair of the search committee. It was during a pivotal transition in my career at a time when my wife and I were open to making a cross-country move for our family, but we had a couple options and felt little margin for a significant mistake. Wesley hosted that process with what I came to know as some of his characteristic "stabilizing" traits—a warm affability, generous and attentive hospitality, and the kind of respectful candor that moves right into the heart of things. I ended up at Boston University for many reasons, but I experienced Wesley's personable style of leadership in that process as unique and significant in our decision-making.

There is one specific anecdote in that narrative that Wesley might prefer I refrain from sharing, but it encapsulates some key dynamics in my experience of Wesley as a scholar and as a person. During the on-campus interview, we were walking to dinner one night, and Wesley was describing a psychometric measure of spirituality he had been working to develop. I naively asked who was running the factor analysis for him and he said, "I am doing it." I remember laughing with surprise, as when one's plausibility structures have been fractured. I was coming from a school where many of the theologians were uncertain whether psychological research was a legitimate endeavor, and I was shocked that a theologian was doing advanced statistical analyses. Failing to reign myself in, I asked, "Where did you learn to do factor analysis?" Wesley said something like, "Well . . . there are books on it you can read."

The real personal lesson for me in this story came the second time I relayed this experience to someone in Wesley's presence when he quite tactfully communicated to me that my amazement was less validating than condescending. He was not harsh but candid. And that is when I really put it together—Wesley Wildman is, quite simply, a seeker of insight, synthetic understanding, and practical transformation. He respects academic disciplines and the limits of his own expertise, but he does not subscribe to modernistic intellectual segregation through rigid disciplinary boundaries. When he wants to engage a certain question, he exercises the agency to learn the literatures and methodologies necessary to pursue that quest, whether that involves science, religion, or other disciplines. He is not looking for acknowledgement of his interdisciplinary talent and agility and would prefer we stay focused on what he considers the deeply compelling questions we get to explore as human seekers. In this chapter, I affirm a number of Wildman's ideas and contributions, but mostly I hope to do so with the seriousness and commitment that is consistent with his values.

Below, I consider some of Wildman's work in relation to psychological research on humility, so I want to note a couple of personal points about Wildman and humility. First, reading his recent works helped me better understand and appreciate the strengths and limitations of my own theological perspective, which is different from Wildman's ground-of-being theology. Rather than prompting theological defensiveness, Wildman gets me to wrestle with myself. I was actually moved by Wildman's intellectual humility in portraying other theological orientations with such respect, fairness, and generosity while still offering critique, and this led me to reconsider some of my own scholarly tendencies that can be less charitable.

At the interpersonal level as his faculty colleague, I have also clashed with Wildman on a couple of occasions, though he and I have been on the same side of the table in other conflicts. At the end of the day, he offers the same relationship either way—he asks about my family, invites me to lunch, or proposes some new collaborative project. It would be nice to experience more of that in academia.

As a psychologist, I am unqualified to fully engage Wildman's multidisciplinary expertise as a philosopher, theologian, and ethicist. But his work makes considerable use of psychology and other social sciences, and he even occasionally ventures into the terrain of mental health, which is my field of professional practice. We also share a particularly strong interest in interdisciplinary understandings of spirituality, intense spiritual experiences, and spiritual transformation. Thus I consider some of his work in that area in conversation with my research on a model of relational spirituality and humility.[1] I work across several scholarly domains: (a) the psychology of religion, (b) the integration of psychology and theology, (c) positive psychology, and (d) clinical and counseling psychology. Wildman's contributions have relevance for each of these fields of inquiry; thus I highlight some points of potential rapprochement or bidirectional influence in these areas organized around (a) relational interdisciplinarity and (b) relational spirituality and ultimacy manifestations (i.e., loneliness, intensity, and bliss).

Relational Interdisciplinarity

I start by offering a relational reading of Wildman's approach to interdisciplinarity and suggest points of connection to a *relational integration* approach to religion and science and theology and psychology, more specifically. The framework of relational integration emerged from my interdisciplinary work on psychology and theology with two theologians—F. LeRon Shults and Jeannine Brown.[2] This framework starts by foregrounding the actual relational dynamics between scholars or professionals attempting (or resisting) interdisciplinary collaboration. By "dynamics," I mean various systemic, interpersonal, and emotional processes that impact possibilities of cooperation and collaboration, such as anxiety, trust, power, curiosity, envy, respect, prejudice, generosity, and social privilege, among others. These kinds of complex emotional and relational dynamics are clearly relevant to theologically and psychologically informed views of human nature, yet they draw barely any consideration in literature on interdisciplinarity.[3]

The relational integration model also emphasizes attention to the epistemological ordering and power dynamics (i.e., the forms of relationality) conceptualized between the disciplines.[4] Some approaches to the conversation between psychology and theology tend to privilege one of the disciplines to regulate or colonize the other.[5] For example, the Christian psychology view prioritizes the recovery of historical Christian theological and biblical resources to shape research on a distinctively Christian psychology, with theology playing a "prophylactic" role to "bracket the substance of twentieth century psychologies."[6] Other approaches to the psychology and theology conversation take more exclusionary relational stances. For example, both biblical counseling[7] and classical Freudian psychoanalysis promote a strong hermeneutic of suspicion toward one of the disciplines, which is viewed as inferior, largely unhelpful, and even epistemically distorted. Levels-of-explanation approaches have held some prominence in psychology and theology conversations,[8] and these views tend to affirm differing disciplines as independent sources of knowledge for examining different levels of reality to set up interdisciplinary dialogue or "parallels."[9] Integrative approaches involve a deeper level of bidirectional influence and interpenetration between psychology and theology than these other approaches and typically attempt to achieve a high level of interdisciplinary coherence amid disciplinary differences.

The integration movement related to psychology and theology started within evangelicalism in the United States, so it might seem odd to bring Wildman's work into conversation with this field of study because his institutional affiliations have not been evangelical. Moreover, his philosophical and theological perspective of religious naturalism would be quite problematic for those who hold to evangelical theological convictions. It is also not completely clear how Wildman might describe his own efforts at interdisciplinary engagement between psychology and theology in light of the approaches summarized above, although he has spoken of integrating "evolutionary biology, cognitive psychology, the social sciences, and religious studies" in the study of intense religious and spiritual experiences.[10] Shults and Neville (chapter 1) have pointed out the systematic nature of Wildman's thinking or how thinking in one domain impacts thinking in another. He has offered a major proposal of religious philosophy as multidisciplinary comparative inquiry (MCI) with the goal of bringing multiple disciplines into scholarly interaction; thus he is interested in comparing and connecting disciplines and does not limit himself to two disciplines.[11] However, for my purposes here I describe him as an interdisciplinary integrationist who brings together highly resonant and coherent perspectives from psychology and theology in ways that are textured, well-grounded in research, and evocative for fresh intellectual constructions. In fact, if we take the process of "integration" to involve exploring potential bridges between differing disciplines or perspectives, it is striking to see how his corpus of work is filled with this kind of bridging of (a) religion and science, (b) differing religious traditions, (c) philosophy and theology (and other disciplines), (d) differing philosophical methodologies and traditions, and (e) liberal and evangelical Christian traditions. Below, I outline four reasons I commend Wildman's relational style of interdisciplinarity to scholars and students interested in (a) the integration of psychology and theology and (b) the psychology of religion.

First, Wildman offers an example of strong conceptual resonance and coherence as an integrationist. Warren Brown has promoted a resonance model of the integration of psychology and theology that does not expect an exact fit between the disciplines but uses resonance as a metaphor for a goal of relative fit within a particular set of interdisciplinary conversation partners.[12] This also makes sense within a relational integration framework, as it would be unrealistic to try to integrate all of psychology and theology or to expect an exact fit between disciplinary perspectives. Rather, it makes more sense to bring particular psychological theories and bodies of research into conversation with particular theological traditions to explore resonance, and this is what Wildman does.[13]

While he touches on a wide variety of psychological literatures, my reading of his recent works makes it clear his formal engagement is strongest with evolutionary and cognitive branches of psychology, which he relates to his ground-of-being theology. He also has a committed existential sensibility that infuses his psychological, philosophical, and spiritual perspectives. My own theoretical preferences within psychology and theology are generally rather different from Wildman's aside from our mutual appreciation for existentialism, but his ground-of-being theology and philosophy combined with a kind of evolutionary existentialism make for a very unique, and I would say coherent, integrative perspective. I see few integration-of-psychology-and-theology scholars achieving this kind of coherence, so Wildman offers a helpful example even if readers do not share his theoretical and theological orientations.

Second, Wildman's ground-of-being theology strongly resists anthropomorphism and does not conceive of the divine as personal in any sense. He explains, "God is not in the caring business" (64). As suggested above, I think this is quite consistent with his primary choices of psychological literatures drawing from evolutionary and cognitive psychology, in addition to neurobiology and certain existential perspectives. Wildman notes Pew survey data indicating nearly that one-third of respondents in the United States say they believe in God but do not understand God primarily in personal terms, suggesting there may be an intellectual market for theologies that cast the divine in less personal ways. If Wildman is correct about this, it is also possible that his approach could help expand the intellectual market of those interested in the integration of psychology and theology beyond the dominant agential-being theological options coming from scholars within evangelical contexts. Moreover, theology has historically achieved very minimal interdisciplinary engagement with mainstream psychology in the United States or with psychology of religion as a subfield,[14] and it is possible that Wildman's religious naturalism and ground-of-being approaches might be more palatable to some psychologists who are not interested in theologies with a personal conception of God.

Third, while calling Wildman a conceptual "integrationist," I should also point out that he thoroughly acknowledges the dis-integrative movements within nature, society, and personal embodiment as necessary relational complements to integrative themes. Some of us interested in the integration of psychology and theology have called for greater dialectical (i.e., relational) attention to themes of dis-integration to do justice to the complexities of the processes of human development, negation and loss, and transformation.[15] Wildman is a good example of this kind of integrative-disintegrative dialectical thinking, influenced in part by his engagement of evolutionary biology, apophatic spiritual traditions, existentialism, and dynamical systems theory, among other streams of influence. While referencing the ground-of-being, he also speaks of the abyss and the abysmal. This attention to the *dis*-integrative adds complexity and realism to the relational integration of psychology and theology and resists the pull toward idealistic conceptualizations that are far removed from the traumatic messiness of life and death.

Fourth, I want to highlight Wildman's interreligious expertise and his substantive depth engagement of different spiritual and religious traditions in his multidisciplinary work. The integration of psychology and theology field has been distinctively Christian in the United States, though my recent personal experience has been to note a growing hunger for interreligious dialogue among psychology doctoral students in some evangelical contexts. The psychology of religion subfield in the United States has been a bit more religiously diverse, but not as much as some might expect or desire. It is rare to find a scholar as conversant as Wildman across spiritual and religious traditions who can also dialogue with scholars in psychology, neurobiology, and related scientific disciplines, and Wildman has helped me personally in expanding my religious and spiritual diversity awareness. He would be the first to acknowledge that his theological and religious assertions will not fit with all traditions, but his writings will help readers better understand a variety of traditions and offer intellectual tools for a broader set of integrative constructions.

Philosophical and Methodological Pluralism

Wildman's philosophical and methodological pluralism, as evidenced for example in his MCI approach and his original mixed method research in the psychology of religion, are also noteworthy from a relational integration perspective.[16] For example, he uses frameworks and methodologies from pragmatic, analytical, and continental philosophical approaches, and it would be difficult to find parallels in the field of psychology (at least in the United States). Pragmatic philosophy is underutilized in Western psychology despite the important historical connections to William James and John Dewey, though the emerging strength of practice-based research in psychotherapy indirectly reflects certain pragmatist sensibilities. At the risk of generalization and despite some valuable moves toward more mixed method research in psychology, I view the fields of psychology and psychotherapy in the United States as largely divided between those scholars who would tend to resonate with analytical philosophical modes of reasoning and those who would prefer continental philosophical perspectives. The rational and logical clarity and precision of analytical philosophy could be roughly associated with scholarly modes of thought among those preferring the more objective quantitative methods of research and empirically supported approaches to treatment (e.g., prominent among cognitive-behavioral therapy theorists). Conversely, the continental philosophical emphases on history, context, phenomenology, social critique and deconstruction, and hermeneutics are more popular among qualitative researchers and psychoanalytical and humanistic psychotherapy theorists who value human subjectivity. These differences would also map onto psychologists' preferences for constructivist or realist ontologies. Sadly, these underlying (and often implicit) philosophical differences among psychotherapy researchers too often result in a kind of hostile tribalism and debates about the "gold standard" of psychotherapy, which miss the kind of complex and multitextured scholarly work and creatively probing intellectual attitude we find in Wildman and his MCI approach.

One of the reasons for the segregation of quantitative and qualitative research methods in psychology (and social science, more generally) may be the relative absence of ontological and epistemological paradigms that can help hold and integrate these differing methodologies and orientations toward knowing. In research discussions, it is common to hear stark contrasts offered between quantitative and qualitative methodologies with associations made to positivist and constructivist paradigms, respectively. Researchers are sometimes warned not to try to mix "the two" paradigms.

Some colleagues and I have articulated a hermeneutical realist paradigm for psychological research using quantitative and qualitative methods,[17] and others have described similar integrative perspectives based on critical realism or versions of constructive realism. Wildman's MCI research could be useful for further explicating an integrative philosophical paradigm that can hold differing social science methodologies. His own mixed method research on narratives of religious and spiritual experiences is a very unique example of integrating quantitative, phenomenological, and narrative methodologies and could serve as an example for consideration by psychologists of religion interested in philosophically integrative approaches.[18]

Interdisciplinary Realism

After commending and celebrating Wildman's interdisciplinary work, I feel an obligation to also practice Wildman-like realism in considering some of the challenges of interdisciplinary scholarship. On the positive side, research-funding initiatives are increasingly calling for interdisciplinary submissions with the understanding that multiple disciplines are often necessary to improve solutions to real-world problems.[19] However, it is also clear that not all scholars value interdisciplinary research and epistemological pluralism. Interdisciplinary scholarship can be hard for tenure and promotion committees to evaluate, particularly given the historical expectation in many settings that scholars will accumulate outputs and accomplishments in a single discipline. Wildman's impressive history of teaching science literacy to doctoral students in religion and science is mentioned in the opening chapter of this volume, but it is typically challenging and time-consuming to facilitate learning of multiple disciplines at a level that can promote scholarly collaboration and productivity. Moreover, interdisciplinary gatherings among scholars, in my experience, prove effective about half of the time, with key challenges including the kinds of competitiveness, emotional reactions, and other power dynamics referenced above. Institutional power dynamics can also inhibit interdisciplinary research, such as when leaders of a certain discipline seek to bolster their influence or resources with a zero-sum game mindset and at the expense of interdisciplinary cooperation. A wealth of social psychological research makes it clear that it takes more than mere contact to promote cooperation among different groups, so we cannot just throw scholars of differing disciplines in a room and expect that genuine interdisciplinary cooperation and productivity will happen without the development of relational virtues and shared goals that will give meaning to the sacrifices involved.[20]

I would personally like to see more research on team science and interdisciplinary approaches to scholarship to better identify the processes and practices that facilitate effective collaboration. I would love to see Wildman further contribute to this work based on his extensive experience working with scholars from various disciplines. There is now a fascinating field of dissemination and implementation science that both studies the ways scientific research on clinical interventions can be effectively translated and implemented into frontline clinical practice, and identifies the multiple barriers that often prevent science-practice integration.[21] A parallel body of research might investigate facilitators and barriers of interdisciplinary collaboration. The growing psychological literature on humility offers some interesting possibilities for identifying a key interdisciplinary virtue.

Multidimensional Humility

One morning in 2013 while I was staying with Wildman and his family on a house-hunting trip, I remember asking him if he had written on any of the virtues. He said "no." So I was surprised to later discover that humility was a main theme of his book *Found in the Middle!: Theology and Ethics for Christians Who Are Both Liberal and Evangelical.*[22] This book, along with *Lost in the Middle?: Claiming an Inclusive Faith for Christians Who Are Both Liberal and Evangelical,*[23] represents efforts to articulate the contours of a moderate Christian faith between the extremes of liberalism and conservatism. Perhaps Wildman was being humble when he said he had not written on virtue, or maybe he assumed I meant scholarly writing and was not counting these more popular-level books. Whatever the case, *Found in the Middle* offers many important points about humility and the constructive role of humility in bridging differences between people and different ways of thinking. In 2009, there was very little scientific research on humility available, but psychological research on humility has greatly expanded in recent years, and humility has become a key virtue in my own work on models of (a) the relational integration of psychology and theology and (b) relational spirituality.

Wildman and Garner[24] argue that humility is a cardinal virtue, "essential to all theology" (8) and a "watchword for theology" (18). They seek to describe a type of mature Christian humility that makes room for passion, one that "reduces disappointment and increases resolve" (10) and is more open and curious than closed and defensively arrogant. Humility is included in their proposal of pluralism principles (along with perseverance, empathy, and love), explaining, "the principle of humility recognizes that life is complicated, human wisdom is always partial, and divine reality is beyond human comprehension and control" (92).

Of course, there are different definitions of humility across the history of religious and theological traditions. For example, Calvin[25] described a somewhat different construal of humility from that of Wildman and Garner, saying:

> For I do not call it humility if you suppose that we have anything left . . . We cannot think of ourselves as we ought to think without utterly despising everything that may be supposed an excellence in us. This humility is unfeigned submission of a mind overwhelmed with a weighty sense of its own misery and poverty; for such is the uniform description of it in the word of God. (604)

Calvin's view of humility is hard to differentiate from shame, and this differential is a major concern in contemporary psychological literature on humility. Thus, Calvinist theology would seem to fit with a psychology of humility that would be hard for many contemporary psychologists to understand or endorse. My own preference is for relational process theologies that posit the involuntary self-limitation of God consistent with human freedom. Wildman has critiqued this kind of theology as depicting a God who is "incompetent" (179; and Calvinists would agree); however, I would call this self-limited God an exemplar of humility.[26] Wildman's ground-of-being theology would also be intriguing to integrate more explicitly with contemporary psychological research on humility, and I propose some potential points of integrative research below.

First, Wildman and Garner suggested that religious leaders should set a standard of humility in contrast with temptations to spiritual superiority, self-promotion, and self-protection. Emerging empirical research on humility with seminary students and experienced religious leaders has supported these intuitions with trait levels of humility being negatively associated with spiritual grandiosity, psychological narcissism, and existential defensiveness.[27] While many theological traditions have historically contrasted humility with pride or what psychologists would now call grandiose narcissism, there is now evidence that there are multiple spiritual barriers to humility beyond grandiosity, including insecure attachment to God, vulnerable or shame-prone versions of narcissism, and a hunger to idealize others that often leads to disappointment and hostility.[28] My colleagues and I have developed a relational spirituality model of humility, which suggests that relational development processes of differentiation and attachment are important mediators of connections between humility and psychological and spiritual health to overcome these multiple barriers, and we have also found that a relational spirituality orientation toward questing, seeking, or exploring can be consistent with highly differentiated forms of humility.[29] This model is generally consistent with Wildman and Garner's idea of integrating humility with healthy forms of confidence, selfhood, agency, and the value of spiritual seeking. But there is plenty of room to further elaborate and investigate relational spirituality and humility, and the apophatic leanings of ground-of-being theology may be particularly helpful for conceptualizing the roles of complexity and tolerance of ambiguity in mature forms of humility.

Second, Wildman and Garner[30] proposed the theme of "reverent humility" to inspire the "radical inclusiveness of the Christian gospel, breaking boundaries of class and culture and reaching out in transforming love across political and religious differences" (165). This seems to imply a correlation between humility and commitments to the openness and widening circle of social and intercultural concern. In fact, our research team has published several studies validating positive associations between humility and commitments to (a) intercultural competence (i.e., relating effectively across cultural differences)[31] and (b) social justice (i.e., a concern for equity for all people).[32] Wildman and Garner's casting of humility and openness to diversity also fits into a larger and growing body of psychological literature on cultural humility among helping professionals, which is showing significant effects in predicting psychotherapy outcomes for cultural minorities.[33] However, if those of us in Christian communities in the United States ask ourselves how much of this radically inclusive humility we are witnessing these days, it may challenge our own humility and capacities to contend with disappointment. I think this point brings us back to important issues of definitions and conceptualizations of humility. For example, is humility intended to be primarily an in-group virtue to reinforce hierarchy and submission to powerful deities and leaders? We might call this a downward view of humility. Or does the virtue of humility necessitate practicing out-group humility to ever widening sets of social relationships and in solidarity with those who are oppressed? This may require more complex and dialectical forms of humility that steer a middle path between the ditches of shame and narcissism. I can anticipate Wildman arguing that ground-of-being theologies could be useful for this kind of dialectical humility because particular religious communities cannot rely on their own personal God to privilege them vis-à-vis other communities or specially protect them from the vicissitudes of suffering and other existential realities. In the relational spirituality model, the spiritual seeking dimension involves questing toward more complex spiritual understandings of self and other, and ground-of-being theologies do place a strong emphasis on this kind of existential questing.

Third, Wildman and Garner also suggest that humility requires more than theological awareness and necessarily includes communal practices that encourage humility. They do not specify the kinds of communal practices they hypothesize to be facilitators of humility, but this thesis is generally consistent with the *dwelling* dimension of our relational spirituality model in suggesting that the practice of spiritual virtue is influenced (for better and for worse) by relational dynamics in the surrounding holding environments. Our qualitative research on humility among religious leaders is pointing to the importance of communal or organizational dynamics and the strain it places on leaders to try to practice humility if their surrounding systems do not. On the positive side, leadership teams that foster an environment of humility tend to make it easier for individual leaders to function in humble ways and without excessive egotism. The interesting research questions here involve better understanding specific communal practices that promote humility, as well as further investigating the positive impact of leader humility on various outcomes for organizations.[34]

Fourth, the growing empirical literature on intellectual humility would be interesting to bring into conversation with Wildman's body of work. For example, Wildman and Garner[35] suggest that theological debates should be grounded in a relational ethic of humility and love, which includes "love of opponents and humility before God" (23). This speaks to certain affective and motivational aspects of humility within religious dialogue and debate, but the kind of intellectual humility needed for (a) MCI and (b) interdisciplinary collaboration is surely broader. Whitcomb and colleagues have offered a philosophical definition of intellectual humility as a proper attentiveness to and owning of one's intellectual limitations.[36] Intellectual humility does not involve global negativity toward one's intellectual limitations or a denial of intellectual strengths but rather an openness to other perspectives and intellectual contributions. This is clearly consistent with aspects of humility necessary for intercultural competence, as mentioned above, such as a willingness to contain judgement long enough to empathically consider cultural perspectives other than one's own. There is a striking similarity in the difficulties some individuals have frame-shifting into other cultural and disciplinary/role perspectives, while others have the cognitive and emotional flexibility to do both regularly with minimal stress. Whitcomb and his philosopher colleagues collaborated with psychologists in developing a psychometric measure of intellectual humility based on their theory (and this interdisciplinary accomplishment is certainly suggestive of intellectual humility), which showed incremental validity in predicting openness and close-mindedness over and above other measures of intellectual humility.[37]

A review of research on intellectual humility is well beyond the scope of this chapter, but I want to mention a couple of relevant findings. Among Christian pastors, intellectual humility has been positively associated with religious tolerance (defined as respecting the rights of everyone to choose and practice their religion and the relational attitude toward those of different religious traditions),[38] and religious tolerance was associated with religious diversity exposure but only at high levels of intellectual humility.[39] This invites research questions about (a) the potential limited benefits of religious diversity exposure for individuals lacking intellectual humility and (b) the educational or formative processes that might help leaders integrate intellectual humility and religious tolerance in the ways Wildman and Garner promote.

In a study with religious leaders from the Abrahamic faiths, my colleagues and I found that religion-specific intellectual humility was positively associated with both religious exploration and insecure attachment to God while also negatively associated with spiritual grandiosity. These findings suggest that religious leaders who are questing and stretching into intellectual humility with regard to their religious beliefs may experience increased anxiety without the self-esteem buffering that can come from greater religious certainty and spiritual superiority in relation to others. This risk was attenuated for those with high levels of characterological humility, which suggests the formation-based point that it could be dangerous to encourage growth in intellectual humility without corresponding holistic attention to other emotional and behavioral aspects of more general humility (including accurate self-awareness). Seminaries and other training contexts that expose emerging religious leaders to diverse and deconstructive perspectives on religious traditions would do well to consider the overall developmental process for religious leaders and the formation resources necessary to encourage integrative development and faith reconstruction.

These literatures on intellectual and other aspects of humility might also be useful for developing research on a new construct—interdisciplinary humility—which would seem crucial for MCI. Here I would again insert a personal observation, namely that Wildman embodies healthy attitudes and practices of humility with regard to disciplinary differences. Wildman regularly practices what I would take to be subcomponents of interdisciplinary humility: (a) a willingness to study other disciplines and methodologies, (b) a willingness to acknowledge disciplinary boundaries held in productive tension with exploring the limits of those boundaries, (c) a complex template for understanding within-group disciplinary variance and resisting stereotyping of particular disciplines, (d) regular engagement in interdisciplinary conversations and collaborations with curiosity and respect, and (d) frequent commitments of personal and professional sacrifice necessary to facilitate interdisciplinary collaboration.

Relational Spirituality, Humility, and Ultimacy Manifestations

In his recent book *Effing the Ineffable*, Wildman uses his interdisciplinary commitments for a phenomenological exploration of a trio of ultimacy manifestations—loneliness, intensity, and bliss.[40] He does not explicate an interpenetrating integration of these themes, although I think it could be quite interesting to do so around a process-oriented model of (a) existential predicament (loneliness), (b) transformative process (intensification), and (c) outcome (bliss). But because Wildman is only in his late fifties, I save that contribution for the next festschrift celebrating his work after he puts in another decade of work. Below I offer some reflections and associations on Wildman's account of these ultimacy manifestations, again in light of psychology, relational spirituality, and humility.

Loneliness

Among Wildman's writings, one of my personal favorites is his interdisciplinary meditation on loneliness as a virtue. The field of positive psychology includes research on many virtues, but I do not think many positive psychologists would have considered loneliness to be one of the virtues. Wildman explains that loneliness is a virtue because "we can be better or worse at being lonely" (188). This chapter again reflects Wildman's existential orientation as he depicts loneliness as "death up close and personal" (199) and relates loneliness to our human consciousness of time. Wildman could easily invoke existential psychologists like Moustakas and Yalom, who similarly argued that human growth requires that we face our basic isolation in the world and the existential anxiety that arises from loneliness.[41]

Wildman also makes poignant connections between loneliness and love and loneliness and intimacy, revealing the dialectical orientation toward virtue that is missing from most of the positive psychology literature. He explains that "loneliness and love are co-primal" (207) and that both arise from the "fertile abyss" (213). Again, many existential psychotherapists would say "amen" and draw out the point that loneliness can potentially prompt self-awareness and, ironically, a capacity for empathy to relate well with others. I have not seen any writers bring humility into reflection on loneliness, but it would be possible to draw out these connections between awareness of finitude, courageously processing the existential dynamics of loneliness and associated vulnerabilities, and humility about oneself in relation to others.

Wildman's casting of loneliness "even in the heart of intimacy" (200) and his poetic line that "loneliness haunts intimacy" (201) offers the existential challenge that we cannot escape loneliness through attempts at intimacy with others. This perspective would appeal to some psychodynamic and systems therapists but is exceedingly rare in the couples therapy literature, which too often implies that communication skills or certain forms of emotional validation can prove relationally salvific for couples. Intimacy is rarely problematized in contemporary psychological literature as fraught with risk and loss and the need for courage in the way Wildman contends. Couples and sex therapist David Schnarch is a rare exception, as he embraces many of Wildman's same points about the need to contend with one's loneliness anxiety to develop mature capacities for intimacy.[42] Schnarch relates this capacity to *differentiation of self* or the ability to self-regulate anxiety, balance connection and autonomy, and manage the anxiety of interpersonal differences. Differentiation of self is a key construct in our relational spirituality model and, as mentioned above, is positively associated with humility and numerous other spiritual and psychological indicators of health and maturity.[43] Drawing on Wildman and Schnarch, we could say that it takes high levels of differentiation of self to constructively process loneliness anxiety in ways that do not lead to defensive interpersonal cutoff or desperate attempts at fusion with others. And differentiation is also part of managing the quest for distinctiveness that Wildman mentions, the understandable human desire to be unique without getting twisted into the kinds of narcissistic grasping for uniqueness that can actually perpetuate loneliness.

In our book on spiritual transformation, Shults and I considered the clinical case study of Juan, a Latino man and inmate in a federal prison who was HIV positive and struggling to hide his physical symptoms from fellow inmates.[44] After describing his relational dilemmas about differentiation and the decision to also keep his health status from his family, I asked him if he felt "lonely" in these struggles. With a smile and softened voice, he replied that loneliness had become his "best friend," explaining that the experience of loneliness had bonded him more deeply to Jesus as one who knew the deepest levels of loneliness. His tone was not one of lament, but at that moment I could not help thinking of the closing to the Psalm 88 lament—"darkness is my closest friend." Both Juan and the psalmist found poetic expression, paradoxically, as they related outward even in the midst of their aloneness. This also bears some resonance with Wildman's apophatic spiritual development connections between loneliness and St. John's dark night of the soul, or deepened spiritual intimacy that results from wrestling with losses of immature forms of spirituality. Loneliness is proving to be an important mediating variable in the links between spirituality and health, particularly in recent research with Latinx populations, and therefore a fascinating, underrated topic for spirituality researchers.[45]

But I should also ask if, in our existential mumblings and ruminations, Wildman and I are being too idealistic about the transforming potential of loneliness. Juan's story as a stigmatized but spiritual seeking prison inmate offers a positive story about loneliness, yet most prison inmates in the United States would not have healthcare access to multiple psychotherapy sessions to relate with someone about their loneliness. And what about the countless people who live with chronic, painful loneliness that stokes bitterness, self-hatred, numbing substance abuse, distortions of reality, and suicidality. Bowlby's classic and influential account of research on loneliness among bereaved spouses showed it was much easier to contend with social loneliness and to recover some level of social connection than to overcome the deeper levels of emotional loneliness tied to losing a primary attachment relationship, with some never recovering.[46]

I am thinking also of the social stigmatized who do not find Juan's hopeful frame—elderly folks living in desolate geriatric facilities, children of color in predominantly white schools bearing constant racist harassment, individuals battling mental illness without a supportive family, among others. I remember joining a church visitation team many years ago where we called on a very senior immigrant woman who told us that the previous day she had been on the verge of jumping out the window of her eighth-floor apartment in a public housing project because of despair over her health problems, poverty, and utter loneliness. And the national and international suicide statistics bear testimony to remarkable levels of despair and liminality that move toward death rather than positive transformation. A very large body of public health data show that loneliness is an upstream factor that increases risks for morbidity and mortality through negative effects of physical and mental health.[47] If we are going to speak of the abysmal dynamics of loneliness, I believe we must linger on the devastating and unjust expressions of loneliness until we are troubled. Wildman's theology suggests God is not providing any supernatural "backup" on these issues, so we as humans are responsible for any amelioration of loneliness.

Intensity

Wildman's meditation[48] and broader work[49] on intensity and intense religious and spiritual experiences (RSEs) raise many intriguing issues for psychologists of religion, in general, and our relational spirituality model, in particular. I start by noting that when Shane Moe and I reviewed the psychology of religion literature on conversion and spiritual transformation, I did not come across Wildman's important work in this area because it was indexed as spiritual experience rather than conversion or transformation.[50] This might speak to carelessness on my part, but I believe it also shows how easy it can be to miss an important area of research because of using slightly different terms and operating in different disciplinary networks. In any event, Wildman's emphases on the ways intense experiences can generate the pressure to silence, the pressure to speak, and the pressure to move strike me as highly unique in the social science literature on spirituality and raise issues I had not previously considered. Silence, speaking, and movement are certainly provocative themes and sets of behaviors that could be productively explored in psychological research on RSEs. Hypotheses related to individual differences in attachment styles could be tested in relation to RSEs and the dynamics of silence, speaking, and movement. It would be valuable to identify differing ways silence, speaking, and movement might be related to spiritual and existential anxiety versus spiritual and existential self-regulation. All three dimensions would also be interesting to consider following traumatic forms of intense experience that can sometimes also intensify RSEs.

Wildman does not give much attention to trauma in his interdisciplinary work on RSEs, and the growing spirituality and trauma literature would be important to integrate with RSE research. From a relational spirituality perspective, RSEs might be embedded in a range of psychosocial and spiritual outcomes including healing, growth, and pathology.

Wildman has also proposed a set of five different core descriptive markers (depth, horizon, scale, complexity, mystery) of intense experiences that should be of interest to psychology of religion researchers and have implications for the relational spirituality model. Depth experiences register dilemmas of surrender, trust, and grace, and I would add to Wildman's account that attachment research in the psychology of religion has much to contribute to understanding RSE depth phenomenology. Horizon experiences involve interpersonal and intersubjective experiences of difference (i.e., different horizons), and this relates to the alterity dimensions of our relational spirituality model and wider scholarly discussions bringing the psychology of religion into conversation with multicultural/intercultural competence and intersectionality. Scale experiences involve feelings such as awe, vastness, emptiness, and compassion, and this dimension is relevant to the widespread integration of mindfulness practices into contemporary psychology and psychotherapy. Complexity references experiences of confusion, curiosity, disorientation, exploration, and surprise and nicely maps onto the seeking dimension of our relational spirituality model and the wider and complicated body of psychology literature on quest religiosity. Mystery pulls for reverence, ignorance, and incomprehension. Mystery themes are underdeveloped in psychology literature, although this might be another place for integration with certain dimensions of humility.

These five dimensions of intense experiences would be interesting to study further in narratives of religious and spiritual experiences. This model has already challenged me to see that our relational spirituality model has basically focused on depth, horizon, and complexity dimensions without sufficient attention to scale and mystery, and I can see ways this reflects certain theological and religious biases and omissions. It would also be intriguing to further consider how transformative RSEs might shift the relations between these dimensions, as suggested from my relational spirituality study of Christian seminary students with Link and Jankowski, where we found that a simple self-report of a spiritual transformation in the past year or not (dichotomous variable) moderated or changed the curvilinear relationship between measures of spiritual dwelling and seeking.[51] Using Wildman's categories, I would say we were indexing depth and complexity dimensions and that a report of a recent spiritual transformation appeared to involve some integration (perhaps a kind of semiotic transformation) of those dimensions compared with students not reporting a recent transformation.[52] These kinds of research questions would be particularly valuable to track longitudinally over time and in situations that might intensify experiences of existential themes and predicaments. Wildman mentions the potential of information theory to further illuminate research on intense experiences; however, my own preference is for relational development theories reflecting more relational and ecological ontological assumptions and an emphasis on affect in processes of change.[53]

As a clinician working from a relational approach to psychotherapy, I am also curious about ways Wildman's five dimensions of intensity might be applied for a more nuanced integrative understanding of intense experiences within the relational dynamics of psychotherapy. Most relational approaches to psychotherapy involve seeking to use intense client-therapist encounters to facilitate corrective experiences of healing and growth. But I am beginning to consider ways that different relational theorists could be read as foregrounding a particular intensity dynamic. For example, clinical theorists highlighting relational dilemmas of trust, attachment, dependence, and repairing ruptures to the working alliance might be indirectly touching upon Wildman's depth category. I have in mind theorists like David Wallin and Jeremey Safran. Intersubjectivity and cultural humility clinical theorists represent two groups focusing on intensifications of the horizon dimension, and examples would include Jessica Benjamin and Jesse Owen, respectively. Clinical theorists probing scale-like intensifications might include Buddhist theorists like Pilar Jennings and Mark Epstein, as well as less explicitly religious mindfulness and compassion theorists such as Ronald Siegel. The complexity dimension is central in emphases on curiosity, searching, exploration, and therapist humility in mentalization-based approaches to therapy, as well as the disorientating crucible intensification process in David Schnarch's model. The mystery dimension might seem a more uncommon intensity theme within psychotherapy models but is clearly present in Jung's work. Wildman's observation that mystery can also be thematic in certain hierarchical religious contexts that place constraints on complexity and existential questioning leads me to consider whether a certain implicit form of mystery might be encouraged in some conservative Christian approaches to therapy that are so common in certain regions of the US mental health treatment landscape. Of course, these different intensity markers might emerge in any treatment approach, and Wildman's model could help clinicians avoid privileging certain experiential themes and neglecting others.

Bliss

I suggested above that, in addition to his poignant meditation on loneliness, Wildman can help psychologists deepen and diversify our understanding of the varieties of views of suffering across the human landscape. In my opinion, this is particularly important for psychologists and psychotherapists in the United States, where, I argue, we tend to have rather limited and thin templates for interpreting suffering and are dominated by a reductionistic medical disease model. Reflection on the differing views of suffering across the cultures and religions of the world will be quite decentering for many clinicians like me because we will begin to see that our treatment models often hold implicit assumptions that are radically different from the worldviews of many of our clients. But, oddly, I bet the dissonance of diversifying our suffering awareness will be preferable for many of us psychologists than reflecting deeply on bliss.

Why are topics like bliss, happiness, and flourishing particularly uncomfortable for some psychotherapists? Actually, I raise these topics in courses with seminary students and often find similar levels of discomfort. My best guess is that this partly reflects some common existential anxiety and ambivalence about happiness, enjoyment, and many positive goals in life. I may deeply want bliss but am also afraid of losing it once I find it. Or what if I never really find It? What does that mean about me or ultimate realities or both? Wildman's notion that ultimate reality is wild and untamed adds another angle on the existential discomfort, and psychology is surely one of the disciplines that often serves the kind of regulation of bliss that Wildman discusses.

Those of us in the helping professions (therapists, spiritual leaders, educators, etc.) may also be so oriented to helping and trying to alleviate suffering or ignorance that bliss might seem like a distraction from the main work of overcoming problems, crises, and deficits. But another thing I appreciate about Wildman is that he boldly probes extremes in various directions, including both suffering and bliss. And I am now convinced that, as a psychotherapist, I really should gain greater clarity about my own views of suffering and bliss and those of my clients.

There is now a large set of scientific literatures in positive psychology on the diverse definitions of happiness, well-being, and flourishing, although very little of that research has been integrated with mental healthcare practice or research on serious mental health problems. There is some emerging work in positive clinical psychology that integrates the subfields of positive psychology and clinical psychology, as well some treatment research on virtues and well-being in psychotherapy.[54] Yet much more research is needed in this area, and it would be helpful if psychological researchers would pursue understandings of bliss, flourishing, and happiness that conceptualize complex interconnections between positive and negative affect, desire, and pain (as Wildman proposes).

As with my comments on loneliness, a relational spirituality conceptualization of bliss would also require moving beyond individual factors to attend to systemic, sociocultural, and contextual factors. We should seek to understand how well-being and happiness characterize some in contexts of oppression, while also being sober about the power of systemic dynamics such as poverty, racism, sexism, homophobia, and other forms of discrimination to impact the psychosocial and spiritual health of people. The diversity sensitivity and overall relational hospitality in social systems like schools, universities, and religious congregations can impact levels of happiness and bliss, particularly for nondominant groups. This brings us back to some needed dialectical perspective—when dominant group members insist on always feeling happiness or bliss without discomfort, it will often mean nondominant groups will be unjustly pressed to tolerate a lack of bliss and the "existential crush" (228) of a lack of understanding, mutual recognition, and intersubjectivity (not to mention the impact on material resources).[55] For those like me with high levels of social privilege, the question becomes whether I can develop the differentiation, emotion regulation, and resilience to work through socially decentering experiences so I might develop the capacity to enjoy more diverse relationships and contexts. When conversations arise about diversity and injustice, if I demand positivity and immediate bliss (e.g., "But things are getting better, right?"), as dominant group members too often do, I am enacting a version of that New Testament text Wildman cites of seeking to build shelters to try to dwell in constant bliss (Matthew 17:4). This is a diversity version of William James's healthy-minded religious bliss, with the inability to really perceive and spiritually contend with evil in myself and in the world. And this means I will not move toward capacities for intercultural bliss and will reveal a fragility and empathic failure that will cause me to seem untrustworthy to those familiar with intercultural loneliness.

There is also interesting potential in exploring ways humility might be related to bliss (or not). Wildman (274) engages the book of Job, which

I take to be among the most important biblical texts for ground-of-being theology, to consider how Job is reduced to humility after his overpowering encounter with bliss (i.e., YHWH).[56] While a much different level of consideration than Wildman's version of bliss, our empirical research with religious leaders found a small positive correlation between humility and well-being.[57] Among the various virtues studied by positive psychologists, humility would probably rank rather low in terms of positive associations with happiness, well-being, and bliss. But, like the Job narrative, humility may be more important for well-being and bliss among those experiencing traumatic levels of suffering and loss or those with William James's sick soul temperament who feel torment within. A study with religious mental health clients at the clinic where I practice found that humility moderated the relationship between religious salience (or commitment) and well-being, meaning clients needed a moderate or higher level of humility to demonstrate a positive relationship between religion and well-being.[58] For clients low in humility, the relationship between religion and well-being was negative, which offers some indirect support for the notion that it may be psychosocially hazardous to pursue religious bliss without humble containment.

Wildman also provocatively and sympathetically associates the quest for bliss with mania and other forms of psychopathology in ways that echo some past humanistic theorists. I share Wildman's desire to recognize and affirm the spiritual impulses within mental illness. Yet similar to my comments on loneliness, I also feel some clinical obligation and "pressure to speak" of the destructive and even violent impact untreated mania has on many lives. Thus, humility may not be a virtue that facilitates bliss as much as it potentially helps counterbalance or contain destructive potential within the human quest for bliss. Dahlstrom's work is helpful in this regard, as he draws on Aquinas to advance the dialectical perspective that humans need both magnanimity and humility—magnanimity to pursue our potential for flourishing balanced by contending with our finitude through the grounding in humility.[59] Or, placed back into Wildman's framework, I would say we need a dialectical integration of humility and bliss.

Conclusion

As a psychologist, I have offered a reading of Wildman as a kind of multidimensional interdisciplinary integrationist. He offers a complex yet coherent relationality in his conceptualization of interdisciplinary methods and models, and his various other scholarly and applied efforts to bridge differences. Wildman's unique scholarly approach in areas such as suffering, spiritual experience, and bliss offer generative ideas for numerous areas of psychological and clinical research. Humility is a motif that provides an integrative window into Wildman the person and the scholar, and the multidimensional nature of humility is also useful for elaborating many areas of his work from a relational spirituality interpretation.

Notes

1. Some of the research described in this chapter was supported by grant #60622 from the John Templeton Foundation on Developing Humility in Leadership.

2. Steven J. Sandage and F. LeRon Shults, "Relational Spirituality and Transformation: A Relational Integration Model," *Journal of Psychology & Christianity* 26 (2007): 261–69; F. LeRon Shults and Steven J. Sandage, *The Faces of Forgiveness: Searching for Wholeness and Salvation* (Grand Rapids: Baker Academic, 2003); F. LeRon Shults and Steven J. Sandage, *Transforming Spirituality: Integrating Theology and Psychology* (Grand Rapids: Baker Academic, 2006); Jeannine K. Brown and Steven J. Sandage, "Relational Integration, Part II: Relational Integration as Developmental and Intercultural," *Journal of Psychology and Theology* 43, no. 3 (2015): 179–91; Steven J. Sandage and Jeannine K. Brown, "Monarchy or Democracy in Relation Integration? A Reply to Porter," *Journal of Psychology and Christianity* 29 (2010): 20–26; Steven J. Sandage and Jeannine K. Brown, "Relational Integration, Part I: Differentiated Relationality between Psychology and Theology," *Journal of Psychology and Theology* 43, no. 3 (2015): 165–78; Steven J. Sandage and Jeannine K. Brown, *Relational Integration in Psychology and Christian Theology: Theory, Research, and Practice* (New York: Routledge, 2018).

3. For a review, see Sandage and Brown, *Relational Integration*.

4. Sandage and Brown, *Relational Integration*.

5. David N. Entwistle, *Integrative Approaches to Psychology and Christianity: An Introduction to Worldview Issues, Philosophical Foundations, and Models of Integration*, 2nd ed. (Eugene: Cascade Books, 2010); for differing views on relating psychology and theology, also see Eric L. Johnson, ed., *Psychology & Christianity: Five Views*, 2nd ed. (Downers Grove: InterVarsity Press, 2010).

6. Robert C. Roberts, "A Christian Psychology View," in *Psychology & Christianity: Five Views*, ed. Eric Johnson (Downers Grove, InterVarsity Press, 2000), 156; Robert C. Roberts and P. J. Watson, "A Christian Psychology View," in Johnson, *Psychology & Christianity: Five Views*, 2nd ed., 149–78.

7. David Powlison, "Biblical Counseling Response," in Johnson, *Psychology & Christianity: Five Views*, 2nd ed., 194–98.

8. David G. Myers, "A Levels-of-Explanation View," in *Psychology & Christianity: Four Views*, ed. Eric L. Johnson and Stanton L. Jones (Downers Grove,

InterVarsity Press, 2010), 54–101; for the broader interface of science and religion, see Ian G. Barbour, *Religion and Science: Historical and Contemporary Issues* (New York: HarperCollins, 1997).

    9. Sandage and Brown, *Relational Integration in Psychology and Christian Theology*.

    10. Wesley J. Wildman, *Effing the Ineffable: Existential Mumblings at the Limits of Language* (Albany: State University of New York Press, 2018), 219.

    11. Wesley J. Wildman, *Religious Philosophy as Multidisciplinary Comparative Inquiry: Envisioning a Future for the Philosophy of Religion* (Albany: State University of New York Press, 2011).

    12. Warren S. Brown, "Resonance: A Model for Relating Science, Psychology, and Faith," *Journal of Psychology and Christianity* 23, no. 2 (2010): 110–20.

    13. Sandage and Brown, *Relational Integration in Psychology and Christian Theology*.

    14. Sandage and Brown, *Relational Integration in Psychology and Christian Theology*.

    15. Sandage and Brown, *Relational Integration in Psychology and Christian Theology*; F. LeRon Shults, "Dis-Integrating Psychology and Theology," *Journal of Psychology and Theology* 40, no. 1 (2012): 21–25.

    16. Wesley J. Wildman and Patrick McNamara, "Evaluating Reliance on Narratives in the Psychological Study of Religious Experiences," *International Journal for the Psychology of Religion* 20, no. 4 (2010): 223–54.

    17. Steven J. Sandage et al., "Hermeneutics and Psychology: A Review and Dialectical Model," *Review of General Psychology* 12, no. 4 (2008): 344–64.

    18. Wildman and McNamara, "Evaluating Reliance on Narratives in the Psychological Study of Religious Experiences."

    19. John H. Aldrich, *Interdisciplinarity: Its Role in a Discipline-Based Academy* (Oxford: Oxford University Press, 2014).

    20. John F. Dovidio, Samuel L. Gaertner, and Kerry Kawakami, "Intergroup Contact: The Past, Present, and the Future," *Group Processes & Intergroup Relations* 6, no. 1 (2003): 5–20.

    21. Shannon W. Stirman et al., "Bridging the Gap between Research and Practice in Mental Health Service Settings: An Overview of Developments in Implementation Theory and Research," *Behavior Therapy* 47, no. 6 (2016): 920–36.

    22. Wesley J. Wildman and Stephen C. Garner, *Found in the Middle!: Theology and Ethics for Christians Who Are Both Liberal and Evangelical* (Herndon: The Alban Institute, 2009).

    23. Wildman and Garner, *Lost in the Middle?: Claiming and Inclusive Faith for Christians Who Are Both Liberal and Evangelical* (Herndon: The Alban Institute, 2009).

    24. Wildman and Garner, *Found in the Middle!*

    25. John Calvin, *Institutes of the Christian Religion*, trans. H. Beveridge (Peabody: Hendrickson Publishers, 2008) (original work published in 1536).

26. Wesley J. Wildman, *In Our Own Image: Anthropomorphism, Apophaticism, and Ultimacy* (Oxford: Oxford University Press, 2017).

27. Chance A. Bell et al., "Relational Spirituality, Humility, and Commitments to Social Justice and Intercultural Competence," *Journal of Psychology and Christianity* 36, no. 3 (2017): 210–21.

28. Steven J. Sandage, David Paine, and Peter Hill, "Spiritual Barriers to Humility: A Multidimensional Study," *Mental Health, Religion & Culture* 18, no. 3 (2015): 207–17; Steven J. Sandage et al., "Vulnerable Narcissism, Forgiveness, Humility, and Depression: Mediator Effects for Differentiation of Self," *Psychoanalytic Psychology* 34, no. 3 (2017): 300–10.

29. Peter J. Jankowski et al., "Humility, Relational Spirituality, and Well-being among Religious Leaders: A Moderated Mediation Model," *Journal of Religion and Health* 58, no. 1 (2019): 132–52; Elizabeth G. Ruffing et al., "Humility and Narcissism in Clergy: A Relational Spirituality Framework," *Pastoral Psychology* 67 (2018): 525–45.

30. Wildman and Garner, *Found in the Middle!*

31. Bell et al., "Relational Spirituality, Humility, and Commitments to Social Justice and Intercultural Competence"; David R. Paine, Peter J. Jankowski, and Steven J. Sandage, "Humility as a Predictor of Intercultural Competence: Mediator Effects for Differentiation-of-Self," *The Family Journal* 24, no. 1 (2016): 15–22.

32. Bell et al., "Relational Spirituality, Humility, and Commitments to Social Justice and Intercultural Competence"; Peter J. Jankowksi, Steven J. Sandage, and Peter C. Hill, "Differentiation-Based Models of Forgivingness, Mental Health and Social Justice Commitment: Mediator Effects for Differentiation of Self and Humility," *Journal of Positive Psychology* 8, no. 5 (2013): 412–24.

33. Joshua Hook et al., *Cultural Humility: Engaging Diverse Identities in Therapy* (Washington, DC: American Psychological Association, 2017).

34. Bradley P. Owens and David R. Hekman, "How Does Leader Humility Influence Team Performance? Exploring the Mechanisms of Contagion and Collective Promotion Focus," *Academy of Management Journal* 59, no. 3 (2016): 1088–1111; Lin Wang et al., "Exploring the Affective Impact, Boundary Conditions, and Antecedents of Leader Humility," *Journal of Applied Psychology* 103, no. 9 (2018): 1019–38.

35. Wildman and Garner, *Found in the Middle!*

36. Dennis Whitcomb et al., "Intellectual Humility: Owning Our Limitation." *Philosophy & Phenomenological Research* 94, no. 3 (2017): 509–39.

37. Megan Haggard et al., "Finding Middle Ground between Intellectual Arrogance and Intellectual Servility: Development and Assessment of the Limitations-Owning Intellectual Humility Scale," *Personality and Individual Differences* 124 (2018): 184–93.

38. Robert D. Putnam and David E. Campbell, *American Grace: How Religion Divides and Unites Us* (New York: Simon & Schuster, 2012).

39. Joshua N. Hook et al., "Intellectual Humility and Religious Tolerance," *Journal of Positive Psychology* 12, no. 1 (2017): 29–35.

40. Wildman, *Effing the Ineffable*.
41. Clark E. Moustakas, *Loneliness* (Englewood Cliffs: Prentice-Hall, 1961); Irvin D. Yalom, *Existential Psychotherapy* (New York: Basic Books, 1980).
42. David M. Schnarch, *Constructing the Sexual Crucible: An Integration of Sexual and Marital Therapy* (New York: W.W. Norton, 1991); David Schnarch, *Intimacy & Desire: Awaken the Passion in Your Relationship* (New York: Beaufort Books, 2009).
43. Peter J. Jankowski et al., "Humility, Relational Spirituality, and Well-Being among Religious Leaders: A Moderated Mediation Model."
44. F. LeRon Shults and Steven J. Sandage, *Transforming Spirituality: Integrating Theology and Psychology* (Grand Rapids: Baker Academic, 2006).
45. Monica L. Gallegos and Chris Segrin, "Exploring the Mediating Role of Loneliness in the Relationship between Spirituality and Health: Implications for the Latino Health Paradox," *Psychology of Religion and Spirituality* 11, no. 3 (2019): 308–18.
46. John Bowlby, *Attachment and Loss: Vol. 3: Sadness and Depression* (New York: Basic Books, 1980).
47. Nicholas Leigh-Hunt et al., "An Overview of Systematic Reviews on the Public Health Consequences of Social Isolation and Loneliness," *Public Health* 152 (2017): 157–71.
48. Wildman, *Effing the Ineffable*.
49. Wesley J. Wildman, *Religious and Spiritual Experiences* (New York: Cambridge University Press, 2014).
50. Steven J. Sandage and Shane P. Moe, "Spiritual Experience: Conversion and Transformation," in *APA Handbook of Psychology, Religion, and Spirituality (Vol. 1): Context, Theory, and Research*, ed. Kenneth I. Pargament, Julie J. Exline, and James W. Jones (Washington, DC: American Psychological Association, 2013), 407–22.
51. Steven J. Sandage, Peter J. Jankowski, and Deborah C. Link, "Quest and Spiritual Development Moderated by Spiritual Transformation," *Journal of Psychology and Theology* 38, no. 1 (2010): 15–31.
52. Wildman, *Effing the Ineffable*.
53. Wildman, *Effing the Ineffable*.
54. Alex M. Wood and Judith Johnson, eds., *The Wiley Handbook of Positive Clinical Psychology* (West Sussex, John Wiley & Sons, Ltd., 2016).
55. Wildman, *Effing the Ineffable*.
56. Wildman, *Effing the Ineffable*.
57. Jankowski et al., "Humility, Relational Spirituality, and Well-being among Religious Leaders."
58. David R. Paine et al., "Religious and Spiritual Salience, Well-being, and Psychosocial Functioning among Psychotherapy Clients: Moderator Effects for Humility," *Journal of Religion and Health* 57 (2018): 2398–2415.
59. Daniel O. Dahlstrom, *Identity, Authenticity, and Humility* (Milwaukee: Marquette University Press, 2017).

12

Wildman's Contributions to the Neuroscience of Religious and Spiritual Experiences

PATRICK MCNAMARA

Wildman's contributions to the neuroscientific study of RSEs are both practical and scientific. His practical contributions include the training of graduate students, the cofounding of the flagship journal for the field *Religion Brain Behavior (RBB)*, and the cofounding of the Institute for the Biocultural Study of Religion (now under the Center for Mind and Culture) and its monthly research digest (*Research Review*), which is emailed each month to most of the active researchers in the field. His scientific contributions include his curation and review work for RBB and his editorials in RBB, particularly on methodological issues relevant to the field and his experimental demonstration that memories of religious and spiritual experiences (RSEs) exhibit a unique set of phenomenological properties that reliably distinguished them from non-RSE memories. He later followed up these phenomenologic studies with some collaborative work on RSEs in patients with Parkinson's disease. His scientific approach to RSEs has been influenced by his religious naturalism. This anti-supernaturalist position is contrasted with the supernaturalist position to highlight the controversial role of supernatural agents in RSEs.

Introduction

I am very happy to contribute to a volume honoring Wesley Wildman's work on the scientific, philosophical, and theological study of religion. It is rare to meet someone who is an expert in the huge array of disciplines (science, philosophy, theology, humanities, etc.) required to do justice to the complex biocultural phenomenon we call religion. But Wesley is that person. He is as good a scientist as he is a philosopher and theologian.

I first became aware of Wesley Wildman's work on the neurology of religious and spiritual experiences (RSEs) by reading his paper with Leslie Brothers on a semiotic approach to the neurology of RSEs.[1] Impressed by that paper, I later invited him to write a commentary on the papers in a volume of essays I had edited on the new neurologic and evolutionary approaches to religion beginning to emerge in the early 2000s.[2] Impressed again by that commentary, I sought out a collaboration with the man himself in approximately 2007. In the next couple of years, our collaborative work resulted in new experimental work; new papers, the creation (with Richard Sosis) of the journal *Religion, Brain and Behavior* (RBB) and its monthly digest of new papers, *Research Review*; an edited three-volume collection of essays on *Science and the World Religions*; and the foundation of the Institute for the Biocultural Study of Religion (now the Center for Mind and Culture in Boston). It should be noted that while I helped create and launch RBB and the Institute, I quickly had to curtail my efforts and contributions to both, and thus their phenomenal growth over the years has been due primarily to Wesley's herculean efforts and the people he collaborated with in those enterprises. Those two enterprises, the Institute and RBB, must be construed as very significant practical contributions to the research infrastructure of the field of the neuroscience of RSEs. Readers can obtain some sense of the practical contributions of the Institute and RBB to the field by visiting its website, mindandculture.org. I focus in this chapter on Wesley's scientific contributions to the field. These have been equally impressive and include his work on the phenomenology of RSEs, which I describe more fully below, as well as his editorials in RBB, as they have helped shape the questions and methodological rigor of the field. Here is a philosopher/theologian who is also an excellent scientist.

As the collaboration between Wesley and me began to bear fruit in the mid- to late 2000s, I recall more than one reporter wishing to write stories about the collaboration, titled something like "The Neuroscientist and the Theologian," Indeed, Wesley and I briefly considered a book with a similar title. Luckily we ditched that idea. In the case of the reporters, my recollection is that they invariably became flummoxed when they discovered that the neuroscientist was something like a traditional theist and the theologian was something like a new atheist! They expected the theologian to carry on about God and the neuroscientist to utter skeptical bromides in the background, but neither Wesley nor I was interested in these script-driven "interviews." Wesley's position on RSEs is subtle and, in my estimation, strongly influenced by his version of "religious naturalism." It therefore is necessary to review his work on RSEs with an eye toward illuminating the naturalism informing the work. Roughly speaking, religious naturalism is religion without a ghostly supernatural realm or supernatural agents. I cannot do justice here to Wesley's subtle philosophical naturalism. Suffice it to say that he sees humanity's penchant for anthropomorphically ascribing agential or mental properties to God or to what is considered "ultimate" to be both intellectually vacuous and possibly socially pernicious. Like other "ground of being" theologians, Wesley wishes to resist the idolatrous temptation to impose our anthropomorphized image on the ineffable mystery that is the ultimate source of all. He does not accept the idea/experience that ultimate reality could be or is personal. What follows from this religious naturalism for his position on religious and spiritual experiences (RSEs)?

Religious Naturalism and RSEs

Wesley strongly rejects "supernaturalism" or the idea that disembodied, immaterial agents are, in any sense, *real*. For him, therefore, *RSEs need not reference a supernatural agent*. To understand the subtlety of his position and its relation to the scientific study of RSEs, it is worth contrasting it with a more traditional supernaturalist position like my own. In the tradition of the great Boston University personalists who populated the theology and philosophy departments before Wesley's arrival at BU, I consider myself a personalist. Like the atheist philosopher J. M. McTaggart as well as the BU personalists, I find that the scientific and philosophic evidence concerning consciousness force one to conclude that something like "conscious persons" (embodied and disembodied immaterial agents) are fundamental to reality. Wesley apparently subscribes to an impersonal "ground of being" ontology or theology as the *whence* or source of all things. I, on the other hand, do not believe you can derive personhood from an impersonal and mysterious ground of being. You can, on the other hand, reach impersonality from personality via "depersonalization." We see it happen every day in the neurology and psychiatry clinic. It is therefore not wholly unreasonable to take the personal as ultimate ground rather than the impersonal. I, like most other theists, admit that the personalist position is paradoxical. *Personal reality* as the ultimate reality gives us a vague kind of intuition about reality because we experience the personal within and without via interaction with others. It can also be argued that personalism actually resists anthropomorphism and idolatrous errors because the personal is almost as difficult to understand and characterize as the indeterminate "ground of being" or the "God beyond God" apophatic ontologies of the religious naturalists. "The infinitude of the private man" is not just a slogan of the Emersonian pragmatists. Be that as it may, the two positions seem to yield significantly differing scientific approaches to the study of RSEs.

For me (and I assume the more traditional theist), the biocultural, evolutionary default for religious cognition necessarily involves reference to supernatural agents (SAs). This necessity to refer to SAs stems not only from the fact that consciousness is fundamental, but also from the overwhelming empirical evidence that RSEs for most people across most epochs have always involved reference to supernatural agents. Now for the religious naturalist, this record of most peoples invoking SAs in their religious experiences merely underlines the fact that most peoples have always been inclined to idolatry. Most peoples are not capable or not willing to do the extra work required to overcome the massive internal urge to anthropomorphize. Then the great axial age came along and people began to overcome this infantile stage in humanity's understanding of the ultimate . . . or so the naturalist story goes.

But if the supernaturalist position is correct, then the story is not just a simple story of the gradual and upward progression and enlightenment of humankind; the gradual freeing of humanity from its anthropomorphic fetters and biases. Instead, those anthropomorphic biases function occasionally as reliable handles on the real. Yes, evolutionary forces do not require that the organism always produce veridical perceptions of the real, but for the most part and over the long term veridical perceptions are required. Humanity's tendency to perceive agents all over the place is sometimes illusory and sometimes not. Therefore, we need to take people's perceptions of agents seriously.

In fact, the supernaturalist will argue that once we note that the default cognitive setting for humankind is to promiscuously postulate supernatural agents, then we should take that fact into account and include something like "perception of SAs" in our definitions of, and scientific approach to, RSEs. After all, if most people in most cultures across most historical epochs have referred to SAs in their religious experiences, then we as scientists should allow for SAs as fundamental to RSEs. For me, therefore (along with the personalists), religion, and RSEs in particular, primarily involve an encounter with an Other, a "Thou," another person that most traditions call God or a god, an ancestor spirit, or spirit being, et cetera. Now if RSEs, by definition, should involve an encounter with another being or person, then one would predict that the brain regions involved in RSEs would often include regions traditionally referred to as the "social brain." That is one reason why I originally avidly read Wesley's paper with Leslie Brothers—one of the early investigators into the social brain. In fact, most of the neuroimaging studies of RSEs to date have indeed implicated the structures in the classic social brain network. Perceptions of persons, minds, or agency are what this social brain network specializes in. Whenever people undergo what they deem to be an RSE, some or all components of this "mentalizing" network will be activated, thus underlining the social perceptual aspects of the RSE itself.[3]

While Wesley's religious naturalism allows for RSEs that involve supernatural agents, it does not require it. Because supernatural agents are not real, you can have RSEs without reference to these agents. Naturalism therefore logically implies that RSEs involving supernatural agents are somehow less valid and certainly less veridical than RSEs that make no reference to supernatural agents. After all, if SAs do not exist and are illusory, the RSEs that reference these illusory agents must be deemed hallucinatory or at the very least a kind of "misfiring." Scientific studies on RSEs that involve supernatural agents therefore should in principle be treated differently than RSEs that reference supernatural agents.

The commitment to religious naturalism also implies that a significant space must be carved out for RSEs that involve no specific reference to SAs, that is, no specific social content. After all, can't atheists have RSEs? In my view, they can and do, but they have to do extra cognitive work to strip these experiences of their social-personal content, as that content conflicts with their worldviews. When atheists and naturalists have RSEs, it may create a kind of cognitive dissonance that needs to be handled, and thus the extra cognitive reflective work to explain away the social content of the experiences. They will see this extra cognitive and analytic work as virtuous. They are freeing themselves of the compulsive and idolatrous anthropomorphic tendency to postulate a big man in the sky as part of their RSE.

Thus, we have two diametrically opposed predictions flowing from the logic of the religious naturalist versus the traditional theist positions regarding the role of supernatural agents in RSEs. From the point of view of the traditional theist, when a naturalist or atheist has an RSE, he or she has to do extra cognitive work to strip it of its social/supernatural content, while that is not the case for traditional theists. Whereas from the point of view of the naturalist, it is the theist who has to do the extra cognitive work because he or she has to produce a hallucination, that is, the supernatural agent. If we induce RSEs in two groups of participants (theists versus atheists) and then observe the amount of analytic/reflective work that takes place in the two groups after each induction, then we can measure the extent to which RSEs in the naturalist versus the theist evoke the analytic style. Or we could look at accounts and narratives of RSEs in naturalists versus theists and code the reports for analytic/reflective phrases in each and then quantify analytic content is each, and so forth. Of course, the naturalist or atheist will never consciously report supernatural agents, so the claim from the theist point of view is extremely strong: it suggests that whenever the atheist or naturalist thinks he or she is having an RSE, there will be social content, but that content will need to be suppressed, as it will conflict with the belief system of the individual and that suppression should be detectable, perhaps with priming or some other technique.

Now if the evolutionary default for religious cognitions necessarily involves social content, then a priori exclusion of that social content of RSEs on metaphysical grounds (e.g., embrace of naturalism) seems scientifically premature. But again, religious naturalism can be read in such a way as to allow social content in RSEs. It's just that that social content has to be judged negatively—as illusory, hallucinatory, and then suppressed. And therefore the epistemic value of theistic RSEs, in turn, has to be summarily dismissed as nugatory. It is no surprise therefore that the philosophic position one adopts with respect to RSEs will necessarily color one's scientific approach to the phenomena. This is true obviously for both the naturalist and the theist.

But surely not all RSEs need have supernatural agents—even unconsciously suppressed agents. It seems reasonable to suppose that people have always had and will always have some *intense* experiences that they deem religious but that do not reference supernatural agents. After all, can't we have RSEs that sometimes do not reference fantastic beings of any kind? The evidence we have at hand from all of the world's traditions is that RSEs everywhere have in the past tended to spontaneously invoke supernatural agents. When these traditions begin to reflect on these experiences (as in the axial age), all kinds of impersonal explanations begin to emerge. But those reflections are secondary to the spontaneous default that invokes supernatural agents. Thus, the most sensible scientific stance to take with respect to defining and studying RSEs is to adopt the default position as our first-pass definition of RSEs—to wit, they necessarily involve SAs.

Nevertheless, the default position and the traditional personalist position can allow for "intense experiences" as part of the spiritual landscape. Here is where Wesley's scientific contribution to spiritual experiences comes in, as he has mapped out these intense experiences in some experimental and philosophical detail.

Wildman's Work on the Neurologic and Phenomenologic Properties of RSEs

Wildman and McNamara[4] studied a sample of thirty-nine volunteers who recalled an RSE (as well as a happy experience and an ordinary experience that was neither religious nor intense), described it, and filled out the Phenomenology of Consciousness Inventory for each recalled experience (see Pekala[4]). This yielded a quantitative profile of the subjective phenomenological features of the recalled experience along twenty-six subdimensions, which can be collected into twelve major dimensions. Results of these phenomenologic analyses revealed that RSEs exhibited a distinct phenomenology. Relative to happy experiences, RSEs exhibited larger alterations of experience, heightened altered state of awareness, more outward focus toward some Other and stronger attention, more imagery, and more active internal dialogue. These results were consistent with past research on RSEs, which emphasized altered consciousness and reduced volitional control. People undergo RSEs—they do not manufacture them. It also became clear that RSEs dominate attention, including abundant mental imagery and interestingly marked internal dialogue—a feature not always noted in previous research.

These results are significant in that they give the neuroscientist a quantitative profile of phenomenologic dimensions that pick out RSEs distinctly. These phenomenologic dimensions, furthermore, are in principle relatively easy to map onto the brain. Reduced volitional control likely involves reduction in activation of frontal lobe regions implicated in agency. Internal dialogue likely involves left-sided speech productions regions and so forth. Thus Wesley's empirical work on RSEs has laid the foundation for a hypothesis-driven research program on brain correlates of the fundamental dimensions of RSEs.

Interestingly, this same study revealed significant sex differences in dimensional analyses of RSEs. The twenty-four women in our sample reported significantly higher alterations in perception, higher physical arousal, higher negative affect (especially anger), and lower positive affect (especially joy) than the fifteen men. There were also five left-handed participants in the sample, so we were able to provisionally identify RSE differences as a function of handedness (recall that handedness indexes brain organization). The five left-handed participants reported that RSEs were significantly less memorable and significantly lower in positive affect (especially joy and sexual excitement) than for right-handed participants.

Following up on the neurologic dimensions of this research, Wesley later contrasted the thirty-nine healthy participants with three patients with Parkinson's disease (PD). The patients with PD reported significantly lower meaningfulness, physical arousal, and internal dialogue, and greater volitional control than healthy controls.

One of the strengths of Wildman's naturalist and pragmatist approach to RSEs is that it can accommodate some aspects of the role of axiologic apprehension in these experiences. Whatever else religion is, it is a biocultural capacity to identify, create, and grasp value—especially things of the highest possible value. The organ that specializes in this sort of "axiologic apprehension" is of course the mind/brain. Here Wildman's interests coincided with my neuroscience approach to RSEs, as I was looking at the evolution and current role of mesocortical dopaminergic systems in value apprehension and RSEs. There is now a very solid body of evidence derived from the neurosciences, including the new discipline of neuroeconomics that locates the key system for the mediation of these axiological perceptual capacities in neostriatal and mesocortical dopaminergic neural systems. These systems encode salience properties of incoming sensory information and in addition construct predictive models of the nature and intensity of both seen and imagined values, including values invested with the highest possible significance. My colleagues and I suggested that when these systems are pathologically upregulated, an individual is overwhelmed with the feeling that everything he or she does or experiences carries intense significance (as in some cases of schizophrenia or temporal lobe epilepsy). When these systems, on the other hand, are pathologically downregulated (as in some cases of Parkinson's disease), very specific deficits in access to religious concepts and experiences may emerge.[5] Wesley and his graduate student Jonathan Morgan actively contributed to one of these studies.[6] In very severe states of downregulation, the individual finds no meaning or value in life at all—a state of suffering that eventuates in major depressive disorder.

Conclusion

Although Wesley and I have clashed many times over basic philosophic positions concerning religion, he has been gracious and patient with my philosophical naivete. Regardless of our philosophic differences, we share a passionate interest in the nature of RSEs. We both also agree that investigation of brain correlates of RSEs can tell us something about the nature of RSEs. We also both agree that any scientifically adequate approach to RSEs must be cross-cultural, sampling reports from as many different religious traditions as possible, including religious traditions of the past. In addition, investigation of RSEs must be multidisciplinary, involving scholars from a variety of disciplines including anthropology, humanistic studies, religious studies, theology, philosophy, sociology, economics, and all of the sciences. Finally study of RSEs should be broadly biocultural because religion is not merely a biological or a cultural phenomenon. Rather, it encompasses both.

Notes

1. Wesley J. Wildman and Leslie A. Brothers, "A Neuropsychological-Semiotic Model of Religious Experiences," in *Neuroscience and the Person: Scientific Perspectives on Divine Action*, ed. Robert J. Russell, Nancey Murphy, Theo C. Meyering, and Michael A. Arbib (Vatican City State, Vatican Observatory, Berkeley, CA: Center for Theology and the Natural Sciences, 1999), 347–416.

2. Patrick McNamara, *Where God and Science Meet* (3 vols.) (Westport, CT: Greenwood Publishing Group, 2006).

3. The "social brain" network is that set of interconnected brain regions that handles or mediates all of the perceptual, thinking, and emotional work we have to do to perceive and understand the intentions of other persons, and to keep track of and regulate our social interactions with others. The network of structures that makes up the social brain includes the amygdala, which is known to be involved in emotional memory, threat appraisal, and fear; the fusiform gyrus, which supports rapid recognition and processing of faces; and the ventromedial and dorsomedial prefrontal regions, which are known to support processing of self-related information as well as understanding the mental states of others (i.e., theory of mind or ToM tasks). The frontopolar region (BA 10) is involved in multitasking, working memory, and cognitive branching and likely supports processing of 3rd, 4th, et cetera orders of perception of others' social intentionality. The superior temporal sulcus contains mirror neurons that support social imitation behaviors and possibly emotional empathy, while the temporal-parietal junction supports ToM tasks and language processing. The insula supports empathetic responses as well as moral emotions, and the precuneus is involved in a range of activities from mental simulation to self-awareness. In short, the social brain is a hugely elaborated perceptual device that specializes in the pickup and processing of the personal states of others.

4. Wesley J. Wildman and Patrick McNamara, "Evaluating Reliance on Narratives in the Psychological Study of Religious Experiences," *International Journal for the Psychology of Religion* 20, no. 4 (2010): 223–54.

5. Paul M. Butler, Patrick McNamara, and Raymon Durso, "Deficits in the Automatic Activation of Religious Concepts in Patients with Parkinson's Disease,"

Journal of the International Neuropsychological Society 16, no. 2 (2010): 252–61; Paul M. Butler et al., "Disease-Associated Differences in Religious Cognition in Patients with Parkinson's Disease," *Journal of Clinical and Experimental Neuropsychology* 33, no. 8 (2011): 917–28.

6. Jonathan Morgan et al., "Impacts of Religious Semantic Priming on an Intertemporal Discounting Task: Response Time Effects and Neural Correlates," *Neuropsychologia* 89 (2016): 403–13.

13

Religious and Spiritual Experiences

An Imagined Dialogue with Wesley Wildman

ANN TAVES

Note: Because Wesley Wildman (WW) and I share a common interest in religious and spiritual experience (RSE), this imagined dialogue focuses on how WW approaches the topic of RSE and why he does it that way. In the process, I reflect on similarities and differences in our approaches to RSE in light of our differing professional identities and intellectual goals. The dialogue is based on relevant writings, comments I prepared for a session on *Religious and Spiritual Experience* at the 2012 Annual Meeting of the AAR, and Wildman's email responses to those comments and an earlier draft of this imagined dialogue. Given the back and forth, the dialogue reflects a real process of coming to understand WW's aims with respect to RSE and the overlap and divergence in our approaches.

> **AT:** I will open our dialogue with a brief description of how you (Wesley Wildman) conceive the relationship between various types of "religious and spiritual experiences" (RSEs). As this diagram indicates (see Fig. 13.1), you view RSE as comprising three intersecting types of experiences that subjects characterize as religious, vivid ("constituted by ultimacy"), and anomalous. You highlight two subclasses of ultimacy experience: mystical experiences, which lie at the center of the Venn diagram, and "intense experiences" (IEs), which you take as your particular focus.
>
> The first thing we need to notice, then, is that your argument focuses not on RSEs, but on "intense experiences" (IEs).

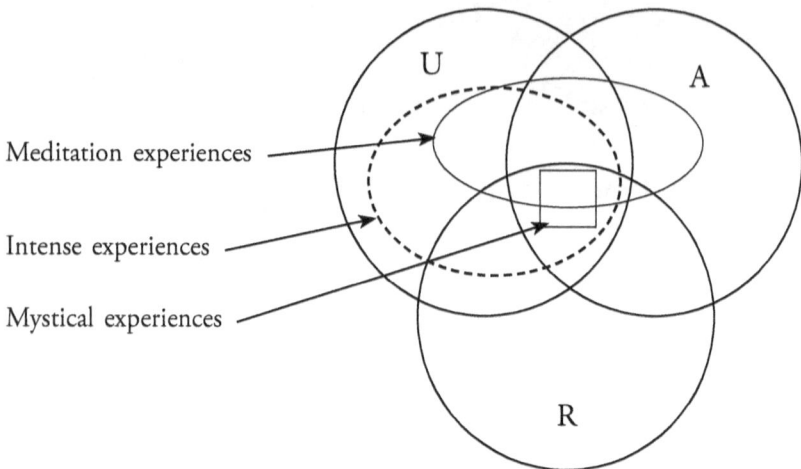

Figure 13.1. Relationships between types of experiences: religious [R] experiences, vivid experiences (constituted by ultimacy [U] and anomalous [A] experiences), meditation experiences, and two subclasses of ultimacy experiences (intense experiences and mystical experiences). RSEs are the union of the ultimacy and religious experiences.[1]

You do so because you view IEs as "a doorway into a broadly based understanding of RSEs," even though IEs, as you conceive them, however, include many experiences that people would not *normally* view as religious or even spiritual, e.g., peak experiences and flow experiences. Ultimately, as I understand it, your aim is to see if it is possible to generate "a theological account of ultimate reality" from the human capacity for IEs (RSE, 132). If, under some conditions, IEs reliably provide access to ultimate reality, they are of potentially immense theological or philosophical significance (rather than "just" delusional or hallucinatory).

In taking an attributional approach to RSEs, you do not focus solely on the attributions others make, but claim that right for yourself in your capacity as a philosopher and theologian. In your theological capacity, you—in your own words—take "an aggressively attributional approach," applying the term "religion" to "a large chunk of the domain intense experiences." As you acknowledge:

This is far from typical usage, but it is theoretically productive because of the evolutionary importance of intense experiences, and it is permitted precisely because I adopt an attributional approach. Coincidentally (not!), it also suits my theological interests in supporting naturalist, anti-anthropomorphic, anti-supernaturalist worldviews as potentially religious in character.[2]

Your focus on IEs as a doorway into a broad understanding of RSEs points to an underlying difference between us. Although we both want to take a scientific and attributional approach to the study of RSEs across cultures and traditions, you choose to focus on IEs in light of your constructive aims as a theologian and philosopher, while I focus on the wide range of experiences that people deem religious or spiritual in light of my historical and theoretical interest in how people construct their cultural worlds. As a theologian, you embrace the right to attribute religious meaning to intense experiences and on that basis argue that the "big questions" of philosophy are religious and, thus, that humans are inherently religious (*homo religiosus*). I too am interested in the big questions, but I view them as a means of defining a core feature of worldviews and ways of life. I refrain from defining religion or spirituality in order to focus on how people characterize their worldviews and ways of life.

Despite those differences, I think that much of the work that you have done on RSEs is very exciting and that your focus on IEs is very promising. In light of your theological interests, I think it would be helpful to distinguish between your naturalistic account of IEs and your claim that under some conditions IEs reliably provide access to *ultimate* reality. The former sounds plausible to me, but I would question the latter.

WW: Hold on here! You are fundamentally misinterpreting me. I am arguing that under some conditions IEs *may* reliably provide access to ultimate reality and for that reason are of potentially immense theological or philosophical significance. This is a much more nuanced claim. I am not making an assertion about ultimate reality; I am making a claim about the potential benefits of investigating IEs.

AT: Hmm, so if that is the case, why are you referring to the "Whence of IEs" and inferences from "intense experiences to their ultimate environmental Whence" (RSE, 134), which I took as a claim to ultimacy? Capitalizing "Whence" suggests an ontological claim, which you say you are not making.

WW: Right, I view the Whence as a logical object of inquiry. As such I hold no assumptions about its character in advance of inquiry. By contrast, you seem to have a vague conception of its nature from the outset (that's prejudgment) as well as a somewhat less vague conviction that something of that kind can't exist (also prejudgment). You might be right, but, on my account, you can't know this in advance of scrupulous inquiry, which in my experience is a grueling process of comparative multidisciplinary analysis (thus *In Our Own Image* and its companion, not yet published, *Science and Ultimate Reality*).

AT: It sounds to me like you are taking "a *possible* Whence" as your object of inquiry. If that is what you mean, I want to refine where I think our differences lie. At bottom I think there are two: first, whether there is any (practical) point in talking about "ultimate reality" and, second, whether it makes (pragmatic) sense to characterize the "big questions" (BQs) of philosophy as R/S. You would say yes to both; I would say no. Our difference on the first, I think, is a matter of philosophical disposition. As we are both invested in how we and others answer the BQs, I think the difference between us may lie in how we prioritize them. Your focus on IEs is driven by your interest in the ontology question, given your hunch that IEs may reveal something significant about ultimate reality. My focus on experience, more broadly conceived, is driven by my interest in praxeology, that is, the effect that different interpretations have on people's lives and our collective human well-being. Our difference on the second issue is shaped, I think, by our intellectual priorities. As a theoretically inclined historian, my focus is on the past, whether in terms of deep, evolutionary history or more recent human history, where it looks to me like your focus—as a constructive theologian and philosopher—is on shaping the future in light of what we can learn from the past.

AT: But before getting into these deeper issues, let's discuss the way you build your argument, specifically your use of Gibson's ecological psychology and McNamara's concept of decentering.

In making your claim about the ultimacy of RSEs, you follow Alston in shifting the focus from experience to perception, but you reject Alston's depiction of ordinary sense perception in favor of an understanding of sense perception as dynamic environmental engagement, building on Gibson's ecological psychology. Although your shift to perception and concern with the reliability of IE is linked, like Alston's, to overcoming the critique of IEs as delusional or hallucinatory, your adoption of an ecological perspective allows you to conceive the "whence of perception" in a much more nuanced fashion. In criticizing Alston, you highlight Alston's point that "X [can appear] in a way that differs from what X actually is" (RSE, 158) and acknowledge that what appears could be a "vivid mental image." You helpfully expand Gibson's understanding of perception to encompass an "ecology of value" and acknowledge that "sometimes perception is all about values and very little about navigating a physical environment" (RSE, 173). Most notably, an ecological perspective allows you to envision a natural process of discernment, such that people can test the veridicality of IEs, such as "big dreams" or visionary experiences ("hallucinations"), in the world (the environment) to determine what is real. Can you explain how you would describe that process in more detail?

WW: Yes, the ecological perspective forces the naming of the logical Whence first, and bracketing questions of the precise characterology of the Whence from the outset, until evidence allows for a judgment. The idea of "external reality" gets exactly the same treatment in an ecological-psychology analysis of perception; we call the whence of our perception a world but we don't know what it is in itself until we explore. That's how the distinction between reliable perception and perceptual illusion gets slightly blurred in ecological psychology; you actually have to explore the environment to figure out what is going to count as real. In the case of intense experiences, exploring the environment often takes the form of institutionally borne experiments on a grand scale. I suspect you can see here how I would incorporate potent dream states more fully into my argument.[3]

AT: Actually, I'm not sure I understand yet. Can you explain what you mean by "institutionally-borne experiments" and spell out how you would incorporate potent dream states?

WW: I spelled this out in the method book, *Religious Philosophy as Multidisciplinary, Comparative Inquiry*. The associated inquiries are incredibly complicated, always socially embodied and so filtered through contexts and socially constructed worlds of understanding and behavior. Very often (I mean almost always), people adopt an orientation to intense experiences that seems plausible because of their local worldview investments; on the basis of the plausibility structure and conceptual apparatus delivered by the worldview group to which they are attached, they are able to answer pressing existential questions about intense experiences bearing on their meaning and reliability. Potent dream states are instances of intense experiences with uncertain meaning. Though some interpret such dreams in relation to custom-built worldviews, that is unusual. In both shamanistic cultures and large-religion cultures, there is an apparatus for interpretation available through accrual of wisdom and insight over a long period of time and refined through application to many different kinds of people and life circumstances.[4]

AT: So what happens when a worldview is challenged?

WW: When the worldview cracks and the plausibility structure starts dissolving, it becomes easy to see the socially constructed character of the reflexive process of inquiry that the person had been engaged in, and maybe he or she tries some other orientation that helps make sense of intense experiences. For most of human history, in most places, these kinds of disruptive unmaskings of the socially constructed plausibility structures don't occur with enough force that the local worldview can't adapt. In such settings, while there might be a few weird philosophers scurrying around with independent inquiries, the worldview itself functions as a socially borne experiment, floating its postulated plausibility structure and conceptual apparatus on the waters of history. Its real value is manifested as worldview boosters adapt the life outlook to changing circumstances and relate it to billions of individual lives. This is the most comprehensive testing our species has ever achieved, and yet it is so disorganized we scarcely know how to make use of it for formal processes of inquiry.[5]

AT: OK, so this comprehensive testing is what you mean by "institutionally-borne experiments." You seem to be suggesting that this is a complex means of knowing, which we have not yet figured out how to use. This seems very important and I want to come back to this later, along with your use of the term "worldviews"—rather than (say) "religions" or "philosophies"—later in our conversation. We might also want to consider the role that "weird philosophers" might play in this process. But for now I would like to highlight another aspect of your psychology of ultimacy: the suggestion that IEs trigger "decentering," a concept you take from McNamara's neurocognitive model of religious experience. McNamara's model is built on the psychological research on play.[6] Both play and dreaming are spaces in which the ordinary sense of self is "decentered" and new associations are more freely generated than usual, either via dream processes or imagination. Other animals play and dream and may also have IEs in that context, which suggests that we might root the capacity for IEs in a long evolutionary history.

WW: Yes, exactly; I think there is a link, however nuanced and conditional, between IEs and perceptions of reality that emerged in early human evolutionary history. More specifically, "the capacity for IE opened human beings up to *the valuational depths of reality*, helping them construct social arrangements as lattice-like structures above a vast abyss of meaning and power. . . . If the intensification of sense experience in early modern humans allowed them to perceive *formerly hidden valuational worlds of meaning* and to picture new forms of social life, then their ritual attempts to control this awesome reality, and to regulate access to it, created an energy source that was capable of powering the realization of new possibilities for social life they were picturing" (RSE, 259 emphasis in original).

AT: When you refer to IEs opening human beings up *to the valuational depths of reality*, are you assuming that these depths are preexisting? I don't think we need to presuppose the preexistence of "valuational depths of reality," hidden from other animals, to which early humans gained access. We could simply presuppose that with expanded forms of cognition humans acquired the ability to anticipate death and think about questions of meaning. I think it is more parsimonious to suggest that the expanded capacity for IEs emerged in tandem with an expanded capacity for neural connectivity and the associated ability to reflect on (ask questions about, perceive the problem of) the meaning of things (e.g., life, death, etc.). The capacity for IEs may be an intense form of meaning perception no more grounded in reality than are dreams, but like intense dreams, affording perceptions of meaning that people can *construe as perceptions of the meaning of what is (and/or always has been) or as perceptions of what might be*. In the latter case, they provide "models for" (in Geertz's sense) what might be and thus the capacity to envision alternatives to what currently is and to generate change.

WW: I agree! I think the capacity to experience IEs leverages ordinary sense perception to open up awareness of the very questions of meaning that make those experiences worthy of the qualifier "intense."

AT: This clarification is very helpful, but I think there is a tension between "valuational depths of reality," which I still think suggests a preexisting reality, and "valuational worlds of meaning," which suggests a new awareness of questions of meaning. Perhaps if you referred to IEs as opening people up to a greater awareness of questions of meaning and, as a result, to new insights into what they construed as the valuational depths of reality, your meaning would be clearer.

At any rate, I think this interpretation fits well with the connections you make between IEs and new insights, new behavior patterns, and new values (RSE, 94). Whether the claims are framed as insights into what really is or what really could be, claims about the "valuational depths" usually have consequences for everyday life lived more on the surface of things. However the claims are framed, I think they most likely can be linked to the ability to envision alternative scenarios and new possibilities, thus linked to human creativity in its broadest sense. The ability to envision, prepare for, and/or realize alternative scenarios, sometimes referred to as "mental time travel," has potentially great adaptive value.[7]

How we characterize such perceptions—whether as religious, spiritual, scientific, or artistic—surely has more to do with our current cultural conceptions than with underlying mental processes.[8] Linking IEs with perceptions of meaning and value, and beyond that with the ability to envision alternatives, not only makes sense in its own right, it also allows us to reflect on the evolutionary significance of imagination, play, dreams, and visionary experiences, especially in relation to anticipating danger, devising alternative strategies, and adaptive change. It also gets us out of the forced choice between real versus hallucinatory or delusional perceptions, where the former are understood as veridical external sense perception and the latter as nonveridical external sense perceptions.

Since I know (from your comments on an earlier draft) that you would agree with this characterization, I still don't get how this allows you to make ontological claims about the Whence.

WW: "Since my approach imagines that what we are engaging in [with respect to] intense experiences is precisely the valuational possibilities of reality, I don't see a lot of difference between granting an ontology of the Whence of intense experiences (an extremely abstract and formal way of specifying an ontology) and rejecting such an ontology in favor of one that acknowledges the reality of concrete meanings in human life (which is what you presume). Unlike Alston, I seriously doubt that this Whence takes coherent shape as anything remotely like a personal being in the manner of traditional theisms, and indeed I think there is a decent case that the Whence may not be especially coherent at all—which [leads] Phil [Clayton to] say that I shouldn't call myself a theist; it is just too confusing."[9]

AT: Given your focus on possibilities rather than outright claims, it sounds to me like your position echoes William James's idea of the More, which he thought might open up to a More beyond the subconscious self. Like you, he viewed this as a matter of empirical investigation, which explains his interest in psychical research. In light of that, I'd like to ask why you call yourself a theist. It seems that you ascribe religious or theological significance to "engaging . . . [with] the valuational possibilities of reality." I would have thought that engaging with valuational possibilities was a core task of a philosopher. Isn't axiology one of the big questions with which philosophers wrestle? Why do you characterize it as religious or theological?

WW: Yes, certainly, axiology is a core philosophical question. I view "religious philosophy [as] . . . inquiry aiming to answer the big philosophical questions of metaphysics, epistemology, and ethics *insofar as they possess religious significance*. [I admit that] the idea of 'religious significance' is difficult to pin down because the interests of religious groups and individuals vary dramatically across cultures and contexts and eras."[10]

AT: But don't you have to pin it down a bit more, if you are going to make that distinction? I am pushing you on this because you want to make the distinction.

WW: Yes, certainly. I do think humans are inherently religious and I've written a book arguing that this follows from the sort of naturalism that I embrace. Specifically, I would argue that "religious behaviors, beliefs, and experiences—understood sufficiently broadly—constitute human nature not only historically, culturally, and circumstantially, but also ontologically, essentially, and inescapably. *A thoroughgoing and consistent naturalism is inevitably also profoundly spiritual and religious*" (RPMCI, xv). I would go further and argue: "A properly generous interpretation of human religiosity inclusive of the full variety of spiritual and axiological sensitivities of the human condition . . . <u>requires a metaphysically minimalist framework that registers species-wide features of the human condition</u>" (RPMCI, xvii).

AT: Ah, I think I see the point where we differ. I agree with the underlined part, but I would prefer to conceive of the "full variety of spiritual and axiological sensitivities" as worldviews rather than human religiosity. Your approach seems to presuppose that philosophy is inherently religious or theological, which you might argue given your definition, but I think most philosophers would embrace axiology without adopting a religious or theological stance. By defining "religious" expansively, you impose that label on all of us and suggest that it is impossible to reflect on axiological issues without being religious. I want to use a more open framework that does not impose that label on people.

WW: Here you begin to name the reasons for your attributional strategy. Keep going. Project it forward into the future.

AT: You are challenging me to think about this in ways that I confess I don't think about much as a historian! But I'll give it a shot. As a historian, I want an open framework that allows me to clearly distinguish between my views as a scholar and those of the people I am studying. I also value a more open worldviews framework for understanding the range of views people hold in the present. It strikes me as significant that you lapsed into more general language of worldviews at an earlier point in our discussion. If we adopt a worldviews framework defined in terms of the big questions, as Egil Asprem and I are advocating, we can subsume worldviews that people characterize as religious, nonreligious, and/or philosophical under that heading without having to specify a definition of religion ourselves (as scholars).[11]

But I realize my inclinations may be rooted in my sense of myself as a historian and scholar of worldviews and that your interest in projecting further into the future than I tend to go may be grounded in your constructive impulses. So can you explain what exactly is at stake for you in your expansive definition?

WW: Yes, like many social scientists, you seem to adopt "the posture (if not the actual achievement) of . . . metaphysical neutrality."[12] In doing so, I think we risk losing sight of "the philosophical interest in evaluative questions of meaning and purpose . . . [after which] there is no possibility of producing a properly *religious* or *theological* interpretation of the human condition." When I ask you to push your approach into the future, I am asking you to test it or try it out (as an imaginative experiment) in relation to how you envision the future is likely to unfold. That is something I am doing and want to explain more fully in my response.

AT: I see you have brought us back to your sense that a "worldview functions as a socially borne experiment, floating [a] postulated plausibility structure and conceptual apparatus on the waters of history, [but that] its real value is manifested as worldview boosters adapt the life outlook to changing circumstances and relate it to billions of individual lives."

WW: Yes, I am betting that there is value in working from the inside of the traditional religions to help them adapt to a coming age of post-supernaturalism.

AT: Hmm, your spelling that out makes it easier to see where our backgrounds lead us to differ. My present-day concern is with those who view themselves as nonreligious, nonspiritual, and/or secular. In defining themselves primarily in opposition to supernaturalism, I worry that they are left without a way to think about the larger questions of meaning and purpose. One of my aims in promoting a worldviews framework is to create a meta-framework that allows such people—my people actually—to take up questions of meaning and purpose on their own terms. A worldviews framework in my view can engage us all in pondering such questions simply as "big questions."

Notes

1. Wesley Wildman, *Religious and Spiritual Experiences* (Cambridge: Cambridge University Press, 2011), 101. Hereafter cited as RSE.
2. Wesley Wildman (WW) to Ann Taves (AT), comment on earlier draft, June 23, 2018.
3. WW to AT, email, October 14, 2012.
4. WW to AT, comment on earlier draft, June 23, 2018.
5. WW to AT, comment on earlier draft, June 23, 2018.
6. Ann Taves, "McNamara's Cognitive Model of Self-transformation," *Religion* 41, no. 1 (2011): 85–89, http://dx.doi.org/10.1080/0048721X.2011.553136.
7. T. Suddendorf and M. C. Corballis, "The Evolution of Foresight: What Is Mental Time Travel, and Is It Unique to Humans?," *Behavioral and Brain Sciences* 30 (2007): 299–313. http://dx.doi.org/10.1017/S0140525X07001975.
8. Maurice Bloch, "Why Religion Is Nothing Special but Is Central," *Philosophical Transactions of the Royal Society of London Series B, Biological Sciences* 363 (2008): 2055–61. http://dx.doi.org/10.1098/rstb.2008.0007.
9. WW to AT, email, October 14, 2012.

10. Wesley Wildman, *Religious Philosophy as Multidisciplinary Comparative Inquiry: Envisioning a Future for the Philosophy of Religion* (Albany, NY: State University of New York Press, 2010), 1–2. Hereafter cited as RPMCI.

11. Ann Taves and Egil Asprem, "Scientific Worldview Studies: A Programmatic Proposal," in *A New Synthesis: Cognition, Evolution, and History in the Study of Religion*, ed. Anders K. Petersen et al. (Leiden: Brill, 2018); Ann Taves, Egil Asprem, and Elliott Ihm, "Psychology, Meaning Making and the Study of Worldviews: Beyond Religion and Non-religion," *Psychology of Religion and Spirituality* 10, no. 3 (2018): 207–17.

12. Wesley Wildman, *Science and Religious Anthropology: A Spiritually Evocative Interpretation of Human Life* (New York: Ashgate, 2009), xvii.

14

The Man Who Receives Too Many Emails

*Exploring the Construction
of Wildman's Institutional Reality*

RICHARD SOSIS

My Colleague Riding Shotgun

In May of 2015, Wesley Wildman and I drove from Boston to Montreal to attend a conference titled *Religion in the Text and in the Ground* at McGill University. Although Wesley and I had been in weekly contact for almost a decade, and resided within a half-hour drive of each other, we had only met a handful of times prior to this trip. There is nothing like a six-hour road trip to get to know a colleague, and I was looking forward to the opportunity.

 At one point during the trip, Wesley turned to me earnestly and said that he had a serious problem and was hoping that I could offer some advice. My initial thought was that I was about to hear about a grim marital or fatherhood predicament, and I was quite nervous about the prospect of weighing in on such an affair. Our relationship simply had not explored this kind of territory. I kept my eyes on the road, cautiously nodding for him to proceed. I was surprised and confused by his next question: "Rich, how many emails do you receive each day?" I told him that I receive around thirty to forty per day, probably inflating the number to sound important. "Why?" I appropriately asked, still anticipating a question about how to repair a crumbling marriage or discipline a wayward child. He responded, "Because I receive hundreds of emails daily, and I don't know what to do about it." Confused, I wondered if he was asking me for advice about an effective spam filter. "Wesley, what do you mean?" No, I learned from his response, he was not referring to junk mail, as I had considered. He receives more than two hundred work-related emails daily, all of which require responses from him. I knew I was a contributor to this glut, but who else felt the need to regularly bother my passenger? He proceeded to tell me about the various outreach projects in which he was involved and the organizations that he was running or contributing to, all of which demanded his unwavering attention. Thank goodness I had six hours to kill.

By necessity, this chapter is a little unusual; its peculiarity is a result and reflection of the individual whom we are celebrating. While the other chapters in this volume will engage with Wesley Wildman's diverse academic writings, this chapter focuses on his institutional accomplishments. Indeed, to understand and appreciate our prolific colleague, we must explore this side of his academic life; in other words, we need to grasp why this ageless polymath, Wesley Wildman, receives and responds to more than two hundred emails every day. No volume that claims to celebrate Wildman's academic accomplishments would be complete without a discussion of the institutional structures that he has built and maintains.

Unfortunately, I am not sure if there is anyone, other than Wesley himself, who has a full grasp of what his various organizations are pursuing and achieving. That said, my credentials to write this chapter appear adequate, even if Wesley's institutional empire is so vast I feel rather inadequate for the task. I have been a senior research fellow at Wesley's Institute for the Bio-Cultural Study of Religion since 2008, and I have continued this position in his recently established Center for Mind and Culture, which I believe makes me the longest tenured fellow of Wesley's organizations. Moreover, I cofounded and currently coedit the journal *Religion, Brain & Behavior* with Wesley. There have been six coeditors of *Religion, Brain & Behavior* since its inception, and Wesley and I are the only ones who have served in this role throughout the journal's entire existence. I know Wesley and his institutions best through our joint work for *Religion, Brain & Behavior*, so it is through the birth of this journal that I explore Wesley's commitment to creating institutions aimed at advancing the bio-cultural study of religion and disseminating its findings.

Entering Wildman's Wild World:
The Birth of a Journal

INTERNATIONAL CONFERENCE ON THE EVOLUTION OF RELIGION

In January of 2007, with Joseph Bulbulia and Armin Geertz, I co-organized a week-long conference in Hawaii that brought together many of the leading scholars engaged in researching the origins and evolution of religion. This conference, the *International Conference on the Evolution of Religion*, did not inaugurate the evolutionary science of religion, but it did mark the field's arrival as a serious area of inquiry.[1] The number of prominent scientists and religious studies scholars who attended the conference suggested to all observers that this young area of study had a very promising future.

Shortly after the conference, I was contacted by neuroscientist Patrick McNamara, whom I had known for several years. One of Patrick's graduate students, Erica Harris, had delivered a paper in Hawaii and was crucial in running the conference; she kept the organizers organized. Patrick asked me, in the wake of the success of the conference, what I thought about developing a journal devoted to evolutionary religious studies, as we often referred to the field at that time. This was an exciting opportunity, and I realized that a journal devoted to the biological study of religion could be a vital resource for advancing this burgeoning but fledgling field. The conference had clearly demonstrated that there was excitement surrounding this area of study, so the time was ripe for such a venture.

During our conversation, Patrick mentioned that he had recently cofounded, with Wesley Wildman, the Institute for the Bio-Cultural Study of Religion (IBCSR). The goal of the institute, as its name suggests, was to advance the bio-cultural study of religion. Patrick wondered whether the three of us could pursue the journal together, with the institutional backing of IBCSR. I had not yet entered Wesley's world and was admittedly unfamiliar with him or his work, but the combination of a philosopher-theologian, neuroscientist, and evolutionary anthropologist working together sounded like the right mix to start up an interdisciplinary scientific journal on religion. I recognized that the journal should not only engage multiple disciplines, but if developed appropriately, it could serve as an intellectual space for scientists and humanities scholars to collaboratively explore the biological foundations of religion. To succeed, a credible editorial voice on the humanities side of the discussion would be essential, and a philosopher-theologian working in a Religious Studies department seemed perfect. Little did I realize at the time that Wesley was no ordinary humanities scholar—indeed, such a label as "humanities scholar" would prove to be far too limiting. Nor did I realize that I would be beginning one of the longest and most fruitful collaborations of my career.

Publish or Perish

The next several years involved the mundane details of writing a prospectus for submission to publishers, working up a business plan, inviting eminent colleagues to serve on the editorial board of the journal, picking the brains of any journal editor foolish enough to respond to our queries, and countless other tasks that I never thought I would do in my academic career. Despite our enthusiasm, publishers were less sanguine about the potential of our proposed journal. We submitted our proposal to various publishers; I have lost count of the actual number, probably to dull the pain of the experience. The external reviews of our proposal were consistently positive, yet the publishers nonetheless repeatedly declined our proposal to establish a new journal.

The problem was not the topic, which was surprisingly easy to sell. As someone who had spent his earlier career studying and writing about the foraging decisions of remote subsistence fishers, I could not believe how different academia was when studying a sexy and newsworthy topic such as religion. And scientists interested in religion? Now that was intriguing! No, our problem was not our area of study but rather that, in the eyes of the publishing industry, we were doing things backwards. Every publisher wanted to know about the academic society that would be supporting the journal. In our naivete, we assumed that the quality of the research we would ultimately publish was our primary concern. We of course had a business plan, but it was a plan for how we could sustain a journal, not how a publisher could sustain *their* business with our journal. It was evident that creating a new journal required a whole new type of thinking on our part.

Thank goodness for Wesley. I have no head for business. Indeed, my fiscal irresponsibility has deprived me of access to my own bank account—and my wife is completely justified on this matter. But the polymathic hero of this volume saved the day. We were running out of potential publishers when some of my work on religious violence led me to a scholar who had recently founded an interdisciplinary journal on terrorism with publisher Taylor & Francis. During our discussions he was encouraging and most notably, he indicated that while his journal was supported by an academic society, Taylor & Francis seemed unconcerned by the size of the society, which was quite small. Despite the low subscription rates of his journal, Taylor & Francis was pleased with the journal's progress because the Pentagon had taken out a subscription. A publisher who was not obsessed with subscription numbers sounded promising.

We submitted our proposal and began negotiations with Taylor & Francis. Like our previous experiences, Taylor & Francis wanted to know about the academic society that would be backing our journal. But this time, when describing IBCSR, rather than reveal that IBCSR had no membership that could financially support the journal, Wesley volunteered that IBCSR would create a membership society in concert with the publication of the journal. Shockingly, Taylor & Francis thought this was acceptable, and they decided to support the journal. To this day I do not know why they decided to take a chance on three young scholars with a memberless membership society. Could it have been Wesley's angelic and trustworthy face?

Wesley set to work on building the membership society that Taylor & Francis required. This was my first glimpse at Wesley's institutional genius. Logic would suggest that to get people to join anything you need to offer them something. The truth was, however, that we did not have anything to offer other than a journal that did not yet exist. Academic societies typically run scholarly meetings, but we had no desire to organize meetings; we simply wanted to develop a journal. Nonetheless, Wesley was undeterred.

Institute for the Bio-Cultural Study of Religion

Before proceeding, I need to provide a little background about IBCSR. IBCSR was founded by Wesley and Patrick in 2006 and its mission is threefold: research, training, and outreach. It is fair to say that at this point in IBCSR's history, around 2009, IBCSR's novel contribution to the scientific study of religion was its outreach work. Wesley and Patrick, along with their associates from the Boston area, conducted research at an extraordinary pace and mentored countless students, but at the time it was difficult to distinguish these activities from their expected obligations as faculty of Boston University. What was different, and most salient, about IBCSR was its attempt to educate laypeople about the bio-cultural study of religion. Outreach included extensive public talks by Wesley, Patrick, IBCSR affiliates, and students, but the most visible outreach consisted of building and maintaining the Science on Religion website (ScienceOnReligion.org). The website contains short blog posts aimed at educating laypeople about the latest findings in the scientific study of religion. The site attracts thousands of readers each month and cumulatively, as of this writing, the site has received well over 2.5 million visitors.

IBCSR Research Review

Let's return to our membership society problem. Academics, including me, have certainly paid attention to postings on Science on Religion, but academics are not the primary target audience for this website. At this point in IBCSR's history, the main thing that IBCSR offered to academics was a recently established monthly review of the literature on the scientific study of religion and spirituality. This monthly electronic publication, *IBCSR Research Review*, annotates articles and books that have been published over the last month related to the bio-cultural study of religion. The aim of *IBCSR Research Review*, in the words of its founding and current editor, Joel Daniels, is "to publicize the work being done in the scientific study of religion and contribute to the development of the field" (personal communication). *IBCSR Research Review* was established in 2009 and has been run continuously by Wesley's former students, such as Joel Daniels, and current students, such as Kate Stockly, who presently serves as *IBCSR Research Review*'s assistant editor.

The search for materials for each issue is extensive and impressive. *IBCSR Research Review*'s promotional website (www.ibcsr.org/index.php/publications/ibcsr-research-review) describes their search methods as follows:

> Articles for each issue are located by searching a variety of databases, such as Applied Science and Technology, ASFA Biological Sciences, ATLA Religion Database, General Science, Medline (PubMed), Psychology and Behavioral Sciences Collection, PSYCinfo, ScienceDirect, and Web of Science. The search terms are similar to the following: ((religio* OR meditat* OR pray*) AND (psycholog* OR neurol* OR neuros* OR scien* OR cogniti* OR evolutio*)). Books are located on Amazon.com, Google Books, and Worldcat. Articles not directly relevant to the scientific study of religion or spirituality, medicine & health research are excluded, as is correspondence.

The *IBCSR Research Review* is an exceptional resource, and more than six hundred scholars currently subscribe to it. A typical issue runs about fifty pages and is filled with book and article summaries that would otherwise take countless hours to find, compile, and digest. When the *IBCSR Research Review* predictably arrives in my email inbox each month, I just as predictably marvel anew at the effort involved in publishing this invaluable resource. But there is one flaw with the *IBCSR Research Review*, at least as an incentive to attract scholars to a membership society: subscriptions are free. In other words, the one thing that we could use as a hook to build an academic society, the one thing we had to offer, was as free as the air we breathe. Why would anyone pay to gain access to something offered for free?

THE GRATEFUL DEAD SCHOOL OF BUSINESS

When to Rob a Bank[2] is a published collection of more than one hundred blogs written by *Freakonomics* authors Steven Levitt and Stephen Dubner. At the beginning of the book, Levitt and Dubner puzzle over what would seem to be egregiously poor economics: how could they expect to sell a book that contains material that is freely available to any interested reader on the internet? They do not exactly provide an answer, but they do describe how, after driving by a water bottling plant, they realized that one could indeed sell what is readily available for free.

Thankfully, Wesley did not intend to test this theory directly. Rather, although it is hard to imagine Wesley with long hair, sandals, and beads, I think he opted for what might be described as the Grateful Dead business model. To the shock and annoyance of the record industry, the Grateful Dead not only allowed bootlegging of their shows, but they also facilitated it by creating secured space within concert venues for tapers to record their live concerts, which would then be shared freely with other deadheads. As Jerry Garcia famously quipped on *Late Night with David Letterman*, "Once we are done with it, they can have it." What Garcia and the rest of the band appreciated, contrary to most business models, is that by giving away music freely, they were building a dedicated fan base who were committed to attending their concerts and purchasing their conventional albums. Likewise, although I asked Wesley to consider limiting access to the monthly publication to those willing to pay for membership to IBCSR, Wesley was committed to keeping the *IBCSR Research Review* free. Wesley had a better idea than charging membership dues for the *IBCSR Research Review*. His plan was to continue to offer the *IBCSR Research Review* for free, but use the issues of the *IBCSR Research Review* to create a searchable database that only IBCSR members could access. Create fans by offering the product for free, which creates a market, where profit can be earned, for greater access to the product and related items.

IBCSR has fallen short—in both numbers and commitment—of the fan base established by the Grateful Dead, but the creation of the *IBCSR Research Review* searchable database gave us a viable hook to turn IBCSR into a membership society. And thus a new journal was born.

What's in a Name?

But details, of course, still remained. What should the new journal be called? A somewhat ironic name, to honor what at the time was a memberless society, could have been the *Journal of the Institute for the Bio-Cultural Study of Religion Society*, but fortunately we did not entertain this possibility. We did, however, entertain *Journal for the Bio-Cultural Study of Religion*, which is both clear and concise. I had reservations about this title, however. In fact, the situation surrounding this name was a little perilous. While I was impressed by what Wesley and Patrick had accomplished with IBCSR, I was not a fan of the term bio-cultural. At that time, bio-cultural referred to a perspective and approach pursued by cultural anthropologists who recognized that humans are both biologically and culturally informed and constrained. Whether accurate or not, for other evolutionary anthropologists and me, the label was associated with what might be considered soft science; bio-cultural studies lacked the scientific rigor of other subfields working at the nexus of biology and culture, such as human behavioral ecology and cognitive anthropology.

Colleagues in the hard sciences probably giggled at our scientific snobbery, and I now find it a bit embarrassing, but such was the landscape at that time. Explaining my reservations about the term to Wesley and Patrick could have been awkward and prematurely ended our collegial working relationship, but to their credit, they listened to my concerns, and we decided to provide a choice of journal names to members of our editorial board and let them consider which name would best represent the goals of the journal. Ultimately, *Religion, Brain & Behavior* was chosen, and it remains the journal's name to this day. Admittedly, my concerns about the term "bio-cultural" proved to be unwarranted, and it is a term that I now embrace. But I am convinced that part of its acceptance among academics is a result of the high-quality work that has emerged from IBCSR, thus giving the term the credibility that I thought it lacked a decade ago.

Possibly as a consequence of my initial concerns about the term, the IBCSR website dedicates an entire page to explaining the meaning of bio-cultural. The bio-cultural study of religion is summarized as:

> . . . a way of shining a spotlight on the constructive intertwining of cultures, brains, and biology. It assumes that we will find no answer to the chicken-and-egg question that asks whether nature or nurture is primary in religion. Brains and cultures are involved in eons-long feedback cycles without end. Biology constrains culture but cannot dictate it. Culture profoundly influences behavior but does not get the last word. In fact, no one gets the last word—both biology and culture are continually talking. And through integrated research methodologies, we coax out the answers to the questions that matter. (http://www.ibcsr.org/index.php/about/what-does-bio-cultural-mean)

Naked Supernatural Beings

While I was concerned about, and involved with, the naming of the journal, I felt comfortable leaving the cover design of the journal in Wesley's capable hands. Wesley suggested we use William Blake's "Web of Religion" illustration on the cover of the journal. Patrick and I mused whether we should be concerned about displaying a bare buttock on the cover of a religion journal, but we otherwise thought it was an exceptional idea. As we wrote in the editorial of our first issue (McNamara et al. 2011, 3):

> William Blake captured some of the restless, promethean nature of religion in his "Web of Religion" (see cover of this issue). This painting appeared as a plate in his book of visions called Urizen. Urizen was the great demiurgic being. As he moved through the "cruel enormities," the "great astonishments," and the "terrifying majesties" of the creations he witnessed, he was both created by and created the "Web of Religion." What is true of Blake's Urizen is true for all of us: we are defined and transformed by what we behold, and we inevitably change what we engage with our restless energies. Religion, Brain & Behavior stands for expert engagement with the manifold complexities of religion and responsible transformation of the study of religion

as a reliable cultural and biological understanding of religion emerges into view.[3]

Religion, Brain & Behavior

The mission and scope of *RBB* has remained unchanged since the first issue was published in 2011. As printed on the inside cover of every issue:

> The aim of *Religion, Brain & Behavior* (*RBB*) will be to provide a vehicle for the advancement of current biological approaches to understanding religion at every level from brain to behavior. *RBB* will unite multiple disciplinary perspectives that share these interests. The journal will seek empirical and theoretical studies that reflect rigorous scientific standards and a sophisticated appreciation of the academic study of religion. *RBB* will welcome contributions from a wide array of biological and related disciplines, including cognitive science, evolutionary cognitive neuroscience, evolutionary psychology, social psychology, evolutionary anthropology, social neuroscience, neurology, genetics, demography, bioeconomics, neuroeconomics, physiology, developmental psychology, mimetics, behavioral ecology, epidemiology, public health, health effects of religion, cultural evolution, and religious studies. In summary, *RBB* will consider high quality papers in any aspect of the brain-behavior nexus that are related to religion.

I guess the published description of the journal's aims no longer needs to be phrased in the future tense. As of 2019, *RBB* is in its ninth year of publication, and by all accounts it is the flagship journal for the evolutionary and cognitive sciences of religion, even if the field cannot agree on a precise name.[4] The journal, which was originally published three time a year, is now published quarterly. And our page count has increased from 250 pages to more than 400 pages annually. *RBB*'s citation rate exceeds many older and more established religion journals, and the number of authors and ad hoc reviewers who have contributed to the journal currently number in the thousands.

The original coeditors of *RBB* are Patrick, Wesley, and me, but after several years Patrick needed to step down to concentrate on various research projects. At the beginning of our fifth year of publication, we welcomed neuroscientist Michael Spezio and philosopher, evolutionary scientist, and religious studies scholar Joseph Bulbulia as coeditors of *RBB*.[5] Michael of course replaced Patrick as our neuroscience specialist, but we needed to further expand our editorial staff to handle the increasing number of manuscripts we were receiving. The neuroscience seat at *RBB* seems to be a hot one, and after two years Michael needed to step down because of competing responsibilities. Michael was replaced by one of the world's leading neuroscientists studying religion, Aarhus University's Uffe Schjoedt.[6]

While Wesley is active in all aspects of *RBB*, he exclusively manages IBCSR's membership society, which supports the journal. Wesley also deals entirely with the business side of the journal. I think he instinctively knew what it took my wife years to figure out: I was not to be trusted with a checkbook. I should also note, in reference to Wesley's unique roles within the journal, that the consensus among all current and former *RBB* coeditors is that Wesley can sneeze an editorial. On more than one occasion we have missed the deadline for the editorials we publish at the beginning of each issue. Invariably, Wesley has come to the rescue, writing something compelling and relevant, and, most impressively, with great haste.

From IBCSR to CMAC

In recent years Wesley's research interests have extended beyond religion, and consequently he sought to develop an institution that could advance his emergent interests. Thus, in 2017 the Center for Mind and Culture, a nonprofit organization dedicated to nonpartisan interdisciplinary research, was born. CMAC continues IBCSR's commitment to research, training, and outreach, but CMAC represents a considerable expansion in all of these areas. IBCSR did not die with the birth of CMAC; rather, IBCSR was subsumed under the umbrella of CMAC. IBCSR essentially serves as the religion branch of CMAC.

CMAC's research projects are vast and fall within six focus areas: academy, health, history, policy, religion, and security. Current projects include research on illegal child trafficking, proliferation of weapons of mass destruction, and the social integration of immigrants and refugees. These projects are globally oriented and pursued by an international team of researchers, tackling contemporary problems in the United States, Norway, Wales, Turkey, Rwanda, Greece, New Zealand, and Canada. Despite the diversity of CMAC's research projects, at their core they all concern issues of social complexity, or, as Wesley would describe it, all CMAC projects attempt to address societal problems arising out of the "mind-culture nexus." Wesley and colleagues bring their modeling and simulation skills to these projects, as well as their strong commitment to bio-cultural science.

Aside from the extraordinary expansion of topics pursued by CMAC researchers, CMAC also represents a significant step in the development of Wesley's institutions. While IBCSR existed virtually and in various temporary spaces on the campus of Boston University, CMAC maintains a large off-campus office space in the heart of Boston, Massachusetts. The CMAC suite contains multiple state-of-the-art workrooms and offices, as well as a conference room for small events. CMAC employs more than 20 staff members who help facilitate the various projects, publications, and presentations of CMAC researchers. In addition to administrative staff, the graduate students, postdocs, and regular flow of scholarly visitors—and of course Wesley himself—make the CMAC suite not only welcoming, but also an intellectually exciting, rich, and vibrant space.

Anthropologist Plays Psychoanalyst

BRAIN-GROUP NEXUS

Before concluding, it is worth considering the motivations that could spur an academic to build such an extensive and elaborate network of institutions. Most academics, myself included, are content to pursue research, write books and articles that are read by like-minded scholars, and travel the world sharing ideas and presenting findings. On occasion, if we are fortunate, we might kindle the imagination of a few intellectually engaged students. Building institutions is not in any of our job descriptions. So why would an academic veer from the tried and true path of research—publish-present-repeat-cycle—until emeritus retirement? I'm no psychoanalyst, not even on television, but I think Wesley's own writings, which have been admirably explored throughout this volume, provide the key to understanding his motivations and ambitions. Here I specifically focus on his 2009 volume, *Science and Religious Anthropology: A Spiritually Evocative Naturalist Interpretation of Human Life*, which offers a religious naturalist vision of humanity's place in the world.

While it would be imprudent to try to encapsulate Wesley's vast research program within a single idea, if there is one core concept underlying the majority of his work, it would be the brain-group nexus. Wesley's research has, explicitly or implicitly, emphasized that the human condition is a product of a complex web of interactions between neurocognitive structures and group-defined social norms and experiences. Wesley acknowledges humanity's biological constraints, but his writings highlight the human capacity, and responsibility, for creating the social worlds that we inhabit.[7] Wesley's institution-building fetish is largely an exercise in social construction; he is creating the infrastructure for an academic environment in which he, in collaboration with his students and colleagues, can pursue the difficult problems that humanity faces.

Yet Wesley offers a deeper clue to his motivations. Provocatively, he argues that the natural world is not value free, or as he puts it, values "are not merely human fantasies."[8] Wesley affirms an ultimate, albeit unknowable, reality in which value and meaning emerge from the dynamics of human-environment interactions. We all have access to these axiological structures, and this is, at least partially, what makes us human. He maintains that

> Axiological features of reality are accessible to human beings in a uniquely nuanced way among Earth species, thanks to our distinctive cognitive and emotional makeup . . . The world of values awaits discovery, just as the possibilities for engineering living environments lie dormant until creatures arise with the dexterity and intelligence to realize them. Access to the manifold axiological structures and dynamic possibilities of reality, as we are able, is the most precious gift that evolution has bequeathed to us.[9]

Moreover, while Wesley insists that the axiological content of the natural world awaits discovery, humans do not simply stumble upon these values. Rather, we engage nature's axiological possibilities, and we do this via the brain-group nexus. The meanings that inform and give purpose to our lives derive from this engagement: "Understanding the brain-group nexus . . . open[s] up a world of values, which is where we derive so much of the meaning of our lives."[10] As he further writes,

> We never simply encounter the good, the true, and the beautiful somehow abstracted from our interpretations, groups, habits, and choices. Rather, we create the good through generating and

nurturing moral traditions. We create the true through birthing and deploying traditions of inquiry. And we create the beautiful through inventing and savoring aesthetic traditions.[11]

I humbly submit, before doffing my psychoanalyst hat, that Wesley's institutional work is his way of creating a stimulating academic environment in which a scholarly group with respected norms and traditions concerning the advancement of knowledge can pursue goodness, truth, and beauty. In his own words, on the path of religious naturalism, which he passionately affirms, "we become increasingly intentional about habitat engineering projects to relieve suffering, increase justice, and to enjoy the possibilities that life presents."[12] Whether he is aware of it or not, this is precisely what his institutional empire has been accomplishing.

Conclusion

So I conclude with some advice for Wesley, advice that I should have offered three years ago on our road trip to Montreal: Wesley, if you want to reduce the number of emails you receive, the solution is simple: you must refrain from further institutional expansion. The list of your institutions and associated projects is astounding, and frankly it makes the rest of your hardworking colleagues, such as myself, look like slackers. In case you want to refresh your memory, your list of responsibilities includes the Institute for the Bio-Cultural Study of Religion; Center for Mind and Culture; Exploring My Religion; Science on Religion; *Religion, Brain & Behavior*; *IBCSR Research Review*; The Spectrums Project; Simulating Religion Project; Modeling Religion Project; Quantifying Religious Experience Project; and the more than a dozen other projects related to health, history, policy, and security that are listed on CMAC's website. Of course you receive more than two hundred emails a day!

But in truth I am glad I never offered you such advice three years ago. In all seriousness, on behalf of the thousands of scholars and laypeople who have benefited from your organizational network, we hope your institutions and projects continue to flourish and grow. We feel your pain and we apologize, but we ask you to suffer your email surfeit for our sake. From our vantage point, your work is worth the effort. And for me personally, it has been an honor and one of the great pleasures in my academic career to work with you. Here's to the next decade of collaboration!

Acknowledgments

I thank Connor Wood and Joel Daniels for their help with this chapter, LeRon Shults and Robert Neville for useful comments, and the James Barnett Endowment for support.

Notes

1. Joseph Bulbulia et al., *The Evolution of Religion Studies, Theories, & Critiques* (Santa Margarita, CA: Collins Foundation Press, 2008).
2. Steven D. Levitt et al., *When to Rob a Bank: . . . and 131 More Warped Suggestions and Well-Intended Rants* (New York: William Morrow, 2015).
3. Patrick McNamara, Richard Sosis, and Wesley J. Wildman, "Announcing a New Journal: Religion, Brain & Behavior," *Religion, Brain & Behavior* 1, no. 1 (February 1, 2011): 1–4, https://doi.org/10.1080/2153599X.2011.558704.
4. Wesley J. Wildman, *Science and Religious Anthropology* (New York: Routledge, 2009).
5. Richard Sosis and Wesley J. Wildman, "At the Beginning of Year Five . . . ," *Religion, Brain & Behavior* 5, no. 1 (January 2, 2015): 1–2, https://doi.org/10.1080/2153599X.2015.980999.
6. Richard Sosis et al., "Religion, Brain & Behavior's Seventh Year," *Religion, Brain, and Behavior* 7, no. 1 (2017): 1–2.
7. Wildman, *Science and Religious Anthropology*, 213.
8. Wildman, 194.
9. Wildman, 174.
10. Wildman, 217.
11. Wildman, 199.
12. Wildman, 203.

15

Response to Religion in Multidisciplinary Perspective

WESLEY J. WILDMAN

Picture yourself waking up one day, as if newly arrived in the world—fully grown and healthy, perceptive and curious, socially functional and quick to learn language, but with no memories, no history of participation in the socially constructed reality around you, and no accumulated burden of blinkered expectations. What could you do with such a mind? What mysteries could you unravel? What questions could you answer? Philosophers have often tried imaginatively to do something like this, perhaps by peeling back accumulated beliefs with the acid of doubt, by unmasking cultural conditioning using deconstructive critical social theory, or by imagining the life of a developing child. Part of my work as a philosopher of religion involves trying to *understand human beings and the context for human life in the broadest possible sense*, often by destabilizing everything we tend to take for granted in just this way. Of course, sometimes I focus on precisely where we are in our assumption-riddled confusion. Either way, my aim has been to identify the conditions for and the dynamics of human life in the widest possible historical, cultural, and natural interpretative frames.

The result is that I have the marvelous privilege of being able to pursue inquiry into questions that are sometimes matters of ultimate concern for me. These are questions about the meaning of life, the ground of moral reasoning, the wellsprings of value, the origins and destiny of our species, and the depth structures of history and nature. My amazement that this kind of inquiry is culturally and institutionally possible leaves me perpetually filled with wonder and undirected gratitude.

The single most important resource for my attempts to do this has been the wealth of expertise available for me to learn from whenever I take the time to look for it—from university science and humanities disciplines, from culturally borne wisdom traditions, and from careful analysis of the diversity of human experiences. One of the fundamental manifestations in my life of what I'm willing to call "grace" has given rise to the abiding confidence that this veritable host of expert perspectives must cohere to a significant degree—not immediately, to be sure, and certainly not obviously, but ultimately, and in the long run . . . mostly. With sufficient patience, a generous dash of empathic imagination, and a ton of effort, this coherence can become fragmentarily evident in a mental model of reality, one that includes answers to questions of ultimate concern.

The mental model coheres pretty well but never completely, not in my experience anyway, and not in my reading of the history of attempts to build such mental models. For my entire career, I've been puzzling over four possible interpretations of this state of affairs. (1) This failure of demonstrable coherence is a reason to believe that the minds building the models are ill-suited to the task toward which they are ineluctably drawn, like sailors obsessed with the siren cry that dooms them to destroy their ship and their lives on the rocks of imprudence. (2) It is a reason to imagine that the rational heart of reality is itself fractured, and that our expectations need to be recalibrated downward, adopting more modest goals for inquiry better suited to the farcically cracked kernel of reality. (3) It is a reason to conclude that the reality we engage is so resplendent with meanings that perspectival grasping is the best we can do and thus that celebrating the final failure of convergent interpretation is actually a meaningful testimony to the nature of the thing perspectivally glimpsed and fragmentarily grasped. And (4) it is a reason to think we need more time, more experience, more perspectives, more information, and more work in order to claim the golden ring of a coherent model of reality.

Which of these possibilities is more likely? Like Immanuel Kant (he seems so close to me he whispers in my ear, like most of the other guiding voices I mention in this chapter), I worried over #1, which concerns the knowing apparatus, the human mind. Unlike Kant, I have relied on the empirical findings of cognitive psychology to show us how our minds work, subordinating my relatively meager introspective abilities (especially compared to Kant) to that picture of human belief formation. The Codex of Tendencies to Cognitive Error (my preferred name for what has often been called the Cognitive Bias Codex; for a list of biases, see https://

en.wikipedia.org/wiki/List_of_cognitive_biases, and for the illustration see https://upload.wikimedia.org/wikipedia/commons/thumb/6/65/Cognitive_bias_codex_en.svg/1200px-Cognitive_bias_codex_en.svg.png) is the summary of a magnificent intellectual achievement, with a hundred different entries, forever changing the way we think about the way human beings form beliefs and seek to know. I suspect that Kant would have stared in wonder, as I do, to behold this iconic and ironic manifestation of the ingenuity of human reason, turning on itself to manifest its own weaknesses and limitations. It's Kant's trick, of course, but taken as far as it can go, just as he himself attempted to do with far less information than we now possess.

Internalizing this Codex is the single most important practical step we need to take if we are to create a safe and sustainable future for human beings on this spinning blue gem of a planet. Seriously.

It turns out that we can compensate for our tendencies to cognitive error, work around them and with them, and thereby refine our belief-formation processes, our emotion-regulation processes, our perception and memory, our ability to detect when we are being manipulated and deceived, and our capacity for self-awareness. Most advanced forms of education routinely employ cultural learning to limit the deleterious effects of a few tendencies to cognitive error, so we know we can work effectively with the limitations of our own minds. Unfortunately, no existing form of education gets even remotely close to targeting the entire Codex of Tendencies to Cognitive Error. But we now know this must be possible, as soon as we possess the will and the wit to make it happen.

For me, the lifelong journey of cultivating virtue is defined, in part, by mastering all of those tendencies to cognitive error, not just the scattershot selection that my education has forced me to identify and confront. My aim is to refine my instrument, my embodied mind, with all my heart and soul and mind and strength. Every part of the codex, every cognitive bias, needs to be confronted, its effects noticed and diagnosed and regulated. That's not everyone's cup of tea, I realize. But for me it is a critical part of my grown-up Wesleyan quest for holiness.

The upshot of this is that I am relatively confident, contrary to Calvin (another of my ghostly whisperers), that the human knowing apparatus is not so corrupt that we can't work with it effectively, so #1 can't furnish a convincing explanation for the failure of demonstrable coherence in big-question models. I note in passing that I seem never to be more than *relatively confident* about anything, contrary to our esteemed editors F. LeRon Shults and Robert Cummings Neville, both of whom are blessed with astronomical levels of confidence about eternal verities that I only ever experience in my dreams and nightmares, and in my waking battles with the perilous worldviews of fanatical religious zealots. Fortunately, LeRon and Bob are gentle souls rather than violent zealots. Their level of confidence reminds me of Saint Thomas Aquinas (yet another whisperer) prior to his end-of-life mystically driven reevaluation of what he knew and how well he knew it.

Regarding #4, as a finite being soon to shuffle off this mortal coil—and as a naturalist you know that I'm betting (with my characteristically unimpressive level of confidence) that all possible beings are of this finite, bodily, death-doomed kind—I dearly want to believe that my effort is sufficient to optimize the process of inquiry. I confess this as an interpretative caveat to my hard-earned conclusion that human reason can do rather well, and is doing increasingly well, at synthesizing all forms of expert knowledge. The denial of death is often expressed in life projects and, because this synthesis is one of my life projects, it is likely that I overestimate its success. Nevertheless, in our time we have demonstrated greater coherence and predictive accuracy of expert knowledge than ever before, and much of this has been achieved through the investment of resources in inquiry and the organization of inquiry itself. Thus, the fourth option can't *completely* explain the failure of demonstrable coherence in our big-question, model-building quests. Obviously, we need to keep working, but we've done enough to learn something.

Practically, speaking then, I'm down to two fundamental answers to the question about the rational nature of reality: #2, reality is rationally farcical, cracked at its heart, and aspirations to coherent models as answers to life's big questions are comically futile; and #3, reality is replete with surfeit of significance to the point that it necessarily deluges the rational capacities of any possible being, forcing perspectival shattering in every deeply adequate act of interpretation. Deliciously, I have come to think that I don't need to choose between these two. To be more emotionally precise, #3 is a blissful restatement of the sober and sobering #2.

This is merely one person's journey through the thicket that is reason trying to understand itself (or being trying to make sense of itself). But I've thought about this as hard as Kant did and as long as Heidegger (another ghostly whisperer) did, if not as well. I've taken seriously every disciplinary insight I can internalize, much as Kant sought to do in his time and Calvin and Aquinas in theirs. I've honestly appraised the manifest failure of reason in the face of reality, much as Heidegger did in his time, Calvin did in his, and Aquinas did when death drew near. Kant and Augustine, Calvin and

Aquinas, and I: equally obsessed, and arguably equally delusional. But I have followed them in putting my body and mind in the way of the relevant forms of information, regardless of discipline, in order to optimize the one shot at answering big questions that my life energy affords me. Above all, then, my answers are maximally informed, genuinely honest, and hard-won. They're probably wrong, too. And I am perpetually viscerally aware of how marginal my level of confidence is in the conclusions I have drawn. But what can we do? More precisely, what more can I do?

Ann (Taves), Bob (Neville), Kevin (Schilbrack), LeRon (Shults), Miguel (Raposa), Nancy (Frankenberry), Nat (Barrett), Patrick (McNamara), Rich (Sosis), Robert (Corrington), Sarah (Fredericks), Steve (Sandage), Tim (Knepper): thank you. It is my honor to respond to you in this chapter. I refer to you by your given names, as friendship invites, hopeful that Bob and Robert don't get confused along the way with one another.

I intend to tell a story about my tentative answers to big questions, weaving in your insights along the way. My mystical philosophical outlook on the final story of everything makes all this a bit of a lark, a kind of play—hard play, to be sure, but fun. Again, it's not everyone's cup of tea. But it has been mine and will remain my kind of fun for a little longer. What's amazing about this kind of fun—and deeply, deeply peculiar—is that we don't have to do it alone. With Kant and Augustine and Calvin and Aquinas and a thousand other ghosts in one ear, and Ann and Bob and Kevin and LeRon and Miguel and Nancy and Nat and Patrick and Rich and Robert and Sarah and Steve and Tim in the other, and with every disciplinary perspective I can absorb whispering to me in my third ear (unique to Australians, and I can't bring myself to tell you where precisely that third ear is located), I'm haunted in the best of all possible ways. This is play than which no greater play can be conceived. Astonishingly, there are institutions that are willing to be the sandbox for our shovels, the base for our boardgames, and the field for our frisbees. I'm thankful for those institutions, too, especially for Boston University, the site of several tragically lost battles but also the venue of more fun than I can express (and yes, I know, Nancy, that's not really a statement of ineffability, just an acknowledgement of the inadequacy of language, or of the will to find the words, or both).

Back to the story. So far, I'm confessing a 60 percent to 70 percent confidence level (yes, Steve, not 95 percent, as befits psychology publications, and nowhere near LeRon's public declaration of 99.999999999999 percent) in an answer to the big question about why we see things differently, even after allowing for differences of experience and expertise and context and culture and language and discipline and personality and gender and all the rest. Our mental models of reality don't cohere because they can't. Something is stopping the manifold components of those mental models from converging completely. That *something*, which we sense in the failure of demonstrable coherence despite our best individual and corporate efforts, is the *last word on reality*—literally, *the ultimate*. It is not the penultimate word, as if there were some final conclusion we could draw from the mess of slightly but tellingly incoherent mental models; feedback sufficient to take this inquiry further is utterly exhausted, there is nowhere else to go, so we are at the last word, the *ultimate*.

Here's the thing: it's not just me. Lots of other people, across cultures and languages and eras, have come up with more or less the same conclusion: this ultimate, this last word, the Whence of reality in some basic sense, is the furthest that so-called natural reason, unaided by supposed supernatural provisions of wisdom and knowledge, can achieve. It is the thing whose reality Charles Peirce thought we could not fail to acknowledge in sustained musement, the reality John Dewey posited at the root of his naturalistic view of reality, the emptiness that Nargarjuna and Bhavaviveka found hovering within everything, the expression-defying Dao that Laozi found, the attributeless (nirguna) Brahman of Sankara, the perversion-resistant object of worship that Mary Daly believed the Christian Church could never destroy, and the God beyond Gods of the mystics who threw off the limitations of their theistic environments such as Meister Ekhart and Catherine of Sienna and Teresa of Avila. These are my siblings in the intellectual life. It's a small family in the big scheme of things, but it's mine. If Robert is right and there's an afterlife, these are the people I'll hunt down for a coffee and a chat (if I can ever figure out how to enjoy coffee). Maybe a hug, too, because we're all a bit lonely living on the underside of the bright and noisy big traditions whose members seem to know a *lot* more about reality than we do.

This joyous dinner-party–sized crowd of mystical siblings is only the tip of an iceberg, obviously, but it is still small compared to the vast crowds boosting alternative views of ultimate reality. How is it possible that we are not a far larger group, not in the majority?

The most obvious explanation for our status as an ignored, neglected, sometimes persecuted, and always tiny minority is that my little group is wrong and the large majority is right: we can know a lot more and we are just not seeing it or we are stubbornly refusing to accept the supernaturally revealed information that breaks through the limitations of frustrated finite reason. I was prepared to come to that conclusion when I embarked on documenting my journey in religious philosophy with six big books that I thought only four people read (now I know it is slightly more, at least for some of the volumes; my publishers will be so gratified). It's not where I wound up, though. The more wisdom traditions I allowed to whisper sweet nothings into my first ear, the more friends I engaged with my second ear, and the more disciplines I listened to with my third ear, the more I found everything revolving around a mystical Whence.

You see, the final incoherence of mental models of reality is only matched in awesomeness by the stunning fit among the insights tumbling out from a host of disciplines. We are not guessing about a lot of things. Strict relativism is stubborn and stupid, and often enough lazy and leveraged for political purposes, despite the fact that ultimately we are forced to acknowledge a kind of epistemic perspectivalism in reason's best efforts. When it comes to how cars work, how human bodies work, and how human societies work, we know a lot. Not everything, to be sure, not even about the machines we build, but a lot. The disciplines speak in different languages, but they are more than merely commensurable and translatable; they are staggeringly harmonious, despite areas of rough fit or no fit, and despite episodes of ideological blindness with disastrous social consequences. If people who claim otherwise could show me their homework, maybe I could be persuaded. But I see the scattered, no-convergence bottom-line assessment of the striving of human knowledge as a nearly evidence-free zone. On the contrary, from quantum physics to cosmology, from molecular biology to evolutionary theory, from bacterial metabolism to big-animal veterinary science, from developmental psychology to medicine, from social theory to economics—it all hangs together stunningly well. Moreover, the most abstract ventures in human exploration, mathematics and logic, fit reasonably well. The most strongly normative and valuational dimensions of human inquiry, including the humanities disciplines from history to literature, and the arts from music to drama, fit right in there as well, jostling with one another in a nearly harmonious portrayal of reality. As a mental model of reality, it is freaky good.

Now, toss big questions into the mix—via literature and ethics, philosophy and theology, aesthetics and axiology—and this grand assemblage of human wisdom functions as an evidence base. When I dig into the giant mound that is the rough consensus of human efforts at inquiry, the deliverances of my third ear, I see tons of disagreements. But almost all of them are resolvable as perspectives on a complex reality that can't be taken in otherwise, or perspectival conflicts reflecting the cruel dynamics of privilege and oppression, and the breathtaking heartlessness of greed and exploitation. Humming in the depths, however, are a few questions where feedback fails us, the evidence doesn't compel an answer, and disagreements seem intractable. Do we need a solution to the problem of the One and the Many, as Bob thinks, or can we get by just fine without one, as Nancy thinks, along with Alfred North Whitehead (another potent whisperer)? Does the near-harmony of human discovery attest to a rational creator and a world in which human reason isn't quite good enough to hear the perfect music of the spheres, as Miguel and Patrick believe, or does it bespeak a mostly irrational underconscious in nature that no amount of human knowledge will ever be able to tame through demonstrations of coherence, as Robert would have it? We can keep adding to the pile of nearly harmonious knowledge indefinitely, and I struggle to see how we'll get a breakthrough on questions such as these.

Patrick and I have journeyed a long way together, and he has been very patient with my inability to be convinced about the reality of conscious agents without bodies, which he thinks is the necessary outcome of taking the hard problem of consciousness seriously—that is, the problem of explaining the first-person subjective feel of consciousness. I think I do take the hard problem of consciousness seriously, and that does *not* mean merely waving a wand, pronouncing the magic word *emergence*, and pulling a reluctant but conscious rabbit from a hat—an all-too-common form of philosophical self-deception in our era of studying complex adaptive physical and social systems. Rather, I weave the foundations for consciousness into my account of the axiological root of reality, much as William James, Peirce, Dewey, and Whitehead did. It's not panpsychism, but it is an axiological form of dipolar monism, which is the beginnings of a serious answer to the hard problem of consciousness, and consistent with naturalism in my specific sense of ruling out disembodied consciousness. In fact, I think Patrick's disembodied-conscious-agents viewpoint faces extreme difficulties, including in the form of the physical-consciousness coordination problem, which René Descartes struggled so desperately to solve: it seems impossible to explain how disembodied mind and embodied brain sync up.

Now, Patrick is a seriously creative scientist, so I pay attention when he says he thinks that we could run neuroimaging studies to test whether a subpile of evidence better supports his body-free consciousness story or my dipolar-monist, no-disembodied-consciousness, naturalism story. In this case, though, I don't see how his proposal for an experiment could deliver a relevant result. He and I agree that many religious and spiritual experiences

(RSEs) involve personal features, which fit rather naturally under the human cognitive imagination as encounters and communication with invisible conscious beings. He and I agree that those for whom invisible conscious beings are not part of the world's ontological inventory are going to have to contest what their cognitive tendencies invite them to accept by following the dictates of culturally learned conclusions about their naturalistic ontology. He and I would both expect to see signs of all those cognitive processes in neuroimaging studies, along with the weakening of second-order reframings under sped-up conditions for testing. Neither he nor I would expect to see supernaturalists working hard to produce such RSEs, as though they had to create something from nothing in the manner of an effortful hallucination; no, human bodies naturally produce such experiences in mentally healthy people. It's part of what makes us so interesting as a species, and one of the reasons RSEs are so fascinating to Patrick and Ann and me. Because Patrick and I both expect to see the corresponding signs in neuroimaging studies, there is no leverage to choose between our different interpretations. That's not to say we couldn't devise an experiment that could shift the interpretation of evidence, or at least the burden of proof, but I don't think we have found such an experiment yet.

The logic underlying my expectation of no relevant result for Patrick's imagined experiment is akin to the logic at work in using cognitive neuroscience to assess the relative plausibility of invisible conscious agents more generally. Yes, it is true, our minds predispose us to experience ambiguous phenomena in personal ways, attributing intentionality and agency. Yes, realizing this obviously reduces the relative plausibility of the supernatural worldview, at least a little. But it is certainly no defeater of supernaturalism, contrary to LeRon's way of thinking. It is easy to imagine, as developmental psychologist Justin Barrett and others have pointed out, that a conscious supernatural creator deliberately equipped us with brains bearing precisely these cognitive tendencies in order that we would have the best possible chance of interpreting the supernatural world of invisible conscious beings accurately. The price paid in the form of cognitive errors would be well worth it for such a supernatural divine creator if the payoff were correct guesses about the reality of God and the other invisible agents with which we must contend spiritually. This makes a mockery of evolutionary theory by allowing divine intentions to override a natural process, I think, but it is not a completely ridiculous view. Both Patrick and Miguel speak as if cognitive science functions as a decisive consideration in my decision against supernaturalism. This is not so; far from it. Cognitive science contributes, but only as one of a host of considerations, as *In Our Own Image* points out in laborious detail.

When I behold the great assemblage of nearly harmonious human knowledge—which I have tried to absorb and interpret as evidence relevant to drawing conclusions about the ontological inventory of reality and its metaphysical conditions—I don't see what Patrick and Miguel see. But I do understand how they reason about that impressive pile of evidence. While I think they are wrong about their relative plausibility assessments, to me it's a close call (though it's not close for LeRon or Bob or Nancy), something like 60-40 or 70-30 in the direction of naturalism in the sense of no disembodied conscious agents. Aware of the closeness of the argument, I am loathe to do anything other than support the ontological inferences of those who weigh the relevant criteria differently, entering my alternative perspective when the opportunity arises. But my argument cannot be reduced to leaning heavily on cognitive science (Patrick and Miguel), nor can it be deflected by saying that I am not taking the hard problem of consciousness seriously (Patrick). On the contrary, there is only one way through the mound of evidence, and it is a messy and difficult journey.

Even if I'm right about a naturalist ontology, though, I may still be wrong about the surd at the root of things, the Whence that I speak of in mystical terms, the thing that causes the failure of demonstrable coherence. Nancey Murphy (another of my whisperers, though not ghostly!) would agree with the naturalist ontology but argue that I'm misreading the evidence concerning the failure of demonstrable coherence. To her it is completely explained by limitations of human reason and says nothing at all about the nature of the Whence. I have gestured toward my reasons for thinking this is unduly optimistic about the rationality of the Whence and unduly pessimistic about human rationality but, again, it is a close call. She sees a personal supernatural deity behind the scenes, knowable only through divine self-revelation. I respect the inference, despite finding it less plausible than my own. Karl Barth (back to the ghostly kind of third-ear whisperers) does the same: he sees the surd at the root of things, treats it as a sign of human brokenness, and (far more aggressively than Murphy does) asserts that God's self-revelation is the only—literally, the only—way to know that there is a conscious, intelligent divine agent behind the scenes. Barth instinctively knew about many tendencies to cognitive error, including especially the kinds of projective impulses that underwrite so much of religion, and concluded that reasoning our way through that morass is more than futile; it is an impossibility. Natural theology is inert in the face of this problem, for Barth. If there's a basis for believing in a God, it can only be because God lets us know through intentional self-disclosure. Fortunately for us, says Barth, God did exactly that. On the contrary, says Wesley, that never happened; we made it up, and it still lives as a civilization-sized hypothesis, though it is getting ragged around the edges in places where the latest of thousands of versions of theism is losing its grip on human imaginations. In my generous moments, I attribute to Barth something less than LeRonian 99.99999999999999 percent confidence in his belief that divine self-revelation occurred in history and nature; his personal weaknesses in other domains of life encourage me to believe he may have possessed a humane appreciation for the possibility of being mistaken. For me, in contrast to LeRon, the self-revealing supernatural deity is more than a mere logical possibility that is practically negligible in its plausibility; on the contrary, I consider it simply unlikely, in the sense of 30 percent to 40 percent likely. I know this drives LeRon nuts. What can I say? I'm a careful appraiser of plausibility, and I know the massive data pile better than most, yet I lack his gift of confidence.

If Robert is right and there is an afterlife, then he might allow me the indulgence of a vision of the pearly gates and me rocking up for a chat with Saint Peter (not one of my whisperers, by the way). Miguel and Patrick, watching on with Robert, will be gratified at my shocked visage as I realize that, despite having died and been cremated, I am in fact conscious (got the afterlife thing wrong), there are pearly gates (got that wrong, too), there is a Saint Peter (and that), and there is a God who not only made things so tricky to interpret but who also saved the perfect version of creation for later instead of giving us the best of all possible worlds the first time (that's my biggest mistake). I can hear only partly suppressed guffaws from the three stooges in the peanut gallery as I put the pieces together in my mind, figuring out where my reasoning went wrong, trying to decide how angry I should be at God for the reality of divine neglect, and estimating whether I'll be allowed in and, if so, whether I can finally learn to play the cello. In this new world, whether accepted through the pearly gates into the Good Place or deposited Elsewhere, I'm going to feel a bit disoriented for a while. But eventually I'll realize that the great theistic theologians such as Barth and Augustine and Ramanuja (all third-ear whisperers), who also see what I see as an irrational surd at the root of things in the form of the failure of demonstrable coherence of mind-maps of reality, were correct that the problem is almost entirely with human reasoning powers, which I overestimated despite my wholehearted embrace of the Codex of Tendencies to Cognitive Error; correct that a personal, invisible, supernatural, designing, creator deity stands behind the whole, which is an interpretative hypothesis whose plausibility I underestimated; and correct that my big strategic failure was trusting my reason, the evidence of my senses, and what I thought were wise voices whispering in my ears, instead of placing my faith in a supernaturally authorized body of divine self-revelation. Trust me: I really can picture being wrong. I can anticipate where the missteps would be. And I'm still calling the reality-interpretation game in favor of *naturalism* (no invisible intentional agents), *atheism* (no divine being and no gods), *ordinary knowledge accrued effortfully* (no supernaturally authorized divine revelation), and *mysticism* (the damnable surd at the root of things *provokes* the failure of demonstrable coherence of mind-maps of reality because it is a superfluity of significance that limits any finite being to shard-like perspectival glimpses of it—and *that's what I call God*).

My emptiness-oriented mystical brethren, no doubt assigned with me to Elsewhere, sixth circle, would be eager for a chat. Sankara would be cursing Ramanuja who is in the Good Place with Augustine; Sankara hates being wrong. Laozi would say that theism wasn't really even on his radar, and the whole thing strikes him as unfair. That goes double for the alien dude hovering on the edges of our thatch of grumblers. Eckhart would be complaining about Augustine having made it to the Good Place despite his obviously tangled relationship to his own body. And I'd be thinking Eckhart and I had the best shot of getting it right; at least we grew up in Christian cultures, even if we perversely thought our way out of the theistic framework. And rising up from the unexpunged reserves of my stubbornness would come this still, small voice: this very experience is a comical deconstruction of the myth of the invisible personal deity, a reductio ad absurdum so compelling that, if only I could wake up, it would all dissolve into nothingness. In short: I wouldn't be surprised if I were wrong, but I'd be hugely disappointed that the Real is so parochial, so close to anthropomorphic pretensions, so conveniently and horrifically small-minded. Of course, I'm toying here with a childish view of the afterlife. But even this silly story picks up on the most salient features of the divine nature and thus has the requisite reductio-ad-absurdum power.

Honestly, the worst thing about being consigned to Elsewhere might be missing Jesus. I have organized my life around following him, striving to cultivate the virtues I admire in what people remember of his impact on them, and self-consciously adopting a moral orientation to life inspired by him, particularly his disruptive approach to social norms in favor of marginalized people. I disagree with his supernatural ontology and his personalist understanding of God, sure. But he meant the world to me, and I followed him with a seriousness akin to the commitment I have to my beloved life partner, Suzanne. In Elsewhere, I'd miss seeing him and being with him. And I sense I'd feel compelled to still follow him the best I could—the only person in Elsewhere trying to follow Jesus, and doing it all wrong. Maybe that absurdity comes along with the inveterate stubbornness that produces the still, small voice, perpetually promising that the nightmare of Elsewhere and the Good Place and a God who thinks this is all fine will just dissolve.

In 2013–2014 I spent the year at the Center of Theological Inquiry in Princeton. There I had the pleasure making a bunch of new friends, including Christian philosopher Robert Roberts. Roberts was baffled by my worldview, and more baffled the better he got to know it. One day, we were returning from lunch, walking across the Princeton Theological Seminary campus, and he turned to me, obviously frustrated, and asked with his characteristically gentle intensity, "If you believe in an ultimate reality that is utterly unscaled to human moral concerns, then how do you figure out what is right and wrong?" Roberts is, like most Christians, a get-your-goodness-from-God kind of guy. I answered, "By following Jesus the best I can." I think it would be fair to say that Roberts was stunned, as he hadn't considered the possibility that someone he thought of as a naturalist atheist could possibly be a disciple of Jesus, self-consciously choosing a moral framework for life inspired in large measure by a person Roberts himself tries to follow. But I thought I also saw a glimmer of understanding, and maybe even a hint of appreciation for the fact that Jesus belongs not only to Christians of the sort he can easily recognize but to everyone, and that Jesus's significance can't be tamed by doctrinal fantasies about his person and work that some thoughtful people elaborate for good reasons and others criticize for good reasons. Roberts never accommodated himself to my particular kind of theism, with its mystical appreciation for a God beyond the Gods of religion, seeing it as indistinguishable from atheism in the ordinary sense of the word; and I think he would have resisted bestowing upon me the title of Christian, despite my obvious devotion to the Christian churches—I can understand all that. But despite those reservations about my religious and theological credentials, I thought he started to discern in me something more like a strange brother in Christ rather than an utter alien. I hope so.

People with my sort of worldview shouldn't seem so strange to others, especially philosophers. If we were better at articulating this mystical theism, maybe philosophers would understand us more easily, with less struggle and confusion. Well, in Elsewhere, we'll have nothing but time to figure it out.

If Roberts had to struggle to understand me from the ideological and theological right side, then one of the great joys of my life is that Bob, speaking from my left side, got me straight away. My goodness, how amazing that is. I have gotten to know hundreds of academics by now, and I have rarely heard of so rich an intellectual and personal relationship with a departmental colleague. As Bob points out, however, although we inhabit the same family of apophatic mystical worldviews, we don't perfectly agree. He's correct when he says that he's more suspicious than I of the negative effects of STEM disciplines on norms for what counts as good academic work in university cultures. I am a reliable defender of the humanities but think the way through the so-called crisis of the humanities is for humanities scholars to demonstrate the positive value of their disciplines in university cultures, including showing how their hermeneutical sophistication and contextual sensitivity can help scientists do better science, as well as generate priceless insights into the human condition. Don't just assert the importance of the humanities while complaining about marginalization; rather, demonstrate that importance!

Bob's disputes with me over symmetry and asymmetry in metaphysics strike me as talking past one another in search of a point of contact. That point of contact was made in my irony-laden critique of the fundamental argument in Bob's *God the Creator*, which Nancy summarizes in her chapter for this volume. That chapter was inspired as much by trying to get people to see how difficult it is to evade the implications of that splendid argument as it was by trying to demonstrate that it is possible to wind up somewhere else by paying certain prices—the highest possible compliment I can imagine paying another philosopher. I still recall my state of mind when writing it: partly annoyed at people not taking the argument seriously enough (so it seemed to me), partly awestruck at how compelling the argument is, and partly earnest about seeking a way to explain how Bob and I diverge. Bob's inference really may fail, even if the identified premises are solid, if we are contending with a farcically cracked kernel of reality that defeats human reason, that collapses what I sometimes call a "rational floor" for reality (nothing to do with epistemic foundationalism!). That this will not happen is a critical hidden premise of the God-the-creator argument, one that would never need to be stated in most philosophical activity but is critically important in an apophatic theological context. If this difference in perception of possibilities is not a matter of temperament—Bob optimistic about reason, me less so, both of us more optimistic than Barth and Calvin, and both of us less optimistic than Charles Hartshorne and Richard Swinburne—then maybe it is more like a bet on the heart of reality. Bob thinks that he knows enough to clinch the argument, and that the heart of reality with its rational floor is cooperating. I'm just not sure and can't see how to resolve the question about just how farcically cracked is reality's kernel.

Is it temperamental difference or semirational gambling when Bob and I disagree on the meaningfulness of speech about acts without actors (as in Bob's view) and theogonies of infinitesimal manifestation (as in Ray Hart's view)? Again, it's a classic disagreement; we see it between Plotinus and Augustine (the latter purified of his inveterate biblically inspired habit of attributing character to ultimate reality *a se*). Bob's position is that the pile of relevant evidence supports a creative act (without an actor), so we just live with the weird language stretching. My position is that Plotinus's emanation of the One story is no more or less weird than Bob's story so it's a tie on conceptual coherence and we can't tell which is correct for want of relevant evidence so something about (ultimate) reality is preventing us from cleanly teasing apart these two options—and that impediment has been at work since the first moment this contrast was conceived, almost two millennia ago. To behold long-standing, seemingly intractable disagreements of this kind is to speak the last word, to grasp ultimate reality in a fragmentary way. For Barth, it's to miss the comically obvious: God inserts information into the world system to help us vault over the failure of human reason. For Bob, it's to miss the best view, which is his.

Bob's and my entanglement with church institutions has been complex in different ways. I do worry about the survival of those institutions, not for their own sake, but for what they deliver in terms of helping people engage ultimacy authentically and for maintaining some of the necessary conditions for speaking of ultimacy artfully and with existential potency. I found myself sighing with relief when I read Bob's implicit advice: "we do not need to worry as much as Wildman does about the religious fragility of religious communities under threat from wild mystics like us. We will find each other irrespective of religious communities." Bob is probably right, though I wonder how my mystical brothers and sisters banished, tortured, or murdered by their communities would react to this. It is a reminder of the good fortune of our era for mystical philosophical theologians, I guess. But I still worry about the secularism-abetted collapse of such religious institutions for other reasons having to do with continuity of specialized discourse communities.

Another of Bob's and my abiding disagreements results from him trying to get me to inhabit a worldview and explain it from the inside instead of setting up a debate to assess relative plausibility and surface underlying disputes over functional yet hidden criteria for assessing plausibility. Long before I began the Religious Philosophy series, I did what Bob hoped I would do and started writing a systematic philosophical theology that would explain my position from the inside, demonstrating how it relates to and absorbs a host of related considerations. I planned out four volumes and wrote several hundred pages before junking the whole thing. The truth is that I wasn't ready. Bob was born ready and has never really worked in another mode for an extended period of time, not since his early twenties anyway. But I have never possessed his degree of confidence, being constantly aware of the plausibility of arguments other than my own. My pathway has been different, accordingly. I first needed to explain to myself, to imagined Paul Tillich and Mary Daly in the Good Place, and to Eckhart and Sankara in Elsewhere—not to Jesus, note; this is not his cup of tea—why I found the view I hold relatively more plausible than the truly moving and intellectually powerful alternatives. That's what the six volumes of the Religious Philosophy series are all about.

Soon, however, I shall be ready to channel Bob—not his confidence, mind you, because I'll still be hovering at 60 percent to 70 percent while he abides with LeRon in the stratospheric heights of conviction. No, with a smidge less confidence, God willin' and the crick don' rise, I'll be developing my philosophical theology internally to my own position, reconnoitering the landscape from there rather than from a viewing tower I construct to oversee the entire territory. I still like the four-volume design I created decades ago, and I might even be able to rescue some of those hundreds of ditched pages, which at the time of ditching struck me as fatally juvenile. Be that as it may, the point here is that I sense I'm about as ready as I'm ever going to be to write my own systematic philosophical theology. It'll possess a transreligious and mystical orientation, and a bunch of other aspirational qualities that Nancy will patiently point out to me are futile and bordering on nonsense. The fourth volume on method will have to work hard to explain how what I did in the first three volumes was actually doable despite ineffability being impossible and speaking of ultimacy pointless.

Most subtly, I have grown to the point that being unsure doesn't bother me. I have internalized the hypothetical-corrective method I laid out in *Religious Philosophy as Multidisciplinary Comparative Inquiry*, itself a report on what I had already been doing for many years. These days, I derive joy from accurately apportioning intellectual assent in accordance with the strength of evidence, and satisfaction from honoring the best in views whose plausibility I take to pale slightly in comparison with that of my mystical philosophy. And I find multidisciplinary learning absolutely thrilling.

I was stunned to read Steve's reflections on the virtues characteristic of effective multidisciplinary research. He's dead right: the aporia in the research literature around how we are supposed to do this well is really a gaping hole. Of course, we do multidisciplinary research routinely in the several dozen teams working on projects within the Center for Mind and Culture. For seventeen years we have been enacting this and learning to talk about it in the weekly religion and science colloquium at Boston University. And I have learned a ton from people who are really good at this, especially Patrick and Steve himself. But it is all trial and error, bumbling our way through uncharted territory. Seeing this clearly for the first time, thanks to Steve, I am overwhelmed at the underserved trust placed in me by my students and the people who have joined teams to conduct research with me. My sense for how to conduct multidisciplinary inquiry is firmly backed by a pragmatist theory of inquiry, yes, and I have been putting it into practice for decades. But I'm embarrassed to admit that what I've been doing is utterly innocent of any *serious research into best practices*. Maybe Steve can help us all by turning a research spotlight onto that darkened corner of human inquiry. His fresh way of seeing things has been a huge gift for me at Boston University, and I treasure him as a colleague and friend.

Here's another confession, to go along with the confession that I have been winging it all these years in multidisciplinary comparative inquiry. I have grown weary of philosophy, theology, and ethics that posture at transformation but never have any impact. It strikes me as a kind of self-exculpatory evasion of the real force of problems that intellectuals say they want to address. That's fine for scholars when they're starting out, trying to win some standing in their disciplinary homes, but veteran researchers should either make a real difference with their research (i.e., not merely through the classroom or among their scholarly colleagues) or turn their professorships over to someone who will. (Nancy, that's hyperbole, or maybe it isn't . . .) The Center for Mind and Culture (mindandculture.org)—including the Institute for the Bio-Cultural Study of Religion (ibcsr.org) and the Climate, Culture, Conflict, and Cooperation Consortium (c4consortium.org)—exists to rectify this problem. Our informal motto is "rescuing big-brained academics from social irrelevance" and that's just how we operate.

Patrick was the first person to show me how to cross the line and make research count for improving the world. His work on Parkinson's disease

(PD), in which I have been honored to participate, promises to improve the self-understanding of people suffering from that condition, particularly those with the left-onset variety. Time and again I have explained this research to people with PD or living with partners who have PD, only to see them weep with newfound awareness and gratitude as the mystery of their changing spirituality suddenly became intelligible to them. It's more Patrick's job than mine to reach stakeholders and medical practitioners with the findings about how PD interacts with spirituality and religiosity. He has published the results and influenced the PD clinic at the Veterans Affairs Hospital in Jamaica Plain, Boston, and I hope his findings catch on more broadly.

Prior to those boundary-crossing experiences, my most treasured examples of changing the world through research of my philosophical-theology kind were Tillich's way of opening spirituality up to people on the margins and fully outside religious institutions such as Christian churches, Daly's assault on the validity of the self-claimed authority of the Roman Catholic hierarchy, the production of a theology of liberation from experiences of living in base communities exemplified by Gustavo Gutierrez, and the generation of a Black theology of liberation from African-American religious resistance to racist American majority culture by James Cone. These are the third-ear whisperers I would teach in my classes on liberation theology, thinking I was raising consciousness and changing things in my humble way. But the world rolled on despite their best efforts. Tillich's worldview is embraced by a tiny few, Daly's feminist protest was ignored, and Gutierrez's base communities were ineffective on a large scale, ultimately swamped by the mass movement of Pentecostalism in Latin America that changed and is still changing the economic circumstances of millions of poor people—doing by accident what he tried and failed to do on purpose. Cone's efforts don't seem to have changed much, either, remaining mostly confined to the academy and to people who already agree with him within churches. I treasure those visionaries and continue to hope that accumulating changes through academic teaching and scholarly publication might have a trickle-down effect on social circumstances. But that type of change has come to seem too abstract for me, too slow and marginal relative to the big problems we face as a species.

Sarah hasn't worked on any of our CMAC research teams, but she might be reassured to see the care we take to engage stakeholders in the problems we tackle. In doing policy analysis using computational modeling and simulation with LeRon, we quickly learned that engaging stakeholders from the start is essential. Without buy-in to a method that facilitates cost-benefit analysis of policy ideas and virtual experimentation with policies in artificial societies, stakeholders have a difficult time trusting the findings. Thus, in recent years we have always built teams from the outset with researchers and stakeholders combined. This is how we are contributing new insights into the alarming rise of suicide rates, particularly in rural settings; the integration of minority immigrants and refugees into Western cities; the exploitation of children in the commercial sex industry; the proliferation of nuclear materials and expertise to extremists who would use them without hesitation; the mitigation of extremist religious violence; fair access to STEM training and careers among marginalized communities; understanding and acceptance of intersex conditions; social conflict rising on the heels of climate change; and a dozen other issues. In some cases, our inclusion of stakeholders is close to optimal, as in the Tools Against Child Trafficking project; in other cases, such as the mitigation of extremist violence project, we are struggling to recruit the right stakeholders while still preserving our central agenda as practical, change-oriented, yet hard-nosed, data-driven, theoretically astute researchers.

We have a lot to learn about leveraging research for social change, obviously. But we're not sitting on our hands. For every one of our research projects, we try to be explicit about a realistic theory of change, or we don't even start. When I ask myself about the realistic theory of social change associated with my Religious Philosophy series of books, I know the answer: there isn't one. The aim of those books is to perpetuate scholarly cultures as part of the rich cultural tapestries that I think are worth fighting to preserve. That's something. But it's no longer enough for me. So my life is divided between the scholarly part and the practical ethics part. Intellectually, they are tightly knit, but people encountering me on one side rarely know much about the other side.

Rich's witty account of my adventures in institution building, and our shared efforts to found the flagship journal in the bio-cultural study of religion, are on point. Institutions leverage social change when they are set up to do that and when their mission is scrupulously protected from degenerating influences. I use research institutions in that way, like lots of people do. My email volume may be daunting as a result, but I'm doing this on purpose, so I need to accept the side effects—something I'm still struggling to do, not for lack of desire but for lack of actual time and competence. I am very grateful that Rich committed to writing an account of the founding of *Religion, Brain & Behavior*; that really does need to be recorded somewhere. It has been a true joy to work with him all these years. He's a reliable collaborator with impeccable scholarly judgment, and great fun at conferences.

My adventures in practical ethics continue to be extensive and time-consuming, while my philosophical worldview already determines a fundamental ethics in a decisive way and deals with questions about the method of inquiry that makes ethical reasoning and action properly responsive to relevant considerations. But Sarah is right when she points out the lack of ethical writings in the middle territory, between the fundamental philosophical framework and my busy life as an applied researcher seeking ethical social change. I have written and intend to write more on the ethics of new technologies, from computational simulations used for policy analysis to transhumanist aspirations and brain-based technologies of spiritual enhancement. But that's still not the kind of ethics, particularly theological ethics, that Sarah is talking about. Honestly, I don't know if I'll ever get to it. If I do go back to writing on ethics, it will most likely be to write a practical book for regular people on the radical ethics of Jesus, whom I follow; of Gautama (the Buddha), who inspires me to centralize the virtue of nonattachment in my daily spiritual life; and of living into full awareness of humanist touchstones, such as the blessed Codex of Tendencies to Cognitive Error and the emerging cross-cultural consensuses on human rights and ecological sustainability. I think I'm probably going to have to rely on Sarah and her generation of theological ethicists to lay out a pragmatist approach to ethical inquiry that can function effectively for theologically inclined thinkers. Based on the outline Sarah has sketched in her chapter, I think that task will be in good hands.

Concerning my fundamental philosophical ethics, Roberts's confusion about the origins of the good in my philosophical worldview is reflected in LeRon's endorsement of my Nietzschean framework for ethics. It certainly is Nietzschean in respect of rejecting the idea that ultimate reality, the Whence of all moral possibilities, the God beyond all Gods, is fitted out with moral opinions and law-like moral demands. On the contrary, ultimate reality is morally unscaled to human interests and concerns, thereby requiring human beings to find their own moral way in the world. The moral affordances of nature are multidimensional and profoundly ambiguous. If we want to be morally consistent beings, we can—up to a point. If we want morally intelligible societies, we can work for that too—up to a point. The creative depths of nature possess moral character not in the sense of a moral compass telling us which way is moral magnetic north but in the sense of semirational logical structures of the if-then, context-relative kind: if I betray people (in this culture and era, etc.) they will stop trusting me, if I show compassion to my enemies, I maximize the chance of their moral transformation in directions I value, and so forth. In theological language: the reality we symbolize and engage with terms such as "God beyond God" and "Ground of Being" is not morally scaled to human interests; its primal manifestation is as a webbed network of moral affordances with a loose logical structure that constrains without determining what we take to be the good (and the bad). It is up to us to define the good and to implement it in our lives, our families, our communities, our societies, our nations, and our world.

Now, here's where there is a departure from, or at any rate an extension of, Nietzsche's moral philosophy. Given all this, the moral journey is necessarily a complex and exploratory process, simultaneously corporate and individual in nature, which involves complex constraints of vague factors given in reality and vague factors stipulated in socially borne moral practices. That still permits an individual both to choose a moral way that can be woven into a personal identity of virtuous beauty, and to urge corporate bodies to embrace some moral norms and not others. Nietzsche downplayed (or neglected) the social, experimental side of our exploration of the landscape of moral affordances.

If this fundamental philosophical ethics is close to correct, the implications go far beyond noticing that God is not in the morality-stipulation business. Divine-command ethics is a misdescribed recapitulation of deference to the moral norms of existing religious communities. Deontological ethics is an exaggeration of the weak rational structure that persists within the moral affordances of life. Consequential ethics is a practical guide to navigating the partly constrained, never determined, and always ambiguous moral landscape by thinking through the outcomes of our morally relevant decisions and actions, but it is also a kind of pretense at clarity, as if consequences were the only determining factor in moral identity formation for individuals and groups. Even Nietzschean will-to-power ethics, while correct about the moral landscape we roam, is weirdly assertive, like a rebellious teenager, anxious to demonstrate how everyone else exists in slavish enthrallment to unexamined moral norms. I'd want to tell Nietzsche to relax, just as I want to tell LeRon to consider putting down the hammer with which he likes to philosophize now and seeing if building things might be fun, too.

Honestly though, LeRon is right about how beaten up and spiritually eviscerated many people have been because of conservative religion. It hasn't been my experience, and I see other things going on in conservative religious communities than psychic and physical abuse and socially intractable hypocrisy, but when LeRon says he prefers the smashing side of philosophizing with a hammer, I confess to being so enraged on his behalf, and on behalf of so many of my students and friends, that I want to get up into the rubble pile and smash away alongside him. But even as I take out my rage on the structures that harm, I'm also aiming to build—building by renovating, smashing off the dangerous and stupid parts, and nurturing the parts that have a chance of leading people more deeply into engagement with ultimacy, on terms that make sense to them, now as well as five hundred years from now. I know it's probably futile, but I'm going to keep protesting from the inside, or as close to the inside as they'll let me get, and I'll continue to try to infect people with my simple idea of Christlikeness.

In the quieter moments of our many extended conversations, LeRon and I wonder how much our church backgrounds—mine gently loving and kind, his legalisticly loving and harsh—have affected our worldviews and affiliative decisions. He's relieved to be out. I'm relieved to be marginalized but, like any good conservative, loathe to see the dissolution of an institution with significant accumulated value, especially given how much good there is inside, how much wisdom is (perhaps accidentally) carried forward, and how difficult such institutions are to build from scratch. And that goes for religious institutions generally. As a result, I'm content for them to thrive or die in their natural life cycles and I know my efforts won't make much difference either way. By contrast, LeRon sees the future of the human project at stake when he ponders institutions that nurture supernatural beliefs and rationalize the exercise of their social authority with supernatural fantasies. His argument entails that these institutions are a threat to human survival, so, to be consistent, he ought to do whatever he can, consistently with his ethical framework, to end them. In practice, he, too, knows that he won't have much impact, not even with his philosophical hammer, and he can see intermediate benefits in reform and renovation. The statement of goals in relation to all-too-familiar religious institutions—LeRon's fundamental aim to destroy, my fundamental aim to renovate—is not really about strategic interactions with those institutions; it is more about life ways, about personal identity, about rationalizing the apportionment of precious life energy.

What exactly is religion that it is such a deadly threat to the future of our species and its homey planetary habitat? LeRon might not have the basic training in the academic study of religion that I was put through, but he's a quick study. He defines religion as shared engagement with axiologically relevant supernatural agents, which necessarily entails belief in supernatural agents. That's how he picks out religious beliefs, religious experiences, religious rituals, and religious institutions from other kinds of beliefs, experiences, rituals, and institutions. As I've mentioned, while he's certain that there are no supernatural agents, I'm less so, though I am more confident than usual for me, confident enough to say that there are better explanations for what prompts and sustains such beliefs. But I am severely short on confidence that we can use belief in supernatural agents to pick religion out from other human activities. There are supernatural and superstitious beliefs everywhere, after all; they are a lot more common and widespread than religion. So I define religion in a way that comports with the mainstream academic study of religion, offering a family-resemblance definition with five components (LeRon quotes the definition). *Supernatural worldviews are one way of articulating all or most of those five components.* There are non-supernaturalist ways to do that, too, though they've been a lot less popular given the cognitive tendency of our species toward maturationally natural supernaturalism. Supernaturalism is not a necessary condition for being religion, as anti-supernaturalist religious believers demonstrate. Supernaturalism is not a sufficient condition for being religion, as shown by the fact that supernatural beliefs without the characteristic marks of religion are everywhere in the human species. If supernaturalism is neither necessary nor sufficient for religion, there's no way I'm going to define religion in such a way as to necessitate belief in supernatural agents. I might use it as a rough simplification for the purposes of a computational model when we need to focus on measurable constructs with relatively sharp conceptual boundaries, but I'd rather not.

So much for LeRon's definition of religion. As for my definition, LeRon wants me to see that "If religion refers to everything, then it might as well refer to nothing because it fails to pick out any empirically tractable distinction in the real world." But religion does not *refer* to everything or *include* everything; it is *relevant* to everything insofar as everything possesses a dimension of depth. I find Tillich's way of making this point while posturing at explicitly speaking for and on behalf of the Christian church in his theology weirdly contorted. However, the depth dimension of reality, perceived and engaged through what he calls ontological reason, is *everyone's business*, period. His and my naturalistic account of those depths is the basis for asserting the possibility of religious naturalism, which stops being an oxymoronic phrase when you define religion and naturalism as I do. In Tillich's mid-twentieth-century context, naturalism ruled out the depth dimension—it typically meant something like James's "medical materialism," which is invidiously reductive—but time has marched on and new possibilities have emerged. In our time, with our semantic habits, Tillich would have been comfortable with the phrase "religious naturalism" and he would have owned it.

LeRon would have me give up "God" too. I'm not that attached to the word. Give me a depth dimension to ground spirituality, spiritual quests, and corporate religious engagement and I'm content. I happily participate in Buddhist rituals and have even postured at offering teachings in a Buddhist setting. Define "God" as any kind of being—finite, infinite, transcendent, immanent . . . it doesn't matter—and I am a straightforward atheist. I love the twist on this given by Richard Dawkins: everyone is atheist with respect to the vast majority of the thousands of divine beings that have caught the imagination of human beings; he's just atheist about one more divine being than most other people. I am with Dawkins on this, with a theological rider: to me, as with Tillich, treating God as any kind of being is bluntly idolatrous. Being idolaters in this sense doesn't stop people from engaging ultimacy authentically or from cultivating virtuous personal characteristics, but under stressful circumstances it manifests its dark side: authoritarian exclusion and the enshrining of delusional thinking as necessary to belong. Thank God (or whatever fictional being appeals to you) for deliverance from such people and their groups, deliverance in the form of secular cultures with a more inclusive and reasonable basis for social participation.

Why, then, am I fighting so hard for theistic language? Not-less-than-personal-God-believer Philip Clayton and not-more-than-fictional-God-protester LeRon don't agree on much, but they do agree that I should stop using the word "God." I ask myself, however, how do we name the depth dimension of reality in ways that regular people can engage? And what happens when we lose the language needed to be articulate about it? I'm persistently worried about the answers to such questions. And I'm not the only one. The reason theistic mystics and philosophers who reject the idea of God as any kind of being have always fought the good fight to maintain access to the word is that they, too, want the linguistic infrastructure to preserve nuanced reference to the depth dimensions of reality. The decision to side with these folks, my siblings on the underside of supernatural religious institutions, is the flip side of my decision to side with those institutions: their memorial encoding of the depth dimension of life is hugely valuable. Rather than destroy the institutional conditions for the possibility of such a memorial, I'll work on purifying the testimony. So God language it shall be for me, at least when engaging theistic institutional realities, and I'll dispense with the God language when other resources suitable for sustaining richly technical and potently existential discussions of the depth dimension (aka the axiological depth structures and dynamics) of reality are readily available.

I do see that these twin decisions—keep talking about God, keep my oar in the water with religious institutions—are questionable. I can understand why both Clayton and LeRon get annoyed with me, the former because I'm fighting over something he thinks is his and LeRon because I'm fighting over something he thinks is Clayton's. At one level, these decisions define me as a person and express my peculiar way of moving through the world: I'm a follower of Jesus, an ordained minister of Word and Sacrament in a Christian church, a student of the Buddha, a quester for Codex-style holiness, an atheist regarding all divine beings, a philosophical theologian who deploys God language to refer to the depths of reality that are the sources of spirituality, a partner to Suzanne, and a father to Sam and Ben. I chose these things, or the aspects of them I could choose. I'm living on purpose. At another level, these twin decisions are strategic. LeRon can worry about protesting false and increasingly maladaptive supernatural beliefs, and I'll do my bit to help him; but what worries me more, far more, is the loss of the philosophical and linguistic conditions for the possibility of meaningful popular and expert-level speech about the spiritual depth dimension of reality. That's what keeps me awake at night, should we survive the trials ahead and reach a civilizational place where it matters. Continuity with religious wisdom traditions, both theistic and nontheistic, is strategically wise and properly cautious about the potentially catastrophic loss of the technical discourse communities that keep alive expert discussion and debate while peering down into the abysmal and blissful vortex that is the spiritual dimension of life. We only need to ponder what happened to Zoroastrianism to understand how devastating such breakdowns in continuity can be.

I admit: this leads to some serious language stretching, and not just about "God" and "religion." Within the large family of religious naturalisms, I live with Robert in the ecstatic camp, and my particular form of mystical philosophical theology is a specific elaboration of religious naturalism. Nancy wants me to wake up and smell the coffee, because my developed philosophical theology is running awfully close to being nonsensical. Only a fine friend would deliver such a devastating critique with such grace and wit; it's Nancy's way.

I laughed out loud in delight as I read much of Nancy's chapter, including its splendid conclusion. I love analytical ascetics, and I heartily welcome Nancy's defense of the analytical ascetic's mode of spirituality. I have never said a bad word about them because it would impugn part of myself—it's how I was first trained in philosophy, after all. Analytical ascetics take their own kinds of risk, however, including by remaining cautiously mute about what might be adventurously and joyously engaged with a technical philosophical apparatus. The characteristic risk of the comparing inquirer, which is how I spend most of my time, is futile ambition and an overorganized way of engaging the mess of relevant data.

Can we speak rationally about the spiritual dimension of reality, particularly when its abysmal depths perpetually elude our cognitive grasp, as I would have it? I have spent a lot of energy arguing that we can and trying to demonstrate that it is possible, though only in a genuinely peculiar and probably linguistically unique way. Nancy is not convinced. So let's back way up and talk about language. Reading Nancy's chapter brought back delicious memories of classes in the Cal Berkeley philosophy department reading Heidegger with Hubert Dreyfus and learning philosophy of language and philosophy of mind from John Searle. I took all of Searle's classes, and he wrote references for me in my post-PhD job-hunting adventure. I'm sure he, too, would think I'm skirting way too close to the rim of the lava-filled volcano of nonsense, but he readily confessed to being theologically tone-deaf. With time, I built a Searle-influenced philosophy of language into a pragmatist framework deeply influenced by evolutionary biology and acutely aware of the tricks we play with language. In that framework, Nancy's way of talking about meaning is optional for me. I shall explain.

Terrance Deacon has set forth a multidisciplinary theory of the evolutionary origins of language that involves tracing the dynamic correlation between developments in vocal tract physiology and complexification of the brain to permit symbolic thinking. Sadly, analytic philosophers have too often excused themselves from dealing with the evolution of language, so their accounts of reference and meaning are often abstract and biologically ungrounded. That doesn't make them useless; on the contrary, they generate superb insights that help to unweave the rainbow of the phenomenon of language. But the biological framing of human language permits us to see that language models born in philosophy are abstractions from the concrete realities of vocal-fold evolution, environmental embedding, species sociality, and symbolic thinking. Symbol-wielding culture builders are complicated beings with complicated communication to support complicated forms of cooperation and inquiry. It shouldn't surprise us if philosophical theories of reference and meaning easily become untethered from that concretely real, entangled web of biological and environmental and social factors. When Nancy presents her take on the theory of language presented by Donald

Davidson, I think I'm detecting a preference for clarity over concreteness. But clarity is not enough, as H. D. Lewis was fond of saying. Clear part models can typically be abstracted from complex, concrete realities *in several ways* that will complement one another unless they are exaggerated so as to exclude one another—a mistake not beyond the pale for analytic (or any other) philosophers. So, for me, it is always back to the concrete, aiming to keep my head clear while attempting to untangle the insights churned out from the spinning wheel of relevant disciplines.

Symbol wielders do things with language. They intend, they express, they communicate—and when they communicate, they ask, they state, they command, they change states of affairs. Not all language use has intent, not all language use expresses, and not all language use communicates, but these three factors often occur together, as when I intend to express my state of mind to communicate my delight at being able to write this chapter for Ann and Bob and Kevin and LeRon and Miguel and Nancy and Nat and Patrick and Rich and Robert and Sarah and Steve and Tim, and for those whose questionable judgment leads them to pick up this volume. An attentive philosopher will quickly be forced to introduce a host of formal distinctions that help us make sense of our linguistic behavior. For example, we'll distinguish between intention in the sense of a mental state potentially associated with an action plan (I intend, aim, plan to write this chapter) and intention in the sense of the directedness of a chunk of language (the "aboutness" of this sentence). We'll distinguish between what language is doing as an action (illocutionary force), its consequences (perlocutionary effect), its internal structure (syntax), and its meaning (semantics). And we'll make a hundred other distinctions to try to unweave this glorious rainbow and figure out what we're really doing when we do our symbol-wielding thing.

Along the way, if we keep in mind the concrete reality we are analyzing, we come across options—forking paths through the woods of interpretation. A classic instance is in the realm of semantics. We humans, especially Australians, will routinely say something snarky that is provocatively ambiguous. At one level it means something innocuous but at another level it means something aggressive. When British Willy, the colonialist target of Aussie Snarky's snark, demands to know, "What did you mean by that, *exactly*, Snarky?" there is a lot going on and we have choices about how to analyze it. Remember: this degree of complexity is routine for clever symbol-wielding linguistic beings. The illocutionary-force story probably involves Willy commanding Snarky to back off, Willy expressing anger and confusion, Willy communicating that he's not an idiot and he can read subtle snark just fine—*simultaneously*.

The least important part of Willy's question may be its syntactical form as a question, in fact. So now we come to the forked path in the forest. What does Willy's sentence *mean*? Option #1 (Nancy's and Davidson's): the sentence means what its syntactic form suggests literally. The literal meaning might be the *least important* aspect of the speech act, but nevertheless focusing on literal meaning is at least *clear*, and everything else going on is about how the speech act is deployed. Option #2: (Decidedly Not Nancy's): Willy's spontaneous use of meaning in his word "mean" is taken seriously, so that the meaning of Willy's sentence and the meaning of Snarky's sentence are both tied to what they intended to communicate. In other words, just as philosophers distinguish between the two meanings of *intention* (above), they could distinguish between two meanings of *meaning*. Option #2 makes phrases such as "levels of meaning" and "symbolic meaning" and "intended (nonliteral) meaning" perfectly intelligible.

We could fight over which pathway of analysis is better and for what purposes but, with my eyes fixed firmly on the concrete complexity of the evolutionary emergence and actual use of human language, I usually don't have a dog in races of this sort. So I happily embrace multiple modes of analysis, struggling instead to demonstrate the complementarity of properly chastened, nonexclusive versions of their respective claims. But I am less indifferent to the effects of insisting on the exclusive relevance of one pathway over another, particularly when this insistence is not accompanied by a careful comparative analysis of pros and cons of the different analytical pathways. In Nancy's case, her analytical pathway of choice leads, she argues, to conclusions that I focus on here: there is no such thing as symbolic meaning; ineffability is impossible; and speaking of an ineffable reality, if it is not nonsense, is certainly useless. On these points, I think Nancy speaks also for Tim and Ann, and maybe others in this volume.

First, Nancy can't rule out symbolic meaning by defining meaning in Davidson's way; that's cheating. Her claim should be: "If we define meaning in Davidson's way, then there is no such thing as symbolic meaning." That's not controversial, and it's not informative.

Second, to assert that "X is ineffable" for any X is either to commit a philosophical faux pas or to deliver a hilarious one-liner (hilarious by bizarre philosophical standards, mind you). You can't both assert something of X and say X is ineffable given the usual meaning of "ineffability." That's why I work so long and hard to develop an entire architecture of ideas merely to express the idea that "ultimate reality is ineffable" in a coherent way—and that's even before I get to arguing that it is a true statement. Swinburne did the same thing when he worked on the *Coherence of Theism* before working on the *Existence of God*; I'm following in his footsteps. Nancy doesn't engage that architecture of ideas and seems to believe that she can generate a meaningful critique just based on the final claim that ultimate reality is ineffable. If I thought she were right about that, I wouldn't have bothered. The architecture involves trajectories of propositions, inspired by Pseudo-Dionysus, who is always whispering in ear #1; disintegrating metrics that permit more-or-less rigorous comparison of preliminary formulations of ultimacy models while also gradually falling apart the closer you get to the last word on reality, the logical object of "ultimate reality"; specialized discourse communities that build ways to sustain technical language on makeshift platforms extending over the abyss of ineffability long after normal language users have given up trying to say what they sense about ultimate reality; and a dynamic conception of inquiry that changes what's possible to express with time, and alters what's worth saying given the prospects of advancing understanding. Maybe this machinery doesn't work. But without taking it into account, an assessment of "ultimate reality is ineffable" cannot be applicable or relevant to my understanding of religious language.

Third, Nancy and Tim and Ann and others are spot-on when they suspect that an ineffable ultimate reality is, in itself, contentless and thus practically useless. I don't mean "almost useless"; I mean "useless in practice." Tim says it beautifully: "I cannot help feeling that there is not enough recognition in Wesley's religious philosophy of the linguistically bewitching non-issue that tempts the scholar into a fruitless line of inquiry, keeps her there entranced (for fear of abandoning a hypothesis too hastily), and has her chasing feedback potential in some will-o'-the-wisp." Marvelous! Given this practical uselessness, the risk of conceptual incoherence, and the dismaying specter of wasting time and energy on futile lines of inquiry, I've always found it surprising that so many literate and non-literate cultures have spent so much effort on developing and talking about such useless and tantalizingly-close-to-incoherent concepts. Maybe those of us who indulge will-o'-the-wisp games are falling prey to a widespread cognitive error, and we should get serious and follow the analytical ascetics out of the wonderland of delusion and *just stop talking about an ineffable ultimate.*

But here's the Jamesian thing that makes a pragmatic difference: the idea of an ineffable ultimate is *indirectly* useful. To say that the last word on reality (aka ultimate reality) is an ineffable content-free zone is *to dislocate and invalidate every other assertion about ultimate reality.* Ultimate reality isn't a person, or an infinite not-less-than-personal being, or a committee of gods, or a non-organized gaggle of nature spirits, or a karmic principle, or a gaia principle, or any other principle, or an entelechy, or nature itself, or nature naturing, or creativity, or axiological depth structures and dynamics, or a fecund emptiness, or any other specifiable thing. To my way of thinking, that *indirect* implication of the assertion that ultimate reality is ineffable is rather important. This goes way beyond the atheistic refusal to accept a God at the root of things; it is a spiritual and theological and political line in the sand, refusing any and every characterization of the whole of reality. It is not an ungrounded, whimsical guess, either: it is a solid inference from the long-standing grappling with the wealth of insights encoded in and asserted by wisdom traditions, literate and not, ancient and contemporary, science-informed and science-innocent—the kind of inference to which only an aggressively multidisciplinary, comparative form of inquiry will afford reasonable access. The spiritual and theological and political nature of this apophatic line in the sand is what makes an ineffable ultimate capable of also being an ultimate concern, and thus worthy of worship and devotion. As I follow Jesus, am inspired by Gautama, and strive to cultivate Codex-relevant virtues, so I keep my eyes firmly fixed on the content-free nothing that is ineffable ultimacy.

So, Nancy and Tim, beloved analytical ascetics, I haven't yet seen a compelling reason to think that multidisciplinary, comparative inquiry is getting us nowhere in the task of speaking of ultimacy. I haven't seen a reason to conclude that the idea of an ineffable ultimate is incoherent. I haven't seen a reason to dismiss the spiritual, theological, and political relevance of an ineffable ultimate. And, weirdly enough, I haven't run out of things to say about it. In fact, I savor the freedom this view of ultimacy confers on the philosophical theologian to deploy a range of symbols to conjure the indirect meaning of an ineffable ultimate (yes Nancy, that's taking pathway #2 through the woods right there, abandoning Davidson to find his way along pathway #1; you might explore along my pathway a little, just to see what it's like). Some of my favorite symbols—emerging from the mists late in the journey toward silence, as measured by the collapsing mystical metric—are God beyond God, One, Dao, Sunyata, axiological depths and dynamics, and landscape of moral affordances. I'll even use God language to get at what I'm trying to say if that's what's going to lead people toward some measure of understanding. This is *uppaya*, as well as the conceptual framework that justifies and demands artful means to communicate about an ineffable ultimate. And I want it to be a part of the field of philosophy of religion. Where else would it live?!

I wholeheartedly support Tim's and Kevin's efforts to establish a global, critical philosophy of religion, trying to rescue the desperate field of philosophy of religion by making sure it is, at last, actually about *religion*. These two revolutionaries are my kin in this venture, though by my lights they are still operating at some distance from an optimal implementation of a multidisciplinary approach to inquiry. Kevin's statement of his challenge to the cognitivist and Christian biases within philosophy of religion in his chapter for this volume is the clearest and most compact I've seen, and he includes constructive philosophical theorizing of my kind in the mix of what can possibly belong, which is a relief. I'm not sure Tim would go that far, despite his recent conversion to the big-tent approach to philosophy of religion according to which everyone brandishes their biased appraisals like badges. Everyone has such badges, of course; I have done as much as any philosopher of religion in the history of our field to be transparent about mine. But if you're not aiming for objectivity as a regulative ideal for inquiry, please go somewhere else. In practice, people unwilling to examine their working premises will (and should) find the philosophy of religion—insofar as it embraces the modern academy's secular morality of inquiry—an increasingly inhospitable environment for their labors. Hopefully, they'll wander off voluntarily, looking for a safer, less annoying, more supportive environment for their inquiries, a place that will happily allow them to retain some treasured assumptions to simplify and render more determinate their philosophical exertions.

Aside from *Religious Philosophy as Multidisciplinary Comparative Inquiry*, my main contribution to this reforming venture has been field mapping—a series of unprecedented attempts to generate data about the field that, like a mirror, can guide disciplinary self-evaluation and any attempted makeovers. Two main sources of data are guiding this effort, replacing my earlier and ineffective efforts aimed at tracing job openings in the field. The first is the Values in the Study of Religion (VISOR) project, which I'm undertaking with Ann and LeRon (in this volume), as well as psychologist Ray Paloutzian. Ann and LeRon have been truly heroic in absorbing findings from the massive amount of data I have analyzed and finding ways to communicate those findings to various disciplinary stakeholders. Our first paper is out ("What do Religion Scholars Really Want? Scholarly Values in the Scientific Study of Religion"), and others will follow.[1] Second, my colleague David Rohr and I invited professional philosophers of religion to present their thoughts in blogs at PhilosophyOfReligion.org. These blogs, as well as the entire collection of more than six hundred philosophers of religion in the site's database, generate many valuable insights. Fifty-four philosophers blogged about the question "What is the philosophy of religion?" and we have published an analysis of their thoughts ("North American Philosophers of Religion: How They See Their Field"). Sixty-seven philosophers wrote on the question "What does philosophy of religion offer to the modern university?" and even more philosophers have contributed their thoughts on "What norms or values define excellent philosophy of religion?" We're still gathering, publishing, and analyzing that material.

What I've learned about philosophy of religion from these field-mapping efforts is every bit as disturbing as Tim's and Kevin's reform efforts are Herculean. VISOR presents powerful evidence of what our experience suggests: philosophy of religion positions are disappearing. Respondents born in the 1950s or earlier are represented in the VISOR sample to the same degree both inside philosophy of religion (31.4 percent) and outside (32.1 percent). But people born in the 1970s or later amount to 2.9 percent inside philosophy of religion and 23.3 percent outside—the difference is a shocking factor of 8. Ouch. My own institution is a case in point. In the period that I have been there, Boston University's philosophy department has gone from three philosophers of religion to zero, though we are fortunate to still have a few talented philosophers interested in religion-related matters; and the religion department has also gone from four philosophers of religion to one or two who are recognized as such within the field, depending on whether the blessed Steven Katz is still in the saddle with the inimitable David Eckel—here again, though, we are blessed to have some brilliant religion experts who are deeply interested in philosophy. Most of the philosophers of religion left in the university are in the School of Theology.

The explanation for this catastrophic shrinkage is complex, and the relevant factors vary from institution to institution. Typically, however, the reasons for shrinkage seem *not* to be about the alleged impossibility of the form of inquiry in question; rather, the factors are mostly political. A particularly acute consideration is that philosophy of religion is associated in the minds of people in both religion and philosophy departments with covert Christian ideology, and they understandably don't want anything to do with that. This association is weakening as philosophy of religion shrinks, however, and torch bearers such as Tim and Kevin are in a position to help religion and philosophy departments grasp the importance, feasibility, and reality of a different kind of philosophy of religion, one truer to the name. Meanwhile, our PhD graduates are launched into an academic environment with virtually no relevant job openings. We can't contract PhD admissions fast enough to keep up with the dire placement realities. But there is good news, too: the big questions that call philosophy of religion into existence are not going anywhere, and the new generation of people who actually do philosophy of *religion* (i.e., in conversation with the academic study of religion) are seriously talented.

Tim worries over my use of the phrase "religious philosophy" for what Kevin calls descriptive and evaluative and constructive philosophy of religion. But I'm doing that specifically to protest the distortions in philosophy of religion that Tim himself complains about. I happily employ "philosophy of religion"—it's where I have my PhD, after all—but I'm not beyond using other phrases to mess with people's heads. I note that my interest in the multidisciplinary aspect of inquiry is barely registered in Tim's global, critical philosophy of religion (GCPR)—it is present in the way that consideration of non-Christian religions has been a mere appendage in the disappointing trail of traditional philosophy of religion textbooks—and it's only present that way because I kept complaining about its absence—so maybe I should keep using "religious philosophy as multidisciplinary comparative inquiry" a bit longer. The GCPR crew knows that multidisciplinarity is a thing, but they don't know how to do it except in a truncated way and seem determined not to think about it very hard. Tim is responsive when I point out the problem, but he doesn't know how to integrate it either, and can do no more than support the halfhearted appendage solution. I wish him all the best with what he's doing in GCPR and hope he wins in the context of the discipline's historic survival challenge. But it is all going to have to be redone to take account of the realities and unmatched opportunities of multidisciplinary inquiry.

The theory of inquiry inspiring my insistence on multidisciplinary as well as comparative methods in philosophy of religion is the aspect of my writings that most contributors to this volume wanted to engage. Both Miguel and Nat mention their suspicion that I am rather too much in thrall to survival-oriented practicalities (and the corresponding aesthetics of agreement) while not making sufficient allowance for survival-irrelevant curiosity (and the corresponding aesthetics of intensity). Nat helpfully puts it this way: "Novelty is permitted only insofar as it is demanded by the problem at hand. There is no allowance for the possibility that novelty can be sought for an increase of satisfaction." *Religious Philosophy as Multidisciplinary Comparative Inquiry* focuses on the biological origins of inquiry, much as my comments about philosophy of language above begin with biological origins. But that book explicitly allows for cultural elaborations of the human capacity for inquiry, intensity is taken up as an aesthetic mode of inquiry in *Religious and Spiritual Experiences*, and inquiry as play is the dominant theme in *In Our Own Image*.

In all things, I am mindful of how biological and cultural evolution play on cognitive resources refined under selective pressures. Nat says, "Now, ideally, what we want is a comprehensive theory that [both] encompasses . . . aesthetics and helps us to understand and adjudicate this divergence of ideals [between an aesthetics of agreement and an aesthetics of intensity]. Does this divergence reflect a deep tension inherent to the pursuit of value, or is it simply a product of an inadequate aesthetics? I have argued elsewhere for the former view." I think it is the former, too, and I think that the former is also the *explanation* for the latter, the prevalence of inadequate aesthetics. Evolutionarily, the former makes sense. The aesthetics of agreement is evolutionarily much older and pervasive; its relevance to survival is painfully obvious. A higher degree of neural complexity is required to pass the threshold necessary to realize and express an aesthetics of intensity. *Religious and Spiritual Experiences* discusses this threshold, treating intensity as the fundamental driver of RSEs. The aesthetic implications of that discussion are not spelled out, but they could be—as a tension between two drives within higher organisms: the drive to agreement (powering inquiry) and the drive to intensity (also powering inquiry), with different kinds of satisfactions. The vague category of "disturbance" still works as comprehending both, and indeed, the younger, later-arriving drive for intensity co-opts the older, earlier-arriving, organismically more basic drive for agreement. Even the novelty of play has a kind of restless quality. Play might occur in secure situations where survival is not at stake, but it does depend on a kind of restless wondering, exploring the space of affordances as a kind of luxurious activity.

Nat is aware of how this fits together in my mind but worries that I'm not fighting back hard enough against the specter of invidious reductionism in cognitive science applied to religion. I love the way he says this: "Sometimes, when writing in a more theological vein, Wildman adopts a stance that seems very close to the aesthetic perspective that I am advocating. But I find this stance difficult, though certainly not impossible, to reconcile with his generally welcoming stance toward cognitive and evolutionary theories of religion, a field that is thoroughly dominated by 'functionalist-adaptationist' thinking and utterly blind to aesthetics." Dear Nat, why would I have to agree with everything happening in a field in order to engage it? Such a "purity of engagement" criterion would spell the death of effective multidisciplinary inquiry. So I engage, and I also push back: I engage computer engineering, and push back on ethics; I engage cognitive and evolutionary theories of religion, and push back on aesthetic and hermeneutical naivete; I engage theology, and push back on isolationism and cognitive self-deception; I engage philosophy, and push back on theological tone-deafness. And I demonstrate in my writings what I think I mean to convey when I push back, presenting concrete evidence that disciplinary parochialism is unnecessary and unproductive. Sometimes my personal pushing back meets self-correcting movements within a field. For example, contrary to Nat's guess that "as it stands, cognitive science has no theory of the unique axiological sensitivity of the human species, let alone a theory that treats this sensitivity as the main driver of human evolution," I think cognitive neuroscience is actually getting somewhere on aesthetic sensitivity and value apprehension. For instance, we know (I learned this first from Patrick) that the dopamine system is a critical part of the brain's value-detection system, differentially assessing value possibilities with the aim of guiding action plans and deepening aesthetic intensity of ordinary perception. Oversights typically get noticed within a discipline, eventually, even if people such as Nat and me jumping up and down trying to point out the lacunae have no effect.

Miguel is trying hard to be polite, but I think his politeness is obscuring his main complaint about my theory of inquiry. He gets close to being frank when he writes, "The concern here again is one about disciplinary boundaries. Wildman is dedicated to building them higher and stronger in some cases, for example, when he wants the distinction between religious philosophy and an apologetic or confessional form of theology to be made clear. But he is interested in keeping the walls quite low when one turns to the range of disciplines clustered under the general label of 'religious studies.'" But I am super clear about the blurriness between religious philosophy (as a tendency) and apologetic theology (as a tendency) with markers to indicate which tendency receives the most emphasis. The reason to say even that much relates to institutional realities, and the positive things I say about the value of apologetic theology are intended seriously, not merely to pacify theologians resentful about being left out of some sort of intellectual club. They don't want to do the multidisciplinary comparative inquiry thing in a wholehearted way, so they carefully truncate natural inquiry activities by adopting very large hypotheses that deliver a great deal of information that simultaneously improves the efficiency of inquiry directed to articulating and extending the hypothesis, and supports the interests of institutions they love. They can do whatever they like! But they rarely stay long at the inquiry parties I host in the secular academic environment because they are not comfortable with the prevailing morality of inquiry. Fine with me. Just don't break anything on the way out. (Australian candor is almost always more efficient than American East-Coast subtlety and American West-Coast kindheartedness, but it is perpetually questionable as social strategy.)

Miguel joins Patrick in wanting me to rethink the plausibility of personal theism and supernaturalism. I responded above to Patrick's concern about my rejection of invisible conscious agents not taking proper account of the hard problem of consciousness—I do take the hard problem of consciousness seriously by advocating an axiologically voiced, dipolar monist ontology. I also responded to their mistaken estimate of how decisive cognitive science is for my rejection of supernatural worldviews. Regarding personal theism, the limit of my support is to confess that my confidence in my working view runs around 60 percent to 70 percent, and to back that up with truly appreciative accounts of such views in *In Our Own Image* and elsewhere that are so empathic that they make LeRon blanch, if not actually upchuck. Miguel, in particular, focuses on the problem of evil (not my terminology): "Because he is quite philosophically precise about what it must mean to believe in God as personal, Wildman is convinced that the traditional form of such belief must ultimately be shipwrecked on the rocky shores of the problem of evil." Well, no, not really. *The problem of evil is not a defeater of personal theism.* I am ponderously clear about this in lots of places, including *In Our Own Image*, where dozens of criteria are in play simultaneously for judging the reverent competition among theories of ultimate reality, and the problem of divine neglect and the problem of suffering (as I name the relevant considerations) are among them. Indeed, quite in line with what Miguel recommends, I do not attempt to "solve" the problem of evil; on the contrary, by rendering ultimate reality as the ontological ground of all axiological possibilities, including what we call good and evil, I render suffering as *suchness*: a fact of life to be navigated, not a problem to be solved. Moreover, God, on this view, has no determinate moral nature so the problem of theodicy is irrelevant.

Ann's astute analysis of our divergent intellectual interests is right on target. She's a theoretically inclined historian and I'm a theologically inclined philosopher, and that difference has downstream consequences for how we approach religious and spiritual experiences, among other topics. It follows that I will struggle to answer praxeological questions related to the role of such experiences in people's worldviews and lifeways, just as

Ann will struggle to answer philosophically pointed questions about the cognitive reliability and theological relevance of these experiences. But we have common interests, too, which allow Ann to grasp my strategic use of the evolutionary derived category of intense experiences to furnish biological grounding for the analysis of cognitive reliability of religious and spiritual experiences. Likewise, those common interests lead me to endorse Ann's fascination with worldviews and, over a series of dinners, to encourage her to use the word "lifeways" in parallel. Just as, she argues, we need to reconceptualize what passes for religious studies as the systematic study of human worldviews and lifeways, which will naturally include both religious and nonreligious types, and both naturalist and supernaturalist variations within each type. To use Bob's terminology, "worldviews and lifeways" is a *better vague comparative category*, involving less distortion of similarities and differences and more clearly acknowledging the mutually contradictory instantiations encompassed by the category. If the contributors to this volume were to sit down and hash it out, we might well conclude that "religious studies" should be renamed "academic study of worldviews and lifeways," and "philosophy of religion" should be called "philosophy of worldviews and lifeways." I would not stand in the way of such a change.

The generosity I detect in these chapters is profoundly gratifying. Just spending time trying to penetrate the thought-world of a friend is a gift, but then to engage in writing, committing yourself to saying what you think in hopes of spurring a fruitful conversation—well, that is simply beautiful. Ann and Bob and Kevin and LeRon and Miguel and Nancy and Nat and Patrick and Rich and Robert and Sarah and Steve and Tim: you know that you are always whispering in ear #2, right? Your whispered advice and protests are cumulatively potent, competing with what's coming in through ear #1 from the host of mostly ghostly voices.

Given the purpose of this volume, though, it's useful to acknowledge that ear #3—where I hear the multitude of disciplines of human inquiry speak to me—is unusually important in my intellectual work. I don't mean *more* important than the deliverances of ears #1 and #2; I mean *distinctively* important. And I sense that its impact on the plausibility assessments I make of extremely complex interpretative hypotheses is difficult for most people to gauge—even my friends contributing to this volume—certainly more difficult than comparative considerations or philosophical considerations, where the relevant forms of expertise are more common. That's worth noting, surely, in a volume dedicated in part to investigating the effects of multidisciplinary approaches to the interpretation of human religion. It'll take teamwork to unlock the full potential of multidisciplinary comparative inquiry in the philosophy of religion, and, as I know from my own intellectual journey, teamwork is often frustrating and humbling. Nevertheless, until we take the multidisciplinary plunge, we're simply not engaging all resources relevant to advancing inquiry. And squandering resources for inquiry is the unforgivable sin for the pragmatically minded inquirer.

Note

1. F. LeRon Shults, Wesley J. Wildman, Ann Taves, and Ray Paloutzian, "What Do Religion Scholars Really Want? Scholarly Values in the Scientific Study of Religion," *Journal for the Scientific Study of Religion* 59, no. 1 (2020): 18–38.

Author Bios

Nathaniel F. Barrett is a research fellow and member of the Mind-Brain Project at the Institute for Culture and Society, University of Navarra (Pamplona, Spain). Barrett completed his doctoral degree in science, philosophy, and religion at Boston University under the direction of Wesley Wildman. His research has since covered diverse topics in Chinese philosophy, environmental philosophy, and the cognitive science of religion. Since joining the Mind-Brain Project in 2012, his work has focused increasingly on philosophy of mind, cognitive science, and consciousness studies, and within these areas on topics related to affect, motivation, and value.

Robert S. Corrington is the Henry Anson Buttz Professor of Philosophical Theology in the Graduate Division of Religion. He received his BA in philosophy from Temple University and his MPhil and PhD from Drew University in theological and religious studies with a concentration in philosophy. He has taught at Penn State and the College of William and Mary before returning to Drew to join the faculty. Corrington has authored twelve books and numerous articles as well as edited several volumes. His concentrations include American philosophy, phenomenology, aesthetics, and psychoanalysis. Starting in 1992 in his book *Nature and Spirit* (Fordham University Press), he has created a philosophical perspective that has come to be called "ecstatic naturalism."

Nancy K. Frankenberry is the John Phillips Professor in Religion Emeritus at Dartmouth College. She spent a total of fifty years in higher education, on one side of the podium or the other, and is the author, editor, or coeditor of five books, as well as more than sixty journal articles, book chapters, and critical reviews. She is currently working on a book that combines her interests in philosophy of religion, American pragmatism, and method and theory in the academic study of religion.

Sarah E. Fredericks is Associate Professor of Environmental Ethics at the University of Chicago Divinity School. Fredericks's research focuses on sustainability, sustainable energy, environmental guilt and shame, and environmental justice; her work draws upon pragmatic and comparative religious ethics. She is the author of *Environmental Guilt and Shame: Signals of Individual and Collective Responsibility and the Need for Ritual Responses* (Oxford, 2021) and *Measuring and Evaluating Sustainability: Ethics in Sustainability Indexes* (Routledge, 2013), and many articles and book chapters. Fredericks coedits a book series, Religious Ethics and Environmental Challenges (Lexington Press), with Kevin O'Brien.

Timothy D. Knepper is Professor of Philosophy at Drake University, where he directs The Comparison Project, a public program in global, comparative religion and local, lived religion. He is the author of books on the future of the philosophy of religion (*The Ends of Philosophy of Religion*, Palgrave, 2013) and the sixth-century Christian mystic known as Pseudo-Dionysius the Areopagite (*Negating Negation*, Wipf & Stock, 2014). He is also the editor of student-written photo-narratives about religion in Des Moines (*A Spectrum of Faith*, Drake Community Press, 2017) and in Beijing (*Religions of Beijing*, Bloomsbury, 2020), and of The Comparison Project's lecture and dialogue series on ineffability (*Ineffability: An Exercise in Comparative Philosophy of Religion*, Springer, 2017) and death and dying (*Death and Dying: An Exercise in Comparative Philosophy of Religion*, Springer, 2019).

Patrick McNamara is Distinguished Professor of Psychology at Northcentral University, Adjunct Associate Professor of Neurology at the University of Minnesota School of Medicine (UMSM). Until 2018, McNamara was based for twenty years at Boston University School of Medicine (BUSM), where he was Associate Professor of Neurology at BUSM. In 2018 he moved to Minneapolis to take up positions in NCU/UMinn and other opportunities. He is the editor of *Where God and Science Meet* and, with Wesley: *Science and the World's Religions*; and is the author of *The Neuroscience of Religious Experience* (Cambridge University Press, 2009), *Religion, Neuroscience and the Self: A New Personalism* (Routledge, 2020), and numerous publications on the neurology and psychology of religion. He is, with Wesley and Rich Sosis, a founding editor of *Religion Brain & Behavi*or, the flagship journal for the emerging field of neuroscience of religion. He is a cofounder (along with Wesley) of the Institute for the Biocultural Study of Religion—a nonprofit research institute dedicated to the study of the neurologic and evolutionary correlates of religious beliefs, behaviors, and practices, now grown into CMAC. He is a past recipient of a JTF award on the "Neurology of religious cognition" and several NIH Awards and is a Merit Review Award Recipient in the VA Medical System.

Robert Cummings Neville is a professor emeritus of Philosophy, Religion, and Theology at Boston University where he is also Dean emeritus of the School of Theology and Chaplain emeritus of Marsh Chapel. The author of over 30 books and 300 articles, he is past president of the American Academy of Religion, the Metaphysical Society of America, the Institute for American Religious and Philosophical Thought, the International Society for Chinese Philosophy, and Charles S. Peirce Society, among others.

Michael L. Raposa is Professor of Religion Studies and the E. W. Fairchild Professor of American Studies at Lehigh University, where he has been a member of the faculty since 1985. He is the author of four books, most recently, *Theosemiotic: Religion, Reading, and the Gift of Meaning* (Fordham University Press, 2020). In addition, Raposa has published numerous articles and reviews, many of the articles focused on the thought of Charles S. Peirce and the relevance of pragmatism for contemporary theology and philosophy of religion.

Steven J. Sandage, PhD, LP, is the Albert and Jessie Danielsen Professor of Psychology of Religion and Theology with appointments in the School of Theology and the Department of Psychological and Brain Sciences at Boston University. He is Research Director and Senior Staff Psychologist at the Danielsen Institute and also Visiting Faculty in Psychology of Religion at MF Norwegian School of Theology, Religion, and Society in Oslo. His recent books include *Relational Integration of Psychology and Christian Theology: Theory, Research, and Practice* (Routledge), and *Relational Spirituality in Psychotherapy: Healing Suffering and Promoting Growth* (American Psychological Association). Sandage does research in positive psychology, psychology of religion, intercultural competence and social justice, psychotherapy processes and outcome, psychopathology, clergy formation and well-being, and clinical training. He also practices as a licensed psychologist with clinical specializations that include couple and family therapy, multicultural therapy, and spiritually integrative therapy.

Kevin Schilbrack is Professor and Chair of the Department of Philosophy and Religion at Appalachian State University (https://philrel.appstate.edu/schilbrack). He is a philosopher of religion who is presently writing on the relevance of embodied cognition and social ontology for understanding what religion is and how it works. The author of *Philosophy and the Study of Religions: A Manifesto* (Blackwell, 2014) and the contributing editor of *Thinking through Myths* (Routledge, 2002) and *Thinking through Rituals* (Routledge, 2004), he has been a visiting scholar at Harvard University, the University of Uppsala, Vrije University Amsterdam, and the University of Birmingham.

F. LeRon Shults is professor at the Institute for Global Development and Planning at the University of Agder in Kristiansand, Norway. He has published 18 books and more than 140 articles and book chapters on topics such as philosophy of religion, philosophy of science, computer simulation, and cognitive science of religion. Shults's recent books include *Practicing Safe Sets: Religious Reproduction in Scientific and Philosophical Perspective* (Brill, 2018) and *Human Simulation: Perspectives, Insights, and Applications* (Springer, 2019, coedited with Saikou Diallo, Wesley J. Wildman, and Andreas Tolk).

Richard Sosis is James Barnett Professor of Humanistic Anthropology at the University of Connecticut. His work has focused on the evolution of religion and cooperation, with particular interests in ritual, magic, religious reproductive decision-making, and the dynamics of religious systems. To explore these issues, he has conducted fieldwork with remote cooperative fishers in the Federated States of Micronesia and with various communities throughout Israel. He is cofounder and coeditor of the journal *Religion, Brain & Behavior*, which publishes research on the bio-cultural study of religion.

Ann Taves is Research Professor and Distinguished Professor (Emerita) of Religious Studies at University of California, Santa Barbara, and PI of the Inventory of Nonordinary Experiences Project. A historian by training, she has long-standing interests in theory and method as they relate to the study of unusual experiences. She is the author of numerous books and articles, including *Fits, Trances, and Visions* (Princeton, 1999), *Religious Experience Reconsidered* (Princeton, 2009), and *Revelatory Events* (Princeton, 2016). She is a Fellow of the American Academy of Arts and Sciences (2011) and a past president of both the American Academy of Religion (2010) and the International Association for the Cognitive and Evolutionary Science of Religion (2016–18).

Index

Aarhus University, 283
Abduction, 118–20
Absurdity, 168–73
Abyss, 21, 167
Academy, 56, 155–56; secular, 46–50; and Wildman, 2
Adaptation, 88–100
Adelaide, 1
Advaita Vedanta, 137–38, 175
Aesthetics, 81, 83–100; of agreements, 87–100; intensity, 87–100
Affordances, 309
Agency, 5, 19, 228; in God, 4; model, 145–46, 158–62; supernatural, 26–31, 249–56
Agreement, 86–100
Aldrich, John H., 246
Allah, 133
Alston, 267
Alzheimer's Disease, 68
American Academy of Religion, 13, 259
Anselm, 145
Anthropology, 22, 130, 280; scientific and religious, 209–19
Anthropomorphic promiscuity and prudery, 27–29
Anthropomorphism, 4, 8, 18–21, 27–28, 31, 111, 117–25, 147, 162–64, 176–77, 183–85; in Peirce, 108
Apologetics, 323–24
Apophasis, 4–5, 14–31, 174–77
Aquinas, Thomas, 146, 149, 165, 244, 292
Arbib, Michael A., 257
Arbitrary, 171
Aristotle, 163, 177
Art, 95, 102; of theology, 154
Arts, Bachelor of, 2
Ascetics, analytical, 186, 204–205, 313–18
Asprem, Egil, 269, 271
Asymmetry, 167, 171, 173–77, 302–303
Atheism, 23–24, 205, 250–51, 300, 313, 318
Atkins, Richard Kenneth, 86–100, 102
Atman, 137–38
Attention, 108, 117–25
Augustine, 146, 292–93, 299–300, 303
Austin, J. L., 206
Autobiography, 6
Axial Age, 18–19, 23
Axiological folds, 165
Axiology, 77–101, 268–70, 285–86
Axiotheology, 4, 48–49

331

Index

Bagger, Matthew, 126
Bangladesh, 218–19
Barbour, Ian G., 55, 58, 73, 246
Barrett, Justin, 297
Barrett, Nathanial, 2, 7, 79–104, 293, 315, 322–23, 325
Barth, 210–11
Barth, Karl, 178, 210–11, 298–99, 303
Beauty, 89–100
Beethoven, Ludwig, von, 195
Being-itself, 193, 212
Bell, Chance A., 247
Bellah, Robert, 206
Belonging, 91
Benjamin, Jessica, 241
Berger, Peter, 178, 206
Berthrong, John, 178
Berve, Aljoscha, 103
Bhavaviveka, 294
Big Bang, 167
Big Bang, 5
Big Guy in the Sky, 162, 253
Big questions, 3–4, 54–60, 79, 129–30, 155–56, 170, 261–62, 270, 293, 295–96
Biology, 5, 50, 114
Blake, William, 281–82
Bliss, 8, 242–45
Bloch, Maurice, 270
Blum, Jason N., 148, 207
Bodies, 5
Boston, 2, 9
Boston University, 5, 30, 38, 48, 74, 153, 155, 181–82, 223–24, 251, 274, 277–78, 293, 320; Departments of Philosophy and Religion, 320; School of Theology, 2
Bowlby, John, 238, 248
Boydston, Jo Ann, 102–103
Brahman, 4, 137–38
Brain, 5, 39, 41; social, 257

Brandom, Robert, 126, 189, 207
Breakdown, 16
Brothers, Leslie, 250, 253, 257
Brown, Delwin, 149, 151
Brown, Jeannine K., 225–26, 245–46
Brown, Warren S., 227, 246
Bucar, Elizabeth, 70, 75
Buddha, the, 308, 313
Buddhism, 156, 164, 175
Bulbulia, Joseph, 283, 287
Burks, Arthur, 126
Bush, Stephen, 195–96, 207
Butler, Paul M., 257–58
Buttock, 281

Cady, Linell E., 149–50
Callicott, J. Baird, 76
Calvin, 232, 246, 292–93, 303
Cambridge University, 115
Campbell, David E., 247
Caputo, John, 150
Catalhoyuk, 22
Catherine of Sienna, 294
Causation, 5
Cavell, Stanley, 206
Cello, 299
Center for Mind and Culture, 2, 9, 153, 249–56, 274–86, 305–307
Center for Theological Inquiry, 301
Chicago, 13
China, 146, 164
Chinese religions, 156
Christianity, 112, 154, 156–57, 163, 188, 223–45, 294, 300–301, 320
Christology, 2
Clayton, John, 150
Clayton, Philip, 267, 312–13
Cleanthes, 186–90
Clingerman, Forrest, 76
Clinicians, 233–45
Clooney, Francis X., S.J., 148, 178

Cobb, John Jr., 2, 4
Codex of Tendencies to Cognitive Error, 290–91, 308
Cognitive error, 96, 162–73, 290–91, 300, 317
Coherence, 80, 290–91, 303
Collaboration, 250–56
Community, 51, 174–77, 234
Comparative Religious Ideas Project, 2, 18, 59–60, 153, 156–57
Comparison, 1, 4–7, 18–20, 37–50, 55–73, 110–25, 129–47, 183–85, 325
Compatibility, 91
Comprehensiveness, 91
Computer science, 2, 22–26
Cone, James, 306
Confessional theology, 110, 113, 154–56
Conflict, 91
Confucianism, 164, 175
Congregations, 176
Consciousness, 98, 164, 296
Consensus, 107–25
Conservatism, in inquiry, 40
Continua, 175–77
Contrast, 91
Cooey, Paula, 133–34, 149
Corballis, M. C., 270
Correction, 53–73, 107–25; of hypotheses, 38–50
Corrington, Robert S., 8–9, 165, 178, 209–19, 293, 296, 299, 313, 315, 325
Cosmology, 4–7, 184
Cosmotheology, 4, 48–49
Costly symbols, 21–22
Courage, 13
Creatio, ex deo, 165–66; *ex nihilo*, 165–66, 169
Criteria, 159–60
Critical realism, 40

D'Costa, Gavin, 150
Da Vinci, Leonardo, 181–85
Dahlstrom, Daniel O., 244, 248
Daly, Mary, 294, 304, 306
Daniel-Hughes, Brandon, 101
Daniels, Joel, 278–79, 287
Danielsen Center, 5
Dao, 133, 164, 294
Dark night of the soul, 125, 238
Darwin, Charles, 94, 115, 126
Dasenbrock, R. W., 206
Daveney, Sheila Greeve, 150
Davidson, Donald, 182–205, 314–16
Davis, Scott, 126
Dawkins, Richard, 30–31, 188, 312
Deacon, Terrance, 314–15
Dearing, Ronda I., 76
Death, 292
Demea, 187
Depth, dimension, 5–6, 14, 209, 312–13; psychology, 240
Descartes, Rene, 207, 296
Desolation, 125
Determinateness, 173–77
Devi, 133
Dewey, John, 57, 82–83, 99, 102–103, 108, 111–12, 116–26, 218, 229, 294
Dialectic, 171–73, 228, 240–45
Dialogues Concerning Human Understanding, 186
Diamond, Malcolm, 187–88, 206
Dimensions, 165
Dionysus the Areopagite, 38, 46
Disciplines, boundaries, 1
Disintegrationism, 229–30
Diversity, 90
Divine command ethics, 309
Divinity, Bachelor of, 1–2
Doctor of Philosophy, 2
Doubt, irritation of 82–83
Dovidio, John F., 246

Dream states, 263–70
Dreyfus, Hubert, 314
Dubner, Stephen, 279–80
Dullness, 91
Durso, Raymon, 257

East Asia, 112
East Asian religions, 164
Ecclesiology, 2
Eckel, M. David, 178
Eckhardt, A. Roy, 109–10
Eckhart, Meister, 294, 300
Ecology, 5
Ecstatic naturalism, 209–19
Editorials, 283
Effing the Ineffable, 3, 6, 9, 17, 154–79, 183–85, 194, 236
Eliade, Mircea, 213
Emails, 273–74, 286
Emerson, Ralph Waldo, 211–13
Endurance, 91
Engagement, 16–17, 168–77, 223–45
Enlightenment, the, 2
Entwistle, David N., 245
Environment, 28, 62
Episcopal Church, 109
Epistemology, 26, 61–62
Epstein, Mark, 241
Eternity, of creation, 157
Ethics, 1, 7, 26, 53–73
Evaluation, 48, 129–47
Evangelicalism, 2–3, 226
Evil, 124–25
Evolution, 4–5, 15, 50, 95–100, 114, 122–23, 162, 203, 209–19, 262, 275–86
Exclusion, 91
Exline, Julie J., 248
Experience, religious, 2–3, 6, 8–9, 237–45, 249–58
Explanation, 130–47

Expression, 91

Face, Wildman's, angelic and trustworthy, 277
Faith seeking understanding, 155
Fallibilism, 7, 54–73, 112, 168–69
Family, Wildman's, 1
Feedback, 80, 99, 123
Fidelity with Plausibility, 9
Fidelity, 2, 134–44
Finitude, 4
First Amendment, 71
Flinders University, 2
Floor, rational, 169–71, 302–303
Folk religion, 20
Ford, David, 151
Form of the Good, 163
Forman, 39
Forster, E. J., 206
Found in the Middle!, 2, 9, 231–32
Frankenberry, Nancy K., 8–9, 181–207, 293, 296, 298, 304–305, 313–18, 325
Fredericks, Sarah, 2, 7, 53–77, 293, 306–308, 315, 325
Frederickson, Paula, 178
Freedom, 93
Freeloaders, 28
Freud, Sigmund, 122, 127, 203, 208, 215, 226
Friendship, 13, 153–54, 172–73, 177
Frodeman, Robert, 76
Frontal lobes, 255–56

Gaertner, Samuel L., 246
Gallegos, Monica I., 248
Garcia, Jerry, 279
Gardiner, Stephen M., 76
Garner, Stephen Chapin, 2, 231–34, 246–47
Geertz, Clifford, 206, 266
Gill, Sam, 144, 151

Index

Globalization, 37
God, 4, 13–31, 111, 121–25, 145–47, 157, 176–77, 232, 239, 299–300, 312–13; God beyond God, 4, 301, 308–309; modeling, 18–21
God Is . . . , 6, 10
Godlove, Terry, 207
Gould, Stephen Jay, 203–204
Grace, 290
Grading, 95–100
Graduate students, 249
Graduate Theological Union, 2
Gratitude, 171, 289
Graysord, 187–88
Griffin, David Ray, 101
Griffiths, Paul, 150
Ground of being, 4, 6, 25, 226–45, 251, 309; models, 145–46, 158–62; theories, 184
Guanilo, 145
Gustafson, James M., 63, 75
Gutierrez, Gustavo, 306

Haggard, Megan, 247
Hammer, 14, 29–30
Hanks, Tom, 182
Haq, Nomanul, 178
Harmonics, 90, 171–72
Harris, Erica, 275–76
Hart, David, 150
Hart, Ray, 303
Hart, William, 150
Hartshorne, Charles, 126, 303
Heaven, 164
Heidegger, Martin, 118, 212, 292–93
Hekman, David R., 247
Heltzel, Peter, 177
Hermeneutics, of suspicion, 226
Hick, John, 2
Hill, Peter, 247
Hinduism, 133, 156, 164

History, 94, 113, 143, 269–70; of religions, 4, 130
Hodder, Ian, 22
Holiness, quest for, 291–92
Holism, 184
Holy Grail, 182, 189
Holy, 21
Homo religiosis, 5, 25, 209–19
Homo sapiens, 15, 27, 29
Hook, Joshua, 247
Houser, Nathan, 101
Human condition, 59–60
Humanities, 22–23, 117, 250, 275–86, 290, 302
Hume, David, 186–90
Humility, 8, 223–45, 294–325
Hyperactive agency detection, 163
Hypothesis, 54, 112, 124, 157–62; external vs. internal, 160–62; in religious studies, 38–50

IBCSR Research Review, 278–79
Ibn Sina, 146
Iconoclasm, 34
Iconoclastic Trajectory, 27–29
Identities, intellectual, 259–70
Ignatius, of Loyola, 125
Ihm, Elliott, 271
In Our Own Image, 3–4, 9, 154–79, 205–206, 262, 298, 322–24
Inclusion, 91
Incompleteness, 91
Indifference, 91
Individuation, 91
Ineffable, 6–7, 17, 38–39, 315–18
Inference to the best explanation, 119, 168
Infinitesimal steps, 166
In-groups, 28–29, 31
Inquiry, 3–4, 7, 53–73, 79–101, 292; art of, 118–19; frustrations of, 170

Institute for the Bio-Cultural Study of Religion, 249–50, 274–86
Institutions, 1, 273–86, 303
Integration, 223–45
Intensity, 8, 90–100, 239–45, 259–70
Intentionality, 4, 19–21, 315–18; attribution of, 145–47
International Conference on the Evolution of Religion, 275–77
Intimacy, 236–40
IOOI-AAU, 162
Islam, 133, 156–57, 163

James Barnett Endowment, 287
James, William, 4–5, 115–26, 159, 229, 243–44, 267–69, 296, 317–18
Jamieson, Dale, 76
Jankowski, Peter, J., 240–41, 247
Jaspers, Karl, 213–14
Jenkins, Willis, 76
Jennings, Pilar, 241
Jesus, 238, 300–301, 308, 313
Job, Book of, 243–44
John of the Cross, 125
John Templeton Foundation, 23
Johnson, Eric L., 245
Johnson, Judith, 248
Jones, James W., 248
Jones, Stanton L., 245
Journal for the Bio-Cultural Study of Religion, 280
Journal of the Institute for the Bio-Cultural Study of Religion Society, 280
Juan, 238
Judaism, 112, 156, 163
Jung, C. G., 215, 218, 241
Justice, participatory, 66–73

Kahneman, Daniel, 85
Kankowski, Peter J., 248
Kanofsky, Joseph, 178
Kant, Immanuel, 49–50, 81, 86–90, 97, 102, 187, 290–92
Karma, 164
Katz, S., 39
Kavka, Martin, 148
Kawakami, Kerry, 246
Keenan, James F., 77
Kinaris, Jim, 151
Klein, Julie Thompson, 76
Kloesel, Christian, 101
Knepper, Timothy, 7–8, 37–53, 293, 315–22, 325
Kohler, Wolfgang, 103
Kohn, Livia, 178
Krishna, 217–18

Lakatos, Imre, 102
Langdon, Robert, 181–85, 189–90, 205
Language, 6–8, 60, 95, 182–205, 314–18
Laozi, 294, 300
Late Night with David Letterman, 279
Leadership, 13
Left, to Wildman's, 174
Lehigh University, 109
Levitt, Steven D., 279–80, 287
Lewis, H. D., 315
Lewis, Thomas, 148, 152, 205
Liberalism, 3
Liddell and Scott, 46
Life, goals of, 93–100
Lifeways, 325–26
Lilley, Christopher, 101
Link, Deborah C., 240–41, 248
Liquor, hard, 31
Logos, 133, 157
Loneliness, 8, 236–45
Lost in the Middle?, 2, 9, 231–32
Lotus Sutra, 164
Love, 124–25, 153, 233–34, 237–38
Loyalty criterion, 42–50

Macdonald, Paul A., Jr., 140–41, 150–51
Madhyamika, 137–38
Maimonides, 146
Mapping, 15–17
Mary Magdalen, 183
Massen, Helmut, 103
Massiveness, 90
Materialism, 113, 165
Mathematics, 5, 95; Wildman in, 2
McCutcheon, Russell, 150
McNamara, Patrick, 8–9, 246, 249–58, 262–63, 265, 275–86, 293, 296–99, 305–306, 315, 323–25
McTaggert, J. M., 251
Meaning, 111, 181–205
Mengzi, 145
Mentality, 97
Mesocortical dopaminergic, neural systems, 256
Metaphor, 182–205
Metaphysics, 26, 108, 214
Method, 108–25
Methodism, 1, 154
Meyering, Theo C., 257
Meyers, David G., 245
Michelangelo, 162
Microbes, 5
Milbank, John, 150
Miller, James, 178
Miller, Richard B., 151
Milton, John, 195
Mind, God's, understood for Peirce, 121–22
Ministry, 1–2, 154, 313
Mitcham, Carl, 76
Modeling, 4, 7, 13–35; of cosmos, 158–62; of God, 157–62; mental, 294–304
Modeling Religion in Norway, 23
Modeling Religion Project, 23
Moe, Shane, 239, 248

Moe-Lobeda, Cynthia D., 76
Monotheism, 4
Morality, 18–21
Morgan, Jonathan, 256, 258
Mortality salience, (death), 23
Moustakas, Clark E., 237, 248
Mu'tazilite, 137–38
Multidisciplinarity, 1, 4–7, 25–26, 37–50, 54–73, 110–25, 183, 202–205, 229–45, 321–22, 326
Murphey, Nancey, 257, 298
Musement, 118–19, 123–24
Musgrave, Alan, 102
Music, 95
Mutual enhancement, 91
Mysticism, 16, 38, 176, 205, 293, 301–303
Mysticotheology, 4, 48–49

Nagarjuna, 294
Narcissism, grandiose, 232–33
Narrative, 4, 19–21, 146–47
Native Americans, 71
Naturalism, 5, 8, 14, 21, 184–85, 228, 249–56, 268–71, 298–300, 311–12
Nature, 209–19; naturing and natured, 211–19
Neo-Confucianism, 133
Neolithic humans, 22
Neo-pragmatism, 114
Neurology, 285–86
Neuroscience, 4–6, 8–9, 249–58
Neville, Robert Cummings, 1–10, 18, 59–60, 74–75, 80–81, 101, 103, 153–79, 184, 188, 205–207, 226, 287, 291–93, 296, 298, 301–304, 315, 325
Nicholson, Hugh, 178
Niebuhr, H. Richard, 63, 75
Nietzsche, Friedrich, 14, 29–30, 308–10

No silos positions, 142–43
Normativity, 3–4, 119, 130–47
Novelty, 91
Numinous, 193
Nussbaum, Martha, 134

O'Brien, Kevin J., 76
Odin, Steve, 101
Ogden, Schubert, 143, 149, 151
Oliver, Mary, 204
One and Many, 161, 169–70, 173–77, 296
One and the Same, 182, 205
One, the, 166–67, 173–77
Ontological context of mutual relevance, 165–66, 168, 171
Ontological creative act, 161–62, 165–66, 168, 171
Ontology, 214, 262–63
Ontotheology, 4, 48–49
Operational definitions, 162
Orisa, 133
Otto, Rudolf, 213
Out-groups, 28–29, 31
Owens, Bradley P., 247

Paine, David R., 247–48
Paley, 14
Paloutzian, Ray, 319, 326
Pantheism, 212–13
Pargament, Kenneth, I., 248
Parkinson's Disease, 249, 256
Participation, 91
Pastor, Wildman as, 2
Peace, 91
Pedersen, Daniel, 101
Peirce, Charles S., 4, 57, 59, 82–83, 86–90, 92, 97, 99, 107–27, 168, 171–72, 294
Pekala, 255
Perennialism, 39

Person, 123–24, 158–64; divine, 227; in God, 4, 324
Personalism, 251–56
Peter, St., 299
Petersen, Anders K., 271
Pew data, 227–28
Phenomena, 217
Phenomenology, 6, 130, 143, 155–57, 230
Philo, 186–90, 205
Philosopher, 224–25, 275–86
Philosophical Theology, 3–4, 107–25, 154–55
Philosophy, 1–2, 26–31, 250, 256–57, 269–70, 325; analytic, 3–4, 143; cenoscopic, 111, 114; contextual, 29; Continental, 3–4; department of, 320; of language, 26; perennial, 4
Philosophy of religion, 3–4, 6, 20, 26–31, 37–50, 53–73, 107–25, 129–47, 183–85, 212, 289–326
PhilosophyOfReligion.org., 319
Physicotheology, 4, 48–49
Piedmont, California, 2
Place, for CMAC, 284
Plato, 163, 177
Plausibility, 2, 143–44
Play, cognitive, 118–19
Plotinus, 146, 165–66, 173, 212, 303
Plum, 103
Plural criteria positions, 142–43
Pockets of order, 170–73
Points regarding criteria, 164–65
Politics, 176
Polytheism, 4
Positivism, 185–86
Postmodernism, 43, 141, 157
Powlison, David, 245
Practical ethics, 308

Practical pious but perilous parlance pervading priestly philosophy, prevaricated on, 30
Practice, 4, 19–21, 307
Pragmatics, 192–95
Pragmatism, 1, 4, 7, 58–60, 79–101, 107–25, 169–70, 219, 229–45
Prehension, 90
Presuppositions, 80
Problem solving, 4, 55–60, 81–100, 107–25, 157
Process, model, 236; theology, 159–62
Projections, 210–19
Protestantism, 2, 209
Proudfoot, Wayne, 195, 207
Prum, Richard, 97–98, 100–101
Pseudo-Dionysus, 317
Psychoanalysis, 214–15
Psychology, 8, 223–45; qualitative and quantitative, 229–45; of religion, 227–29
Psychotheology, 4, 48–49
Public, 37
Publishers, 276–77
Pure Act of To Be, 163
Putnam, Robert D., 247

Quine, Willard, 189, 207

Ramanuja, 299
Raposa, Michael L., 7–10, 107–27, 293, 296–99, 315, 325
Rational Practicality, 146–47
Rawls, John, 134
Realism, 123, 230–31
Reality, cracked and farcical, or superabundant, 291–93
Reasonableness, 87–100
Reconstruction, of philosophy of religion, 37–50
Reflection, critical, 80

Reich, Wilhelm, 218
Relations, 5, 8, 223–45
Religion and science, 53
Religious and Spiritual Experience, 3
Religion and spiritual experiences, 259–70
Religion department, at Boston University, 109, 320
Religion in multidisciplinary perspective, 289–326
Religion, 2, 5, 7, 13–31, 116, 168, 250, 276–86; bio-cultural study of, 24; scientific study of, 9, 81; study of, 1, 13–14, 22–26; religionless, 168
Religion, Brain, & Behavior, 2, 249–58, 274–86, 307
Religions, East Asian, South Asian, West Asian, 52
Religious and Spiritual Experiences, 5–6, 9, 18, 322
Religious Philosophy as Multidisciplinary Comparative Inquiry, 3–4, 9, 18, 42–43, 49, 53, 57, 70, 108, 112, 154–79, 205–206, 264, 304–305, 319, 321
Religious philosophy, 3–6, 45–50, 107–25
Religious studies, 129–47, 276
Research Council of Norway, 23
Responsibility, 63, 68–73
Revelation, 16, 111, 140–42, 213, 300
Reynolds, Frank, 75
Richardson, W. Mark, 73
Ricoeur, Paul, 189
Rituals, 23
Robbins, Jeffrey, 150
Roberts, Michelle Voss, 149
Roberts, Robert, C., 245, 301, 308
Robins, Richard W., 76
Rohr, David, 206–207, 319–20

Roman Catholicism, 70, 111, 181
Rorty, Richard, 126, 150, 189, 202, 208
Rosch, Eleanor, 104
Ruffing, Elizabeth G., 247
Russell, Robert J., 257

Sacerdotal Trajectory, 27–29
Sacred folds, 209, 214–17
Safran, Jeremey, 241
Saldarini, Anthony, 178
Sanchez-Canizares, Javier, 103
Sandage, Steven J., 8, 223–48, 293, 303, 315, 325
Sankara, 300
Satisfaction, 92–100
Saussure, 185
Schelling, 179, 211–12
Schilbrack, Kevin, 8–9, 129–52, 205, 293, 315, 319–22, 325
Schiller, F. C. S., 120
Schizophrenia, 256
Schjoedt, Uffe, 283
Schleiermacher, Friedrich, 176, 209–11, 217
Schnarch, David, M., 237–38, 241, 248
School of Theology, at Boston University, 30, 155, 320
Schopenhauer, Arthur, 212
Schweiker, William, 64–65, 75
Schweitz, Lea F., 68, 75
Science, 1–2, 4–5, 13, 108–25, 167, 183, 219, 250, 290; primitive, 163, in study of religion, 94–101; technology, engineering, mathematics (STEM), 156, 302
Science and Religion Program, 153
Science and Religious Anthropology, 3, 5–6, 9, 284
Science and Ultimate Reality, 3–5, 262
Science and world religions, 250
ScienceOnReligion.org, 277–78

Scotus, Duns, 169
Searle, John, 136, 150, 314
Secularism, 21
Segrin, Chris, 248
Sellars, Wilfrid, 191
Semantics, 184, 189–95
Sermons, 6
Sexuality, 4–5
Shakespeare, William, 202
Shame, 232
Shangdi, 146, 164
Shepardson, Tina, 178
Sherburne, Donald W., 101
Sheveland, John N., 148
Shi'i, 70
Shults, F. LeRon, 1–10, 13–35, 162–63, 225–26, 238, 245–46, 248, 287, 281–93, 287, 299, 304, 306, 308–13, 315, 325–26
Sideris, Lisa H., 62
Sidney, University of, 1–2
Siegel, Ronald, 241
Silence, 17, 20
Siloes, of disciplines, 61
Simulations, 2, 15–18
Smart, Ninian, 131, 148
Smith, Barbara Herrnstein, 104
Smith, Jonathan Z., 178
Sociality, 50, 116–25, 175–76, 285–86
Sociographic Promiscuity and Prudery, 27–29
Solomon, Robert, 150
Sorley, 187–88
Sosis, Richard, 2, 9–10, 250, 273–87, 293, 307–308, 315, 325
South Asia, 112
South Asian religions, 164
Spezio, Michael, 283
Spinoza, Benedict, 148
Spirit Tech, 6
Spirituality, 223–24, 45
St. John of the Cross, 238

Stability, 91
Statistics, 2
Stirman, Shannon W., 246
Stockly, Kate, 6, 278–79
Stoicism, 133
Stout, Jeffrey, 152, 189
Subjective form, 90
Subordinate deity, 4, 19, 145–46, 158–62
Suddendorf, T., 270
Suffering, 242–45; as suchness, 324–25
Sullivan, Winnifred Fallers, 148
Supernaturalism, 5, 24–31, 163, 184, 209–19, 251–56, 310–11
Superstition, 26
Supranaturalism, 209
Supreme Principle, 133
Surfer-dude, laid back, 169–70
Swinburne, Richard, 49, 303, 316–17
Symbols, 8, 17, 181–205, 315–18; broken, 174–77, 184–85; religious, 117
Symmetry, 167, 171, 173–77, 302–303
System, 168
Systematic theology, 154

Tangney, June Price, 76
Tanner, Kathryn, 141, 149–51
Taves, Anne, 9–10, 259–71, 287, 293, 315–18, 324–26
Taylor & Francis, 276–77
Technology, 6
Temperament, 161–62
Temporal lobe epilepsy, 256
Temporality, 167–68
Teresa of Avila, 294
Thatamanil, John, 149, 178
The Da Vinci Code, 183
The Future of an Illusion, 203
The Grateful Dead School of Business, 279–80

Theism, 7, 38, 43–50, 96, 121–25, 129–47, 251–56
Theism, 96
Theodicy, 125
Theogony, 167
Theologian, 224–25, 275–86
Theologies, internal and external, 172–73
Theology, 1, 4, 8, 37–50, 53, 109, 129–52, 250; internal and external, 172–73; trajectory of, 165; Wildman's and Neville's, 153–77
Theosemiotic, 125
Thompson, Evan, 103
Thought Thinking Itself, 163
Tian, 146
Tiger, 163
Tillich, Paul, 4, 145–46, 154–55, 158, 174–78, 182, 187–206, 209–19, 304, 306, 311–12
Togetherness, 91
Tolk, Andreas, 15
Topics, for CMAC, 283–84
Torrance, Iain, 150
Tracy, Jessica I., 76
Traditions, 4
Transcendence, 209–19
Transformation, Wildman's, 224
Tritten, Tyler, 171, 179
Triviality, 91
Troeltsch, Ernst, 2
Truth, 16, 111; religious, 59–60
Tsai, Jeanne, 76
Tu, Weiming, 178
Turkey, 22
Turner, Denys, 151

Udayana, 146
Ultimacy, ultimate reality or realities, 2, 4, 14–31, 59–60, 110–25, 157–73, 183–205, 260, 289–326; ultimates, five, 173

Unconditioned, the, 17
Unconsciousness, 54–56, 212–19, 296
United Methodist Church, 154
United States, 238
Uniting Church of Australia, 1, 154
Universal criteria, 142–43
Universalism, 210
Universities, secular, 8, 29, 129–52, 154
Urizen
Use, of language, 191–95

Vada, an Indian tradition, 45–46
Vagueness, 18–19, 108, 110–25, 167
Valuational depths, 264–70
Value, 79–101, 165–73, 265–70, 285–86; ecology of, 263
Values in the Study of Religion (VISOR), 319–20
Van Gogh, Vincent, 194
Van Huyssteen, J. Wentzel, 95, 101
Varela, Francisco J., 103
Varieties of Religious Experience, 5
Variety, 91
Violence, 22–23, 213, 216
Vulnerability, 112–25, 172

Wallin, David, 241
Wang, Lin, 247
Water, 31
Watson, P. J., 245

Web of Religion, 281
Webster, John, 150
Weiss, Paul, 126
Whence, 260–70, 295, 298–99
Whitcomb, Dennis, 235, 247
Whitehead, Alfred North, 4, 80–81, 87–100, 296
Wiebe, Donald, 148, 150
Wiener, Philip, 126
Wildman, Sam and Ben, 313; Suzanne, 301, 313; Wesley, 1–326
Williams, Michael, 207
Wine, red, 31
Wisdom, 40, 264
Wish-fulfillment, 122
Wittgenstein, Ludwig, 43, 192, 202, 206
Wong, Ying, 76
Wood, Alex M., 248
Wood, Connor, 287
World, issues in religion, 129–47; the way it is, 42–43
Worldviews, 129–47, 263–65, 325–26

Yalom, Irvin D., 237, 248
Yong, Amos, 177
Yoruba, 133

Zeus, 216
Zoroastrianism, 313

www.ingramcontent.com/pod-product-compliance
Lightning Source LLC
Chambersburg PA
CBHW031704230426
43668CB00006B/107